ACTIVISM AND THE FOSSIL FUEL INDUSTRY

In less than a decade, activism against the fossil fuel industry has exploded across the globe. While environmentalists used to focus on legislative goals, such as carbon emissions trading or renewable energy policies, today the most prominent activists directly attack the fossil fuel industry. This timely book offers a comprehensive evaluation of different types of activism, the success and impact of campaigns and activities, and suggestions as to ways forward.

This book is the first systematic treatment of the anti-fossil fuel movement in the United States. An accessible and readable text, it is an essential reference for scholars, policymakers, activists, and citizens interested in climate change, fossil fuels, and environmental sustainability.

The entire book or chapters from it can be used as required or supplementary material in various courses at the undergraduate and graduate level. As the book is not technically challenging but contains a comprehensive review of climate change, fossil fuels, and the literature on environmental activism, it can be used as an accessible introduction to the anti-fossil fuel campaign across disciplines.

Andrew Cheon is Assistant Professor of International Political Economy at Johns Hopkins School of Advanced International Studies, USA.

Johannes Urpelainen is Prince Sultan bin Abdulaziz Professor of Energy, Resources and Environment at Johns Hopkins School of Advanced International Studies, USA.

ACTIVISM AND THE FOSSIL FUEL INDUSTRY

Andrew Cheon and Johannes Urpelainen

Routledge
Taylor & Francis Group

LONDON AND NEW YORK

First published 2018
by Routledge
2 Park Square, Milton Park, Abingdon, Oxon OX14 4RN

and by Routledge
711 Third Avenue, New York, NY 10017

Routledge is an imprint of the Taylor & Francis Group, an informa business

British Library Cataloguing-in-Publication Data
A catalogue record for this book is available from the British Library

Library of Congress Cataloging-in-Publication Data
Names: Cheon, Andrew, author. | Urpelainen, Johannes, author.
Title: Activism and the fossil fuel industry / Andrew Cheon and Johannes Urpelainen.
Description: Abingdon, Oxon ; New York, NY : Routledge, 2018. | Includes index.
Identifiers: LCCN 2017045730 | ISBN 9781783538089 (hbk) | ISBN 9781783537549 (pbk)
Subjects: LCSH: Energy industries—Environmental aspects. | Fossil fuels—Environmental aspects. | Fossil fuels—Political aspects. | Green movement. | Environmentalism. | Environmental policy—Citizen participation.
Classification: LCC HD9502.A2 C4634 2018 | DDC 338.2/72—dc23
LC record available at https://lccn.loc.gov/2017045730

ISBN: 978-1-78353-808-9 (hbk)
ISBN: 978-1-78353-754-9 (pbk)
ISBN: 978-1-351-17312-4 (ebk)

Typeset in Bembo
by Apex CoVantage, LLC

CONTENTS

List of figures   viii
List of tables   ix
Preface   x

1   Introduction   1
    1.1 Fossil fuels and the future of human civilization 6
    1.2 Understanding the movement against fossil fuels 8
    1.3 Mobilization potential and impact: evaluating the
        movement 11
    1.4 Ideas, implications, and contributions 15
    1.5 A road map 19

2   Fossil fuels in the world economy   23
    2.1 Industrialization, globalization, and fossil fuels 24
    2.2 The problem with fossil fuels 25
    2.3 The fossil fuel industry 29
    2.4 Future prospects 33

3   Perspectives on the movement against fossil fuels   39
    3.1 Study of activism: the state of the art 40
    3.2 Environmental activism in America before campaigns
        against fossil fuels 46
    3.3 Goals of campaigns: why mobilize against fossil fuels? 51
    3.4 Explaining the momentum: why does the campaign
        catch on? 56

*3.5 Counting chickens while they hatch: the impact
of the movement 63*
3.6 The four campaigns 64

4   Keystone XL   67
    4.1 Significance 68
    4.2 Overview 70
    4.3 Activism in motion 74
    4.4 Motives 85
    4.5 Mobilization potential 86
    4.6 Impact 89

5   Divestment   93
    5.1 Significance 94
    5.2 Overview 97
    5.3 Activism in motion 103
    5.4 Motives 113
    5.5 Mobilization potential 117
    5.6 Impact 119

6   The campaign against coal in the United States   126
    6.1 Significance 127
    6.2 Overview 127
    6.3 Activism in motion 135
    6.4 Motives 143
    6.5 Mobilization potential 146
    6.6 Impact 147

7   Mobilizing against fracking   154
    7.1 Significance 155
    7.2 Overview 156
    7.3 Activism in motion 159
    7.4 Motives 169
    7.5 Mobilization potential 170
    7.6 Impact 171

8   Campaigns against fossil fuels: a global view   174
    8.1 Historical precedents 175
    8.2 Against fossil fuels: international dimensions 178
    8.3 Case study: coal and development 185
    8.4 Summary: from America to the world 189

9   Conclusion   192
    9.1 *Understanding and evaluating the campaign against fossil
         fuels 195*
    9.2 *Implications for research on activism and social
         movements 203*
    9.3 *The campaign against fossil fuels and the politics of climate
         change 208*

Bibliography   *215*
Index   *235*

FIGURES

1.1   Public concern about global warming among Americans,
1999–2017   9

2.1   Historical trends in fossil fuel consumption, 1965–2013   25

2.2   Electricity, oil, gas, and mining share of annual lobbying
in total energy and resources, 1998–2014   32

4.1   Headlines containing KXL pipeline, 2011–2014   75

5.1   Colleges, universities, and cities and faith-based judicatories
act on divestment   100

5.2   Divestment actions by faiths   107

6.1   Recent and planned retirements of coal plants   131

6.2   Defeated coal plants by state   135

6.3   Map of defeated coal plants   136

7.1   Municipal bans by county   160

7.2   Municipal moratoriums by county   161

7.3   Municipal anti-fracking movements by county   161

7.4   Municipal bans and moratoriums over time   162

7.5   Fracking wells by county   166

7.6   Drilling violations by county   167

TABLES

3.1 Evaluation matrix for the four campaigns 66
8.1 Summary of similarities and differences between American and international campaigns against fossil fuels 189
9.1 Evaluation matrix for the four campaigns 196

PREFACE

This book is perhaps the culmination of a collaborative partnership that began at Columbia University eight years ago. As an incoming graduate student and a self-proclaimed generalist, Andrew was looking for a specialization. With his enduring passion for all things energy and the environment, Johannes had a suggestion.

The urgent need to balance the growing demand for energy with the clear and present danger of climate change was the driving force behind our early scholarship on subjects such as energy technology innovation and the role of interest groups in renewables deployment, as well as the role of geopolitical threats in motivating energy investments.

Though our initial success in top journal hits was certainly rewarding, both of us wanted to explore other platforms for conveying our ideas and concerns more directly to an even wider audience. In the end, we agreed that a book about climate change politics would be the best medium for contributing to the public debate. While social scientists by training, we wanted to write this book as concerned citizens.

We understand the complexity of the issue at hand. While mobilization against the fossil fuel industry, as our book seeks to demonstrate, has been strikingly effective, it is too easy to forget that we ourselves are also contributors to climate change. We have both left too many lights on at night to claim a clear conscience. In one of life's ironic moments, Johannes, a lifelong environmentalist, has recently been named Prince Sultan bin Abdulaziz Professor of Energy, Resources and the Environment at the Johns Hopkins School of Advanced International Studies, where we both now work.

These ironies and complexities are what make activism against the fossil fuel industry so interesting to study. There is something quintessentially human about the political tactics we examine in these chapters, and we believe that there is value in studying them on their own terms. While we are not writing with the aim of directly contributing to a theoretical literature in Sociology, Political Science, Psychology, or Economics, we liberally draw from and seek to build upon their insights because our book is an extension of social science, much more broadly defined.

While it is no secret that we share many of the activists' concerns about climate change, we have made conscious and systematic efforts to examine their campaigns as dispassionately as we can. We also examine their campaigns for what they are – political tactics. What are the motivations? Who are the target audiences? How successful have they been in drawing recruits? Has the message resonated? Ultimately, we believe that an objective analysis on our part – of their successes and shortcomings – will ultimately be of greater use to these activists than an unqualified endorsement.

We have accumulated numerous debts along the way. In particular, our editor at Greenleaf Publishing, Rebecca Marsh, has been a difference-maker, carefully reviewing our manuscripts and suggesting productive new directions for the book. Judith Lorton at Routledge made our transition to the Routledge platform seamless. Jessica Green and Doug McAdam gave us detailed comments on the entire manuscript at a workshop at Columbia University. Our greatest debt, of course, is to the activists we interviewed, and especially Steve Knight.

1

INTRODUCTION

Following the release of the US State Department environmental impact assessment on the Keystone XL pipeline, ranchers, indigenous leaders, and allies from across the country descended on Washington, DC, to engage in civil disobedience. From August 20 to September 3, 2011, 1,253 people were arrested in sit-ins outside the White House, calling on President Barack Obama to stop the construction of the pipeline that would run from Alberta, Canada, to the Gulf of Mexico. James Hansen, a prominent climate scientist among those arrested, argues that the construction of the pipeline would solidify America's addiction to fossil fuels, essentially a "game over" scenario for the global climate (McGowan, 2011, August 29).

Far more than just a spectacle, the protests unified a range of environmental organizations with different political orientations, such as the Natural Resources Defense Council, the Sierra Club, the Environmental Defense Fund, the National Wildlife Federation, Greenpeace, Friends of the Earth, and the Rainforest Action Network. They took to the press and jointly declared, "there is not an inch of daylight between [their] policy position on the Keystone XL pipeline, and those of the protesters being arrested daily outside the White House" (Henn and Kessler, 2011, August 24). It was a feat unsurpassed until February 17, 2013, when 35,000 gathered at the National Mall in Washington, DC, for "the largest climate rally in history."

Titled "Forward on Climate," the rally drew from organizations such as the Tar Sands Blockade, the Sierra Club, 350.org, aboriginals from British Columbia, and the Hip Hop Caucus. Bill McKibben captured the excitement perfectly: "All I ever wanted to see was a movement of people to stop climate change, and now I've seen it! You are the antibodies kicking in as the planet tries to fight its fever" (McKibben, 2013). On that day, companion rallies broke out across the country, including California, Colorado, Illinois, Iowa, Michigan, Montana, Oregon, Texas, and Olympia and Seattle, Washington (Spear, 2013, February 12).

The fighting spirit found its way to institutions of higher learning. On May 1, 2014, Brett A. Roche, a member of the campus group Divest Harvard, was arrested by Harvard University Police around 7:15 a.m. for blocking the entrance to Massachusetts Hall, the offices of University President Drew G. Faust and the administration. Roche and other fellow students who rotated shifts that morning demanded an open meeting with the Harvard Corporation to discuss divestment from fossil fuel companies (Hashimi, 2014, May 1). They were only the tip of the iceberg. In an Undergraduate Council referendum in 2012, 72 percent of participating Harvard College students supported divestment from fossil fuels. Since then, more than 200 faculty members, almost 1,100 alumni, and around 65,000 community members cosigned the campaign (Divest Harvard, 2015, February 12).

These actions are all part of today's most dynamic and controversial climate movement. While the greens have for decades advocated for various climate policies, a large-scale national movement that focuses on the *exploration and extraction of fossil fuels* is a newcomer to the crowded field of environmentalism. In fewer than 10 years, activism that specifically targets the fossil fuel industry has grown bigger than traditional advocacy in favor of conventional climate policy in America.

The movement against fossil fuels consists of individuals who are all deeply worried about climate change. For anti-fossil fuel activists, the link between climate change and humanity's ravenous consumption of coal, oil, and natural gas is an emergency that necessitates immediate action. These activists are willing to dedicate countless hours, travel thousands of miles, and get arrested by the authorities. They do so fully aware of the global scale of the problem and the long odds of winning.

The centrality of fossil fuels themselves in the world's environmental crisis is undeniable. Fossil fuels release greenhouse gases, such as carbon dioxide, into the atmosphere, preventing the release of heat to space. Cumulative emissions among the 20 largest energy companies between 1854 and 2010 total 428,439 metric tons of carbon dioxide equivalent (MtCO2e), or 29.5 percent of global industrial emissions from 1751 to 2010. Ninety companies are responsible for contributing 63.04 percent of global industrial CO2 and methane between 1751 and 2010 (Heede, 2014). At current pace, the global mean temperature may increase by more than 4 degrees Celsius by some estimates, disrupting ecosystems and bringing in its wake crop decline, freshwater depletion, diseases, flooding, and rising sea levels (World Bank, 2014; IPCC, 2013: 20–21).

The political power of the fossil fuel industry is equally obvious to anyone following contemporary politics. With millions of dollars in annual spending and an official outpost on K Street, ExxonMobil deploys career lobbyists to secure meetings, executive orders, and favorable laws in Washington, DC (Coll, 2012). Perhaps the most prominent example is the close friendship of former Vice President Dick Cheney and ExxonMobil's Lee Raymond, who share a public disdain for climate scientists and government regulations (Coll, 2012). According to OpenSecrets.org, the vast majority of campaign contributions from oil, gas, electricity, and mining industries have found their way to Republican candidates, at least since the 1990 election cycle (OpenSecrets.org, 2016).

And yet, the debate on the merits of the movement against fossil fuels is heated. To its supporters, this new movement gives a spark of hope in an otherwise depressing climate policy landscape. The proponents of going after the fossil fuel industry believe this approach has unique mobilization potential, tackles the root case, and will ultimately cause a profound social transformation for more sustainable human communities. To its detractors, however, this new movement is a fatal misstep away from policies that promise genuine effectiveness, such as carbon taxes. If activists focus their energies on opposing individual pipelines or calling for the divestment of small financial endowments in colleges, the opponents of the movement against fossil fuels argue, then they are wasting valuable time and energy that could have been aimed at campaigning for enlightened public policy. Even worse, the movement against fossil fuels may sharpen the already vexing problem of partisan polarization over the environment and energy in the United States. If anti-fossil fuel activists label corporations as evil, then there may not be much hope for reasoned and respectful debate among differing views.

Regardless of these diverging assessments, nobody can deny the impressive achievements of the national organizers. Where does all this activist energy for social change come from? In an account of his own activism against the Keystone XL pipeline, activist and writer Samuel Avery beautifully captures the fundamental puzzle of activism:

> What is the spark within? What impels ordinary people to go forth, carry signs, attend rallies and hearings, write letters, walk miles, disturb the peace, and submit to arrest? What sort of mad citizen's disease grabs hold of people and moves them against the wisdom of their leaders? Why do otherwise sane people spend free time opposing directions society is taking for their benefit?
>
> *(Avery, 2013: 8)*

The difficulty of motivating large groups of people to become activists for political and social change has been a fundamental, and usually elusive, problem for American environmentalists and their global peers. How can it be that this new movement against fossil fuels has reinvigorated so many sleeping and disillusioned activists?

In this book, we describe and evaluate the growing grassroots movement against fossil fuels. As we show, the rapid growth and unexpected dynamism of the movement reflect first and foremost the nature of the issue. While the technicalities of emissions trading and renewable energy portfolio standard have proven boring enough to put everyone, save the most enthusiastic of policy wonks, to sleep, the movement against fossil fuels offers a more exciting prospect: tackling the root cause of climate change. Fossil fuel companies are today's Goliath, a large and visible enemy that is destroying everything that environmental activists consider sacred and beautiful. For activists, the disconnect between today's frenzy of fossil fuel extraction and the urgency of reducing our greenhouse gas emissions to stop global warming is a call to arms.

This framing of the movement against fossil fuels taps into the core beliefs of what Avery (2013) calls the "ecological paradigm." People who are potential participants to the movement against fossil fuels share a common set of values that emphasize the importance of protecting ecosystems and human societies from destruction, even if such protection comes at the expense of profits and economic growth. To them, the movement against fossil fuels is a tremendously exciting opportunity to take a strong stand for something they truly believe in. What is more, the movement against fossil fuels does promise achievable "small wins" (Weick, 1984) in the short run, as every halted pipeline construction or closed coal mine counts as a victory to the activists. Campaigns against fossil fuels promise results here and now, even if the ultimate goal of stopping climate change requires a healthy dose of patience. For the adherents of the ecological paradigm, the steady stream of small wins against a powerful and fearsome enemy responsible for unprecedented global ecological destruction is irresistible.

The call to arms for anti-fossil fuel activists was Bill McKibben's (2012) *Rolling Stone* article, "Global Warming's Terrifying New Math." Drawing on research conducted by the Carbon Tracker Initiative (CTI), McKibben shows that if humanity were to extract and burn all known reserves of fossil fuels, we would see rapid global warming during this century, with potentially devastating consequences. In the words of America's most prominent environmentalist, "We have five times as much oil and coal and gas on the books as climate scientists think is safe to burn. We'd have to keep 80 percent of those reserves locked away underground to avoid that fate. Before we knew those numbers, our fate had been likely. Now, barring some massive intervention, it seems certain" (McKibben, 2012, August 2). According to anti-fossil fuel activists, this is a logic of planetary emergency, calling for draconian limits on the use of fossil fuels. The measures required to stop dangerous climate change, says McKibben, are an existential threat for the fossil fuel industry. So, "what all these climate numbers make painfully, usefully clear is that the planet does indeed have an enemy – one far more committed to action than governments or individuals. Given this hard math, we need to view the fossil-fuel industry in a new light. It has become a rogue industry, reckless like no other force on Earth." In other words, the anti-fossil fuel campaigners abide by what K. C. Golden, the policy director of Climate Solutions, calls "the Keystone Principle" (Golden, 2013, February 16). According to this principle, Keystone XL is "not just a pipeline":

> *Specifically and categorically, we must cease making large, long-term capital investments in new fossil fuel infrastructure that "locks in" dangerous emission levels for many decades.* Keystone is both a conspicuous example of that kind of investment and a powerful symbol for the whole damned category.
>
> *(emphasis original)*

The same factors that make the movement engaging for activists are also driving its dynamic growth. Because the campaigners can promise concrete action and rapid results that are deeply tied to larger global concerns, the movement contains a lot of potential for recruitment and sympathy among the target audiences. While conventional climate campaigns have often lost their momentum because they do not offer concrete means of participation to grassroots activists or much hope for results for the hard work of mobilization, the movement against fossil fuels has so far avoided this fate. At the same time, the movement against fossil fuels is not detached from policy or legislative concerns. By undermining the legitimacy and removing the social license of the fossil fuel industry, ecological activists are doing political work to level the playing field and turn the tide against the seemingly invincible adversary: oil and gas interests.

Our research also reveals several critical limitations of the movement. Most importantly, strong evidence that the movement against fossil fuels has not resonated with the political right or the middle. Although there is some subtle variation in the target audience of the different parts of the movement, and some actions such as the Nebraska protests against Keystone XL have even attracted by conservative ranchers, on balance the real target audience of the movement is the progressive political base. In America, anti-fossil fuel activists are gambling on their ability to make climate change a core concern for an increasingly powerful progressive political coalition. If this spectacularly bold gamble proves to be the wrong one, we do not see much hope for the movement against fossil fuels to change the way the political right views climate change. Under President Donald J. Trump and a Republican Congress, for example, the policy impact of anti-fossil fuel mobilization at the federal level is bound to be limited. Indeed, the adversarial and confrontational tactics of the anti-fossil fuel activists may even contribute to polarization on the margin.

Overall, the weaknesses of the anti-fossil fuel movement are overshadowed by the successes. The movement has galvanized activism by giving activists clear and symbolic targets at the root cause of climate change – the powerful fossil fuel industry – and scored important victories against both the legitimacy of the industry and specific energy projects, such as pipelines and coal-fired power plants. Although the anti-fossil fuel movement does not speak to political moderates or conservatives, and the anti-fracking campaign can be criticized for ignoring the benefits of displacing coal, the anti-fossil fuel movement has injected badly needed energy into the much broader campaign to stop climate change.

This book is intended for anyone interested in understanding why there is such a vibrant anti-fossil fuel movement in America, and to what effect. While the book draws on academic literature for ideas and insights, our target audience is not limited to experts with doctoral degrees in the social sciences. We hope that students, professionals, and environmental activists alike can find value in our description, explanation, and assessment of the movement against fossil fuels.

The rest of this chapter summarizes the book. First, we briefly summarize the case for concern about fossil fuels. We begin by discussing the negative environmental and human consequences of our civilization's addiction to coal, oil, and natural gas. Next, we illustrate what our research has taught us about the motivation and dynamism of the movement. We follow with an evaluation of the movement's successes, failures, and future prospects. The remaining two parts offer a summary of the implications of the study and provide the reader with a preview of the chapters to come.

1.1 Fossil fuels and the future of human civilization

Why fight against fossil fuels? The answer to this question requires understanding what fossil fuels are and how the industry extracting and selling them operates. For more than three centuries, fossil fuels have played a central role in human development and the growth of the industrial society. Ever since the British industry began to use coal to power various machines and transportation, the expansion of the global economy has depended on larger and larger amounts of coal, oil, and gas. As a whole, the world used more fossil fuels in 2014 than ever before and, with booming demand in the emerging economies of Latin America, Asia, and Africa, this trend is sure to continue in the absence of a massive intervention. Fossil fuels provide large amounts of energy in a convenient package. Fossil fuels do not require a lot of space and they can be burned for energy whenever necessary.

Over hundreds of years, the efficiency of power plants, heaters, and automobiles has increased dramatically, meaning that industrial, agricultural, and residential users get more out of fossil fuels than ever before. And with the rapid growth of an increasingly wealthy global population craving for higher standards of living, the growth in global energy demand is projected to rise sharply over the coming years (Asif and Muneer, 2007). According to the International Energy Agency's (IEA) projections based on existing and planned government policies in the 2014 *World Energy Outlook*, world primary energy demand is set to increase by 37 percent between 2012 and 2040 (IEA, 2014). Almost all of the growth in energy demand comes from non-OECD (Organisation for Economic Co-operation and Development) countries, such as China and India.

If it were not for ecological destruction, the increased use of fossil fuels would be but one facet of abundance. For centuries, the increased use of energy – in practice, fossil fuels – was considered an indicator of all things good and beautiful. But today, there are many reasons to worry about fossil fuels. Most importantly, they are the primary cause of climate change. Fossil fuels release carbon dioxide into the atmosphere, preventing the release of heat to space. Unless our civilization can dramatically reduce our reliance on fossil fuels, the global mean temperature may increase by more than four degrees Celsius by some estimates, disrupting ecosystems and wreaking havoc in human settlements across the world (World Bank, 2014; IPCC, 2013: 20–21). The consequences for international development would be severe, as crop yields decline, freshwater resources dwindle, diseases move into new ranges, heavy precipitation causes flooding, and rising sea levels threaten urban settlements along the coastlines. The poorest countries would be hardest hit, seriously jeopardizing development goals, such as ending poverty, increasing global prosperity, and reducing global inequality (World Bank, 2014).

The production and consumption of fossil fuels also bring other ecological consequences. The burning of coal is a major source of air pollution, as evident in major cities in China (Chan and Yao, 2008). Transportation, fueled by diesel and gasoline, is another major source of air pollution (Mayer, 1999). Coal is often extracted from the ground through techniques called "surface mining," which involves removing the soil and rock overlying coal deposits, visibly changing the geological landscape (Beynon et al., 2000; McNeil, 2011; Montrie, 2003; Nace, 2010). When oil is found in populated or biodiverse areas, such as the Yasuni National Park in Ecuador, a conflict ensues between oil companies and environmentalists (Martin, 2011). Oil pipelines and maritime transportation create risks of oil spills, as exemplified by activist concerns surrounding the Keystone XL (Avery, 2013). Fracking, an unconventional method of extracting natural gas, has been accused of spoiling the local water (Davis, 2012).

Rapid reductions in the use of fossil fuels are needed to avoid dangerous climate change. According to IPCC (2013: 28), emissions pathways that would keep the global average temperature from rising more than two degrees Celsius, the United Nations target for avoiding dangerous global warming, would require a reduction in carbon dioxide emissions of about one-half from 2010 levels by 2050. By the end of the century, they will need to be close to zero. At a time of rapidly growing carbon dioxide emissions, this is an incredibly difficult target to meet, and many detractors say the game is already over. David G. Victor and Charles F. Kennel write in *Nature*: "Owing to continued failures to mitigate emissions globally, rising emissions are on track to blow through this limit eventually. . . . Because it sounds firm and concerns future warming, the 2°C target has allowed politicians to pretend that they are organizing for action when, in fact, most have done little" (Victor and Kennel, 2014).

What is worse, there is no technological fix in sight. Technologies such as fusion power or carbon capture may become commercially viable in the future – or not. Renewable energy can be deployed already, but it will not replace enough fossil fuels to stop climate change without ambitious policies and massive investments. For anyone worried about the status of the global environment, the situation is dire and demoralizing. The world is making little progress toward solving the world's great problem. A global transition to an economy without fossil fuels is far from becoming a reality, and we are not even moving toward the goal.

The fossil fuel industry is itself an important reason for why we are making little progress. The fossil fuel companies have fortified their profitable positions through a strong presence in politics, particularly through well-funded lobby groups. With millions of dollars in annual spending and an official outpost on Washington's K Street, ExxonMobil relies on career employees to secure meetings with politicians, executive orders, and favorable laws (Coll, 2012). In fact, hundreds of millions of dollars are spent each year on "Energy and Natural Resources" lobbying in the United States. The oil and gas industry leads the sector in regularly pumping the vast majority of campaign contributions into Republican coffers (OpenSecrets.org, 2016). Other big contributors include electric utilities and mining, both of which are associated with coal (OpenSecrets.org, 2016).This challenge is what motivates campaigns against fossil fuels. Our primary source of energy is a major source of ecological destruction and political leaders are doing little to solve the problem, in large part because of the political activities of the fossil fuel industry. The social movement against fossil fuels is dedicated to changing all this.

1.2 Understanding the movement against fossil fuels

There is no denying that campaigns against fossil fuels have grown big – and fast. While the environmental destruction caused by fossil fuels is itself a powerful image for motivating action, the same could be said about any campaign on climate change. What is special about targeting fossil fuels? Why is this movement mobilizing large crowds of grassroots activists in America and elsewhere?

The answers to these questions are not obvious. If anything, at first sight, there is something puzzling about campaigns against fossil fuels. The fossil fuel industry is the world's largest and heavily concentrated. Major producers of oil, gas, and coal have immense resources at their disposal. Environmentally destructive or not, the demand for the industry's product has grown fast and consistently over the past three centuries. High energy prices, a rapidly growing world economy, and the absence of an effective global climate agreement conspire to raise the profits of the fossil fuel industry. Why are grassroots activists keen to take on such a powerful enemy?

Supportive public opinion certainly cannot explain this outburst of activism. Gallup's polls on public opinion about global warming as a threat suggest no change over time, as shown in Figure 1.1. While there was a temporary uptick of concern until the year 2007, the concern decreased rapidly beginning in 2008. And yet, the anti-fossil fuel mobilization grew rapidly in the years after the global financial meltdown of the fall of 2008, suggesting that the movement's evolution cannot be ascribed to secular trends in public opinion. What is more, the growth of the anti-fossil fuel movement is puzzling even from the perspective of models that emphasize crisis-induced grievances (Davies, 1962; Dryzek and Goodin, 1986; Gamson, 1975; Piven and Cloward, 1977; Skocpol, 1979). While hard times may render redistribution popular, it is unclear how taking on a Goliath of a fossil fuel industry is the fastest means of achieving this goal.

In the scholarship on social movements, the timing of movements is often linked to conducive "political opportunity structures" (Kitschelt, 1986; McAdam, 1999). As McAdam and Boudet (2012: 13–16) explain, drawing on the work of Gamson (1975), Tilly (1978), and others, the presence of a threat is itself not enough to generate mobilization. Instead, an opportunity to effect change is needed to turn grievances into action. In the case of the anti-fossil fuel movement, President Obama's election in 2008 and the success of the Democratic Party in the Congress can certainly explain why the anti-fossil fuel campaigners saw an opportunity to influence the views of the progressive elite in the federal political system – and

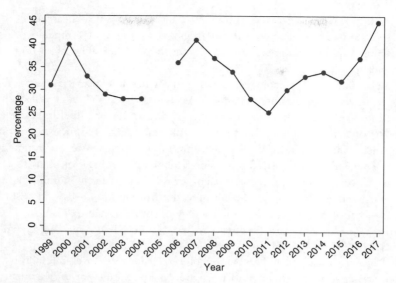

FIGURE 1.1 Public concern about global warming among Americans, 1999–2017. The question wording is as follows throughout the surveys: "I'm going to read you a list of environmental problems. As I read each one, please tell me if you personally worry about this problem a great deal, a fair amount, only a little, or not at all. First, how much do you personally worry about: global warming or climate change?" The graph shows the percentage of Americans choosing "a great deal." The 1999 number is the average of two polls, one in March and the other in April. See www.gallup.com/poll/1615/environment.aspx (accessed December 15, 2017) for details.

President Trump's choice to approve the Keystone XL pipeline shows the limits of activism under a deeply hostile administration. However, such an account cannot explain why the campaign against coal began to grow rapidly already in the early years of the 2000s (Nace, 2010). Indeed, the dynamo of 350.org, Bill McKibben, had himself already begun to emphasize fossil fuels in August 2007, during President George W. Bush's tenure, when he called for a moratorium on coal-fired power plants (McKibben, 2007).[1]

We argue that to understand the popularity and growth of activism against fossil fuels, it is essential to see the world through the activist's eyes. What makes the people who participate in campaigns against fossil fuels tick is not a rational computation of costs and benefits. The typical anti-fossil fuel campaigner believes in what we, following Avery (2013), call the "ecological paradigm." The ecological paradigm in essence is a worldview that emphasizes the primacy of life and nature over economic growth. For the adherents of the ecological paradigm, activism against fossil fuels is a natural choice because it closely reflects their identity and fundamental beliefs about themselves and the world. Because the use of fossil fuels for economic growth is fundamentally incompatible with the goal of ecological preservation and the sanctity of nature, each and every fossil fuel project must be opposed. Anti-fossil fuel activists thus respond to a strong moral imperative. Their activism is driven by considerations of what qualifies as ethical behavior under the ecological paradigm.

The centrality of the ecological paradigm provides an explanation to the rapid growth of campaigns against fossil fuels. As soon as leaders such as Bill McKibben created an organization and a strategy to combat the fossil fuel industry, large numbers of activists found a way to transform their energy and urge to do something into concrete action. While the conventional approach to environmentalism in America has emphasized professional lobbying and litigation (Dowie, 1995; Shabecoff, 2003), anti-fossil fuel campaigns greatly expanded the number of environmental activists by tapping directly into the frustrations, needs, and wishes of masses of sympathizers who were alienated by the professionalism, pragmatism, and rigid structure of what anti-corporate activist Naomi Klein dubs "Big Green" in America (Klein, 2014).

For those who accept and embrace ecological values, the fossil fuel industry is a perfect target. It is a clearly identifiable opponent responsible for the vast majority of global greenhouse gas emissions. By setting their sights on the fossil fuel industry, activists turn climate change from a complex global problem into a simple battle between good and evil. The economic and political activities of the fossil fuel industry have indisputable negative ecological effects. In the eyes of activists, the heavy-handed political tactics of the world's largest fossil fuel producers, frequently called "carbon majors" (Heede, 2014) by their detractors, bear a family resemblance to the policies and behavior of apartheid governments in South Africa and Big Tobacco in the United States.

Far from deterring activists, the global nature, heavy concentration, and centrality of the fossil fuel industry together inspire and encourage the social movement. The goal of anti-fossil fuel activists is to stigmatize the industry and remove the "social license to pollute" that has allowed the fossil fuel industry to reap tremendous profits at the expense of human societies and nature. Through a variety of campaigns, the anti-fossil fuel activists want to make *coal*, *oil*, and *gas* dirty words that provoke unpleasant images in the eyes of the public. This change in public perceptions, activists believe, will force policymakers to enact policies that put an end to fossil fuel extraction.

These insights suggest that the high energy prices of the 2000s were a key motivation behind the movement against fossil fuels. In the 2000s, international oil prices grew rapidly until the financial crisis that began in the fall of 2008, and natural gas and coal prices followed suit. As energy prices increased, both the *threat* and *opportunity* presented by fossil fuels were magnified. On the one hand, high fossil fuel prices drove American energy companies to increase their investments into nonconventional and environmentally destructive projects, such as tar sands. This increase in the salience of the threat motivated activists to mobilize. On the other hand, the rapid escalation of extraction activity in

North America created an opportunity by allowing activists to delay or stop specific projects.

The reasons for the dynamism of the anti-fossil fuel movement are related to the primary motivations behind action, yet a distinction must be made between activist motivations and the movement's ability to grow and succeed. These reasons can be best understood with the help of the concept of "small wins" (Urpelainen, 2013; Weick, 1984). A small win is essentially a feasible but meaningful achievement that gives activists the experience of success and improvement. For example, closing a coal export terminal would be a small win because it can be achieved by activists in the near future and supports the broader effort to combat climate change. In contrast, a global carbon tax is not a small win because it cannot be achieved by activists except over a very long period of time and with a lot of luck.

As Weick (1984) argues, social movements are dependent on small wins for maintaining their momentum and dynamism. This is a critical reason for why anti-fossil fuel campaigns thrive. Activities against individual energy projects, no matter how local, are essentially small wins that can be easily tied to a truly global story about activism for a good cause. The social movement against fossil fuels can sustain and expand itself because campaigns such as divestment from fossil fuels and actions against pipelines, coal mines, and power plants enable a continuous stream of small wins. What is more, these small wins can be easily tied to a broader account based on the ecological paradigm. Whereas traditional environmentalism struggles to motivate its supporters in a society that is heavily biased against ecological values, as is the case in today's America, campaigns against fossil fuels use small wins to keep going.

1.3 Mobilization potential and impact: evaluating the movement

Understanding campaigns against fossil fuels is but a first step toward a satisfactory analysis. The second, perhaps more important, step is assessing whether the campaign has made a difference for global efforts to reduce the rate of climate change. Campaigns against fossil fuels are one approach to mitigating climate change, and anyone who is concerned about climate change should ultimately care about their effect on global temperatures. If the anti-fossil fuels movement makes a lot of noise without reducing climate change, then the campaign should be considered a failure. In this case, activists should use other means to pursue their goals.

In our assessment, we distinguish between two aspects of the campaign: *mobilization potential* and *substantive impact* (Amenta and Caren, 2007; Kriesi, 2007). On the one hand, a necessary condition for the success of the anti-fossil fuel campaign is the mobilization of activists. We shall show that for the reasons we have given above, the anti-fossil fuel campaign has enjoyed considerable success across the United States, and in all of the four issue areas we consider: Keystone XL, divestment, coal, and fracking. By targeting the fossil fuel industry and concrete energy projects on the ground, the campaign has mobilized adherents to the ecological paradigm, while also creating "hybrid" (Heaney and Rojas, 2014, 2015) alliances with other causes, such as local concerns about water pollution and property rights. However, a high degree of mobilization is not enough to call a movement a success (Andrews, 1997, 2004; Kitschelt, 1986). As Tarrow (2011: 216) notes, a correlation between mobilization and changes in outcomes is not itself evidence of an effect: "Movement actions often coincide with changes in public opinion, interest groups, parties, executives, and administrators, not to mention the impact of other movements." We, therefore, also evaluate each of the campaigns for substantive impact on immediate outcomes (e.g., energy projects) and more diffuse achievements (e.g., changes in public opinion or state/federal policy). In conducting this analysis, we acknowledge that the campaign is still ongoing and any substantive impacts are focused on the short run. Some of the movement's achievements could prove short lived, while others could grow more impressive over time (Koopmans, 2007).

Are campaigns against fossil fuels effective? Our answer to this question is a qualified "yes," with stronger evidence for mobilization potential than for impact, at least so far. At this time, the campaign against fossil fuels has done more to raise visibility and provoke concern about climate change and the practices of the fossil fuel industry than any other campaign. Anti-fossil fuel campaigners have reinvigorated environmental activism in the United States and scored a series of important victories. For example, the Sierra Club and other activists have played an important role in defeating planned coal power plants across the United States, preventing the construction of costly infrastructure that would lock in high levels of emissions for decades to come. Even actions such as protests against Keystone XL, which are frequently criticized, have created a vibrant movement that now targets other issues, such as fossil fuel divestment and defeating planned export terminals for coal or natural gas.

The case of divestment from fossil fuels illustrates the power of this kind of campaigning. This campaign urges various institutions, ranging from congregations to universities and foundations, to sell their shares of the fossil fuel industry, often emphasizing the 200 largest companies in the industry. Since divestment sends a powerful moral message and emphasizes the responsibility of individuals and institutions for how they use their resources, it has resonated among religious organizations more than just about any other campaign against climate change. According to GreenFaith, a nonprofit group dedicated to promoting environmental stewardship among faith-based communities, already by June 25, 2015, there were 73 divestment resolutions in the United States and 31 outside the country.[2]

Although much of the action against fossil fuels is ultimately symbolic, we do not see this as a reason to criticize the movement. Politics, by its very nature, is symbolic. If campaigners can provoke concern about climate change by attacking the root cause of the problem, fossil fuels, then even a loss or a seemingly small win can turn into a victory in the long run. This same pattern of moving from nothing to rhetoric, and then from rhetoric to action, has underpinned important victories against the apartheid government in South Africa and Big Tobacco in the United

States. Over time, campaigns against fossil fuels increase the likelihood that we see a similar shift in the public debate and discourse on fossil fuels.

The campaign's recentness notwithstanding, the evidence for the campaign's substantive impact is also quite strong. Most obviously, the Keystone XL campaign *did* in the end convince President Obama to reject TransCanada's application for the pipeline itself (Labott and Berman, 2015, November 6).

Although President Trump later re-approved the pipeline in March 2017, President Obama's decision not to approve caused years of delay and may have doomed the pipeline if oil prices remain low in the future. Both the anti-coal and anti-fracking campaigns have also had considerable success in preventing or stopping projects, though in the case of coal some of the credit actually goes to the crowding out of coal in electricity generation because of fracking itself.[3] While the divestment movement has not targeted specific energy projects, the number of divestment decisions both domestically and internationally has grown quickly.

As a counterweight to this generally positive evaluation, we see three potential roadblocks to success for today's campaign against fossil fuels. For one, the campaign remains vague about specific policy proposals. This is understandable for a relatively new campaign that has chosen a strategy of raising awareness and mobilizing the progressive base in America, but organizational inertia may prevent leading organizations such as 350.org from directly shaping policy. In practice, energy and environmental policy is set in a complex political environment characterized by structural and institutional obstacles to change. If the broad movement for moving away from fossil fuels cannot transform its potential into concrete policy demands, it is possible that there will be no legislative response. For example, future federal administrations could continue to emphasize regulatory dealings with individual energy projects, similar to the skirmishes around Keystone XL over the past years. Even if one believes that rejecting Keystone XL or similar projects has a lot of symbolic value and can be used to rally the troops, it is nowhere near as effective in terms of actual climate mitigation as a carbon tax or other comprehensive federal policies would be.

A second bump in the road is the campaign's inability to reach audiences outside the progressive base. As we shall show, local successes notwithstanding, the anti-fossil fuels campaign has not had much success in reaching out to conservatives, or even independents. While local alliances against *particular* energy projects have often attracted conservatives, such as the ranchers in Nebraska who participated in mobilization against Keystone XL, the national campaign has not drawn any interest among conservative elites. The anti-fossil fuel campaign is gambling on the ability to promote social change through increased salience among progressives, and if this gamble fails, the movement's ability to bridge the gap between local success and national change will be limited.

The third challenge for the movement against fossil fuels concerns the global nature of climate change. Even if the movement in the United States remains vibrant, turns the public against fossil fuels, and begins to exert influence on policy, the global hotspots for energy development are found in emerging economies.

With rapid economic growth, large countries such as China and India will continue to grow their energy consumption for decades to come. The energy choices of these countries will determine the future of the global climate, and the ability of an American movement to shape their policies remains unclear. While 350.org and other environmental organizations have offices, members, and projects in emerging economies, they remain small and have had little effect on policy so far. For example, even successful campaigns to stop World Bank funding of coal power plants may not put much pressure on emerging economies, as Chinese and Indian financial institutions are now capable of funding energy projects both at home and abroad.

In this sense, the ultimate goal of the movement against fossil fuels must be to break what Victor (2011) correctly calls the "global warming gridlock" in international negotiations. As activists launch attacks on the fossil fuel industry in America, they cannot expect to effect genuine change without major ripple effects. Even here, though, we see evidence of strategy and shrewdness on part of the activists. The leading anti-fossil fuel organization, 350.org, is active in virtually all countries of the world – not including North Korea, for obvious reasons – and consistently emphasizes the importance of restoring American leadership in international climate policy.

The first key message for the activists is that their strategy of morally condemning the continued extraction and burning of fossil fuels has been strikingly effective, particularly in drawing new recruits. To sustain its momentum in the context of today's low and volatile energy prices, we recommend a calculated shaming strategy, directing social pressure at vulnerable targets to force the fossil fuel industry to consider alternatives to continuous expansion. The recent decline in oil price represents an unprecedented opportunity, as the rapid and unexpected collapse doomed many nonconventional energy projects, such as tar sands and fracking wells, into unprofitable irrelevance. Armed with an understanding of the cost benefit calculus of the fossil fuel industry, activists must increase social pressure on unconventional energy, particularly as the future profitability of fossil fuels comes under question.

The calculated shaming strategy should be pursued in tandem with broader coalition-building efforts around feasible and pragmatic alternatives to fossil fuels. It is one thing to argue and propagate the notion that the continued burning of fossil fuels is morally wrong, and it is another to suggest plausible alternatives. By transitioning recruits from anti-fossil fuel activism to broader green advocacy, the tremendous success enjoyed in the former area could now be used to breathe new life into the latter, forming synergistic linkages with advocates of energy efficiency, green companies, and renewables producers. If energy prices remain low in the future, then the demand for oil, gas, and coal may continue to increase and undermine the ongoing global shift to cleaner sources of energy, rendering vigorous and coordinated activism on behalf of these cleaner sources absolutely critical.

On the topic of revitalizing green activism, the December 2015 climate summit in Paris prompted, for the first time in history, a global agreement aimed at limiting global warming below two degrees Celsius (United Nations Framework

Convention on Climate Change, 2015).[4] Because the agreement relies heavily on decentralized action – countries are allowed to choose their own national action plans to be reviewed periodically – the anti-fossil fuel movement has an unprecedented opportunity to push governments and other decision makers to adopt policies and measures that contribute to global climate mitigation. Every time countries come together to review their national actions, as per the timeline laid out in the Paris Agreement, the anti-fossil fuel movement has an opportunity to demand climate action in a favorable media environment.

As for the major fossil fuel companies, it would actually be in their best interest to acknowledge the reality of climate change. By rejecting science, ExxonMobil (2013) reinforces the narrative that the entire industry is driven solely by myopic self-interest. The anti-fossil fuel movement thrives on this idea, as it seeks to emulate the success of stigmatizing the tobacco industry. As BP (2013) and Shell (2014) demonstrate, energy companies can prevent this worst-case scenario at a relative low cost, simply by acknowledging climate change and adapting their business models to the more modest demands of the activists. This may entail gradually reducing investments in extreme energy and increasing investments in renewables.

If the industry does respond in a constructive fashion and makes a serious effort to move away from fossil fuels, then the anti-fossil fuel movement has an opportunity to identify and support promising plans for change. This, ultimately, is how we envision the best-case scenario for both the anti-fossil fuel activists and the fossil fuel industry itself. If the activists are better able to understand the cost benefit calculus of fossil fuel companies, they should be able to take the long view and encourage burgeoning business ventures that promote sustainability, while condemning those that undermine it. While these companies are unlikely to transition to renewables overnight, our point is that even incremental changes can help them move toward a more prosperous, sustainable future.

1.4 Ideas, implications, and contributions

By describing and assessing what is perhaps the world's largest and most important movement, we situate environmentalism in the larger game of 21st-century climate politics. This is important because most research on the politics of climate change focuses on other issues. Books have been written on the tremendous social challenge that climate change poses (Giddens, 2009), the cultural controversies created by global warming (Hulme, 2010), the difficulty of international environmental cooperation (Barrett, 2003), the sources of skepticism about climate science (Oreskes and Conway, 2010), and climate policy in the American states (Rabe, 2004). As helpful as these books are, they have little to say about how a growing global movement against fossil fuels will shape climate policy in the coming decades. A movement that focuses on fossil fuels is not just about climate change and, due to the local destruction that fossil fuel extraction causes, can mobilize many people who are not interested in the nuances of climate science. Our research shows, for example, that the campaigns against fossil fuels have drawn participants from a variety of other causes, such as religious environmental stewardship, labor unions, anti-corporate mobilization, and opposition to nuclear weapons. The emergence of such "hybrid activism" (Heaney and Rojas, 2014) reflects a confluence of strategic decisions, issue characteristics, and failures of conventional environmentalism.

Indeed, the importance of this story is particularly clear against the backdrop of American environmentalism before 350.org and others entered the game. Over the past two decades, many a scholar has written about the evolution of American environmentalism, often chastising the movement for inertia and a lack of dynamism since the major legislative victories around the 1970 Earth Day (Dowie, 1995; Schlosberg and Dryzek, 2002; Shabecoff, 2003). Since the publication of these studies, American environmentalism has been reinvigorated by the innovations, strategies, small wins, and spirit of campaigns against fossil fuels. Our study is the first to show how American environmentalism has again become a dynamic, vibrant, and lively socio-political force. In a context characterized by the primacy of climate change as an environmental issue, the indirect strategy of attacking fossil fuels instead of carbon emissions has brought environmentalism back to the center of the political game.

While the movement against fossil fuels sometimes calls for international agreements on climate change, a notable feature of this campaigning is its sharp emphasis on local and national politics. The campaign against fossil fuels is ultimately about fossil fuels in various local contexts. Even completely international aspects, such as coal and natural gas exports, are fought locally, terminal by terminal. The analysis of this strategy is important because the literature on social movements and climate change has, by and large, been spellbound by international climate summits, agreements, and governance processes (Hoffmann, 2011). The truth is that these international processes have little to show for themselves in terms of mitigating climate change. Most action remains either national or, at best, regional, as in the case of the European Union. Even the Paris climate agreement of December 2015, which has finally created a global regulatory framework for climate mitigation, calls for countries to choose their own targets and policies – leaving a critical role to domestic activists. As Bill McKibben himself wrote in a *New York Times* opinion piece in the aftermath of the Paris deal:

> We need to build the movement even bigger in the coming years, so that the Paris Agreement turns into a floor and not a ceiling for action. We'll be blocking pipelines, fighting new coal mines, urging divestment from fossil fuels – trying, in short, to keep weakening the mighty industry that still stands in the way of real progress. With every major world leader now on the record saying they at least theoretically support bold action to make the transition to renewable energy, we've got a new tool to work with.
>
> (McKibben, 2015, December 13)

The trials and tribulations of international climate cooperation also emphasize the importance of our evaluation of the campaigns against fossil fuels. From an academic perspective, evaluating a movement that is only a few years old and still growing is, of course, an enterprise fraught with difficulty. But we see no alternative. Climate change is today's most difficult challenge and the science leaves little doubt about the severity of the climate disruption that awaits humanity unless we manage to cut our emissions. From a practical perspective, now is the time to evaluate the campaign against fossil fuels. Our evaluation, which is for the most part positive, suggests that anyone interested in mitigating global warming should support the campaign against fossil fuels. Our research shows that the detractors of the campaign against fossil fuels are mostly wrong, and this is because they misunderstand the challenge of social mobilization.

But the caveats, problems, and challenges that we identify can also help the movement improve its efficacy. It is always challenging for an academic to claim that practitioners can learn something from a book that summarizes research on the activities of these activists. And yet, we believe a comprehensive analysis of the campaign against fossil fuels can improve the campaign itself. Anti-fossil fuel activists lead lives of extreme intensity and constant pressure, leaving little time for genuine reflection and introspection. Our book provides a sympathetic, yet objective and critical, evaluation of the past years. From the grassroots level to national leadership, current and prospective anti-fossil fuel campaigners can learn from our research about what works, what fails, and why.

Of the different strategies adopted by anti-fossil fuel campaigners, divestment is, despite its visibility, perhaps the least understood in the public debate. Our chapter on divestment should remove some of the confusion surrounding this strategy and provide insights into when and how divestment works. The critics of divestment often emphasize that selling shares of fossil fuel companies does not have a direct effect on their valuation. This is true and divestment activists understand well that their actions are symbolic and political in nature. But this is no reason to discount the effectiveness of divestment. As we show, divestment has already had a clear effect on the public debate, drawing attention to the problem of climate change, the deep problems caused by our continued reliance on fossil fuel extraction, and the need for more ethical alternatives. The mobilization of religious groups to demand action on climate change alone is a notable achievement.

While this book is not intended for academic researchers in particular, we do offer four key contributions to researchers. The first concerns motivations for participating in and contributing to social movements. Much has been written about the role of grievances (Barnes, 1984; Klandermans and Oegema, 1987; Walsh, 1981), social networks and connections (Campbell, 2013; Diani, 2007), resource mobilization (Edwards and McCarthy, 2007; McCarthy and Zald, 1977), political opportunity structures (Kitschelt, 1986; Kriesi, 2007; McAdam, 1999; Meyer, 2004), and risks (Dryzek and Goodin, 1986; McAdam, 1986) as factors in activism. We show that, while these factors are important, the intrinsic features of the issue (fossil fuels), the characteristics of the target (global energy industry), and the worldview of potential activists (ecological paradigm) can be decisive in shaping mobilization. Conventional and professionalized environmentalists focusing on legislative action had the same grievances as did the anti-fossil fuel activists. Major environmental organizations had more resources and access to existing social networks. Their activities were certainly not risky or particularly expensive for the members. And yet, it was the more demanding grassroots campaign against fossil fuels that reinvigorated the American environmental movement. While existing scholarship has recognized that "[m]ediating between opportunity and action are people and the subjective meanings they attach to their situation" (McAdam, 1999: 48), we show how a strategic reframing has allowed movement leaders to mobilize ecological activists and reinvigorate the movement.

Our findings are in line with McAdam's (1999: 29–30) emphasis on "the importance of the mass base" for social movements. The national level campaign certainly played an important role in bringing together diverse local campaigns, but the very ability of the movement to do so has depended heavily on the formation of local coalitions to address local grievances. In evaluating the role of local, hybrid coalitions in climate activism, we draw on insights by Jung et al. (2014: 189), who argue that "co-occurrence of issues is more likely to happen between culturally similar movements," where cultural similarity refers to "the extent of tactical overlap between pairs of movements." As we shall see, such similarity in tactics at the local level can explain how conservative ranchers and ecological activists have joined forces to fight fossil fuels.

As we shall see, political opportunity structures did play a role in invigorating the movement during Obama's presidency (Kitschelt, 1986; McAdam, 1999), but ultimately the emergence of the anti-fossil fuel campaign reflects more the threats and opportunities afforded by the explosion of nonconventional fossil fuel extraction. This structural factor enabled a strategic reframing of the climate campaign, with more combative overtones and a more localized approach. Neither public opinion nor the state of the economy were particularly favorable to climate campaigning during the past decade, but the advent of a new era of fossil fuel extraction empowered ecological activists to mobilize. In this regard, and contrary to the recent focus of the social movements literature, our analysis lends support to the emphasis that the "classical model" of mobilization puts on "strain in society."[5] When high fossil fuel prices generated a series of ecologically destructive extraction projects, activists responded with swift mobilization. On the other hand, we also find that the threat presented by nonconventional fossil fuel extraction also created an opportunity for mobilization – the same forces that caused the threat also created the opportunity for local action.

The second contribution pertains to the empirical analysis of what Weick (1984) calls small wins. As we researched the campaign against fossil fuels, we were struck by the prescience of Weick's (1984) analysis. The campaign against fossil fuels has not stopped climate change or driven carbon majors into bankruptcy, yet activists can boast a stream of meaningful small wins. While the concept of small wins is not enough to say what makes anti-fossil fuel activists tick, it is the cornerstone of our account of why the campaign thrives and grows. In this sense, our analysis validates an important hypothesis from the literature on social movements.

On the other hand, we also uncover evidence for the limits of the small-wins strategy. In the latest generation of research on social movements (McAdam and Boudet, 2012; Tarrow, 2011), the distinction between mobilization and outcomes has increasingly drawn attention and become a bone of contention (Amenta and Caren, 2007; Kriesi, 2007). In the case of anti-fossil fuels movement, we show that while small wins have had an unambiguously positive effect on mobilization, their substantive significance is much less clear. The impact is the clearest in the case of anti-coal and anti-fracking mobilization – though the two campaigns seem to have somewhat contradictory goals – and is much murkier in the case of Keystone XL and divestment.

The third contribution pertains to the role of social movements in global climate policy. By now, a body of literature focusing on transnational nongovernmental actors in climate politics has emerged (Betsill and Bulkeley, 2006; Corell and Betsill, 2001; Green, 2014; Hadden, 2015; Hale, 2011; Hoffmann, 2011; Urpelainen, 2009). However, this literature mostly focuses on private governance (Avery, 2013; Green, 2014), local climate policies (Betsill and Bulkeley, 2006), or activism related to international climate negotiations (Hadden, 2015). In practice, though, the most important climate policies are formulated at the national level.[6] Moreover, increased ambition at the international level will probably require more favorable domestic political environments. By focusing on the anti-fossil fuel movement in the United States, we break new ground for understanding the ability of social mobilization to change the domestic politics of climate change.

Finally, our analysis of activism against fossil fuels speaks to broader debates in environmental politics and political ecology. Regardless of whether or not capitalism and ecological sustainability are compatible, an environmental movement that is unwilling to confront destructive economic interests cannot protect the planet from pillage. Similar to results from the analysis of political ecology in the developing world (Martinez-Alier, 2002), we find that explicit confrontation is a powerful force. Some industries, such as fossil fuel producers, are by their very nature environmentally destructive. Although fossil fuels are an engine of economic development, their uncontrolled expansion is bound to worsen environmental degradation in all corners of the world. Recognizing this basic fact, the campaign against fossil fuels tackles the root problem of climate change and ecological destruction. This observation does not validate the claim that capitalism is fundamentally incompatible with ecology (Klein, 2014), but it shows that sometimes antagonism is a force for good.

1.5 A road map

This book has nine chapters. In Chapter 2, we provide an overview of the global fossil fuel industry. First, we provide a brief overview of the significance of oil, gas, and coal for the world economy, both historically and today. The chapter then explains why fossil fuels pose, despite their attractive features as a convenient and abundant source of energy, many problems for humans and ecosystems. Next, we provide an overview of the industry that extracts and sells fossil fuels for profit. Finally, we offer a prospectus on the future of the fossil fuel industry, especially in relation to climate change and the activism against the industry.

Chapter 3 is the analytical core of this book. We review the literature on activism, provide an overview of American environmental activism before campaigns against fossil fuels began in earnest, and offer a discussion of the motivation and drivers of anti-fossil fuel campaigns. The chapter explains how the large existing body of scholarly literature on activism informs our work and summarizes the pathologies of American environmentalism at the turn of the 20th century. The most important parts of the chapter are the next two sections. They explain why the campaign against fossil fuels is so attractive for the adherents of the ecological paradigm by emphasizing the presence of a clear enemy, the availability of feasible intermediate goals such as the termination of an oil pipeline, and the clear connection between local and global campaigning. Along similar lines, we offer a summary of the potential of the campaign by highlighting the importance of movement building, the removal of the social license of the fossil fuel industry, and the possibility of shaping policy formulation through campaigns that seemingly ignore policy. At the same time, we note that the campaign against fossil fuels is ultimately intended to mobilize progressives and turn them into fierce climate advocates. One of the most important weaknesses of the campaign is that there is not much in this campaign to motivate conservatives, or even independents. There is not much in it for conservatives or even independents, and this is among the most important weaknesses of the campaign.

Chapters 4–7 contain the empirical analysis of the campaign against fossil fuels in the United States and, in some cases, Canada. We begin with a chapter on the campaign against the Keystone XL pipeline. Led by the Vermont environmental writer and activist Bill McKibben, who founded the organization 350.org, Keystone XL is arguably the most important reason for why there now is a grassroots climate movement in the United States. The Keystone XL campaign shows how a concrete target that brings together global and local concerns can mobilize a large activist coalition in opposition. While the Keystone XL campaign is repeatedly criticized for failing to grasp the relatively small role of the pipeline in the larger climate game, it is impossible to deny that the pipeline has brought huge crowds of activists from the state of Nebraska to the National Mall in Washington, DC. As such, the Keystone XL shows why campaigns against fossil fuels can grow and bring together large groups of previously passive climate advocates.

In Chapter 5, we set our sights on the divestment campaign. This campaign encourages investors to draw their resources out of the world's large oil, gas, and coal companies. The campaign has gained a lot of popularity on college campuses, among religious communities, and, more recently, even in cities. While the divestment campaign also benefits greatly from the presence of a clear opponent, it draws more strongly on moral and ethical principles than Keystone XL has ever done. Divestment activists are also enthusiastic about the presence of a local target. They have succeeded in drawing attention to the problematic practices of the fossil fuel industry and, most importantly, the incompatibility between continued extraction and international climate targets. Combining ethical arguments with financial ones, such as the possibility that huge fossil fuel deposits become "stranded assets" under international climate policy, divestment activists have begun to shake the confidence of the fossil fuel industry. What is more, divestment activists show an impressive understanding of the arguments of their detractors, such as the irrelevance of divestment for the stock market valuations of the individual companies.

Chapter 6 focuses on the most polluting of fossil fuels, coal. Local campaigns against coal mining, especially strip mines and mountaintop removal, have a long history in America, but a systematic campaign to stop the production and use of coal in the United States is a creature of this millennium. Over the past years, anti-coal activists have attacked hundreds of existing and planned coal power plants across America, often with considerable success. Compared to Keystone XL and divestment, the anti-coal campaign has been more strongly oriented toward local goals. Although campaigning against coal mines and power plants is more directly relevant to global greenhouse gas emissions than blocking one pipeline or encouraging divestment from the fossil fuel industry, climate change only plays a secondary role in the communications of the anti-coal campaign.

In Chapter 7, we delve into the campaign against hydraulic fracturing, or "fracking," of shale gas. This campaign has drawn considerable criticism, as proponents of shale gas use maintain that it is the fastest and most effective way to reduce the use of coal in the United States. At the same time, anti-fracking activists express grave concerns about the effect of fracking on the local environment, especially supplies of drinking water, and highlight studies that suggest the global warming potential of fugitive methane emissions from fracking. If anything, the fracking campaign appears even more strongly local than the other campaigns against fossil fuels, to the extent that the campaign would probably continue in many communities regardless of the climate impact of fracking.

Our analysis so far has focused on North America, but in Chapter 8 we examine the global aspects of the campaign against fossil fuels. This analysis highlights the unique nature of the North American campaigns in the global picture. While campaigns against pipelines are common and have a long history on all continents of the world, their focus even today is exclusively local. International campaigns against fracking are fragmented and shaped by the specific national characteristics of different countries. There is no independent global divestment campaign to speak of. Among the four anti-fossil fuel campaigns we have reviewed, only the international campaign against coal is independent but shares many core features with its American counterpart.

In the concluding chapter, Chapter 9, we bring together and discuss the results of our analysis. We reflect on the applicability of our analysis and the limitations of the study. We also consider the future implications of the campaign against fossil fuels for the broader international effort to stop climate change. Based on the research done for this book, we see the campaign against fossil fuels as an important tactic in the daunting and increasingly urgent struggle to stop global warming.

Notes

1 See www.stepitup2007.org/ (accessed November 20, 2015).
2 These are conservative figures, as we require explicit commitments to divest their own funds and forego further investments in fossil fuels from the concerned entities. For our source, see "Divest and Reinvest Central," available at http://greenfaith.org/programs/divest-and-reinvest/listing-of-known-religious-divestment-efforts (accessed December 13, 2014).
3 As we shall show, there has been tension between the anti-coal and anti-fracking activists for this very reason. The anti-fracking activists, in particular, have resented anti-coal campaigns because they have contributed to the growth of fracking.
4 The text of the agreement can be found at https://unfccc.int/resource/docs/2015/cop21/eng/l09r01.pdf.
5 See McAdam (1999: 11) for a detailed discussion.
6 The European Union is an important exception to this general pattern.

2

FOSSIL FUELS IN THE WORLD ECONOMY

Fossil fuels are the backbone of today's industrial economy. Not only do they represent the world's largest and most valuable industry, but the growing energy demand in the developing world has also prompted the largest fossil fuel companies – the carbon majors – to launch and sustain a relentless effort to locate new reserves of coal, oil, and gas. Since this book is about various campaigns against the fossil fuel industry – their motivation, logic, efficacy, strengths, and weaknesses – we begin with a fairly detailed exploration of the industry itself. The mechanics of this global industry are key to understanding why it provokes so much resistance, why it invites millions to become activists, and whether or not it proves unassailable.

Fossil fuels play a central role in sustaining industrialized economies and modern life itself. This chapter illustrates how fossil fuels became the primary source of energy for the world's leading economies at the onset of industrialization, and, in turn, set them on a seemingly inevitable path of continued fossil fuel dependence. As we illustrate with facts and figures, a shared addiction to fossil fuels has fundamentally shaped the nature of political economic relations among nations. Those to benefit most from these developments, of course, were the major fossil fuels companies, global juggernauts that raked in billions of dollars in profits for supplying the lifeblood of nations. The unfortunate consequence of all this, however, is that their highly profitable industry has also generated significant negative externalities, namely climate change and its harmful ecological effects, that are only now beginning to attract the attention of the international community. Against this backdrop, environmental organizations such as 350.org have embarked on a public campaign to stigmatize the fossil fuel industry – "revoke their license to pollute" – in an effort to tip the balance in favor of renewables and clean energy. The progress of technology, however, has been a mixed blessing. While it has strengthened the case for an economically feasible transition to sustainable energy, it has also equipped the fossil fuel industry with new and unconventional methods of extracting oil at significant costs to the environment. As the thirst for energy among emerging economies, such as China and India, continues to grow, the stakes for environmental activists and their adversaries in the fossil fuel industry could not be higher.

We begin with a section on how the fundamental shaping forces of history, such as industrialization and globalization, have been fueled by and contributed to a global addiction to fossil fuels. Next, we discuss the environmental consequences of this global addiction to fossil fuels, namely climate change and its ecological consequences, and how environmental activists of various stripes have responded to this challenge. Third, we explore the inner workings of the fossil fuel industry, which has benefited tremendously from the global addiction to its commodities and, not coincidentally, become the prime target of environmental activists of late. We conclude with thoughts about the future prospects of the fossil fuel industry and their activist opponents, with a particular focus on technological developments. This analysis sets the scene for a thorough exploration of activism against fossil fuels.

2.1 Industrialization, globalization, and fossil fuels

Fossil fuels are organic matter made from the remains of flora and fauna, subjected to immense heat and pressure while buried deep within the Earth over millions of years. Petroleum, coal, and natural gas are the three major fossil fuels. The global demand for energy is rapidly increasing with human population, urbanization, and modernization. The growth in global energy demand is projected to rise sharply over the coming years (Asif and Muneer, 2007). According to the International Energy Agency's projections based on existing and planned government policies in the 2014 *World Energy Outlook*, world primary energy demand is set to increase by 37 percent between 2012 and 2040 (IEA, 2014). Almost all of the growth in energy demand comes from non-OECD countries. Asia accounts for 60 percent, shifting the locus of energy markets away from the Americas and Europe. China is the dominant force behind global demand growth for the next decade, accounting for more than one-third of the increase. But after 2025, India will take over as Chinese growth slows down noticeably. To be sure, *Outlook* tells us that while energy use per capita in non-OECD countries will rise strongly, by 2040 it will remain well below the level that was reached in OECD countries in the early 1970s, due to technological progress and improved energy efficiency (IEA, 2014).

Fossil fuels such as oil, gas, and coal are providing almost 80 percent of the global energy demand, while renewable energy and nuclear power are contributing only 13.5 percent and 6.5 percent, respectively (Asif and Muneer, 2007). Led by China's ravenous thirst for energy, emerging economies are using more coal, gas, and oil than ever before (Nuttall and Manz, 2008: 1249). This trend is clearly seen in Figure 2.1. The global consumption of all fossil fuels has increased dramatically between 1965 and 2013. Initially driven by the rapid growth in industrialized and

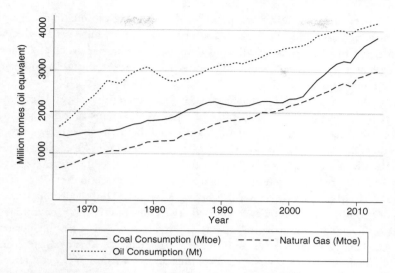

FIGURE 2.1 Historical trends in fossil fuel consumption, 1965–2013.

Source: BP (2015)

socialist countries, China and other emerging economies have since become the key players. Of particular importance is the rapid increase in the use of coal since the year 2000, driven in large part by China's demand for inexpensive electricity, both for the industry and increasingly wealthy households.

2.2 The problem with fossil fuels

The largest source of greenhouse gas emissions from human activities in the United States and globally is, of course, the burning of fossil fuels. According to a recent study, cumulative emissions among the 20 largest energy companies between 1854 and 2010 total 428,439 metric tons of carbon dioxide equivalent (MtCO2e), or 29.5 percent of global industrial emissions from 1751 to 2010. In fact, 90 energy companies are responsible for contributing 63.04 percent of global industrial CO2 and methane between 1751 and 2010 (Heede, 2014). The effect of fossil fuel use on climate change is a particularly salient topic today, but the extraction and use of fossil fuels also cause direct, local environmental damage.

The Earth's climate is changing in ways that affect our weather, oceans, snow, ice, ecosystems, and society. Though disputed by a small minority of skeptics, it is widely accepted that natural causes alone cannot explain all of these changes. Human activities are contributors to climate change, through the release of billions of tons of carbon dioxide (CO2) and other heat-trapping gases, known as greenhouse gases, into the atmosphere every year (IPCC, 2013; Rockström et al., 2009). The most disturbing aspect of the problem is that anthropogenic climate change is still ongoing. What we are experiencing today, the melting of ice caps and the abnormal temperatures, is the product of our past emissions. By the same token, carbon emissions today will contribute to future changes, such as a warmer atmosphere, a warmer and more acidic ocean, higher sea levels, and larger changes in precipitation patterns.

In evaluating the environmental consequences of fossil fuels, it is of course important to distinguish between different types. While comparing the local environmental damage caused by coal, oil, and gas is difficult, their climate effects can be evaluated more easily. To do this, let us consider the case of electricity generation. Relative to the energy generated, coal is far worse than oil or natural gas. One kilowatt hour of electricity from coal generates twice the carbon dioxide of natural gas, and oil carbon dioxide output falls between the two. This calculation, however, does not consider the possibility of high "fugitive emissions" of methane from natural gas in fracking (Howarth et al., 2011). If fugitive emissions are as high as environmental activists fear, then natural gas could be as bad as coal for climate change.

For anti-fossil fuel campaigners, preventing climate disruption is a core priority. For example, 350.org finds its inspiration from James Hansen, a respected Columbia University climatologist, who claims that "[i]f humanity wishes to preserve a planet similar to that on which civilization developed and to which life on Earth is adapted, paleoclimate evidence and ongoing climate change suggest that CO2 will need to be reduced from its current 385 ppm to at most 350 ppm" (Hansen et al., 2008).

The intuition is that when the ratio of carbon dioxide molecules to all other molecules in the atmosphere exceeds 350 parts per million, we are already in the danger zone (Rockström et al., 2009). According to the Intergovernmental Panel on Climate Change (IPCC)'s *Fifth Assessment Report*, the atmospheric concentrations of the greenhouse gases carbon dioxide (CO2), methane (CH4), and nitrous oxide (N2O) have all increased since 1750 due to human activity. By 2011, the concentrations of these greenhouse gases were at 391 ppm, 1803 ppb, and 324 ppb, and exceeded the pre-industrial levels by about 40 percent, 150 percent, and 20 percent, respectively (IPCC, 2013: 11).

At the 2009 United Nations Climate Change Conference, 114 countries, including the United States, China, India, and the United Arab Emirates (later joined by 27 more for a total of 141 countries), recognizing the scientific view that the increase in global temperature should be below 2 degrees Celsius, agreed to enhance their long-term cooperative action to combat climate change (United Nations Framework Convention on Climate Change, 2009).[1] The globally averaged combined land and ocean surface temperature data, as calculated by a linear trend, show a warming of 0.85 [0.65 to 1.06] °C over the period 1880 to 2012, when multiple independently produced datasets exist. The total increase between the average of the 1850–1900 period and the 2003–2012 period is 0.78 [0.72 to 0.85] °C, based on the single longest dataset available (IPCC, 2013: 5).

Already now, many of the observed changes since the 1950s are "unprecedented over decades to millennia." The amounts of snow and ice have diminished, the sea level has risen, and the concentrations of greenhouse gases have increased (IPCC, 2013: 4). Over the last two decades, the Greenland and Antarctic ice sheets have been losing mass, glaciers have continued to shrink almost worldwide, and the Arctic sea ice and the Northern Hemisphere spring snow cover have continued to diminish (IPCC, 2013: 9). The rate of sea level rise since the mid-19th century has been larger than the mean rate during the previous two millennia. Over the period 1901 to 2010, the global mean sea level rose by 0.19 [0.17 to 0.21] mm per year (IPCC, 2013: 11). Carbon dioxide concentrations have increased by 40 percent since pre-industrial times, primarily from fossil fuel emissions, and secondarily from net land use change emissions. The ocean has absorbed about 30 percent of the emitted anthropogenic carbon dioxide, causing ocean acidification (IPCC, 2013: 11).

Changes have also been observed in extreme weather and climate events. It is very likely that the number of cold days and nights has decreased and the number of warm days and nights has increased on a global scale. It is likely that the frequency of heat waves has increased in large parts of Europe, Asia, and Australia. There are likely more regions where the number of heavy precipitation events has increased than where it has decreased. Closer to home, the frequency or intensity of heavy precipitation events has likely increased in North America and Europe (IPCC, 2013: 5). Intensity and/or duration of drought have likely increased in many regions, and so has tropical cyclone activity in some regions since 1970 (IPCC, 2013: 7).

On human impact, World Health Organization (WHO; McMichael et al., 2004) has estimated the likely effects of climate change on exposures to thermal extremes and weather disasters (particularly floods), the distribution and incidence of malaria, the incidence of diarrhea, and malnutrition (through decreased agricultural crop yields) to be more than 150,000 deaths for the year 2000. Climate change was estimated to increase the relative risk of diarrhea in regions comprised mainly of developing countries, and this modest change in relative risk, as it relates to a major cause of ill-health, was associated with a disease burden of 47,000 deaths. Effects on malnutrition, which varied markedly even across developing sub regions, was associated with a disease burden of 77,000 deaths. Floods were associated with 2,000 deaths, whereas falciparum malaria was associated with 27,000 deaths, particularly in Africa. Overall, the effects were heavily concentrated in poorer populations at low latitudes, where malnutrition, diarrhea, and malaria are already common, and vulnerability to climate effects is greatest. Since these diseases mainly affect younger age groups, children in developing countries are most vulnerable (McMichael et al., 2004: 1545).

The effects considered represent only a subset of the pathways in which climate change may affect health, as others include influences of changing temperature and precipitation on other infectious diseases (new pathogens), the distribution and abundance of agricultural pests and pathogens, destruction of public health infrastructure, and production of photochemical air pollutants, spores and pollens. Rising sea levels may cause salination of coastal lands and freshwater supplies, resulting in population displacements. Changes in the availability and distribution of natural resources, especially water, may increase risk of drought, famine, and conflict (McMichael et al., 2004: 1544). Based on more recent analyses, climate change is projected to have substantial adverse impacts on future global mortality rates, even under optimistic scenarios of future socioeconomic development. Under a base case socioeconomic scenario, the WHO estimates approximately 250,000 additional global deaths due to climate change per year between 2030 and 2050 (WHO, 2014).

Indeed, the World Bank reports that new assessments of business-as-usual emissions in the absence of strong climate mitigation policies, as well as recent reevaluations of the likely emissions consequences of pledges and targets adopted by countries, point to a considerable likelihood of warming reaching 4°C above pre-industrial levels within this century (World Bank, 2014). In such a scenario, the report predicts, climatic conditions, heat, and other weather extremes considered highly unusual or unprecedented today would become the new climate normal, a world of increased risks and instability. The consequences for development would be severe as crop yields decline, water resources change, diseases move into new ranges, and sea levels rise (World Bank, 2014).

Climate change is not the only negative consequence of fossil fuels. Both the production and consumption of fossil fuels cause ecological destruction. For example, the burning of coal is a major source of air pollution. In China, the rapid growth of coal-powered electricity generation has reduced air quality in major cities, with negative health and environmental impacts (Chan and Yao, 2008). In the United States, econometric studies indicate that the negative externalities of coal use could outweigh the economic benefits (Muller et al., 2011). Moreover, coal power plants use large amounts of water. Fueled by diesel and gasoline, transportation is another major source of air pollution in urban areas across the world (Mayer, 1999). Among the three major fuels, only natural gas can be considered relatively clean in terms of the pollution its use generates.

The ecological destruction caused by fossil fuels is more visible at the production stage. Studies in political ecology often emphasize fossil fuel projects as the source of local conflicts between communities and project developers (Beynon et al., 2000; Carvalho, 2006; Casper and Wellstone, 1981; McNeil, 2011; Montrie, 2003; Nace, 2010). Today, coal is often extracted from the ground through techniques called "surface mining," meaning that the soil and the rock overlying coal deposits is removed. This technique causes visible changes in the landscape and has been a major source of local opposition, especially in the United States (Beynon et al., 2000; McNeil, 2011; Montrie, 2003; Nace, 2010).

When oil is found in populated or biodiverse areas, a conflict ensues between oil companies on the one side and environmentalists and local communities on the other. In Ecuador, for example, the Yasuni National Park is not only one of the world's biodiversity hotspots, but also sits on billions of dollars' worth of oil (Martin, 2011). Oil pipelines and maritime transportation create risks of oil spills, and often generate resistance. For example, in the campaign against the Keystone XL oil pipeline from Canada to the United States, many local activists are motivated by concerns about the local environmental hazards of oil transportation (Avery, 2013). Natural gas suffers from similar problems, and today there is a heated debate on the environmental consequences of fracking, with anti-fracking activists accusing natural gas companies of spoiling the local water (Davis, 2012).

One area of the world where the tragic consequences of fossil fuel extraction for local communities have been visible for decades is the Niger Delta in Nigeria. A deprived area with major oil assets developed by Shell and other oil companies, Niger Delta has seen some of the worst ecological conflicts in history (Opukri and Ibaba, 2008). Moreover, the value of oil assets has provoked a violent conflict between various groups (Ikelegbe, 2005). In 1995, the prominent human rights and environmental activist Ken Saro-Wiwa, a member of the Ogoni people, who have for decades fought against Shell due to the negative environmental effects of oil extraction, was executed along with other Ogoni leaders by the military government of General Sani Abacha. Nigeria's ecological destruction due to oil extraction continues today. For example, on December 3, 2014, it was reported that a Shell oil facility had spilled 3,800 barrels of oil "across the swamps and into the ocean" (Owolabi, 2014, December 3). A local fisherman, Boma Macaulay, said "We can't go fishing anymore. It has destroyed our fishing equipment." The local communities are now suing Shell for compensation, potentially reaching billions of dollars.

To summarize, fossil fuels create a host of environmental problems. Climate change is probably the most salient of these, but there are also many negative environmental and ecological effects at the local level. We next investigate the nature of the industry behind these problems.

2.3 The fossil fuel industry

We briefly survey the fossil fuel industry, emphasizing its widespread perception as the symbol of the rich and the powerful. The industry has benefited from a global addiction to fossil fuels, even as evidence of the environmental damages and ecological changes wrought by this dangerous addiction continues to mount. To fortify their position, the fossil fuel companies maintain a strong presence in politics through well-funded lobby networks. It is no accident that the fossil fuel industry became a useful target and a rallying point for the activists we study in this book.

Some of the biggest companies in the world today are those engaged in upstream (exploration, production, development) and downstream (refining, distribution) operations in oil and natural gas. The merger of Exxon and Mobil, both direct descendants of Standard Oil, resulted in the birth of ExxonMobil Corporation on December 1, 1999, destined to become the world's largest nongovernmental producer of oil and natural gas and the largest corporation of any kind headquartered in the United States (Coll, 2012: 66). The corporation's revenue in its first year of combined operations, $228 billion, exceeded Norway's GDP. If its revenue were counted as GDP, the corporation would rank as the 21st largest nation-state in the world. Its net profit alone – $17.7 billion that year – was greater than the GDP of more than 100 nation-states, from Latvia to Kenya to Jordan. ExxonMobil, ranked third in the world in a prominent global ranking of the world's top oil and gas companies based on financial and operational measures, is joined by BP, Royal Dutch Shell, Chevron, and Total, which rank sixth, seventh, ninth, and tenth, respectively.

How is it possible that the world's largest producer of oil and natural gas is ranked only third, and some of the biggest names in the business, such as BP, Shell, Chevron, and Total, fall outside of the top five? One key development in recent history has been the rise of resource nationalism, as resource rich governments, particularly in the Middle East and Latin America, reclaimed their oil and natural gas assets from foreign majors by force and forbade future attempts at foreign ownership. Private ownership of the world's oil and natural gas base has accordingly diminished to less than 10 percent (Lewis, 2007). Ninety percent of the oil and natural gas base has been taken up by governments and their national oil companies. Saudi Aramco (Saudi Arabia) and National Iranian Oil Company (Iran) check in at the number one and number two spots, respectively, and state-owned enterprises comprise five of the top ten. As we examine anti-fossil fuel movements with a focus on the United States, the world's largest economy, it is important to keep in perspective the extent to which the control of the world's oil and natural gas actually rests with governments and national oil companies (Energy Intelligence, n.d.).[2]

Coal firms are also global, but they have relatively little diversity for their scale. With few exceptions, national boundaries define a company's resource base and its economic exposure. Thus, while the top coal companies, such as Shenhua (China), Coal India, China Coal Energy, Consol Energy (US), and Shaanxi Coal (China), may hail from different parts of the world, they mainly operate in their home grounds (Bullard, 2014). The heavy Chinese representation among the major coal companies reflects the fact that China is the largest coal producer in the world. It is reported that in 2005, China produced 2.19 billion tons of coal, which represents 37 percent of total coal production in the world and accounts for 75.9 percent and 70 percent of China's total primary energy production and consumption, respectively (Fang et al., 2009).

Within the US, top four coal companies accounted for more than half of the domestic production in 2011, the result of changes in regional production, as well as decades-long trends toward the concentration of coal production around the top few companies: Peabody Energy Corporation, Arch Coal Inc., Alpha Natural Resources LLC, and Cloud Peak Energy together supplied 575 million tons, or 52 percent of total US coal production in 2011, while more than 500 other companies supplied the remaining 48 percent (Kearney, 2011).[3] However, coal companies have much smaller scale than those dealing with oil and gas. Within that smaller scale, there is also less intra-company diversity. The largest coal firm by market capitalization would barely break into the ranks of the top 20 oil and gas firms (Bullard, 2014).

The enormous profits for the fossil fuel industry come at a significant cost to the environment. According to cumulative estimates from Heede (2014) spanning 1854–2010, Chevron ranks as the highest contributor, with 51,096 methane and carbon dioxide emissions (MtCO2e), followed by ExxonMobil (46,672), Saudi

Aramco (46,033), BP (35,837), Gazprom (32,136), Royal Dutch Shell (30,751), and National Iranian Oil Company (29,084). Cumulative emissions among the 20 largest private and state-owned energy companies between 1854 and 2010 total 428,439 MtCO2e, or 29.5 percent of global industrial emissions from 1751 to 2010. The 90 international entities that Heede (2014) labels "carbon majors" are responsible for producing 63.04 percent of global industrial CO2 and methane from fossil fuel combustion, flaring, venting, fugitive or vented methane, own fuel use, and cement between 1751 and 2010. These statistics lend legitimacy to not only the argument for anthropogenic climate change, but also to the goals of the anti-fossil fuel movement.

The fossil fuel companies have fortified their positions through a strong presence in politics, particularly through well-funded lobby groups. With millions of dollars in annual spending and an official outpost on K Street, a lobbying district in Washington, ExxonMobil relies on career employees to work the Capitol Hill, the White House, and regulatory agencies to secure meetings, executive orders, and favorable laws (Coll, 2012). ExxonMobil's Washington strategists typically divide the capital's political populace into four tiers (in descending order of friendliness): those from the oil patch, such as senators and congressmen from Texas, Louisiana, Oklahoma, and Wyoming; sympathetic free market Republicans; industry Democrats or liberal Republicans who might be open to compromise; and finally the lost-cause Democrats and environmentalists. Perhaps the most prominent example of this mentality and the close ties between the government and the oil industry is the close friendship of former Vice President Dick Cheney and ExxonMobil's Lee Raymond, who shared a public disdain for climate scientists and government regulations (Coll, 2012).

The political influence of fossil fuel companies is not limited to ExxonMobil. As seen in Figure 2.2, hundreds of millions of dollars are spent annually on "Energy and Natural Resources" lobbying in the United States. Not surprisingly, among the different categories of "Energy and Natural Resources," electric utilities, which rely on coal as their most important fuel, play an important role. The other major category is oil, gas, and mining (mostly coal). This lobbying structure shows that fossil fuel interests play a central role in American energy policy. Equally notable, energy lobbying expenditures went up sharply when President Obama, a Democrat who has announced new climate and environmental policies and regulations, was elected.

We also find broader evidence for the tier system employed by ExxonMobil's Washington strategists described above (Coll, 2012). According to OpenSecrets.org, the oil and gas industry leads the sector (Energy and Natural Resources) in regularly pumping the vast majority of campaign contributions into Republican coffers. Since the 1990 election cycle, interests from this sector have contributed more than two-thirds of its campaign contributions to Republican candidates. Another big contributor in this sector and Grand Old Party supporter is the electric utilities industry. Less generous, but even more partisan, is the mining industry (OpenSecrets.org, 2016).

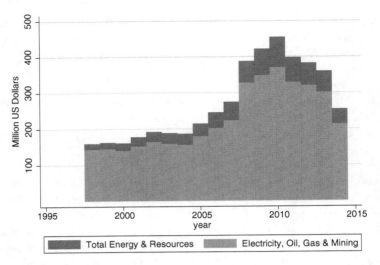

FIGURE 2.2 Electricity, oil, gas, and mining share of annual lobbying in total energy and resources, 1998–2014.

Source: OpenSecrets.org (2014)

Money talks, especially when it is backed by political will. Oil, gas, and coal interests that helped the Republicans reclaim control of Congress in 2014 have moved swiftly to contain President Barack Obama's Environmental Protection Agency (EPA) regulations. Through conservative state policy groups, such as the American Legislative Exchange Council (ALEC), fossil fuel lobbyists representing Koch Industries, Peabody Energy, and others have met with state legislators to discuss potential bills to block or delay the Obama administration's new environmental standards, including limits on power-plant emissions. The fossil fuel industry's full-frontal assault on the EPA has become a cause for concern among many environmentalists, who fear their once bipartisan support may be quickly eroding. When Republicans are slow to respond, the fossil fuel industry can also take to the airwaves. The group Americans for Prosperity began an advertising campaign in two dozen House districts after the November elections, pressing GOP lawmakers to oppose tax breaks for wind energy firms. The organization was founded and funded in part by billionaire brothers David and Charles Koch (Hamburger, 2014, December 7). Not surprisingly, Koch Industries also represents the biggest spender among all of fossil fuel lobbies, pouring in a sum total of $6,439,535 in 2013–2014 alone (OpenSecrets.org, 2014).

Fossil fuel interests are also powerful elsewhere in the world. According to Yergin (1991), global politics in the 20th century has largely revolved around commercial and geopolitical interests in oil. Today, China's interest in Africa is largely driven by Beijing's perceived need to secure oil supplies in the continent

(Taylor, 2006). The largest oil companies, such as ExxonMobil, operate everywhere in the world and are able to shape politics according to their needs and preferences, often relying on political support from their country (Coll, 2012). Concerns about the ability of the Russian energy giant Gazprom to use natural gas prices as a bargaining chip are widespread in Europe (Goldthau, 2008). European climate policy, such as new commitments to emissions reductions and renewable energy, is consistently undermined by Poland's opposition, largely motivated by the country's extensive coal resources and a powerful coal lobby (European Climate Foundation, n.d.).[4]

2.4 Future prospects

The previous sections showed that activists, such as Bill McKibben of 350.org, fear that the fossil fuel industry already has enough total reserves to put our climate in serious jeopardy. The fossil fuel industry, however, continues to scour the earth for oil and gas while investing in unconventional methods of extraction, under the assumption that the demand for fossil fuels will continue to increase. Many of their annual reports reveal their rock-solid confidence in this assumption, particularly bolstered by China and India's insatiable thirst for energy.

Against this backdrop, the impact of technology on the fight against the fossil fuel industry is on balance ambiguous. While it has equipped the fossil fuel industry with new and unconventional methods of extraction at significant costs to the environment, it has also strengthened the case for an economically feasible transition to sustainable energy. What is less ambiguous, however, is the fact that technology has raised the stakes for actors on both sides of the conflict. Moreover, the impact of this high-stakes contest will not be limited to the fossil fuel companies and activists. Should governments decide to act on climate change, the so-called "stranded assets" hold significant implications for the future of the world economy (Ansar et al., 2013).

One way to understand the fossil fuel companies and their visions for the future is to examine what they tell their shareholders in their annual reports. One common theme is the world's continued reliance on fossil fuels for the greatest share of its energy source, driven by China and India's continued growth trajectory. ExxonMobil (2013) predicts that from 2010 to 2040, the world's population will increase from 7 to 9 billion and the global economy will double, driving up energy demand by 35 percent. China and India will account for half of the projected growth, with 9 of the world's 20 most populated cities. In their picture, oil remains the largest fuel type, with natural gas surpassing coal as the second largest. Conventional crude production will decrease, but it will be offset by rising production utilizing new technologies, particularly tight oil, deepwater, and oil sands. By 2040, more than 45 percent of liquids supply will come from sources other than crude and condensate production. Tight oil will grow most rapidly to more than 10 times its 2010 level. Similarly, 65 percent of the growth in natural gas supply by 2040 is expected from unconventional sources, including shale and other tight rock formations. North America will shift from a net importer to exporter by 2025. The largest shift in net imports will occur in Asia Pacific, where gas imports will rise by more than 300 percent by 2025, and 500 percent by 2040 (ExxonMobil, 2013).

Similarly, BP (2013) projects the world population to increase by 1.7 billion from 2012 to 2035, with real income likely to more than double, driving up energy demand by 41 percent, even with technological strides in the direction of energy efficiency. Unlike ExxonMobil (2013), however, BP (2013) acknowledges that action is needed to limit carbon dioxide (CO_2) and other greenhouse gases emitted through fossil fuel use. The solution they propose is achieving energy security and "sustainable transition" through a "diverse mix:" oil sands, shale gas, deepwater oil and gas, and biofuels. BP (2013) believes that oil and natural gas will represent about 54 percent of total energy consumption in 2035. Even under the IEA's most ambitious climate policy scenario, in which governments commit to 450 ppm CO_2 equivalent of greenhouse gases, oil and gas still make up 47 percent of the energy mix in 2035. Oil remains the dominant source for transport fuels, accounting for as much as 87 percent of demand in 2035. Emphasizing that natural gas can reduce CO_2 emissions by half in replacing coal, BP projects that 47 percent of the growth in global natural gas supplies between 2012 and 2035 is likely to come from shale gas. As new sources of hydrocarbons are more difficult to reach, extract, and process, BP acknowledges that the extraction of these resources might be more energy intensive, which may entail higher operating costs and greenhouse gas emissions from operations. BP claims that renewables, the fastest-growing energy source that started from a low base, are "increasingly important" over the long term. By 2035, renewable energy, excluding hydro, is likely to meet 7 percent of total global energy demand (BP, 2013). BP's outlook and plan for the future are largely similar to ExxonMobil's, with the exception of acknowledging the existence of climate change.

Shell (2014) provides another European perspective, with largely similar projections. By 2035, additional supplies needed to meet demand will be twice the size of today's US energy system. The population will increase to 9 billion by 2050 (from 7 billion today), "equivalent to adding another China and India." Urbanization continues as 70 million people move into cities each year for the next 25 years. Global energy demand will grow by 15–20 percent between now and 2020, with nearly all coming from non-OECD nations. Global energy demand could double from 200 million barrels of oil equivalent (mboe) per day in 2000 to some 400 mboe per day by 2050. Shell (2014) cautions that as living standards increase, there will be an increasing stress placed on our food, water, and energy supply, as well as on the climate. Shell (2014) suggests that government, industry, and society must work together to address this "stress nexus." Policies that address CO_2 emissions also help to mitigate water and food stresses, so governments should put a price on CO_2 as a means to promote low-carbon technology, energy efficiency, and the replacement of coal by natural gas in the power sector. Similar to the ExxonMobil and BP, Shell (2014) regards natural gas as part of the solution, occupying "the sweet spot in the stress/opportunity nexus." Similar to BP, Shell prides itself in renewables involvement, distributing biofuels for more than 30 years. In 2011, Shell started producing biofuels. In partnership with Brazil's Cosan, Shell has established a joint venture, Raízen, with annual ethanol production capacity of about 2.2 billion liters (Shell, 2014).

Last but not least, Chevron (2013) projects a worldwide energy consumption increase by more than 40 percent by 2035, fueled by a population increase of 25 percent in the next 20 years, with most of that growth coming from emerging economies, such as China and India. Similar to Shell, Chevron emphasizes that economic output and improved standards of living will put added pressure on energy supplies. For example, in China alone, demand is expected to increase by 75 percent by 2035. The conclusion reached by Chevron is that the world needs all the energy it can develop in many potential forms. Joining the chorus of other majors, Chevron (2013) claims that even if the use of renewables triples over the next 25 years, the world is still likely to depend on fossil fuels for at least 50 percent of its energy needs. Thus, in 2013 they invested $41.9 billion in exploration and production to develop major capital projects. New technologies maximize the production of existing crude oil and natural gas fields, drilling deeper than ever before. Nonetheless, Chevron (2013) claims to invest hundreds of millions of dollars on energy-efficiency efforts in their operations, such as upgrading steam traps, installing more efficient heat exchangers, and constructing more efficient power plants. They are also making "global investments" in renewable and alternative energy to modify their energy portfolio over the long term. Renewables – such as cellulosic biofuels that do not undermine the food supply, geothermal energy, and solar – will provide new raw materials for fuels, sources of power, and benefits for the environment.

From this general comparative exercise, it becomes clear that the world's major fossil fuel companies remain firmly committed to oil and natural gas. While BP and Shell are more explicit about climate change than ExxonMobil and Chevron, there is a consensus that the future demand for energy must be met by oil and gas. While technology may contribute to the growth of renewables, fossil fuel companies see their role in meeting the energy demand for the next 20 to 30 years to be marginal at best. Instead, their investment priority seems to be new and improved technologies for unconventional methods of oil and gas extraction, even at the cost of higher carbon emissions.

The arrival of unconventional oil and gas production at affordable prices illustrates how technology is revolutionizing the fossil fuel industry's scramble for resources. Unconventional oil refers to oil that cannot be "produced, transported or refined using traditional techniques" because of low porosity, permeability, or density. These sources include oil sands, oil shale, heavy oil, and shale oil. These unconventional oils are also found in unconventional geographic locations: North America, South America, and Eastern Europe, rather than the Middle East, Russia, and Africa. When unconventional oil resources are included in oil resource estimates, the OECD Americas region has as much technically recoverable oil as the Middle East plus Eastern Europe and Eurasia (Kalicki and Goldwyn, 2013).

As for environmental impact, the production of unconventional oils is more difficult and energy intensive than the production of conventional oil. Unconventional oils are higher in sulfur and metals, require more processing (more energy and emissions), and have greater impact on water and land use. In addition, the larger carbon footprint of unconventional oil is an issue of growing concern. Life-cycle CO_2 and greenhouse gas (GHG) emissions data for oil sands do not typically include methane losses or emissions associated with land use and infrastructure construction. Additional research is needed to more accurately reflect the GHG emissions associated with unconventional oil in general and oil sands specifically, as well as to develop technologies to reduce these emissions (Kalicki and Goldwyn, 2013).

Technological advancements in unconventional methods of extraction have also enabled a natural gas boom in North America, along with its attendant environmental implications. By 2005, the prevailing political and industry wisdom – as per Alan Greenspan's testimony before Congress in 2003 or Lee Raymond's view expressed in 2005 – was that the United States and North America were running out of natural gas. Policies were adopted and investments were made to substantially increase US gas imports. Fast-forward just a few years and the United States is the number one gas producer in the world and is preparing for gas exports.

The development of technologies to produce shale gas, 20 years in the making, was the result of a highly effective public–private partnership and a time-limited tax credit. The primary beneficiaries of this effort were thousands of smaller independent producers. This profile of players and the speed of the technology development, deployment, and diffusion, however, came with a downside. When the initial deployment rush occurred, best practices and environmental concerns were not well understood by some producers or regulators, and little baseline data were available to analyze potential impacts. Water treatment systems, other infrastructures, and communities were sometimes overwhelmed. Awareness has increased since then, and widely reported environmental incidents associated with shale gas production have mostly resulted from faulty well completions and surface-water management. Air quality and methane emissions are other issues that must be managed (Kalicki and Goldwyn, 2013).

The Carbon Tracker Initiative (CTI) research found that $1.1 trillion of capital expenditure is expected in the next decade in expensive oil sands, deepwater, and Arctic projects but that this investment will be lost if policymakers agree to slash carbon emissions. It found that only the oil expected to cost less than $75 a barrel to produce, much of which is from conventional onshore wells, can be burned within the planet's "carbon budget" (IPCC, 2013). The analysts found even when focusing only on the high-end – oil costing more than $95 a barrel – $1.1 trillion was at risk from 2014–2025. Looking farther ahead to 2050, CTI estimated $21 trillion worth of high-cost oil projects could be wasted. The region with the highest risk of wasted capital in the report was Alberta, Canada. Canada's vast oil sands province is expected to see $400 billion of investment by 2025. The companies with the biggest exposure to risk there are Canadian Natural Resources Limited, Suncor, and Shell.

Deepwater oil projects in the Gulf of Mexico and off Brazil were also seen as high risk, with ExxonMobil and Petrobras set to invest $100 billion each. Ultra-deepwater projects, which drill in ocean depths greater than 1500m, expose Total and BP to the risk of capital being wasted, the report concludes. In the Arctic, Statoil was most exposed, with $22 billion capital expenditure projected by 2025. The report also found that high cost (more than $80/barrel), high-carbon projects comprised between one-fifth and one-quarter of the total capital expenditure expected by the major international oil companies in the next 10 years, with Total at 28 percent and BP at 18 percent. But at least a dozen multi-billion-dollar independent oil companies had 85–100 percent of their capital expenditures targeted at high-cost projects (CTI, 2014).

Already, the markets are reacting. The Bank of England is to conduct an inquiry into the risk of fossil fuel companies causing a major economic crash if future climate change rules render their coal, oil, and gas assets worthless (Carrington, 2014, December 1). The concept of a "carbon bubble" has gained traction since 2013, and is being taken more seriously by some major financial companies, including Citibank, HSBC, and Moody's, but the bank's inquiry is the most significant endorsement yet from a regulator. The concern is that if the world's governments meet their agreed target of limiting global warming to 2°C by cutting carbon emissions, then about two-thirds of proven coal, oil, and gas reserves cannot be burned. With fossil fuel companies being among the largest in the world, sharp losses in their value could prompt a new economic crisis.

In an apt analogy, former Vice President Al Gore likens today's fossil fuels to the subprime mortgages of the last decade that triggered the global credit crisis (Bloomberg, 2014, December 2). Their value "is based on an assumption every bit as absurd," specifically the notion that all known oil, gas, and coal will be consumed. "Investors who haven't yet come to grips with the stranding problem are like the classic scene in the Road Runner cartoons where the coyote runs off the edge of the cliff, and his legs keep moving for quite a long time before gravity takes hold," Gore said. "There are investors out there whose legs are moving in mid-air."

The world had a small foretaste of changes in the investment environment when the oil price took a significant decline near the end of 2014. The days of $90 or $100 dollars per barrel came to a screeching halt, as the oil price suddenly collapsed and the oil industry went into deep recession. Though the oil price did not stay below $30 for long, recovery has been slower than expected, hovering around $50 to $60 and leaving the oil market in a largely unpredictable state (Krauss, 2017, March 10). Analysts pointed to this as the "new normal," attributable to a new business model introduced by American shale oil and gas producers that fundamentally reshaped the global oil landscape. Due to technological advancements, "they can ramp up production in an appraised field in as few as six months at a small fraction of the capital investment required by their conventional rivals." With concerns about Peak Oil now a distant memory, even traditional oil producers like Saudi Arabia, as well as South Africa, China, and Argentina, are hoping to try their hands in unconventional oil and gas business (Hartmann and Sam, 2016, March 28).

The drop in oil price has not dampened the enthusiasm of the green industry. Particularly promising in this regard is the potential widespread adoption of electric vehicles by the 2020s. Research by Bloomberg New Energy Finance suggests that reductions in lithium-ion battery prices will allow electric vehicles to overtake gasoline and diesel cars as an affordable option in most countries. According to their estimates, the sales of electric vehicles will hit 41 million by 2040, representing 35 percent of new light-duty vehicle sales, which is almost 90 times the equivalent figure for 2015. To be sure, these estimates are partly based on "crude oil price recovering to $50, and then trending back up to $70-a-barrel or higher by 2040," and a sustained low oil price is likely to delay the mass adoption of electric vehicles further (MacDonald, February 25, 2016).

This section has provided a forward-looking assessment of the impact of technology on fossil fuel companies. Fossil fuel companies are using unconventional methods of extraction to tap previously inaccessible oil and gas under the assumption that fossil fuels will continue to meet most of our energy needs well into the future. Either governments will remain complacent in the face of climate change, along the lines forecast by major fossil fuel companies, or they will take action, reining in carbon emissions and steering the market toward renewables. Technology has raised the stakes for both sides. If the projections of fossil fuel companies prove to be correct, then humanity will have incurred significant opportunity costs by foregoing renewables in favor of an unsustainable path of fossil fuel dependence and climate change.

Notes

1 See http://unfccc.int/resource/docs/2009/cop15/eng/11a01.pdf (accessed December 12, 2014).
2 See http://www2.energyintel.com/PIW_Top_50_ranking_about (accessed December 13, 2014).
3 See www.eia.gov/todayinenergy/detail.cfm?id=13211 (accessed December 13, 2014).
4 See https://europeanclimate.org/initiatives/regional/poland/ (accessed May 28, 2017).

3

PERSPECTIVES ON THE MOVEMENT AGAINST FOSSIL FUELS

Why campaign against fossil fuels? Why not campaign for a carbon tax instead? To understand why the movement against fossil fuels has grown so large and prominent, we first need to understand what different people to become activists. It is not immediately obvious why people engage in activities that are often controversial, do not produce any direct material gain, and consume lots of time. Every hour spent on pursuing a political or social cause could have been spent pursuing a direct material gain.

In the case of resistance to fossil fuels, the question is even more important. The fossil fuel industry is among the largest and most profitable on this planet. All human societies today depend on fossil fuels, and we have already shown that global demand for coal, gas, and oil is growing. Fighting an industry that can be described as a global behemoth is a thankless and frustrating task. Any victories that activists score are inevitably tiny when shown against the larger, global canvas. So, explaining activism against the fossil fuel industry is about explaining an extreme case of seemingly irrational behavior.

And yet, campaigns against fossil fuels are thriving today. In colleges and seminaries around the world, thousands upon thousands of students demand divestment from fossil fuels. Churches, foundations, and municipalities are also moving their endowments from fossil fuels to more sustainable industries. Campaigns against fracking are vibrant everywhere in the United States. The Keystone XL campaign has drawn hundreds of thousands, maybe millions, of Americans into the vortex of climate activism. In our fieldwork, we encounter optimism, enthusiasm, and resilience.

The key to explaining and understanding campaigns against fossil fuels is found in the activist worldview. People who join campaigns against fossil fuels and stay with them believe that their cause is unique. Drawing on an ecological perspective to life, anti-fossil fuel activists believe that climate change is today's greatest problem, and burning fossil fuels is, therefore, immoral. For activists participating in campaigns against fossil fuels, mobilization and protests are an obvious choice that reflects their values, beliefs, and principles. A rational approach to activism, which emphasizes the costs and benefits of action for individuals, cannot capture the deep moral and ethical commitments that motivate activists to swim against strong tides.

For our analysis of campaigns against fossil fuels, we begin with a general description of the huge and growing body of literature on activism. These works provide us with a series of ideas for why so many activists participate in campaigns against fossil fuels and why these campaigns are growing so fast. Before we delve into campaigns against fossil fuels, we also provide a concise overview of American environmental activism before the boom of campaigns against fossil fuels. This historical background is important for understanding the traditional alternative to grassroots campaigns against fossil fuels in the American context.

Next, we focus our attention on the *internal logic* of campaigns against fossil fuels. By internal logic, we refer to the ideas and motivations that activists themselves give for joining the cause. Here, our goal is not to evaluate or judge the campaigns, but to describe what the world looks like from an activist's viewpoint. To summarize our argument, anti-fossil fuel activists aim to shift the public debate on fossil fuels and undermine the status of the industry in society by stigmatizing them and removing their social license to pollute. While the anti-fossil fuel campaign does not yet have clear policy proposals, this lack of specificity is consistent with the general thrust of the campaign. Indeed, much of the campaigning still focuses on building a movement, with the implicit understanding that specific policy proposals are forthcoming.

In the next section of this chapter, we will show that the *external logic* of campaigns against fossil fuels promotes expansion and commitment, as counterintuitive as this initially may seem. In contrast to the study of internal logic, the analysis of external logic is about the reasons behind the success and growth of campaigns against fossil fuels. Here, we offer an account of why these campaigns have grown so quickly and achieved success in mobilizing activists. Since campaigns against fossil fuels feature local actions that can achieve concrete results, yet also tie into a broader conflict between ecological activists and the global fossil fuel industry, their ability to draw participants and sustain their commitment as members of a broad people's movement is exceptional. We conclude with two sections on measuring the key outcomes of interest (mobilization, impact) and our case selection strategy.

3.1 Study of activism: the state of the art

Following the *Oxford English Dictionary*, we define *activism* broadly as "the policy or action of using vigorous campaigning to bring about political or social change." An activist, then, is someone who campaigns vigorously to effect change in society or politics. In practice, it is important to distinguish between activists, whose goal is broad political or social change, and professional lobbyists, who try to influence policy formulation to the benefit of their clients in exchange for compensation.

Some activists are salaried and affiliated with a formal organization; others campaign voluntarily as members of a broader, less structured social movement. All of them, however, are at least somewhat motivated by political or social change, as opposed to personal gain alone.

Activism and social movements have a long history. When Jesus overthrew the tables of the moneylenders in the courtyard of Herod's Temple, he was in the role of an activist because he advocated for the social norm that temples are not houses of trade. Since the industrial revolution, labor activists have organized countless strikes to demand higher pay and better working conditions for the working class. Activists have protested for and against racial discrimination, women's rights, gay rights, and animal rights.

For contemporary activists, historical precedents and success stories play an important role. Even today, many activism campaigns are inspired and informed by Mahatma Gandhi's *satyagraha* movement in pre-independence India. As a leader of the Indian National Congress, Gandhi drew on his experiences in apartheid South Africa and put pressure on the British to grant home rule to the Indians. Today, many activists find Gandhi's commitment to nonviolence and rejection of tactics such as terrorism appealing. Indeed, one of the most memorable quotes by Gandhi urges people to "[b]e the change that you want to see in the world." This commandment reflects the spirit of activism.

In America, Gandhian tactics were successfully deployed by Martin Luther King Jr. in his struggle against racial discrimination. King fought against racial discrimination by deploying a host of innovative tactics of civil disobedience. During the 1963 Birmingham, Alabama campaign, for example, black youth boycotted downtown businesses, participated in library and lunch sit-ins, entered predominantly white churches, and marched on the streets. In 1966, King deployed similar tactics to combat racial discrimination in housing in the city of Chicago.

An even more recent example that inspires activists is the African National Congress and the campaign to end apartheid in South Africa. A household name among today's activists, Nelson Mandela initially led a violent insurgency against the privileged white minority. Over time, however, Mandela and his supporters moved toward a strategy of civil disobedience, combined with continuous negotiations with the white government. This strategy allowed Mandela to dismantle the apartheid regime without a violent civil war between the majority blacks and the minority whites. When Mandela, before being inaugurated as the president of South Africa, won the Nobel Peace Prize in 1993, he shared the honor with South Africa's last president under apartheid, Frederik Willem de Klerk. This achievement lifted Mandela to fame and made him the hero of political and social activists who believe in nonviolent resistance.

According to Hawken (2007: 2), if we adopt an inclusive definition of environmentalist organizations, globally "there are over one – maybe even two – million organizations working toward ecological sustainability and social justice." Not all of these organizations focus on fossil fuels, of course, but the social justice approach to environmentalism itself creates a bias against fossil fuels. The extraction of fossil fuels causes local environmental destruction and social displacement. Both the transportation and burning of fossil fuels are potent environmental and public health threats. If we accept the Hawken (2007: 2) number as a reasonable estimate of the number of ecological organizations active globally, then it can be considered an upper bound for the number of organizations that mobilize against fossil fuels. In a similar vein, Martinez-Alier (2002) provides a global survey of ecological conflicts around the world, emphasizing that the common thread running through them is the clash between local ecological values and the global economy. Local environmentalists are, even in the poorest of countries, acutely aware of the global economic mechanisms and processes that result in ecological destruction.

To explain activism, it is natural to begin with grievance theories, which predict that dissatisfaction with the political or social situation drives individuals and groups into activism. In the four-stage model of social mobilization that Klandermans and Oegema (1987) propose, the first step toward action is called "mobilization potential." If activism centers on vigorous campaigning for social or political change, then the first question is whether or not an individual or a community wants to abandon the status quo. Walsh (1981) examines the growth and development of grassroots protest organizations in the wake of the Three Mile Island accident in 1979, arguing that the sudden intensification of grievances can be a catalyst for organized protest. Noting that Marxist theories emphasize "alienation" from society as a cause behind activism, Bolton (1972) uses attitudinal survey research to show that student members of the American peace movement in 1962, at the height of anti-war activism during that decade, felt significantly more removed "from the [prevailing] economic-political structure" than did nonmembers. At the same time, the activists also felt empowered and understood themselves as change agents. The "relative deprivation" literature (Korpi, 1974; Smith et al., 2012; Stouffer et al., 1949) finds that groups often generate and air grievances when they consider themselves at an unfair disadvantage relative to other groups. More generally, feelings of "outrage" play a major role in activist campaigns, both as a motivator and as a mobilization technique (Jasper, 2011: 292). Recent sociological work on environmental grievances, such as Auyero and Swistun (2009) on toxic chemicals in an Argentine shantytown and Messer et al. (2015) on polluted communities in the United States, has also recognized the importance of subjective perceptions of hazards.

Other sociologists and political scientists argue that while grievances may constitute a necessary condition, they are not a sufficient condition for the emergence of social movement organizations. According to proponents of the "resource mobilization" theory, originally formulated by McCarthy and Zald (1977), demands for political or social change cannot generate effective mobilization unless organizations channel these demands into collective action. Similar to theories of collective action in political science (Olson, 1965), the resource mobilization approach emphasizes the gap between grievances and mobilization. Since activism requires planning and coordination, it would be naive to assume that individuals and groups engage in effective campaigning simply because they are angry and frustrated. Unless potential activists can mobilize and campaign through an organization capable of managing and directing the activists, the mobilization potential created by grievances and outrage will not produce action. At the center of these approaches is how unequally distributed many kinds of resources are among social groups, and how these durable patterns of resource inequality continue to shape uneven access to those resources among social groups (Bourdieu, 1986; Edwards and McCarthy, 2007). As the scholarship has developed, the typology of resources has been refined to include moral, cultural, social-organizational, human, and material resources (Benford and Snow, 2000; Cress and Snow, 1996; Edwards and McCarthy, 2007; Gongaware, 2010).

Although both grievances and resources are relevant, they neglect the role of broader opportunity structures in society. According to Kitschelt (1986: 58), "Political opportunity structures are comprised of specific configurations of resources, institutional arrangements and historical precedents for social mobilization, which facilitate the development of protest movements in some instances and constrain them in others." He shows that these structures have played a decisive role in the vigor and success of anti-nuclear protests in industrialized democracies. For example, he argues that the success of the anti-nuclear movement in the United States largely reflects the institutional weakness of the federal government and the openness of the political system for challengers of the status quo. Other scholars have similarly found that political opportunity structures play an important role in various kinds of activism (Meyer, 2004; Tarrow, 1998), including the civil rights movement (Gamson, 1975; McAdam, 1999) and local opposition to energy projects (McAdam and Boudet, 2012).

A fourth approach to explaining activism can be described as political economy. Though the literature on grievances can be viewed as micro-level, the political economy literature can better be described as macro-level. This strand of the literature, which draws inspiration from Marxism, points to systems of economic production and class relations that undergird all of social and political life as a source of activist mobilization (McAdam and Boudet, 2012). According to this approach, power is systemic, institutional, structural, and materially grounded, and the various structures of power (e.g., capital, state, the media) are seen as articulated together. Oppression is mainly a matter of material deprivation, exploitation, and alienation; counterpower involves resistance in the sense of concerted opposition to domination in an attempt to transform the system (Carroll and Ratner, 1996). Thus, the focus is squarely on underlying economic factors or processes that shape grievances, organizational structures, and tactical choices of movements. This perspective on social movements and revolutions, particularly relevant during the 1970s when the field was coming together, has largely disappeared in contemporary debates (McAdam and Boudet, 2012).

Another strand of the political economy literature emphasizes the material incentives of activists, social movements, and organizations. While most research on activism emphasizes that participants are motivated by an intrinsic preference for social or political change, others point out that self-interest can also motivate activism. Cooley and Ron (2002: 6) analyze the activities of transnational nongovernmental organizations, arguing that "that dysfunctional organizational behavior is likely to be a rational response to systematic and predictable institutional pressures." Their case studies show that, because activist organizations face considerable fiscal pressures and competition, they must carefully consider the implications of their activities for their funding and reputation. Similarly, Bob (2005) shows that the success of local protest movements, such as the Zapatistas of Mexico, depends largely on their ability to market themselves to major international players, such as Amnesty International or Greenpeace, and the media. While these perspectives do not necessarily contradict the idea that activists are genuinely passionate about political and social change, they add an important dimension to the calculus of activist organizations. Pallas and Urpelainen (2013) show that some nongovernmental organizations run lengthy but ineffective campaigns because their funders actually reward participation instead of outcomes.

In analyzing activism, it is also important to distinguish between low-cost and high-cost variants (McAdam, 1986). Low-cost activism comprises canvassing, petitions, peaceful protests, online "clicktivism," and other legal activities that do not carry high costs or risks. High-cost activism comprises illegal activities, violent protesting, and other activities that put activists at financial, reputational, or physical risk. Since most of the campaigns against fossil fuels in the United States are of the low-cost variant, there is no need to emphasize factors that predict extremism. Even civil disobedience, such as being arrested for protesting in Washington, DC, does not put the participants at any serious risk. The most important cost that anti-fossil fuel activists accept is the opportunity cost of time spent in campaigning.

Since any given issue can mobilize but a subset of potential activists, contemporary scholarship on activism has emphasized the importance of "hybrid" organizations in social movements (Albert and Whetten, 1985; Heaney and Rojas, 2014). These organizations combine issues that are seemingly unrelated, such as women's rights and peace. The attraction of hybrid activism is that the involved organizations can grow their numbers by linking issues that need not necessarily go together. Heaney and Rojas (2014) offer a comprehensive study of the centrality and benefits of hybrid activism for social movements. Studying data on participation in anti-war activism in the post-9/11 period, they find that:

> individuals with past involvement in nonantiwar movements are more likely to join hybrid organizations than are individuals without involvement in nonantiwar movements . . . organizations with hybrid identities occupy relatively more central positions in interorganizational co-contact networks within the antiwar movement and thus recruit significantly more participants in demonstrations than do nonhybrid organizations.
>
> *(Heaney and Rojas, 2014: 1047)*

While earlier research has shown that hybrid organizations in general may suffer from an "illegitimacy discount" stemming from the conflation of different issues (Leung and Sharkey, 2013; Zuckerman, 1999) – imagine, for example, an environmentalist group joining forces with revolutionary anarchists – Heaney and Rojas (2014) find no evidence for this problem, while at the same time uncovering many positive effects of a hybrid identity.

How applicable are these theories to the case of fossil fuels? Clearly, we are talking about a social movement that depends on the mobilization and contributions of a large number of activists. Grievance theories are potentially relevant, as they identify feelings of resentment toward the fossil fuel industry as a critical ingredient of participation. At the same time, the conversion of a grievance into concrete and effective action may depend on the ability of organizations and campaign leadership to mobilize and coordinate action. Broader opportunity structures, such as the open but weak and often-paralyzed federal government that played a critical role in Kitschelt's (1986) analysis of the anti-nuclear movement, shape the strategies and tactics of any savvy campaign against fossil fuels.

McAdam and Boudet (2012), homing in on "communities at risk" rather than realized movements, explore how much collective action actually emerges among 20 communities faced with eighteen proposals for environmentally risky projects, many of which involve liquefied natural gas (LNG) terminals. The authors find little emergent opposition across the 20 cases. By their measure, half of them experienced "mobilization," but the level of mobilized activity was "exceedingly modest." Furthermore, they find that political opportunities and civic capacity help explain higher levels of mobilization, though they work in conjunction with community context variables, such as similar industry, economic hardship, and experience with a past proposal. They interpret the former two causal conditions as reflecting the "objective structural propensity for collective action" (McAdam and Boudet, 2012: 96) within the community and the latter context variables as shaping the "subjective interpretation of project risk" by local residents.

In a chapter particularly relevant for our purposes, they further explore potential mechanisms behind "scale shifts," the geographic expansion or contraction of contention. Why do some movements remain local ("Not In My Back Yard"), while others spread ("Not In Anyone's Back Yard")? McAdam and Boudet (2012) point to two mechanisms, among others, that are particularly helpful for explaining what they found in their cases: coalition building and certification. In some cases, state regulators brokered connections between disparate opposition groups, while working to develop broader oppositional frames to cement the embryonic coalition. In others, particularly ones where the issue has virtually no initial standing with either the general public or policy makers in the region, certification by "neutral experts" or influential public figures becomes instrumental to the emergence and spread of an opposition movement.

Beyond the McAdam and Boudet (2012) study, theories of social movements and activism have been surprisingly invisible in the study of campaigns against fossil fuels. Most studies (Avery, 2013; Beynon et al., 2000; Carvalho, 2006; Hawken, 2007; McNeil, 2011; Montrie, 2003; Nace, 2010) of activism against fossil fuels, or energy project in broader terms, are either descriptive or journalistic, focusing on telling the story of a specific movement without any effort to provide an analytical explanation. However, the rise of fracking has given rise to a growing body of literature. From public opinion (Brown et al., 2013; Theodoria et al., 2014) to policy formulation (Davis, 2012; Rabe, 2014; Rabe and Borick, 2013) and local mobilization (Dokshin, 2016; Gullion, 2015), these studies situate opposition to fracking in a larger canvas of social conflicts. Foreshadowing our findings, they show that policies on fracking at local, state, and national levels emerge from conflicts over economic value and environmental costs. Drawing on research in the Barnett Shale in Texas, Gullion (2015), for example, notes that "extraction of fossil fuels in middle-class communities results in great environmental backlash . . . such communities have more resources at their disposal, including both a legal system in place to protect their interests and an ethos of democratic participation."

While studies of activism against fossil fuels remain rare, there is a large body of literature on anti-nuclear activism (Jahn, 1992; Kitschelt, 1986; Rucht, 1990; Rudig, 1990; Walsh, 1981). These studies report findings that are largely in line with the prevailing theories of activism. Nuclear power is a source of grievance due to perceived health and environmental hazards, especially after the Three Mile Island and Chernobyl nuclear plant accidents, and the existence of organized and resourceful groups facilitates actions and protests against nuclear energy. National opportunity structures are important for understanding variation in the success of anti-nuclear activism, ranging from high influence in the United States and Germany to virtually no effect in France. The critical difference between anti-nuclear and anti-fossil fuel activism is that the former does not have, with the exception of the partially related issue of nuclear weapons, a strong global component; in contrast, anti-fossil fuel activism is ultimately about global energy development, even if specific actions and campaigns are local or national. This sense of a global goal, it turns out, is important for understanding the logic of anti-fossil fuel activism.

Our hope is that, by drawing on contributions of social scientists, we can shed new light on activism against fossil fuels. We want to do so without throwing out the baby with the bathwater, that is, by being bogged down in arcane theoretical debates that divert attention from the substantive logic of the campaigns.

3.2 Environmental activism in America before campaigns against fossil fuels

American environmental activism has a long and varied history, but the basic pattern of action from Ronald Reagan's rise to power in 1981 until the boom of campaigns against fossil fuels is actually quite clear. Before the 2009 legislative battle for a cap-and-trade scheme, American environmentalism became increasingly professionalized, with a growing focus on lobbying in the nation's capital. This strategic drift away from grassroots activism reflected two historical developments. First, the environmental movement scored a series of major legislative victories in the 1970s, creating a precedent for effective strategies of litigation and lobbying. Even today, this golden era of American environmentalism captivates the imagination of the

American environmentalist establishment. Second, Reagan's inauguration as the President of the United States in January 1981 threatened to throw professional environmentalists out of their comfortable and powerful position in the legislative process. Reagan's conservative values and staunch pro-business ideology did not leave much access to environmentalists.

The early success of the environmental movement reflects several developments in American society and politics. The first Earth Day on April 22, 1970, which was celebrated by 20 million Americans (Dowie, 1995: 24), followed the 1962 publication of Rachel Carson's massively popular *Silent Spring* (Carson, 2002), a book that popularized concern about the effects of pesticides on the environment (Shabecoff, 2003: 111). The 1969 Santa Barbara oil spill, the fire on the Cuyahog River in Cleveland because of inflammable chemicals, the problem of smog in Los Angeles and other major cities, and many other negative effects of industrialization created public demand for policies to protect the environment. While environmental concerns were decades, and in some cases, centuries old in the United States, "The modern environmental movement evolved from these many issues and causes in the context of a post-World-War-II urban environment whose degradation had become insistently obvious to people of all classes and races" (Dowie, 1995: 24). Meanwhile, the environmental movement benefited from the explosion of radical, new left youth activism in the 1960s, as "[t]he environmental movement especially seemed to have potential for diverting the energies of a substantial portion of young people away from more bothersome movements" (Shabecoff, 2003: 117–118). During the 1960s, a new generation of environmental movements, most notably the Environmental Defense Fund and the Natural Resources Defense Council, were formed (Shabecoff, 2003: 104).

According to Schlosberg and Dryzek (2002: 789), the initial success of the American environmentalist movement in the early 1970s resulted in a "massive burst of environmental policy innovation." At this time, the United States was a hotbed of effective environmental activism, and environmentalists were the envy of the rest of the world due to their access to and influence in the political system. Both elite ideology and public opinion supported sweeping legislative solutions to problems of air and water pollution, wildlife protection, and habitat conservation. Indeed, today's environmental policies at the federal level continue to rely on the foundation laid by legislation such as the Clean Air Act and Clean Water Act, both of which originated from legislation passed in 1972.

Although the 1973 energy crisis had already begun to slowly erode the influence of environmentalists, it was Reagan's entry into power in 1981 that finally confirmed the waning of environmentalist influence in policy formulation at the federal level. In a scathing criticism of the mainstream environmental movement's strategy, Dowie (1995: 66) writes that "[b]y responding to Ronald Reagan as they did, mainstream environmentalists missed their best and perhaps last opportunity to lead a significant social movement. . . . Ronald Reagan was a counterrevolutionary whose policies and tactics quickly revealed the limits of compromise." During the

Reagan years, environmentalists not only lost their access to policy formulation, but also found their ability to defend existing victories through litigation compromised by Reagan's counter-strategies.

Following their loss of influence, and to safeguard whatever little access they had left, environmentalists began a process of professionalization. Major environmental groups hired scientists, economists, and, most importantly, lawyers. The focus of activity shifted decisively toward the nation's capital, where legislators and bureaucrats were designing – or, perhaps dismantling – environmental policies. The professionalization and increased emphasis on lobbying "came at a time, in the 1980s, where the movement was constantly battling hostile administrations and, for the most part, playing defense. Professionalization was providing access as one interest group among many, but not authentic inclusion in the development of policy" (Schlosberg and Dryzek, 2002: 794).

Perhaps the best example of this strategy is the environmental group Environmental Defense Fund (EDF) under Fred Krupp's leadership. On November 20, 1986, the *Wall Street Journal* published an opinion piece by the 32-year old president of EDF, titled "New Environmentalism Factors in Economic Needs." In the piece, Krupp, who is a lawyer by education, argued that environmentalists must recognize the importance of economic considerations and exploit the efficiency gains that market-based instruments promise. Following the publication of the piece, the EDF has profiled itself as the nation's leading proponent of the economic approach to environmental regulations. For example, it was the EDF that proposed to use emissions trading to reduce the cost of sulfur emission cuts under the Clean Air Act. The EDF does not have grassroots campaigners, and much of its budget comes from the largest corporations in America, especially Walmart. Recently, Krupp has also advocated fracking as an effective approach to reducing greenhouse gas emissions in America (Krupp, 2014). While the EDF has pushed the collaborative, pro-business strategy farther than other organizations, until the explosion of campaigns against fossil fuels, most of the national lobbying by all major groups had turned to seeking increased inclusion in the policy process (Dowie, 1995: 176).

The lobbying strategy made sense for many environmentalists as the tide turned against environmental policy after the golden years of the early 1970s. As environmentalists began to lose their influence, they thought that they must be realists and recognize the new political realities. The growing power of corporations and the lack of a credible counterforce in national politics meant that environmentalists did not see an alternative to seeking access and inclusion ever more vigorously.

This is not to say there were no radicals who chose more combative positions. The "environmental justice" movement, which positions itself against environmentally destructive projects that inflict damage on low-income and minority communities, is explicitly confrontational and emphasizes the inequitable features of projects such as landfills, hazardous waste management sites, polluting factories, and power plants (Bullard, 1990). According to Dowie, the mainstream environmental organizations have largely failed to collaborate with the large grassroots movement for environmental justice:

There is tremendous talent and passion in the mainstream environmental movement and a lot of potential leadership, but too much of it is being spent or misspent on bureaucracy and specialization. Those talents and passions belong on the battlefield, not in the office.

(Dowie, 1995: 173)

Similarly, radical organizations such as Earth First! have engaged in eco-sabotage to stop the economic forces that wreak havoc on the natural environment (Lee, 1995). However, these organizations are clearly fringe elements of the broader environmental movement. Unlike the environmental justice activists, eco-saboteurs have so little influence today that their role in environmental activism is marginal.

The radicals were frustrated with the professionalism and compromise of the mainstream approach. Indeed, the EDF and its followers can hardly be seen as steadfast advocates of the ecological paradigm. If anything, the increasingly pragmatic and professionalized approach advocated by the EDF was considered elitist, remote, and submissive by grassroots activists in love with a much deeper shade of green.

The backlash against the mainstream environmental organizations, sometimes dubbed the "Big Green," was not limited to radical fringe elements. From a practical perspective, the strategy of professionalization and access had two major drawbacks. First, it relegated the membership of environmental organizations to a passive role. This role may be exactly what a wealthy and busy donor wants, but for someone looking to become an environmental activist, frequent calls for more donations without any opportunity to actually participate can be frustrating and demoralizing. Second, the professional strategy leaves the movement open to accusations of cooptation by opponents of environmental policy. If organizations such as the EDF accept money from Walmart, how can they possibly claim to represent environmentalists, who want to constrain unnecessary consumption and protect ecological values?

It was in 2009 that the mainstream environmental organizations finally faced their moment of truth. The Waxman-Markey bill, officially titled the American Clean Energy and Security Act, passed the House but never made it through the Senate, as the 60-vote requirement to avoid a Republican filibuster failed after several moderate Republicans defected from the legislative coalition for the Senate version of the Waxman-Markey bill. The massive campaign for this bill, which would have created a federal cap-and-trade system for carbon emissions trading, was a defining moment for the environmental movement. As Harvard political scientist Theda Skocpol puts it, the "insider movement" of mainstream environmental organizations simply did not have the political clout to push through their preferred legislation:

To counter fierce political opposition, reformers will have to build organizational networks across the country, and they will need to orchestrate sustained political efforts that stretch far beyond friendly Congressional offices, comfy board rooms, and posh retreats. Compromises with amenable business interests will still be necessary. But insider politics cannot carry the day on its own, apart from a broader movement pressing politicians for change.

(Skocpol, 2013: 11)

This is exactly what environmentalists have since realized and what motivates campaigns against fossil fuels: without a strong movement, lobbying efforts will be futile. According to the *Climate War*, a journalistic account of the failure of federal climate legislation in the United States, there was a sense among environmental campaigners that they simply did not have what it would take to win:

> In their least guarded moments, the climate campaigners would tell you what they had always known in their bones: their work was necessary but not sufficient. Climate action was going to happen sooner or later, but they couldn't make it happen.
>
> *(Pooley, 2010: 440)*

The 2009 legislative debacle was a disaster for mainstream environmental organizations, and the criticisms of their compromise strategy were fueled by the spectacular failure of the Waxman-Markey bill and the lackluster result of the 2009 Copenhagen conference. Although Senator John Kerry and his allies were seemingly close to creating a coalition for federal cap-and-trade, they never succeeded and, over time, Republican and Democrat positions on climate policy became increasingly polarized. The notion that increased lobbying efforts would lead America to a legislative solution to climate change was no longer tenable. As the Harvard divestment activist Chloe Maxmin puts it, "The failure of the cap-and-trade bill ... demonstrated the enormous influence from the fossil fuel lobby that overpowered any input from climate organizations" (Maxmin, 2015: 35).

The man who came to symbolize the grassroots alternative to traditional lobbying was Bill McKibben, an environmental author and journalist from Vermont. His efforts to create a grassroots movement against fossil fuels were, from the beginning, based on the understanding that the era of professional environmental lobbying was over. In his famous August 2012 article in *Rolling Stone*, McKibben explains why mainstream environmental organizations are failing:

> Environmentalists, understandably, have been loath to make the fossil-fuel industry their enemy, respecting its political power and hoping instead to convince these giants that they should turn away from coal, oil and gas and transform themselves more broadly into "energy companies." Sometimes that strategy appeared to be working – emphasis on appeared. ... The fight, in the end, is about whether the industry will succeed in its fight to keep its special pollution break alive past the point of climate catastrophe, or whether, in the economists' parlance, we'll make them internalize those externalities.
>
> *(McKibben, 2012, August 2)*

As we shall show, McKibben's combative approach offers a very different alternative to professional environmentalism – one embracing ecological values, emphasizing grassroots mobilization, and encouraging activists to confront the fossil fuel industry in explicitly political terms.

3.3 Goals of campaigns: why mobilize against fossil fuels?

What do anti-fossil fuel activists want? The superficial answer is a rapid reduction in the extraction and use of environmentally and socially destructive fossil fuels. To fully understand what motivates anti-fossil fuel activists to contribute to their movement, however, it is necessary to understand the deeper values and moral commitments that drive activists to focus on fossil fuels in particular. After all, there are many more people in this world who are concerned about the extraction and use of fossil fuels than there are participants to anti-fossil fuel campaigns and protests.

To understand the goals of campaigns against fossil fuels, it is particularly important to consider the environmentalist's worldview. This worldview is based on an ecological paradigm that differs significantly from the views of economists or policy analysts. While a conventional economic analysis of fossil fuels would investigate the quantifiable costs and benefits of each investment, the adherent of the ecological paradigm would reject most, and perhaps all, investments in fossil fuels as fundamental violations of the idea that ecological sustainability requires going fossil free. As the author and environmentalist Samuel Avery puts it in a newspaper interview, in the ecological paradigm,

> economic growth may not be the most important thing that we can do here. Other things we have to do are to live in relation to the natural world, to the forest, the ocean, the land and the weather. The problem with the economic paradigm is that it has no conscience. It can't see life. It can't value life. It looks at a tree and it sees two-by-fours.
>
> *(Papousek, 2013, September 24)*

From this perspective, extraction of fossil fuels is a serious violation of basic ethics. In a wealthy society, the use of fossil fuels for economic growth amounts to sacrificing irreplaceable, priceless natural assets for the increased promotion of luxury goods.

The ecological paradigm explains why the fossil fuel industry is a natural target for today's climate activists. The general, shared grievances that environmental activists hold include the destruction of nature, habitats, and traditional forms of life. The fossil fuel companies are unique among all industries as a source of said grievances. Viewed through the lens of ecology, extracting and burning fossil fuels is fundamentally unethical. For environmental activists, counter-arguments about economic prosperity and poverty eradication are not compelling because these activists accept the fundamental premises of the ecological paradigm. Most activists also believe that a "soft energy path" (Lovins, 1976) paved with renewable energy and conservation can meet our basic human needs or, in the case of green-growth advocates, improve the performance of the global economy in a much more sustainable fashion.

Given this grievance, anti-fossil fuel activists are not going to be persuaded by cost-benefit analyses on the margin. The goals of today's campaigns against fossil fuels reflect a firm commitment to the principle of ecological integrity and a sense of environmental urgency. Both among grassroots activists and campaign leadership, the substantive motives behind anti-fossil fuel campaigns reflect a thorough rejection of a social and economic system that is willing to trade off ecology for faster economic growth. This principled, paradigmatic approach is key to understanding what makes anti-fossil fuel activists tick and why their movement has grown so fast.

To see this principle in action, consider the evolving position of the author and activist Bill McKibben on natural gas. In an April 2012 interview with Elizabeth Kolbert, McKibben explained why he has turned against natural gas, rejecting the idea of a "bridge fuel" between coal and renewable energy:

> Three or four years ago there was a certain part of me that was hopeful that we were going to find a lot of natural gas, and it was going to be a bridge fuel. It just turns out that the math doesn't work. You've got this problem – a big problem, it looks like – with these fugitive methane emissions. We don't know exactly how much. But even if you just converted the whole world to natural gas. . . . The IEA [International Energy Agency] ran what they called a "Golden Age of Gas" scenario, and it had all of us off coal or something by 2025 and we're all on gas. . . . I can't remember all the details, but it was a gas-run world. And the atmosphere then was still 660 parts per million CO2. What we actually need is a bridge away from fossil fuels, or maybe we should dispense with the "bridge" metaphor and just nerve ourselves up to take the jump across the chasm into the new world.
>
> *(Kolbert, 2012)*

The passage illustrates the ecological approach to climate change. While energy analysts talk about immediate and cost-effective environmental gains from replacing some coal with some natural gas, McKibben not only worries about fugitive methane emissions, but also notes that if natural gas succeeds – as it seems to be doing at least in the United States, where fracking is all the rage these days – global greenhouse gas emissions remain high. For someone who aspires to reach 350 parts per million, natural gas is a bridge to nowhere. Proponents of natural gas, such as the Canadian conservative author Ezra Levant, who has written a book titled *Groundswell* on the virtues of fracking, ridicule McKibben for being stubborn and unreasonable (Levant, 2014: 95). But for McKibben, the economic success of natural gas thanks to fracking is a principled reason to reject the fuel – there is too simply too much of it underground.

Equipped with an understanding of this commitment to ecological principles, we are now ready to discuss the substantive goals of campaigns against fossil fuels.

On a general level, these campaigns aim to change the public discourse and status of fossil fuels in society. Activists are aware of the tremendous political power that the fossil fuel industry enjoys today. They know that the world economy runs on oil, gas, and coal. For the activists, however, this state of affairs is not inevitable. If the fossil fuel industry can be forced to retreat, campaigners believe, the solutions for weaning the world off fossil fuels are readily available. For the adherents of the ecological paradigm, our dependence on fossil fuels is not a necessary precondition for human wellbeing. Rather, fossil fuels are an addiction that reflects neither technical nor economic necessity, but rather the capture of the political system by dirty energy interests.

Although the campaign against fossil fuels is motivated by a highly principled approach that emphasizes a nonnegotiable moral imperative, it is also politically savvy. It is perhaps easy to dismiss mobilization against the fossil fuel industry as naive. After all, there is a clear consensus among economists that a simple carbon tax or cap-and-trade system would be a much less expensive solution to the climate crisis. So, why should activists try to block fossil fuel projects or attempt to shut down individual power plants? The answer is that these activities are motivated by a combination of moral commitment and the view that the fossil fuel industry is the primary obstacle to better policy. It is both virtuous and necessary to combat the fossil fuel industry. Virtue stems from the ecological destruction that the extraction and use of fossil fuels bring about; necessity reflects the overwhelming political power of the fossil fuel industry. During our research, activists of all stripes told us that, in their view, the primary obstacle to effective climate policy in America and elsewhere is the ability of oil, gas, and coal companies to capture politicians. Unless activists can mobilize people's power to counter these industries, debates about optimal economic approaches to climate change are purely theoretical, due to their political infeasibility. As one activist put it, "lobbying is wishful thinking" in today's politics because "fossil fuel companies are too powerful."

If campaigns against fossil fuels are successful, they remove the industry's "social license to pollute." From the activist's perspective, today fossil fuel companies get away with the ecological destruction they cause because there is no clear social norm against the extensive use of fossil fuels. If activists manage to stigmatize the fossil fuel industry by both revealing the extent of the damage they have caused and by pulling the alarm about the powerful influence of oil, gas, and coal in today's politics, the argument goes, the tide turns against fossil fuels. Citizens begin to demand policies to constrain ecological destruction, politicians can no longer accept money from fossil fuel interests without a popular backlash, and, as a result, the politics of climate and energy policy will undergo a seismic shift. Never again will fossil fuel interests dictate policy.

The analogy that is on every activist's mind is the fate of the tobacco industry (Wolfson, 2001). As we attended activist meetings and events, and discussed their campaigns with both lay members and the leadership, this one analogy was offered to us repeatedly. For most of the 20th century, smoking was considered in the United States and other industrialized countries a perfectly legitimate habit. Even after the negative health effects of smoking became clear, smoking was initially considered a private vice that was nobody else's business. Over time, however, the tobacco industry lost a number of high-profile lawsuits and developed a negative reputation for spreading misinformation about the effects of tobacco smoke on health. Smoking bans, not only indoors but also outdoors, spread across offices, restaurants, university campuses, and other public spaces. After the tobacco industry lost its social license to sell cigarettes and other tobacco products to the people, its political power was gone. This is the what activists want to befall the fossil fuel industry.

In practice, the foundations of the fossil fuel industry are much more solid than that of the tobacco business. Cigarettes are a vice that is hardly necessary for modern life, whereas cheap and abundant energy is the cornerstone of the industrial society. And yet, fossil fuel companies are vulnerable. Their extractive activities cause widespread social displacement and environmental damage, creating opportunities for naming and shaming. If the public opinion in the United States turns against coal, oil, and gas, then public support for alternatives – renewable energy and conservation, environmental activists would hope – increases. The fossil fuel industry depends on permissive policies for profits, and a strongly negative public opinion would put pressure on politicians to change these policies. For example, a carbon tax would effect a decrease in demand for fossil fuels. If the public opinion is against the fossil fuel industry, such a carbon tax could be popular as a policy, especially in conjunction with redistributive mechanisms that shield households against the effects.

Although activists sometimes target specific fossil fuel companies, such as the oil and gas giant ExxonMobil or the coal empire Peabody, for strategic reasons, there is clearly a widespread understanding among activists that the entire sector – embodied by the 200 global carbon majors – must be held responsible for their activities. Anti-fossil fuel activists are both infuriated and energized by the recognition that much of today's climate change and ecological destruction can be attributed to one industry. This clear attribution of guilt and blame creates an "us versus them" situation, which motivates activists to rally around a common cause and increase their contributions and commitment. Seemingly intractable problems, such as climate change, can now be boiled down to a simple battle between opposing interests. For the activists, these interests are greedy, dirty energy versus people and nature.

In addition to changing the public discourse and removing the social license of the fossil fuel industry, activists also hope to shake its financial foundation. To an outsider, this effort may appear even more hopeless than the effort to stigmatize the industry. However, a certain logic underpins the idea of financial disruption. Activists participating in campaigns against fossil fuels believe that, if our civilization is to truly avoid the disruptive effects of runaway global warming then it is necessary to leave most of the already available fossil fuels underground. Since the ecological paradigm is inconsistent with incremental measures to mitigate climate change, anti-fossil fuel activists must assume that, with some positive probability, the future holds aggressive climate policy at the global and national levels. In such circumstances, fossil fuels become stranded assets and their value is lost. To the extent that climate activists can raise awareness about our small and rapidly diminishing carbon budget, they can hope to destroy the financial health of the fossil fuel industry. In other words, the stranded asset scenario becomes a self-fulfilling prophecy. This strategy is based on raising awareness. If the activists are correct about major climate policies in the future, the fossil fuel industry will be much less attractive as an investment than it would be in a world with little climate change mitigation. Activists believe that such major climate policies are, if not a slam dunk, at least plausible.

By raising awareness about the inherent contradiction between ambitious climate policy and major investments in the fossil fuel industry for new exploration and extraction, activists also show that the fossil fuel business is based on hypocrisy. Fossil fuel companies often trumpet their environmental values and commitments to sustainability, but activists can point out that these values and commitments are a smokescreen for an inherently unsustainable business. Such hypocrisy throws the shaky foundation of the environmental claims of the fossil fuel industry into sharp relief, allowing anti-fossil fuel activists to drive the industry into a corner and demand policies that reduce the rate of fossil fuel extraction and use.

It is quite interesting that some economists actually agree with this emphasis on fossil fuels. One of great negotiation theorists of our time, the Nobel Prize winner Thomas Schelling, actually believes that climate policy should focus on fossil fuels, not on emissions. In an interview with the writer George Marshall, he said that "[t]he way to simplify this is to put the cap on the fossil fuels, not on different industries – a cap on oil and gas at the wellhead, a cap on coal at the minehead" (Marshall, 2014: 170). While Schelling's views of the relevance of the activist tactics for federal bargaining over climate policy are not revealed, he certainly endorses a shift of focus from carbon dioxide emissions to fossil fuels.

The elephant in the room, then, is the lack of specific legislative or political goals. Why are campaigners not demanding specific policies or measures? Why is there no emphasis on a feasible and concrete goal within a clearly specified timeframe? At first sight, this lack of focus appears to undermine the efficacy of the campaign. If the campaign does not have any broader goals than combating individual energy projects, organizing protests, and making a lot of noise, then what can the campaign achieve? Even if the campaign proves wildly successful against the leadership's own yardstick, this may not mean much without specific targets and goals.

The lack of emphasis on specific proposals in anti-fossil fuel campaigns is, however, neither an accident nor an omission. All the activities emphasized in the anti-fossil fuel campaigns have the major advantage of building a movement. Throughout the scores of activist groups and organizations that participate in anti-fossil fuel campaigning, there is a widely shared understanding that action begets action. When seasoned activists mobilize others to join the cause, they are under no illusion that they remain politically too weak to turn the tide against the fossil fuel industry. However, they also believe that their cause is a powerful one. Having learned from the anemic years of the American environmental movement, anti-fossil fuel campaigners are always looking for mobilization techniques that are iconic, symbolic, attractive, and flashy. Perhaps incidentally, the ecological paradigm encourages direct confrontations with the fossil fuel industry, and such confrontations tend to draw more participants than mobilization around more obscure and technical issues, such as federal renewable portfolio standards.

3.4 Explaining the momentum: why does the campaign catch on?

The motivation behind campaigns against fossil fuels is intrinsically linked to their popularity and rapid growth. Since activists are constantly recruiting kindred souls, whatever motivates activists to participate in campaigns is also the engine of expanded mobilization. However, it would be fallacious to conflate the internal and external logics of campaigning. While a description of the internal logic helps us to understand what is going on in an activist's head, even the most elaborate, sympathetic, and poetic description of the ecological paradigm and the role of the fossil fuel industry in global warming would not explain the success and popularity of campaigns against fossil fuels.

So, why does the campaign against fossil fuels catch on? To answer this question, we build on a more general argument about the roots of success in social movements. Published in *American Psychologist*, Weick's (1984) short article noted that activists tend to thrive when they can frequently score "small wins." A small win is an intermediate success that brings activists closer to their inevitable goal. For example, for proponents of a federal carbon tax in the United States, a municipal carbon tax in Seattle would be a small win. As long as activists continue to score small wins, they establish a strong track record and derive psychological satisfaction for their achievements. In a group context, these small wins create a feeling of solidarity and turn activism into a rewarding activity. Without small wins, activists would grow frustrated and give up on their ultimate goal because they would see no signs of progress and fail to reap any rewards from their hard work.

Weick's (1984) insight gives us the missing piece of the puzzle. If campaigns against fossil fuels can use their formidable internal logic to score one small win after another, then activists can turn their compelling moral argument into a dynamic, growing campaign. For potential activists, the ecological paradigm is a solid foundation for sustained participation in campaigns against fossil fuels. However, only small wins can support the continued sense of meaningful, rewarding activity. The key to understanding why campaigns against fossil fuels captivate the activist imagination and expand is found in their ability to score small wins continuously and tell a compelling story about these small wins as parts of something that is larger than life – a collective campaign to save the planet.

What makes small wins possible is the strong sense of tackling the root cause of the problem. When activists stop the construction of a pipeline or push a college to divest its endowment from coal, they are not tinkering at the margins of the problem. Instead, they have just scored a small win. Even limited achievements that do not directly threaten the global balance of power between the activists and the fossil fuel industry are meaningful, because they represent a successful effort to defend the core values of the ecological paradigm. While an economist or financial analyst may sneer at the notion that an individual project would have any relevance to the problem of global climate change, this is not how an activist wedded to the ecological paradigm sees the world. The ecological paradigm calls for a defense of the core values of sustainable human societies, and every action that results in the defeat of a destructive energy project reaffirms the integrity of these values.

The notion of tackling the root cause also lends the campaigns plenty of symbolic power. While self-identified realists and skeptics often ridicule symbolic efforts, activism against the fossil fuel industry gains much from the symbolic nature of the campaign. A small, detached action does not encourage participation, but the powerful symbol of attacking the primary culprit of climate change and related forms of ecological destruction motivates the adherents of the ecological paradigm to join the cause.

The nature of the campaign itself reinforces the powerful notion of tackling the root cause. Consider the following description of being arrested at a Keystone XL action in Washington, DC, by the writer Samuel Avery in his book *The Pipeline and the Paradigm*:

> [B]eing arrested for what you believe in becomes a transformational experience. It is not something you can plan your day around, not something that fits into the rest of your schedule. Everything else in your life comes to a stop. You step out of the normal flow of time – away from your house, your car, your family, your morning routines, and your workday – into an unknowable realm of waiting and wondering. You have no control. Someone else says where you go and what you do. The world no longer looks the same to you, and you no longer look the same to the world. You have been removed from society. After you reenter, you are never fully the same.
>
> *(Avery, 2013: 15)*

This sense of a radical transformative experience, which played a major role in Gandhi's *satyagraha* campaign, is conspicuously absent in traditional environmental lobbying, which relegates grassroots activists to the role of passive donors and, at best, online petitioners.

Conversely, the identity of the powerful opponent, the fossil fuel industry, is also important. When anti-fossil fuel campaigners succeed in their activities, the relevance of their achievement is not limited to defeating a local opponent. The framing of campaigns as a defense of the planet against the fossil fuel industry unifies individual small wins and places them squarely within a grand narrative. If the significance of a successful individual action was limited to stopping a local energy project or passing a municipal policy, it would hardly be the kind of small win that would allow anti-fossil fuel campaigners to do a victory lap and focus on the next action with renewed vigor. However, individual victories against a global fossil fuel industry are much more than local achievements. Each such victory is another contribution to the success of a dynamic global movement.

The unification of small wins in a global movement against fossil fuels is greatly facilitated by the simplicity of the message. The ecological paradigm is itself a sophisticated and subtle framework for analysis and action, yet its message for activists is simple: *dirty energy projects must be stopped*. Equipped with such a message, anti-fossil fuel activists need not justify the significance of their small wins with complex and convoluted arguments. When activists stop a pipeline, their interpretation is that they have defended nature and people by stopping a dirty energy project, full stop. There is no need to engage in complex debates about policy design, unanticipated effects, and so on.

This simplicity is powerful because it avoids confusion. When energy analysts debate the relevance of projects such as Keystone XL, they engage in complex calculations of counterfactuals and scenarios, making and defending dozens of assumptions along the way. Often, energy analysts offer a strong "maybe" or "it depends" as their final argument, with lots and lots of fine print and caveats. Campaigners see no pressure to engage in such arguments, however, because their paradigmatic approach simply calls for an end to fossil fuel development. Since activists understand that potential participants to their movement usually share strong ecological values, a simple message is enough. There is a clear link among the framing of the problem, attainable small wins, and the big dream of a sustainable society without fossil fuels.

The combination of local and global goals is also a powerful unifying force for the movement against fossil fuels. If the anti-fossil fuel activists set their sights only on major global goals, such as driving ExxonMobil into bankruptcy or stopping new coal mining, they would rarely, if ever, have any small wins to report. Since campaigns against fossil fuels have a strong local component, activists have found a way to overcome an important obstacle to success: in addition to mobilizing grassroots support, local actions create potential for meaningful small wins that feed into the broader campaign against fossil fuels at the national, regional, and global levels. The old slogan "think globally, act locally" captures this idea.

Given this argument, it is not entirely surprising that the movement began at a time of high fossil fuel prices. According to the price data reported by the oil company BP, crude oil prices reached $106.94 in the year 2008 (2014 constant dollars), the highest since 1864 (BP, 2015). Despite the global financial crisis, oil prices reached another record of $117.09 in 2011. High oil and other fossil fuel prices were both a threat and an opportunity to the activists. On the one hand, high prices meant that fossil fuel extraction became very attractive for extraction companies in North America, as unconventional resources such as tar sand oil and shale gas were now profitable despite high extraction costs. On the other hand, the fossil fuel projects triggered by unprecedented energy prices also created concrete targets for anti-fossil fuel mobilization, including the Keystone XL pipeline that was to transport tar sands oil from Canada through the United States to the Gulf of Mexico (McAdam and Boudet, 2012).

Besides the local-global connection, campaigns against fossil fuels have a lot of potential for hybrid activism. Recall that hybrid activism combines multiple different issues into a campaign. Resistance to fossil fuels creates many opportunities for such issue linkages. Anti-corporate, anti-globalization, and socialist activists can join because the fossil fuel industry is dominated by a few hundred of the largest, most multinational corporations in the world. The same goes for labor unions. For environmental justice activists, the local damage caused by fossil fuels, which often hurts poor minority communities the most, is a call to arms. Water activists are concerned about the effects of fossil fuel extraction and use on aquatic environments and people's access to clean water. For global justice advocates, the effects of climate change on the least developed countries, along with the concept of "ecological debt," are compelling reasons to mobilize against the fossil fuel industry. The list of potential allies is long.

In our research, we learned that many religious communities were particularly drawn to the arguments of the anti-fossil fuel activists. While various faiths and congregations have sounded the alarm about climate change for a long time, relative to the large size of the faith community in the United States, there has been surprisingly little concrete action. The campaign against fossil fuels has managed to reinvigorate religious climate activism – and not just Christian, but also all other major faiths – by highlighting the moral and ethical aspects of their activities.

To illustrate the notion of a religious approach to campaigns against fossil fuels, consider the case of GreenFaith, a US nonprofit group dedicated to "[i]nspiring, educating and mobilizing people of diverse religious backgrounds for environmental leadership" (GreenFaith, n.d.).[1] GreenFaith promotes the strategy of divestment from fossil fuels and reinvestment into renewable energy, emphasizing the historical commitment of religious communities to this kind of activism:

> Religious groups have chosen to divest if certain companies regularly and intentionally undertake activities that injure or kill large numbers of people, often groups that are vulnerable or marginalized. They've divested because they come to believe that investing in the offending industries violates the essence of their identity. When a company, industry or government behaves in this way, divestment has represented a refusal to profit from activities irreconcilable with a fundamental religious mission and purpose.
>
> *(Harper, 2013: 5)*

The document further emphasizes that, as a target, the fossil fuel industry meets these criteria:

> The suffering and harm caused by climate change will be greater than the harm caused by the targets of all previous religious divestment campaigns combined. The fossil fuel industry's business model ensures nothing but increasing harm. The industry's entrenched resistance to change, expressed through intentionally deceptive public relations and extensive lobbying

against climate legislation, has been extensively documented. A rapid shift away from a carbon-intensive future, urgently needed, won't occur without intense, sustained public pressure.

(Harper, 2013: 8)

In addition to the symbolism of tackling the root cause, the campaign against fossil fuels draws participants who find the climate justice aspect compelling. The social and ecological consequences of fossil fuel use are not evenly distributed. The least-developed countries pay the highest cost for the world's fossil fuel use, both because of their limited ability to adapt to climate change and natural vulnerabilities, such as those of low-lying islands and coastal areas. This framing creates a powerful analogy to earlier campaigns for civil rights and against apartheid, as climate justice highlights the uneven benefits of contemporary patterns of fossil fuel use to the world's wealthy and the poor.

While much of our argument emphasizes the successes of campaigns against fossil fuels, it is important to also consider the downside of the way the ecological paradigm feeds these campaigns. Because the rhetoric and framing of the campaigns emphasize opposition to the fossil fuel industry, activists have a difficult time reaching out to non-progressive audiences. While the arguments used by anti-fossil fuel activists are effective in encouraging and mobilizing kindred souls, these arguments often fall on deaf ears outside a relatively small group of potential activists. The very arguments that create unity among activists by connecting local struggles to a broader global showdown with the fossil fuel industry are potential deterrents to moderate and conservative audiences. For example, the framing of climate change as stemming from excessive "corporate power"[2] is not compelling to a conservative who has a strong pro-business worldview.

Although anti-fossil fuel activists frame their movement as a common "people's" cause, in practice their target audience is found on the progressive, liberal end of the political continuum. How can such a position be justified? A prominent campaigner told us that his team was under no illusion about their limited reach across the political spectrum. He said, however, that in today's environment it would be pointless to reach out to people with a conservative worldview. Since today's conservatives would not listen to a grassroots climate activist in any case, he said, there is no reason to try to develop messages that are so nonpartisan as to appeal to both conservatives and liberals. Such messages would be watered down and ineffective, and yet they would do nothing to truly expand the target audience of the campaign. Since today's politics are highly polarized, it is not possible for campaigners to please everyone.

The profile of today's anti-fossil fuel activists is readily seen in the September 21, 2015, People's Climate March in New York. A major environmental protest with an estimated number of 400,000 people participating, the march was largely led by the anti-fossil fuel activists and their allies (Alter, 2014, September 22). Therefore, understanding the profile of the participants sheds a lot of light on what kind of people join the campaign. We assisted Dana Fisher, a professor of Sociology at the

University of Maryland, in a statistically representative survey of the participants. Sporting "Go Fossil Free" shirts, we and the Maryland team successfully surveyed a total of 468 people from all segments of the march during that day.

The results were striking. First, people with college education were dramatically over-represented in the sample. Four out of five protesters had finished college, and only 5 percent had never had any college education. We suspect that the remaining 15 percent were mostly current students, most of whom will graduate in the future, instead of dropouts. Furthermore, there was a very strong left-wing bias. On a 1–7 scale, as many as 20 percent considered themselves "extremely left" on the political scale and another 53 percent said they were on the "left." Another 16 percent said there were "slightly left." Fewer than 2 percent said they were "slightly right" or "right," and nobody said they were "extremely right." In a country that is evenly split between the left and right, this is a remarkably strong leftist bias. Taken together with the results on education, this observation means that The People's Climate March could have been called The Educated Leftist People's Climate March.

In a report on the march, Fisher (2014) compares the political participation profile of the participants to the American population. Clearly, the participants are much more active than the general population. To give an illustration, 82 percent of the participants said they had signed a petition in the past, whereas only 35 percent of the national population report doing so. Twenty-three percent of the participants had participated in a protest before, while the same number for the national population is 6 percent. In fact, among 10 different forms of participation, the only one that is approximately equal is experience working for a political party, which is 19 percent among the national population and 17 percent among the protesters. Perhaps most remarkable, 9 percent of the respondents report having been arrested in the past.

At the same time, the march seems to have had a lot of success with the hybrid strategy of mobilization among liberals. In her report, Fisher (2014) reports results on prior experience with protests among the participants in the past 10 years. Unsurprisingly, the environment is the largest category, with almost 40 percent of people with prior protest experience saying they have been to an environmental rally. However, the margin of victory over other issues is small. Human rights is above 30 percent and peace is at almost 30 percent. Social welfare, education, local issues, racism, labor, immigration, and globalization all score above 10 percent, as well. This suggests both that many environmental activists are also active on other issues and that the march drew participants who had no background in environmental protest. Indeed, even among experienced protesters, more than 60 percent – a clear majority – had never been to an environmental action before.

Given the progressive emphasis of the anti-fossil fuel campaign, the political opportunity structure argument cannot explain the beginnings of the anti-coal campaigning during President George W. Bush's tenure. However, a favorable shift in opportunity structure with President Obama's inauguration in January 2008 can certainly illuminate why the anti-fossil fuel campaign put so much emphasis on national campaign on issues such as Keystone XL. As opportunity structure theorists would expect (Kitschelt, 1986; Kriesi, 2007; McAdam, 1986; Meyer, 2004), a favorable national political change empowered the anti-fossil fuel movement by improving the odds of success in the federal political system.

It is not entirely clear what the movement against fossil fuels can hope to achieve with a strategy that focuses on progressives alone in the long run. A successful outcome of this kind of campaigning could be a robust consensus on the need to reduce the use of fossil fuels and tackle climate change among the liberal establishment. Even if anti-fossil fuel campaigners cannot expect to convert conservatives into fervent advocates for climate action, a visible and vocal campaign could put heavy pressure on the Democratic Party elite to choose climate change as a top issue on their legislative agenda. If the campaign against fossil fuels grows so powerful that it can shape the outcomes of congressional elections by rallying people behind anti-fossil fuel candidates, then liberals will have to adopt positions that go against the fossil fuel industry. At the municipal level, such a change in the political balance of power would result in fracking bans, denied permits to pipelines, defeated coal power plants, investments in renewable energy and conservation, and perhaps even more comprehensive policies, such as carbon taxes. At the state and federal levels, various climate and energy policies begin to exhibit a new bias toward reduced greenhouse gas emissions and a "soft path" (Lovins, 1976) of energy development based on renewables and conservation.

Over time, a successful campaign against fossil fuels will have to adopt more specific policy goals. If the movement succeeds in mobilizing the progressive base and, therefore, achieves its broad strategic goal of creating a powerful political constituency, then the importance of specific proposals increases. If the campaign against fossil fuels emerges as a powerful force in politics at all levels, the leadership of the movement has an opportunity to shape not only the likelihood, but also the broad contours, of climate and energy policy. However, the movement is still far from reaching this kind of influence in the political system.

It is also possible that the campaign against fossil fuels indirectly contributes to legislative progress through what Haines (1984) calls the "radical flank effect." During the American civil rights movement, the entry of radical leaders and organizations, such as Malcolm X and the Black Panthers, facilitated fund-raising from whites by moderate black organizations, as the appearance of militant forces on the stage made moderate blacks more acceptable to the white majority. When Malcolm X heard that his biographer's brother had become a Kansas state senator, he said that the moderate black activists "who are getting somewhere need to always remember that it was us extremists who made it possible" (quoted in Haley and X, 1992: 423).

If campaigns against fossil fuels make powerful societal interests strengthen their collaboration with less radical environmental organizations, such as the EDF, then the anti-fossil fuel activists may promote progress toward legislation even without any concrete proposals. For example, if business interests worry about their public image and the possibility of costly regulations, they could support less costly alternatives, such as emissions trading, to parry the attacks of anti-fossil fuel activists.

Such a virtuous cycle is possible if anti-fossil fuel activists are able to act strategically and put pressure on moderate environmental groups without provoking a backlash.

To summarize, anti-fossil fuel campaigns are not only consistent with the ecological paradigm that is a shared value among many environmentalists, but also bring together localized small wins and a grand narrative at the global level. Campaigns against fossil fuels can expect to see a series of small wins in their battle with the fossil fuel industry, yet these small wins can be easily woven into a much larger fabric of urgently needed ecological activism. This combination of the local and the global is why the campaign against fossil fuels can sustain itself and grow rapidly.

3.5 Counting chickens while they hatch: the impact of the movement

So far, we have focused the discussion on understanding the motivations underlying mobilization and the ability of the movement to sustain high levels of activism over time. In the end, however, these factors are intermediate products that do not guarantee actual *impact*. If the movement against fossil fuels is to be successful, it must contribute to economic, political, and social changes that reduce greenhouse gas emissions and thus mitigate climate change.

Unfortunately, evaluating the movement's impact is harder than evaluating the degree of mobilization and levels of activism. In the literature on social movements, this difficulty is by now recognized (Amenta and Caren, 2007; Amenta et al., 2010; Kriesi, 2007; Meyer, 2005). As Andrews (1997: 800) puts it, the "tendency to focus on the earliest and most visible phase of a social movement neglects the ongoing dynamics and long-term consequences of social movements."

In the case of the anti-fossil fuels campaign, there are two central challenges. The first is the difficulty of establishing causality. It is entirely possible that the movement's emergence is associated with positive changes, but these changes reflect deeper forces – technically, an omitted variable – that produced both the movement and the desired outcome. For example, we shall see this difficulty in evaluating the relative importance of the movement and fracking as causes of the decline of coal-powered electricity generation in the United States. Because both the movement and fracking have grown rapidly during the past decade, it is difficult to say how important the two have been in the recent troubles of the American coal industry.

The second difficulty is that the movement's story is far from finished. What we can observe at this time is the short-term impact of the movement after less than a decade of activism, whereas the long-term impact remains subject to uncertainty. In this sense, we are counting chickens while they hatch. Our claims about impact, whether praising or condemning, are based on observed trends and estimates of their significance in the long run.

These difficulties notwithstanding, we can still offer useful insights into the role and contributions of the movement. The four campaigns we shall investigate – Keystone XL, divestment, coal, and fracking – all have immediate goals that are in a sense necessary conditions for their long-term success. By evaluating the movement's progress toward reaching these goals, we can say if the movement is on track to reaching its own goals or not. In the case of Keystone XL, for example, we can assess both the movement's ability to delay and increase the cost of the pipeline construction and the ripple effects of this controversy to the more general environmental and energy policy of the incumbent administration. In the case of coal, we can examine the movement's contribution to defeating planned coal power plants in the United States – a substantive outcome of significance. If these evaluations are positive, then the movement has, at the very least, begun to make an impact. If these evaluations are negative, then the movement has not even achieved its immediate goals.

Here we must emphasize that it is important to measure impact independent of the movement's dynamism, as evaluated from an internal perspective. For example, it is possible that the movement achieves considerable success in mobilizing millions of people, draws a lot of media attention, and secures enough donations to sustain activism for a long time in the future. None of these achievements constitute true impact, however, and it is important to avoid the fallacy of conflating aggressive mobilization and substantive influences. While it is hard to imagine that the movement could be effective without mobilization, it is *not* inconceivable that the movement achieves success in mobilization but does not reduce the use of fossil fuels or contribute to climate change mitigation.

Because our argument puts a lot of emphasis on small wins, we pay particular attention to separating small wins in mobilization from small wins in impact. For Weick (1984), small wins are important because they sustain mobilization. In the case of fossil fuels, small wins may not contribute to climate change mitigation in the long run. For example, the movement could succeed in defeating Keystone XL and promoting divestment – only to then see alternative pipelines built and fossil fuel production remaining unabated. In this case, the small wins could contribute to mobilization without having much of a substantive impact. Throughout the discussion of impacts, we will distinguish between the contribution of small wins to mobilization and impact by evaluating whether said small wins could through accumulation reduce the use of fossil fuels. If they could not, then they could still be meaningful as an instrument of mobilization; if they could, then we must consider them in our evaluation of short-term impacts as well.

3.6 The four campaigns

To assess the motivations, mobilization capacity, and impact of the campaign against fossil fuels, we conduct case studies of four key campaigns that constitute the anti-fossil fuel movement: the Keystone XL mobilization, divestment activism, campaigns against coal power plants and mines, and the anti-fracking groups. The campaigns are not independent of each other, but because they have different short-term goals and aim at mobilizing different constituencies, they can be analyzed both comparatively and in a more holistic sense. Within each case, we also conduct a small number of case studies of local campaigns, and thus lower the level of analysis by one (Przeworski and Teune, 1970: chapter 3). On the other hand, the encompassing analysis of each campaign is based on case study analysis and process tracing (Gerring, 2004).

In studying the cases, we mostly rely on publicly available resources, such as writings and statements of activists, along with the burgeoning secondary literature on the topic. Because the campaign against fossil fuels is intended to shape public opinion and stigmatize the fossil fuel industry, the campaigners have left behind an impressive, if often virtual, paper trail. Therefore, most of our analysis draws on transparent, publicly available sources that the reader can easily verify by following the links we provide. We recognize that such sources have an ideological bias in favor of the activists, but given our interest in activists' subjective perceptions and goals, we consider it particularly important to consult these materials – but take them with a grain of salt.

We also draw heavily on the excellent secondary literature on anti-fossil fuels campaigning. The academic literature has not addressed the movement yet, but journalistic accounts provide many helpful accounts and case histories that we can draw on. To complement this study of the evidence, we also participated in public events organized by the movement here in New York City, observing the debates and actions. Finally, we interviewed a small number of key activists, whose identity will remain anonymous throughout this book. The interviews were mostly used for background information and to fill gaps in the sequence of events; with the exception of the People's Climate March (PCM) interviews cited earlier, we did not conduct any formal surveys or test hypotheses through structured interviews.

Because the cases feature different sets of issues and research challenges, we introduce our research strategy on a case-by-case basis. For example, Keystone XL is a campaign aimed to stop a single pipeline. Here the anti-fossil fuel campaigners are targeting a specific, if highly symbolic, energy project – a pipeline from Canadian tar sands to the Mexican Gulf through the United States. In contrast, the number of concrete targets in the anti-coal and anti-fracking campaigns is large. Similarly, the divestment campaign deviates from the others in that it does not target a particular energy project. In assessing the Keystone XL campaign, then, maintaining a sharp focus is easier than in the other campaigns, which have multiple targets across space and over time.

When we assess activist motivations to participate in the campaign, we in essence ask the question of why activists would choose to focus on a specific project, instead of pursuing a broader strategy of anti-fossil fuels policy. Similarly, the question of why the campaign catches on is about the ability of a single, symbolic energy project to sustain high levels of mobilization over time. The impact of the campaign can be evaluated against three yardsticks. First, have the activists been able to delay and reduce the likelihood of Keystone XL approval and construction? Second, has this specific success raised new barriers to other similar projects, be it for political or economic reasons? Finally, has Keystone XL raised the salience of fossil fuels and climate change as problems in American politics?

TABLE 3.1 Evaluation matrix for the four campaigns. In the concluding chapter, the cells will be populated with results from the analysis of the four campaigns for purposes of comparison.

	Activist Motives	*Mobilization Potential*	*Impact*	*Weaknesses*
Keystone XL				
Divestment				
Coal				
Fracking				

The divestment campaign requires a somewhat different approach to understanding motivations for participation. In this case, there is no specific project with great symbolism. Instead, divestment from fossil fuels is a general strategy that different institutions can follow. Why, then, are activists motivated by divestment in particular? Why are so many divestment activists among college students? Moving from motivations to sustaining mobilization, we ask whether individual successes in divestment can be thought of as small wins for the anti-fossil fuels campaign. The impact of the divestment campaign can be measured in two ways. First, how much divestment have activists prompted? Second, and more important, have these divestment decisions and the publicity surrounding them actually begun to turn public opinion against fossil fuels?

In a sense, the campaigns against coal and fracking are easier to evaluate. In the case of coal, motivation is about the ability of the movement to create local mobilization, supported and publicized by the national campaigners, against coal mines and coal power plants. In particular, how powerful is a local fight against coal as a motivation when compared to alternatives, such as local renewable energy investment or state-level or national campaigning for climate policy? The ability of the movement to sustain high levels of mobilization can be evaluated by asking if the successes and failures of local coal campaigns have, in the context of the national campaign, an effect on other local campaigns. The case of fracking, finally, is analogous to the coal campaign and can be evaluated using similar yardsticks. When we put these different approaches together, we obtain an evaluation matrix for all four campaigns. The matrix, which we fill with data in the concluding chapter, is illustrated in Table 3.1.

In the concluding section of this book, we return to explicit comparisons between the cases. Moving beyond individual evaluations, we contrast the motivations, mobilization capacities, and impacts of the four campaigns. While we hesitate to rank the campaigns explicitly, we can compare their strengths and weaknesses and use this comparative angle to derive implications for the social movements literature, for climate policy, and for the anti-fossil fuel campaign.

Notes

1 See http://greenfaith.org/ (accessed November 17, 2014).
2 See Hayden (2012, November 13) for a typical example of this framing.

4

KEYSTONE XL

What issue is pressing enough to bring together Native Americans and ranchers in South Dakota, a state often compared to Mississippi for its racial tensions (Schweigman, n.d.)? The answer is the environment, and the enormous damage the two groups foresee should TransCanada be allowed to construct Keystone XL, a pipeline that would run from Alberta's tar sands to Texas Gulf Coast refineries. Leading the charge are Beth Lone Eagle, a Lakota woman with a history of local activism, and Paul Seamans, a lifelong rancher who once accepted TransCanada's terms for the pipeline under the threat of expropriation. In April of 2014, many activists would ride horses side-by-side through Washington, DC to present a painted tipi symbolizing the protection of water to President Barack Obama (Lukacs, 2014, November 18).

Native Americans and ranchers would not be the only ones pressuring President Obama on Keystone XL. The Dalai Lama and Archbishop Desmond Tutu, along with seven other fellow Nobel Peace Prize winners, called on President Obama:

> We – a group of Nobel Peace Laureates – are writing today to ask you to do the right thing for our environment and reject the proposal to build the Keystone XL, a 1700-mile pipeline that would stretch from Canada's Alberta tar sands to the Texas Gulf Coast. It is your decision to make. The night you were nominated for president, you told the world that under your leadership – and working together – the rise of the oceans will begin to slow and the planet will begin to heal. You spoke of creating a clean energy economy. This is a critical moment to make good on that pledge, and make a lasting contribution to the health and well being of everyone of this planet.
>
> *(Sheppard, 2011, September 7)*

How did a business proposition by a Canadian energy company become a rallying point for environmentalists? As the symbol of the political debates surrounding fossil fuels in North America, Keystone XL is an excellent point of departure for our study of the campaign against fossil fuels. It is the largest coordinated campaign that specifically targets fossil fuels in recent US history. More recent campaigns, such as the call for divestment from fossil fuels, all build on the experience with Keystone XL. Because activism against Keystone XL has continued for more than three years, we also have a lot of material for drawing inferences and learning about the internal and external logics of activism against fossil fuels.

The campaign against Keystone XL highlights the central elements of our argument. The organizers of the campaign have managed to turn the pipeline into a lightning rod of controversy by presenting its construction as a blatant violation of the core ecological principles that call for an immediate halt to fossil fuel extraction. This rhetorical move has allowed local anti-pipeline activists to join forces with those who worry about the global problem of climate change. In turn, this approach has allowed the 350.org leadership and their allies to reap huge benefits in the form of grassroots mobilization and movement building.

At the same time, the Keystone XL campaign also showcases the weaknesses of the mobilization. The campaigners have neither shown that Keystone XL is actually critical to tar oil development in Canada – there are many other pipelines in construction and the oil could also be shipped to Asia – nor used the campaign to effect decisive change in the American political establishment. The impact of the campaign has been substantial mainly because President Obama's campaign promises, as well as his desire to leave a green legacy, provided a political opportunity that the activists were able to exploit. The heated contests in Congress over the issue reflect its divisive nature. The nature and the impact of the campaign, as it unfolded, would have looked very different in the absence of a receptive Obama. With this political advantage now gone, the strength of the campaign will truly be put to a test.

4.1 Significance

Keystone XL is a pipeline that would run from the Canadian province of Alberta all the way to Texas ports in the Gulf of Mexico. According to the company that proposed to build the pipeline, TransCanada, "The pipeline will have capacity to transport up to 830,000 barrels of oil per day to Gulf Coast and Midwest refineries, reducing American dependence on oil from Venezuela and the Middle East by up to 40 per cent" (TransCanada, 2013).[1]

The main significance of Keystone XL lies with its potential to export tar sands oil from Alberta, Canada, to the United States and, through Texas, to other countries. Writing in *Nature Climate Change*, Swart and Weaver (2012) quantify the effects of Alberta tar sands on the global climate. They find that if all of the estimated 1.8 trillion barrels of unconventional Alberta oil were used, the global temperature would increase by 0.36 Celsius – almost half of the observed warming during the 20th century. To be sure, the numbers are smaller if only proven reserves are used. These reserves are only one-tenth of the estimated total, and so they would increase the global temperature by 0.03 Celsius.

Climate scientist James Hansen, who was arrested in August 2011 for his participation in a rally against Keystone XL, goes so far as to argue that Keystone XL would be "game over" for the global climate:

> If released all at once, the known tar sands resource is equivalent to 150 parts per million. As is the case with other fossil fuel sources, the amount in the air declines to about 20 percent after 1,000 years. Of course, only a small fraction of the resource is economically recoverable at the moment. But if you decide you are going to continue your addiction and build a big pipeline to Texas, the economically extractable oil will steadily grow over time. Moreover the known resources would grow because there is plenty more to be discovered.
>
> (McGowan, 2011, August 29)

This claim is based on the ecological paradigm. Hansen understands that "only a small fraction of the resource is economically recoverable at the moment," but he says that the construction of Keystone XL is essentially a slippery slope, as "the economically extractable oil will steadily grow over time." In his view, Keystone XL is "game over" for the climate because it irreversibly sets the United States and Canada on a path toward increased reliance on tar sands.

Most energy policy analysts disagree with this claim. In their view, activists greatly overestimate the importance of Keystone XL. Consider, for example, Michael Levi, who was the director of the program on energy security and climate change at the Council on Foreign Relations during most of the Keystone XL campaign. In January 18, 2012, he wrote the following about the claims made by Hansen and other Keystone XL activists:

> The additional emissions generated by replacing conventional oil with the crude that the pipeline could have carried would have been no more than a small fraction of 1 percent of total annual U.S. greenhouse gas pollution. Meanwhile, it would take more than 1,000 years to burn all the oil sands, even if extraction were ramped up threefold from its current pace. The fate of the climate will be determined long before that.
>
> (Levi, 2012, January 18)

According to Levi, activist claims about the significance of the Keystone XL pipeline – as well as the hypothetical burning of all of Alberta's tar sands, which he considers unrealistic – are overblown.

Are the activists right or wrong? There is no easy answer to this question. It is certainly true that Keystone XL itself cannot carry enough oil to make a large difference, but this does not mean that the construction of the pipeline would not have broader implications. Therefore, a conclusive answer would require telling the future. The decision to build Keystone XL would not only influence tar sands extraction in Alberta, but also influence attempts to build other pipelines and ship oil from the Pacific coast of Canada and the United States to East Asia. Hansen's argument is based on the assumption that Keystone XL is pivotal. If it is not built, then the use of tar sands will be significantly reduced, as compared to a Keystone XL scenario. The energy policy analysts, on the other hand, mostly assume that Keystone XL has little effect on total fossil fuel use in the world. In their view, Keystone XL is an individual project with at best marginal significance in the big picture.

Besides the climate pact, opponents of Keystone XL have raised other concerns. In particular, the construction of the pipeline would affect natural landscapes across the United States. In Nebraska, the envisioned route of Keystone XL has already been changed by TransCanada because local activists mobilized to oppose the plan to construct the pipeline through the ecologically sensitive Sandhills wetlands and the Ogallala aquifer, which is one of the largest freshwater reserves in the world. According to Tar Sands Blockade, an NGO that opposes Keystone XL and related tar sands projects in North America, "The Keystone XL pipeline threatens Texas's Carrizo-Wilcox Aquifer which supplies drinking water to more than 12 million people living across 60 counties in drought-stricken East Texas" (TarSands Blockade, n.d.).[2] Native American groups along the planned route of the pipeline have also mobilized in opposition because they worry about the effects of the pipeline on the natural landscape and consider the construction plan a violation of tribal sovereignty (Lukacs, 2014, November 18).

4.2 Overview

The Keystone XL campaign consists of many actions, events, and smaller campaigns. It has been constantly in the news at least since August 2011 and the number of activist participants must be in the hundreds of thousands, if not millions. Amid the rapid growth of a shale gas and oil boom in the United States and Canada, the Keystone XL campaign has come to symbolize grassroots activism against fossil fuels and climate change in North America.

The campaign dates back to a 2011 paper by James Hansen, calling the development of the tar sands "essentially game over" for the climate (Hansen, 2011). In July 2011, environmental leaders, including McKibben, Tom Goldtooth, and Naomi Klein, answered Hansen's call by inviting the public to join in civil disobedience in Washington, DC, to deny Keystone XL, "a 1,500-mile fuse to the biggest carbon bomb on the continent." This metaphor conveys the sense of urgency needed to mobilize grassroots activists in Washington.

The first prominent action, as promised, came in front of the White House during the last week of August 2011. The timing of the action was no coincidence, as the "final environmental impact assessment" – hardly the last word on the topic, as we shall see – of the pipeline was released on August 26 by the Department of State. From August 20 to September 3, some 1,253 people were arrested sitting in as part of the Tar Sands Action, calling on President Obama to stop the pipeline. Ranchers, indigenous leaders, and allies from across the country joined in the historic two-week action.

The CEOs of every major US environmental organization co-signed a letter stating that "there is not an inch of daylight" between their stance on the pipeline and that of the protesters risking arrest. Nine Nobel Peace Prize laureates, including Archbishop Desmond Tutu of South Africa and the Dalai Lama, wrote to President Obama to reject the pipeline. President Obama and Vice President Joseph Biden were greeted by Keystone XL protesters in cities such as Richmond, Portland, Columbus, Boston, Cincinnati, Seattle, Denver, Raleigh, Pittsburgh, St. Louis, New York City, and San Francisco.

On November 6, 2011, another 15,000 protestors gathered around the White House, calling on President Obama to stand for a healthy climate by rejecting the Keystone XL tar sands pipeline. A small win came on November 10, 2011, when President Obama and the State Department announced that a decision on Keystone XL would not be made until 2013, citing the need to assess alternative routes and effect on climate change. Toward the end of 2011, Republicans in Congress made a major push to secure the approval of Keystone XL. Arguing that the project would create 20,000 jobs "directly" and "support hundreds of thousands of jobs in coming years," Senate Republicans proposed a bill that would require the Secretary of State to grant a permit for the controversial project within 60 days, unless President Obama were to publicly determine that the pipeline is "not in the national interest" (Madison, 2011, November 30).

On January 18, 2012, the Obama administration responded in kind by denying the permit for the Keystone XL pipeline, citing the arbitrary deadline and inability to conduct a full review. TransCanada was given permission to reapply. On February 13, 2011, Senate Republicans introduced an amendment to a federal transportation bill that would speed the construction and operation of the controversial new leg of the oil pipeline between Canada and the United States (Eilperin, 2012, February 13). The anti-fossil fuel movement responded swiftly and decisively. More than 800,000 people contacted their senators within 24 hours, urging opposition to the pipeline. More than 500,000 signatures against Keystone XL and a letter by prominent climate scientists were delivered to the congressional leadership (350. org, 2012, February 13).[3] With his own credibility on the line, President Obama called Senate Democrats to oppose the amendment. The amendment was narrowly defeated on March 8, 2011 (Miller, 2012, March 8).

Following the rejection of their proposal, TransCanada broke their proposal into two parts, a southern segment and a northern segment. After visiting Cushing, OK, President Obama announced on March 22, 2012, that he was ready to support the southern segment of Keystone XL, while still committing to a review of the northern segment. On May 4, 2012, TransCanada submitted a new application to the State Department for the northern segment of Keystone XL with a slightly modified route that would run from the Canadian border to Steele City, Nebraska. Following President Obama's re-election, thousands would descend upon Washington, DC, on November 18, 2012, calling on the president to reject the tar sands pipeline as a critical piece of tackling climate change during his second term (Samuel, 2012, November 12).

In what was heralded at the time as the largest climate rally in US history, 40,000 people gathered at the National Mall for the "Forward on Climate" rally on February 17, 2013, calling on the president to lead on climate action, beginning with stopping Keystone XL (Gerken, 2013, February 17). The event came days after a bipartisan group of US senators made the latest call for Obama to approve the pipeline. What Van Jones, President Obama's former green jobs adviser who participated in the rally, had to say aptly illustrates the "game over" sentiment that the leaders of the movement had embedded into the movement: "There is nothing else you can do if you let that pipeline go through. It doesn't matter what you do on smog rules and automobile rules – you've already given the whole game [a]way" (Volcovici, 2013, February 17).

On March 2, 2014, the US Park Police arrested hundreds of young people protesting the Keystone XL project, as demonstrators fastened themselves with plastic ties to the White House fences and called for President Obama to reject the controversial oil pipeline. Consistent with the symbolic nature of the campaign, the young activists capitalized on the theatrics. Participants held signs such as "There is no planet B" and "Columbia says no to fossil fuels," referring to the university in New York City. Another group, donning white jumpsuits splattered with black ink symbolizing oil, staged a mock spill. Organizers estimated 1,000 people came out to protest and, according to US Park Police figures, almost 400 people were arrested (Stephenson, 2014, March 2).

This would be a running theme throughout 2014, a back-and-forth between spurts of mass protests and political wrangling in Congress, as President Obama continued to mull over the Keystone XL decision. As the final public comment period on the pipeline drew to a close, opponents claimed to have gathered 2 million voices urging the rejection of the pipeline. As nationwide protests continued, a group of activists also gathered in front of the State Department that month, calling on Secretary of State John Kerry to oppose Keystone XL. More than 86,000 signed a "Pledge of Resistance" to commit civil disobedience otherwise (DemocracyNow.org, 2014, March 10).

Meanwhile in Congress, Senate Democrats staged an all-night filibuster urging congressional action on global warming, though Keystone XL was not the main focus. Senators Edward Markey of Massachusetts and Barbara Boxer of California said Republicans who deny global warming are ignoring an existential threat. Three hours into the filibuster, Senator Tim Kaine of Virginia finally brought up Keystone XL: "Why would we embrace tar sands oil and backslide to a dirtier tomorrow?" (DemocracyNow.org, 2014, March 11).

In April 2014, the Obama administration announced a delay on the Keystone XL decision, and the State Department said it was waiting on the results of legal challenges to the pipeline's route through Nebraska, making it less likely that the matter would be concluded until after the midterm elections (DemocracyNow.org, 2014, March 11).

A week later, the Cowboy and Indian Alliance brought thousands to Washington, DC, as ranchers, farmers, and tribal communities stood in solidarity against the pipeline under the slogan "Reject and Protect" (DemocracyNow.org, 2014, April 28a). Among the protestors was the Canadian musician Neil Young, who commented: "I feel that the fossil fuel age is ending. It's having its first death gasps, and we need to keep pushing. We need to stop this pipeline [bringing] this really bad fuel from the tail of the snake in Canada all the way down to the head of the snake in Texas" (DemocracyNow.org, 2014, April 28b).

The following month, to highlight the degree of internal divisions in Congress, a bipartisan Senate measure to encourage energy efficiency in federal and private buildings collapsed, as Republicans tried to add the approval of the Keystone XL oil pipeline and block new US Environmental Protection Agency regulations (DemocracyNow.org, 2014, May 13).

The Congressional tug of war would continue well after the People's Climate March, an historic mass protest in September that brought more than 300,000 people to New York City in advance of a UN summit on climate change. As the midterm elections in November brought momentum to Republicans in Congress, the stage was set for another Republican push. The Obama administration declared that it would await the State Department's review before making any decision on Keystone XL (DemocracyNow.org, 2014, November 6).

In November, the House of Representatives approved the Keystone XL pipeline, while the Senate narrowly voted against it (DemocracyNow.org, 2014, November 17). It was a Democrat, Louisiana Senator Mary Landrieu, who tried to push the pipeline, hoping its passage would help her in the December runoff election against her challenger, Congressman Bill Cassidy, who sponsored the Keystone XL bill in the House (DemocracyNow.org, 2014, November 20). Incidentally, Senator Landrieu would lose her seat to Cassidy in the runoff contest (DemocracyNow. org, 2014, December 8).

In the interim, the battle for the pipeline heated up in Nebraska. On January 9, 2015, the Supreme Court of Nebraska controversially approved the construction of the pipeline through the state (Davenport and Smith, 2015, January 9). This development coincided with a House vote of 266 to 153 in favor of the pipeline, sending the measure to the Senate for approval.[4] On January 16, landowners filed new lawsuits in Holt and York counties, challenging the constitutionality of the state pipeline routing law and seeking to stop TransCanada from using eminent domain (Harris, 2015, January 16).

Four days later, TransCanada filed court documents in nine Nebraska counties to initiate eminent domain proceedings (Schulte, 2015, January 20). The Republican-dominated Congress would continue to pressure the president on this issue, as the Senate voted 62 to 36 in favor of building the pipeline on January 29, 2015. Nine Democrats joined 53 Republicans in passing the bill. This sent the measure back to the House, and House leaders had to decide whether to pass the Senate bill as was or to hold a conference merging the House and Senate versions into a new bill to be voted on by each chamber (Davenport, 2015, January 29). The House voted 270 to 152 in favor of a bill approving the construction of the Keystone XL pipeline. Twenty-nine Democrats voted with Republicans in favor of the measure. The president was given a 10-day window to act on the bill, though the Congress did not have enough votes to override a presidential veto (Davenport, 2015, February 11).

Holt County District Court Judge Mark Kozisek issued a temporary injunction on February 12, 2015, halting condemnation cases along the proposed route of the pipeline (Duara, 2015, February 12). Perhaps in a sign that the company was losing ground, TransCanada announced a change in strategy on September 29, 2015, suspending its efforts to force Nebraskans to give up easements and restarting its bid for route approval by the state's Public Service Commission (Bergin, 2015, September 29). However, the momentum turned against TransCanada near the end of 2015. On November 2, TransCanada asked the Obama administration to pause its review of the project (Davis, 2015, November 2). The Obama administration denied TransCanada this lifeline (Davis, 2015, November 3). President Obama publicly announced the rejection of the Keystone XL pipeline on November 6, 2015, stating that it did not serve the national interest.[5]

To summarize, the campaign produced years of delay in the approval of Keystone XL, eventually resulting in President Obama's rejection of the pipeline. Initially envisioned as a simple process of regular bureaucratic review, the approval of Keystone XL has become the cornerstone of the campaign against fossil fuels. Obama's rejection, which came at a time of a global oil price plunge, may have been the nail in the coffin, but the seven-year delay certainly played a vital role in the campaign's success. We now delve into the details of the campaigning by analyzing select case studies of individual events, actions, and local mobilization.

4.3 Activism in motion

To discern potential patterns in outbreaks of protests against the Keystone XL pipeline, we used the source *Democracy Now!* to compile major headlines related to the pipeline by month, beginning in August 2011.[6] As the clustering of events in Figure 4.1 illustrates, media coverage for the pipeline came in fits and starts. Consistent with our overview, the peaks in media coverage came in the months of August 2011 (the opening salvo), January to February 2013 (the "Forward on Climate" rally), February to April 2014 (the Cowboys and Indians march in Washington), and November 2014 (the Republican push following the midterm elections). Less obvious from the graph are developments in Nebraska, where locals mounted protests in opposition to the pipeline.

Among these prominent events, we discuss at length the first three months of the campaign (August – November 2011), the developments in Nebraska, and the Forward on Climate rally. The first three months of the campaign provide many insights into the logic of the campaign and how it grew. We will recount these three months while identifying five different mechanisms – visibility, opportunity, activation, bandwagon, and prestige – that helped the Keystone XL become the lightening rod that it is. Despite a Republican-dominated Congress, President Obama came down decisively against the pipeline, closing the pipeline debate until

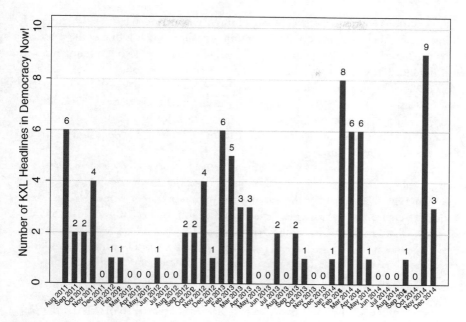

FIGURE 4.1 Headlines containing KXL pipeline, 2011–2014.

Source: Democracy Now!

the arrival of his successor, Donald J. Trump. Bold Nebraska's activities and the Forward on Climate rally provide an in-depth look at the hybrid nature of the coalition that formed against the pipeline.

In late August 2011, as anti-Keystone XL protestors descended on Washington, DC, to engage in civil disobedience, the leaders of the nation's largest environmental groups came together to publicly declare their support for the protestors (Greenberg, 2011, August 24). It unified a range of environmental organizations with different protocols for political action – some familiar with civil disobedience and others relative strangers: Natural Resources Defense Council, the Sierra Club, the Environmental Defense Fund, the National Wildlife Federation, Greenpeace, Friends of the Earth, and the Rainforest Action Network. How was such solidarity achieved and what are some of its implications? Bill McKibben's statement is revealing:

> On an issue as complicated as climate, there will often be disagreements over tactics and goals – just recall the differences over the Senate climate bill this time last year. But there are some projects so obviously dangerous that they unify everyone, and the Keystone XL pipeline is the best example yet. For those of us out there in front of the White House, the best thing about this ringing statement is that the administration won't be able to play one group off against another by making small concessions here and there.
>
> *(Greenberg, 2011, August 24)*

This candid statement sheds light on an important reason why the Keystone XL pipeline became a rallying point for environmental groups: It is one of the most *visible* projects the fossil fuel industry is currently pushing that also holds implications of potentially dystopian proportions for those concerned about climate change, a major "lock in," whereby North America becomes more dependent on unconventional fossil fuels. For 350.org and other environmental organizations that subscribe to the ecological paradigm, Keystone XL provides ready-made, smoking-gun evidence that the fossil fuel industry, with its unlimited endowment and nefarious intentions, is already on the move.

Such visibility is aided by an element of *political opportunity*: the pipeline is a large-scale international project that requires the explicit consent of the American government, in 2017 under the administration of a president whose electoral base includes environmental activists. If the activists can mobilize around this cause and beat the fossil fuel lobbyists at their own game, that would be a victory of considerable symbolic value. McKibben, once again, is quite candid on this point: "[The protesters] have all shown that there is one way to demonstrate to the environmental base that the rhetoric of Obama's 2008 campaign is still meaningful – and that's to veto this pipeline. Since he can do it without even consulting Congress, this is one case where we'll be able to see exactly how willing he is to match the rhetoric of his 2008 campaign" (Henn & Kessler, 2011, August 24). To see the true value of this, we can fast forward to Donald Trump's presidency. Would the same strategy of encouraging protests in front of the White House be as effective today?

Indeed, the protesters at the White House provide another important clue to the political dynamic at work – the *activation* of local interests. Due to its expansive nature, the proposition for the pipeline activated local interests in various parts of the United States (and Canada), who proceeded to make their way to Washington, DC, to protest the issue on a national stage. The Cowboys and Indians Alliance is more than just a catchphrase, as it aptly describes the hybrid nature of the coalition that formed as a result of Keystone XL. In many ways, the political mobilization process was organic, as grassroots movements often are. This is not to suggest that Keystone XL, based on the nature of the issue alone, is sufficient to explain the degree of success enjoyed by the campaign. While Keystone XL is the most prominently debated, it is hardly the only major pipeline in North America. In fact, one of the ancillary consequences of the politicization of Keystone XL has been to raise the profile of some of the less known pipelines currently being pursued by companies, such as TransCanada and Enbridge.

That the Keystone XL became one of the most potent symbols of the fossil fuel industry's latest transgressions was by no means inevitable. The effort benefited from a deliberate, national effort by Bill McKibben and his organization, 350.org, specialists in grassroots mobilization. As evident in their call to civil disobedience in June prior to the Washington protests, widely disseminated through social media, McKibben and his allies consciously engineered the rhetorical move from arguments against a pipeline (one among many) to arguments against climate change:

A wonderful coalition of environmental groups and concerned citizens has built a strong campaign across the continent to fight the pipeline – from Nebraska farmers to Cree and Dene indigenous leaders, they've spoken out strongly against the destruction of their land. We need to join them, and say that even if our own homes won't be crossed by this pipeline, our joint home – the Earth – will be wrecked by the carbon that pours down it. . . . And we need to say something else, too: It's time to stop letting corporate power make the most important decisions affecting our planet. We don't have the money to compete with those corporations, but we do have our bodies, and beginning on Aug. 15, many of us will use them.

(McKibben, 2011, June 23)

The movement is not just about the pipeline and those who are immediately affected by it. The pipeline represents a threat not only to the communities through which it traverses, but all citizens of the world, current and future generations, who are affected by climate change. The fossil fuel industry is to blame for this latest effrontery. The rhetorical move is subtle but highly potent. The movement begins at the local level, but it quickly becomes a part of a larger narrative, namely the good fight against catastrophic climate change brought about by the fossil fuel industry.

The symbiotic relationship between the protesters and the environmental organizations that later threw their weight behind 350.org and the Washington protesters can be captured by two mechanisms, *bandwagon* and *prestige* strategy. It is hard to dispense with the notion that there may be an element of opportunism at work, even in the decision of environmental organizations to lend their support to the burgeoning protest movement in Washington, DC. This charge is particularly tempting to make against environmental organizations that, unlike 350.org, have no prior record of participation in civil disobedience. At the same time, jumping on the bandwagon is not necessarily the same thing as free-riding, and these organizations, if they are prominent enough, bring additional prestige to the movement. The exchange of prestige can be politically relevant when facts are up for contestation.

Nobel prizes are all about prestige. It is no small matter that not one, but nine Nobel Peace Prize laureates, the Dalai Lama and Desmond Tutu among them, penned an open letter on September 7, 2011, endorsing the protesters in Washington and calling on President Obama to reject the Keystone XL pipeline (Sheppard, 2011, September 7). Echoing many of the themes already mentioned, the laureates write: "In asking you to make this decision, we recognize the more than 1200 Americans who risked arrest to protest in front of the White House between August 20th and September 3rd. . . . They represent millions of people whose lives and livelihoods will be affected by construction and operation of the pipeline in Alberta, Montana, South Dakota, Nebraska, Kansas, Oklahoma and Texas." If this debate had been merely about the pipeline, this paragraph would have been sufficient. However, we also find in the letter a curious paragraph seemingly replete with rhetorical strategies worth analyzing:

> All along its prospective route, the pipeline endangers farms, wildlife and precious water aquifers – including the Ogallala Aquifer, the US' main source of freshwater for America's heartland. We are aware that Nebraska's Governor Dave Heineman – as well as two Nebraska Senators – has urged you to reconsider the pathway of the pipeline. In his letter to you he clearly stated his concern about the threat to this crucial water source for Nebraska's farmers and ranchers. The aquifer supplies drinking water to two million people in Nebraska and seven other states. We know that another pipeline that covers some of the same route as the proposed pipeline, and built by the same company proposing to build Keystone XL, already leaked 14 times over its first year of operation. Like you, we understand that strip-mining and drilling tar sands from under Alberta's Boreal forests and then transporting thousands of barrels of oil a day from Canada through to Texas will not only hurt people in the US – but will also endanger the entire planet. After the oil fields of Saudi Arabia, the full development of the Alberta tar sands will create the world's second largest potential source of global warming gases. As NASA climatologist James Hansen has said, this is "essentially game over for the climate.
>
> *(Sheppard, 20011, September 7)*

Why do the Nobel laureates indulge in such regurgitation of facts? Surely the president must be aware of the contents of a letter addressed to him by Nebraska's governor, Dave Heineman. As the phrase "Like you, we understand" conveys, the laureates themselves are aware that the talking points contained in this letter should not strike any informed president as novel. What do these cues, such as "we are aware," "we understand that" and "we know that" achieve rhetorically, especially when the intended reader is already well informed on the issue? As is often the case, the intended audience is much broader than the one to whom the letter is addressed.

This letter serves multiple political purposes, the most prominent among them lending legitimacy and prestige to a particular set of facts and interpretations of such facts that are currently being contested in the public sphere. It provides fresh ammunition to anti-fossil fuel activists, as they can now appeal to the authority of a group of highly recognized, accomplished individuals. The political strategy the nine Nobel laureates employ in this letter arguably mirrors the political role Nobel Peace prizes have served in the recent past, lending legitimacy to a nascent but desirable cause by bestowing prestige upon an individual or an organization that best represents it. The intent is not only to reward that individual or organization for the contribution, but also to help the cause flourish and find more political support.

To be sure, it also serves the more immediate political purpose of raising the stakes of the Keystone XL decision for the president, a fellow Nobel Peace Prize laureate, by sending a signal to the public that Obama is (or should be) aware of the concerns they have raised. "Like you, we understand" is a phrase that conveys this very well. These words immediately draw President Obama into the sacred trust of Nobel laureates, who define the terms of the climate debate from the ecological perspective. While the letter does precisely what it claims to do, which is to keep President Obama accountable to his environmental supporters, it also defines the terms of and shapes the larger climate debate.

As hinted above, there is also a local element to the national campaign. Local resistance to Keystone XL has played a pivotal role in stalling and delaying pipeline construction. Nowhere can the importance of local resistance be seen as clearly as in the state of Nebraska, where a coalition called Bold Nebraska has led the charge against the pipeline throughout the campaign's existence. Bold Nebraska is an organization that wants to transform Nebraskan politics by presenting a viable alternative to the dominant conservative ideology that, according to Bold Nebraska, places the interests of big business above of those of ordinary Nebraskans. How does the Keystone XL pipeline fit this mission? According to the coalition's website, Keystone XL is a critical threat to the economic and environmental sustainability of the state:

> The TransCanada export pipeline, called Keystone XL, is a risky and bad idea for our state, our land, our water and our economic activity. We do not want to see it built. We want to see investments in American-made energy, including domestic oil and sustainable biofuels, wind, solar and efficiency programs, which bring long-term jobs to rural and urban Nebraska (Bold Nebraska, 2012, February 6).[7]

The Bold Nebraska objection to Keystone XL revolves around concerns about oil spills, damage to the Ogallala freshwater aquifer and the Sandhills ecosystems, and American energy independence.

A notable feature of Bold Nebraska is a strong commitment to activism. Here are some organizations that have collaborated with Bold Nebraska on activism against Keystone XL (Bold Nebraska, 2011, May 27):[8]

- Audubon Nebraska
- Nebraska Farmers Union
- Nebraskans for Peace
- Sandhills Beef

As this short list shows, the opposition against Keystone XL in Nebraska is not limited to environmental activists. Indeed, the local agricultural groups have expressed concerns about the pipeline and, in an unusual move, joined forces with anti-fossil fuel campaigners.

What makes such hybrid activism possible? Avery (2013: 117–118) sheds light on this question by interviewing Nebraskan farmers who have joined this coalition. Consider, for example, Joe Moller, a farmer whose land was on TransCanada's planned route for Keystone XL. Previously employed at a natural gas company,

Moller says he has many reservations about the pipeline because of oil leaks: "Tar sands oil is corrosive. It's not like natural gas. They get a lot of the sand out before it goes in the line, but they don't get it all. That silicate will scrape the inside of the pipeline; it's abrasive and corrosive, too." Although he does not have a background as an environmental activist, he is aware of the risks that the pipeline presents to the land and water on his property, and he is ready to act to protect these resources on behalf of his family.

If anything, Bold Nebraska's activities preceded the August 2011 action of the national campaign by over a year. Bold Nebraska was founded in March 2010 by Jane Kleeb, a "Southern Florida transplant" who at the time was not aware of the Keystone XL plans and has herself admitted that, at the time, "energy and the environment were not on our radar" (Bergin, 2014, September 15). A few months later, however, she attended a meeting about the Keystone XL and learned about the risks that possible oil spills would pose to the land and water in the Sandhills area. By July 2010, Bold Nebraska's website was issuing calls for members to participate in official pipeline hearings and to voice their concerns (Bold Nebraska, 2010, July 27).[9]

The Keystone XL soon became Bold Nebraska's main action item, while Bold Nebraska appeared in the national spotlight as perhaps the most active local group opposing the pipeline. In a remarkable turn of events, Bold Nebraska's hybrid activism went so far that the entire organization's nascent *identity* changed toward environmental issues. While Kleeb and other Bold Nebraska activists were initially skeptical about environmental issues as a platform in their locale, the grievances and concerns of the local farmers showed that, in this particular instance, environmentalism would resonate with rural communities. Environmentalists were there to protect land and water, and landowners had identical interests. In such a setting, it was not difficult to generate support for a campaign to oppose Keystone XL and, as an alternative, promote the local generation of renewable energy.

For the Nebraska campaign, January 2011 was a milestone for political impact, both at national and local levels. When the Nebraska legislative session was opened, "125 anti-pipeline activists representing about 10 different groups, including Bold Nebraska, greeted them" (Bergin, 2014, September 15). The campaign succeeded in drawing the political establishment's attention to the pipeline, and in August 2011 – at the time of the first major protest against Keystone XL at the national level – Governor Dave Heineman sent a request to President Obama to reject Keystone XL. In November 2011, under constant political pressure to act, the legislature passed new laws to ensure that Keystone XL could not be built without an explicit approval by the state.

In an interesting account of the Nebraska fight against the pipeline, the famous writer and a local pipeline activist, Mary Pipher, notes that large groups of people in Nebraska began to see TransCanada as an arrogant and greedy company. In the first University of Nebraska college football game of the 2011–2012 season,

> eighty-five thousand fans booed when a TransCanada ad flashed on the jumbo screen in the stadium. The next day the University of Nebraska's

chancellor announced that TransCanada would no longer be allowed to advertise at university events.

(Pipher, 2013: 194)

This incident shows how successful the local activists were in turning the local population against the corporation and the pipeline despite operating in a deeply conservative state that has mostly had little patience for environmentalists and their views of natural resource exploitation and economic development. Given this success, it is no wonder that even a conservative Republican governor saw the urgent political need to do something.

To be sure, the local activists never thought Heineman was genuinely in favor of rejecting the pipeline. According to Pipher, Heineman expected President Obama to approve the pipeline and hoped to avoid blame for the approval:

> Bowing to popular pressure and looking toward his next election, Governor Heineman wrote a letter asking President Obama to reroute the pipeline so that it wouldn't go through the Sandhills and over the aquifer. Members of our coalition knew Heineman was playing a political game. He wrote his letter to pass the buck to President Obama. Then, when the White House supported TransCanada's decisions about the route, which he fully expected the president would do, Governor Heineman could blame Obama for not protecting us. But much to the governor's surprise, Obama responded to his letter by delaying the pipeline process and calling for more environmental reviews. In fact, the president often cited our Republican governor as his reason for denying the pipeline permit.

(Pipher, 2013: 195)

This instance shows that even a hostile political elite, in this case the governor's office, cannot necessarily stop local activists from achieving success. Governor Heineman's political blunder and President Obama's willingness to support the environmentalists resulted in a major victory for the activists.

Ever since these two years of campaigning, Bold Nebraska has remained vigilant. In September 2012, the first hearings of a lawsuit, Thompson v. Heineman, were heard. Led by farmer Randy Thompson, activists sued Governor Heineman, along with the director of the Nebraska Department of Environmental Quality and the State Treasurer, for unconstitutional legislative measures to avoid review of the Keystone XL by the Nebraska Public Service Commission (Kleeb, 2014, December 11).[10] Though a district court had initially ruled in favor of the plaintiff, meaning that any pipeline construction would be delayed or prevented by the review of the commission, the Nebraska Supreme Court could not reach a super majority to uphold the decision (four of seven judges voted in favor, but needed five) (Valentine, 2015, January 9).

TransCanada filed nearly 90 eminent domain cases against landowners in January of 2015. Landowners sued to stop the land acquisition. Holt County District

Court Judge Mark Kozisek issued a temporary injunction on February 12, halting TransCanada's eminent domain cases (Duara, 2015, February 12). TransCanada would eventually be forced to reconsider its strategy, suspending its efforts on securing easements and redoubling its efforts for getting its route approved by the state's Public Service Commission (Bergin, 2015, September 29). The momentum turned decisively against TransCanada near the end of year. On November 2, TransCanada asked the Obama administration to pause its review of the project (Davis, 2015, November 2). The Administration said no (Davis, 2015, November 3). President Obama sealed its fate, publicly announcing the rejection of the Keystone XL pipeline on November 6th on the basis of the national interest.[11]

The leader of the lawsuit, Randy Thompson, is the public image of the Bold Nebraska campaign against Keystone XL (Avery, 2013: 115–118). A Republican with no background in environmentalism, Thompson says his views have changed significantly since he became a key player in the Bold Nebraska campaign against the pipeline. Although his own interest lies primarily with the defense of his property, he says that there is a natural connection between the goals of environmentalists and local farmers. Indeed, a particularly important contribution of local opposition in Nebraska is that it has allowed the broader campaign to grow by disposing of the image of environmentalists as an isolated interest group. The hybrid coalition of climate activists, cowboys, and farmers in Nebraska has allowed the Keystone XL movement to significantly expand its support base and draw supporters from large segments of the American population.

Returning to the national level, the movement against Keystone XL built impressive momentum in fewer than two years of campaigning. Tens of thousands gathered at the National Mall, Washington, DC, on February 17, 2013, for what was hailed at the time as "the largest climate rally in history" (Alter, 2014, September 22). The location of the rally within walking distance from the White House aimed not only to ensure Obama's audience, but also to generate as much noise as possible in the eyes of the fossil fuel industry and the nation, as well as potential recruits. Some 35,000 people marching on a storied political space such as Washington, DC, would send a resounding statement to the world. Some of the activists' strategies and rhetoric on display at the event aptly illustrate how activists seized upon the politically vulnerable position of the Keystone XL pipeline to hold the fossil fuel industry responsible for climate change (Broder et al., 2013, February 17).

Consistent with the hybrid nature of the coalition, activists from diverse backgrounds marched on Washington, embedding multiple and rather familiar narratives into the larger narrative that is the ecological paradigm. To sustain such a motley coalition, the leaders focused on a concrete objective, namely to convince President Obama to oppose the Keystone XL pipeline (or at least make it politically costly for him to support it). Titled "Forward on Climate," the rally drew from the experiences and tactical arsenals of multiple organizations, such as the Tar Sands Blockade, Sierra Club, 350.org, and the Hip Hop Caucus. These activists were united in their determination to effect a major swing in momentum in an otherwise uphill battle against the fossil fuel industry. For the activists, this represented a win–win proposition.

If President Obama were privately against the pipeline, the rally would provide additional assurance that his political base was behind him, and that together they could deal a major blow to the big polluters. If President Obama were privately in favor of the pipeline, the rally would not only be a demonstration of power to a president who may have lost touch with his political base, but it would also be an opportunity to mobilize and recruit additional activists for future attempts to keep President Obama accountable to his campaign promises. It is no accident that the official emblem of the Forward on Climate campaign appropriates that of Obama for America, with the important addition of a hurricane to emphasize the urgency of climate change. "Forward," of course, was Obama's re-election campaign slogan in 2012. Most important for the activists, keeping Obama accountable to his campaign promises represents a feasible and legitimate objective (Zornick, 2013, February).

In some ways, this rally represented the convergence of multiple familiar historical narratives, such as those of civil rights activists and first nations, but with a focused objective of convincing President Obama. First, the Tar Sands Blockade provides the overall blueprint for the day of action. The word blueprint is quite appropriate, as the rally represents a carefully crafted political act. On its website, the organization offers its rationale in no uncertain terms: "nonviolent direct action . . . is a way of seeking justice that is strategically successful and celebrates the values that move us to action. The bottom line is that nonviolent direct action works. History shows this to be true and so does our collective personal experience inside of various movements for justice across the globe" (TarSands Blockade, n.d., Nonviolent direct action).[12]

Moreover, Tar Sands Blockade emphasizes how the nonviolent direct action is almost a scripted ritual, weaving together the present and a storied past in a tapestry of activism: "Gandhi called it *satyagraha*, 'truth or soul force.' Judaism calls it *Tikkun Olam*, 'to heal the world.' Henry Thoreau called it civil disobedience. Others just call it people power. Underneath all of these definitions there is a history of tactics that lie[s] outside of our orthodox political institutions and shares a commitment to refraining from violence in order to resist violence" (TarSands Blockade, n.d., Nonviolent direct action). As will be seen below, other organizations participating in the rally were quickly encouraged to adopt this tactic. 350.org, of course, was well familiar with this tactic and thrived. As per usual, McKibben lent his star power and eloquent rhetoric to rouse the participants of the rally: "All I ever wanted to see was a movement of people to stop climate change, and now I've seen it! You are the antibodies kicking in as the planet tries to fight its fever" (McKibben, 2013).

The Sierra Club, on the other hand, was in unfamiliar territory. "Twenty years from now on President's Day, people will want to know what the president did in the face of rising sea levels, record droughts and furious storms brought on by climate disruption," said Michael Brune, executive director of the Sierra Club. "President Obama holds in his hand a pen and the power to deliver on his promise of hope for our children" (350.org, 2013, February 17).[13] Brune also made history himself, as he was one of about four dozen pipeline protesters arrested at the White House in an act of civil disobedience that was a first for the 120-year-old Sierra Club.

However, Sierra Club's efforts seem to have been insufficient to convince the skeptics. When asked to address concerns that 350.org and Sierra Club are "opportunists," Tar Sands Blockade's response was telling: "350 has backed us up a lot," @KXLBlockade tweeted after the march. "Sierra club is who you should be tweeting at" (Kilkenny, 2013, February 18). While 350.org, a younger organization with a platform built on grassroots mobilization, could demonstrate its solidarity with concrete action, it seems much harder for Sierra Club, an established environmental organization in the traditional mold, to shed its old image.

An indispensable place in the hybrid narrative belongs to the Aboriginals who came all the way from Canada: "The Yinka Dene Alliance of British Columbia is seeing the harm from climate change to our peoples and our waters. . . . We see the threat of taking tar sands out of the Earth and bringing it through our territories and over our rivers," said Chief Jacqueline Thomas, immediate past Chief of the Saik'uz First Nation in British Columbia (350.org, 2013, February 17).[14] The rhyme of history would not be missed on the audience: The imagery of "watching their homelands being destroyed" sets up a powerful analogy between the destruction of the Native American homeland at the hands of the settlers and the destruction of the climate at the hands of fossil fuel companies and their lobbyists.

The Hip Hop Caucus similarly used an analogy to forge historical linkages. Referencing the March on Washington for Jobs and Freedom, in which Martin Luther King Jr. famously delivered the "I have a dream" speech, Rev. Lennox Yearwood, president of the Hip Hop Caucus, exclaimed: "This rally 50 years later is as important or more important as the rally then. Because while they were fighting for equality, we are fighting for existence, so that in 2063, 50 years from now, they will look back at this rally . . . they will look back then, and say 'Thank you.' So we've come too far to turn around now. As we say in hip hop, 'can't stop, won't stop!'" (Yearwood, 2013, February 17).[15] In a sense, by reenacting the civil rights movement, same place, different time, the activists associate the ecological paradigm with one of the most important and celebrated examples of social activism of our time.

In this way, multiple narratives across time and space would converge on Washington, adding momentum to a movement united against climate change. The movement, however, would not be contained. On that same day, there were companion rallies erupting across the country, including California, Colorado, Illinois, Iowa, Michigan, Montana, Oregon, Texas, Washington, and Seattle, organized by chapters of the Sierra Club, 350.org, and numerous other organizations, often featuring prominent keynote speakers (Spear, 2013, February 12).[16] The historical record set by the "biggest climate rally" would remain until September 21, 2014, when 400,000-strong converged on New York City for the People's Climate March to demand climate action from the U.N.

4.4 Motives

Having described the campaign against Keystone XL, we now turn to the questions of why and to what effect. To begin with, what motivates so many activists to join the campaign against Keystone XL? To gain a deeper understanding of the motivations behind activism against Keystone XL, we collected data from various sources. We reviewed the public statements of 350.org and other organizations, participated in local meetings and events in the New York City metropolitan area, and conducted a series of anonymous interviews with activists. Combined, these data sources allow us to paint a vivid image of what makes activists tick.

Simply put, Keystone XL has many attractive features for activists who subscribe to the ecological paradigm. A pipeline to transport oil extracted from the Canadian tar sands to the United States, Keystone XL symbolizes the environmental destruction associated with what activists call "extreme energy." It paints vivid images of destroyed landscapes, massive amounts of greenhouse gases, excessive water use, and risks of oil leakages across North America. For people who were arrested in August 2011, Keystone XL is not an individual pipeline, rather it is the cornerstone of a destructive drive to exploit dirtier sources of energy at a great environmental cost. This logic is best seen in Hansen's claim that Keystone XL would be "game over" for the climate – a call to arms for anti-fossil fuel activists.

The idea of fossil fuels as the root cause of climate change and other environmental problems has also been a powerful impetus to act. As we have shown above, there is a lot of skepticism among experts about the claim that Keystone XL is somehow decisive for the global climate. How can activists see Keystone XL as a powerful impetus to act, while many energy analysts consider the implications of the pipeline for the global climate trivial? This is where the role of the ecological paradigm is critical. The more general idea of extracting nonconventional fossil fuels for the global growth engine is clearly a major threat to climate stability, and that is what counts for the legions of people who have become climate activists because of Keystone XL. The pipeline is a concrete target that motivates climate activism in a way that other targets in America have failed to do.

Contrast this powerful idea with a legislative focus, such as a carbon tax. Clearly, the climate mitigation afforded by a carbon tax could also be achieved through many other policy instruments, ranging from cap-and-trade to direct regulation and massive public works for clean energy. Moreover, if political obstacles were somehow overcome and a carbon tax were implemented in a meaningful way, its impact on climate mitigation would be quite substantial. While the Keystone XL certainly does not hold similar promise, it carries a lot of symbolic power and motivates activists in a way that a campaign for cost-effective carbon pricing could never do.

As we have seen above, a firestorm of controversy surrounds the climate impact of Keystone XL. For adherents of the ecological paradigm, stopping Keystone XL amounts to stopping an avalanche of dirty energy development in North America; for energy experts relying on cost-benefit analysis, stopping Keystone XL is tinkering at the margins. Both sides make valid arguments, but we think this is ultimately a controversy that cannot be resolved empirically. It is simply not possible to test the validity of the fundamental premises of the ecological paradigm in the long run. Therefore, we are going to have to leave this question open.

And yet, there is a different way of looking at the whole issue. As an interim goal and a piece of the broader puzzle of climate mitigation, Keystone XL appears attractive. Stopping a major pipeline shows that the fossil fuel industry cannot count on being able to build the infrastructure for new fossil fuel exploration and extraction in the future. This anticipation of future opposition and resistance is itself significant, as it reduces the profitability of fossil fuel extraction and raises barriers to investment in this sector.

The detractors of the Keystone XL campaign respond to this by emphasizing the opportunity cost of focusing on an individual pipeline. What if activists would have instead pushed for climate policies at the national or state level, a choir of critics says. As Harvard environmental economist Robert N. Stavins put it, "The political fight about Keystone is vastly greater than the economic, environmental or energy impact of the pipeline itself. . . . It doesn't make a big difference in energy prices, employment, or climate change either way" (Davenport, 2015, January 8). According to this logic, even if the campaign on Keystone XL is not directly harmful, it means that the environmental groups are wasting their time. We disagree. Environmental organizations in America have tried countless other approaches, but none of these has inspired so many to mobilize as Keystone XL. Without Keystone XL, there might be no movement against fossil fuels, and so the question of opportunity cost would never arise. Without Keystone XL, we might have nothing but deafening silence.

Michael Brune, the executive director of the Sierra Club, probably says it best in an interview on the significance of President Obama's February 2015 decision to veto an effort by the Congress to remove executive authority:

> Most actions that have been taken on climate change have been about smokestacks and tail pipes. . . . [Keystone XL] has been the first major public fight to argue that we have to begin to curtail production. . . . Over the course of the last six years, concerns about climate change have grown to the extent that we now have pressure campaigns against every form of extraction, every operation on the supply side – from drilling and mining, to pipeline fights, to refineries, all the way to the tailpipe.
>
> *(Mooney, 2015, February 25)*

This simple observation captures the idea that Keystone XL is the first campaign to shift the focus from fossil fuel consumption to production, in effect turning the logic of climate change campaigning on its head.

4.5 Mobilization potential

No wonder, then, that McKibben had already achieved his first major goal of building a national climate movement in the United States by November 2011.

Notwithstanding the question of substantive relevance, Keystone XL is undoubtedly a masterstroke in political mobilization and environmental activism. McKibben and his associates have managed to bring to light the problems associated with tar sands, and fossil fuels more generally, in a way that had previously eluded environmental organizations. Indeed, one of the frequent criticisms of McKibben is that he has been *too* successful in creating hype around Keystone XL. Such criticisms, we contend, miss the point. Keystone XL has always been about building a movement against fossil fuels, and in the chapters to follow we shall show that the movement has done much more than fight this individual pipeline.

For activists, the symbolism of "us versus them" further strengthens the case for action. As we have argued, it is easier to rally the troops when there is a concrete target. In the past, that target may have been a hostile tribe or a hostile nation; today, the target is a pipeline being built by a faceless and powerful company for the simple purpose of profit. In the Nebraska case, we saw that one of the key reasons behind widespread local activism was the way TransCanada ignored local concerns and tried to force the pipeline on the rural communities along the route (Schulte, 2015, January 20). This strategy created a strongly antagonistic situation, allowing progressive environmentalists and conservative farmers to form a powerful coalition.

In spite of facing a Goliath, taking on Keystone XL as a target actually allows activists to retain their optimism. Throughout the campaign, activists have scored notable victories by forcing TransCanada to change the route of the pipeline and by causing years of delay in the environmental review and approval process on Capitol Hill. Here the principle of "small wins" (Weick, 1984) is particularly potent, though obviously more salient for mobilization than policy impact. Once activists internalize the notion that Keystone XL is a critically important target in the broader campaign against fossil fuels, any delay in environmental review at the national level or legal victory at the local level is a reason to celebrate. Because such victories have been frequent, the campaign against Keystone XL has been a positive, and often transformative, experience for the participants. Some of the student activists who had participated in Keystone XL activities said that the protests and the arrests were among the defining moments of their lives and changed their perspective and identity entirely.

The importance of local–global connections has also become abundantly clear in the case of Keystone XL. While the most salient events were organized at the national level, robust and vigorous activism in Nebraska and other local sites gave the campaign a boost of relevance and legitimacy. In Nebraska, for example, the local activists had a genuine opportunity to thwart TransCanada's plans and cast a dark shadow of doubt on the entire project. What is more, the local grievances against TransCanada were the key reason why conservative farmers and ranchers joined the coalition (Lukacs, 2014, November 18). A campaign run by progressive, vegetarian environmentalists with college degrees would never have been received as positively as a campaign that brings together Americans of all stripes. The combination of global and local motivations has allowed the campaign to grow and retain its dynamism over the years. In addition to mobilizing traditional environmental activists, Keystone XL has drawn opposition from many other interests, further expanding the coalition against fossil fuels. Without a sharp focus on the pipeline, such an expansion of the coalition would probably not have been possible.

Together, these advantages make Keystone XL a powerful instrument for movement building, but is expansion for the sake of expansion all there is to the campaign? Is the campaign little more than an organism that tries to grow itself as fast as possible? Not really. Activists see Keystone XL as an important precedent. Any consideration of policy impact begins with winning the hearts and minds of those in power. While the rejection of the Keystone XL pipeline per se is no silver bullet, it can turn the tide politically. If the campaign succeeds and Keystone XL is not built, it reduces the likelihood that similar pipelines – or tar sands projects, more generally – will be planned in the future. Success in stopping Keystone XL sends a clear message to the fossil fuel industry that their activities are constantly under the threat of falling to Blockadia.

What is more, the pipeline campaign has put dirty energy and climate change on the political map. Anti-fossil fuel activists believe that, on balance, public attention to Keystone XL has already had a positive effect on the public discourse on fossil fuels and climate change. People are more aware of the environmental consequences of continued fossil fuel extraction, both locally and globally, and public perceptions of the fossil fuel industry are growing more negative because of Trans-Canada's activities.

Finally, the Keystone XL campaign clearly shows that the activists are already setting their sights on state and federal legislation. The efforts of Nebraska campaigners to bring President Obama's support into their fold, for instance, illustrates how the grassroots campaigns often commence with the national stage in mind. We have also seen that, while the campaign itself focuses on the pipeline, activists are continuously highlighting the significance of the pipeline in the broader context of measures to reduce fossil fuel extraction and use. For the activists, the significance of the campaign is not so much in stopping an individual pipeline, but in creating a movement to stop many more pipelines, mines, and power plants in the future, initially through mobilization and later through state and federal policy.

Indeed, there is no question about Keystone XL's contribution to the growing climate movement. Virtually all Keystone XL events both in the national and local contexts have been smash hits in terms of participation and mobilization. Both typical environmental activists and their unusual allies, such as farmers worried about property rights, have joined the campaign in hordes – a stark contrast to the anemic performance of major green environmental organizations in America at the turn of the millennium.

And as we shall see below, many of these activists have since made pivotal contributions to the campaigns on divestment from fossil fuels and against fracking. Our assessment here must be overwhelmingly positive, confirming and validating the perception of McKibben about the importance of Keystone XL for the growth of the American movement against fossil fuels in his autobiographical *Oil and Honey*

(McKibben, 2013: 139): "The Keystone fight had demonstrated that we could rally people to go to jail. And at least for a little while we'd actually won something." Obama's rejection of the pipeline seemed to provide somewhat of a storybook ending to reward their efforts.

After all, the activists had framed the issue from the beginning in progressive-populist terms. Courageous, ordinary Americans were opposing the greedy machinations of faceless transnational corporations with unlimited resources and no conscience. And yet, it was clear that the Keystone XL campaign was aimed at two primary constituencies. First, any campaign against fossil fuels must win the hearts and minds of potential ecological warriors. Second, the Keystone XL campaign skillfully targeted unusual allies who had a direct local stake at rejecting Keystone XL, with great success in the hybrid coalition that Nebraskans formed.

4.6 Impact

Having started our evaluation with one of the harder questions, we can now answer an easier question: has the campaign achieved its own immediate goals? Here, the answer must be positive, as the Keystone XL campaign has clearly raised high barriers to the construction of the pipeline. Without the campaign, there is no reason to believe the Obama administration would not have simply approved the pipeline, as no administration has ever rejected a pipeline construction application. Without the activists in Nebraska, it is hard to imagine that state politicians would have gone out of their way to challenge a powerful energy corporation on an issue that is not even traditionally under state jurisdiction.

We believe a positive evaluation is justified, but there is an important caveat that we still have to consider. For one, if Keystone XL is delayed indefinitely or simply cancelled, how will the fossil fuel industry react? TransCanada, for instance, is redoubling its efforts to build a domestic oil sands pipeline that would increase western Canadian oil producers' access to East Coast and offshore refineries (King, 2015, December 17).

If another pipeline is built or tar sands oil shipped to China through export terminals on Canada's Pacific Coast, can we still say the activists achieved their immediate goals? That depends on the definition of the word *immediate*. If we narrowly focus on what the Keystone XL activists say about the pipeline itself, then the answer continues to be "yes." But if we consider the broader mosaic of pipeline construction and fossil fuel extraction in North America, then our evaluation must be less positive.

At the same time, we also cannot discount the fact that any social movement must continue to secure small wins to maintain dynamism and momentum. Sometimes an appropriately timed loss can also be valuable. As we have seen in the Nebraska case, for example, some of the most spectacular challenges that Bold Nebraska faced stemmed from ethically questionable moves by the state administration to circumvent proper legal safeguards on the pipeline approval process. Such losses contribute to the growth of moral outrage and the strengthening of the "us versus them" mentality. When activists lose because of what they consider dirty tricks by the fossil fuel industry, their moral apprehension fuels increased mobilization against what is considered an unfair and unsustainable status quo.

Even more important is the relationship between the immediate goals and the ultimate goal of climate stability. To what extent can the movement's success in delaying Keystone XL contribute to climate change mitigation? Setting aside James Hansen's claim that Keystone XL itself is "game over" for the planet, answering this question requires considering two aspects of securing climate stability: the enactment of new policies and the growth of a mass movement to support new policies in the future through political activism.

As to new policies, it would be difficult to claim that the Keystone XL campaign itself has, through channels other than the building of a climate movement, influenced federal policy. President Obama's new regulations, such as constraints on air pollution and carbon dioxide emissions from the power sector, are not directly related to Keystone XL. In the debate on Keystone XL, serious legislative bargains for a package – pipeline in exchange for renewable energy, for example – have yet to emerge. If anything, Keystone XL may have contributed to the polarization of the House and Senate along party lines. According to Abby Johnston, who was writing in *The Independent Mail*:

> Somehow the bill became a symbol for both sides – one claiming the pipeline would surely destroy the earth as we know it, and the other talking about it as if it delivers America's economic rebirth. But here's the thing – it didn't have to be that way.
>
> *(Johnston, 2015, February 26)*

If this view is correct, then Keystone XL activists may have, whether deliberately or by accident, contributed to one of the major obstacles behind federal environmental legislation in the United States. This outcome would be even worse than the concern that the Keystone XL is diverting attention from more worthy causes.

No sophisticated data analysis is necessary to show that the Keystone XL activists achieved great heights of success in their efforts to reach the target audience. Anyone even remotely aware of climate and energy issues in America has heard of Keystone XL, and no other campaign has drawn so many new people into environmental activism. In the Nebraskan case, we showed that TransCanada received an icy reception even in events such as football games, where one would not expect traditional environmental activists to be in the majority, or even in a significant minority. The Nebraskan activists were not afraid to take their cause to the national level, and the movement was eventually rewarded with the incumbent president's rejection of the pipeline.

The success of Keystone XL campaigners in reaching their target audience largely reflects the auspicious characteristics of the issue itself. A concrete pipeline project, the destructive nature of oil extraction from tar sands, a scary and powerful opponent, and the wonderful ease of forging local-global connections across

America have all conspired to make the work of Keystone XL campaigners easier than is often the case. At the same time, the decision to focus on Keystone XL despite the naysayers was a strategically smart move, showing that the movement leadership has understood the potential of the issue for environmental mobilization for climate change mitigation and against fossil fuels.

The limitation of the Keystone XL campaign's communication strategy, of course, is the relatively narrow choice of the target audience. Although the campaigners deserve kudos for going beyond the standard strategy of reaching out to the niche constituency of committed environmental activists, the fact remains that those conservative farmers in Nebraska are opposed to the pipeline only because of local land and water issues. Elsewhere in the country, the conservative public and the conservative political establishment are strongly in favor of Keystone XL, and the campaign has done nothing to weaken this sentiment.

Indeed, the strength of a campaign forged under a favorable president will now be put to a test. On March 24, 2017, President Trump directly contradicted his predecessor by issuing a Presidential Permit to TransCanada for the construction of Keystone XL. The US State Department announcement cited the national interest, including but not limited to foreign policy, energy security, environmental, cultural, and economic impacts, and compliance with applicable law and policy (U.S. Department of State, 2017, March 24).[17] Appropriately, the fight has now returned to the grassroots heartland of Nebraska, where the construction of the pipeline needs the approval of the Nebraska Public Service Commission and local landowners (Krauss, 2017, March 24).

To summarize, Keystone XL has been a highly successful campaign in many different ways. Energy analysts who obsess over the pipeline's limited direct effect on greenhouse gas emissions miss the larger point of encouraging climate activism and creating an effective climate movement in North America, where traditional environmental organizations have not had much success in grassroots mobilization. These achievements may not have immediate policy impact comparable to a carbon tax, but they represent the opening salvo of a larger national standoff against the fossil fuel industry.

Notes

1 See www.keystone-xl.com/wp-content/uploads/2013/09/Keystone-XL-Pipeline-Fact sheet.pdf (accessed May 28, 2017).
2 See www.tarsandsblockade.org/about-2/why-oppose-kxl/ (accessed January 2, 2015).
3 See http://350.org/top-climate-scientists-warn-congress-over-keystone-xl/ (accessed May 28, 2017).
4 See U.S. House of Representatives Office of the Clerk voting records available at http://clerk.house.gov/evs/2015/roll075.xml (accessed May 17, 2017).
5 See the official announcement available at www.whitehouse.gov/the-press-office/2015/11/06/statement-president-keystone-xl-pipeline (accessed January 1, 2016).
6 We thank Jennifer Hadden for initially providing us with the protests data based on *Democracy Now!*
7 See http://boldnebraska.org/transcanada-pipeline/ (accessed January 21, 2015).

8 See http://boldnebraska.org/transcanada-pipeline-background-and-resources/ (accessed January 21, 2015).

9 See http://boldnebraska.org/attend-pipeline-hearings/ (accessed January 22, 2015).

10 See http://boldnebraska.org/lawsuit/ (accessed January 22, 2015).

11 See the official announcement available at www.whitehouse.gov/the-press-office/2015/11/06/statement-president-keystone-xl-pipeline (accessed January 1, 2016).

12 See www.tarsandsblockade.org/about-2/non-violent-direct-action/ (accessed January 17, 2014).

13 See http://350.org/amazing-35000-march-forward-climate-rally-dc/ (accessed January 17, 2014).

14 See http://350.org/amazing-35000-march-forward-climate-rally-dc/ (accessed January 17, 2014).

15 See full remarks at www.c-span.org/video/?c4363223/forward-climate-rally-21713 (accessed January 17, 2015).

16 See http://ecowatch.com/2013/02/12/forward-on-climate-solidarity-rallies/ (accessed January 17, 2015).

17 See www.state.gov/r/pa/prs/ps/2017/03/269074.htm (accessed April 22, 2017).

5

DIVESTMENT

To many, Harvard University is not the kind of institution where one would expect to see students arrested for blocking the entrance to the president's office. Nor is a college president's office the first thing that comes to mind when thinking about environmental activism. These are strange times, but this chapter will show that there is a method to the madness. On May 1, 2014, Brett A. Roche, a member of the environmental activist group Divest Harvard, was arrested by Harvard University Police around 7:15 a.m. for blocking the entrance to Massachusetts Hall, home to the offices of university president Drew Gilpin Faust and members of the administration. Before 6 a.m., eight students rotated shifts so that at least two were present at all hours. At 6 a.m., more supporters arrived, including environmental activist Bob Massie and Harvard's Quaker Chaplain John Bach (Hashimi, 2014, May 1st).

So, what did the protesters want? Their stated demand was for an open and transparent dialogue with the Harvard Corporation – Harvard's main governing body – on fossil fuel divestment, as President Faust and Harvard University had previously rejected the case for divestment and refused to hold a public forum on divestment and climate change.[1] Citing robust support from the student body, the leaders of Divest Harvard made their case in the *Huffington Post*:

> Alongside the 72% of Harvard undergraduates and 67% of Harvard Law students, as well as the students, faculty, and alumni of Divest Harvard, we refuse to accept our university's unwillingness to hold a public meeting on this critical issue. We are here today because we believe in a better Harvard. We are here because it is our duty to act. We are here today because it is our moral responsibility as students to ensure that Harvard does not contribute to and profit from the problem but instead aligns its institutional actions and policies with the shared interests of society.
>
> (Clark, 2014, June 30)

Roche, the student who was arrested, later remarked in the student newspaper:

> The fact that I wasn't even spoken to at the door, that microscopic example of [the administration] avoiding interaction with the students, upset me a bit . . . What we're trying to do out there was show the administration that this is something that should be expected of them. They should be expected to listen to and engage with their students.
>
> *(Hashimi, 2014, May 1)*

The strong moral overtone among the participants of the campaign, as we will demonstrate, is the hallmark of a much bigger divestment campaign that is engulfing campuses across America.

The widely publicized campaign calling for Harvard to divest from fossil fuels is but one example among hundreds, maybe thousands, of similar local campaigns. McKibben and his grassroots organization, 350.org, from the previous chapter reprise their roles. McKibben's influential "Global Warming's Terrifying New Math" article in the *Rolling Stone* that went viral was the catalyst for this campaign, and his organization 350.org continues to play a vital role in continuing the momentum (McKibben, 2012, August 2).

5.1 Significance

There are a number of reasons for studying divestment. First, it is an ongoing campaign with its fair share of media coverage still searching for a long-term direction. While the campaign has not fully run its course, many observers see far-reaching ramifications that warrant a closer examination. Second, we will make the case that the divestment campaign places a stronger emphasis on stigmatization than others. According to the activists, every divestment decision challenges the very idea that the continued extraction of fossil fuels constitutes a legitimate business activity. Third, a striking feature among all divestment activists is a strong sense of historical continuity. Readers will understand why the historical precedent that divestment activists commonly invoke is the campaign against apartheid in South Africa. Fourth, a study of divestment will shed light on the concept of stranded assets.

Similar to the last chapter, we first provide an overview of the divestment campaign, delve into a select few cases to examine the tactics employed by activists, and evaluate the campaign in that light. To summarize, we find that while the divestment campaign also benefits from a clearly defined objective, it is based on a logic that is different from that of the Keystone XL campaign. The divestment activists and their target audience are much more concerned about moral and ethical arguments, their strategy builds on the availability of a large number of local small wins, and the connection between divestment and the fossil fuel industry as a whole is clearer than in the case of Keystone XL. At the same time, divestment cannot draw activists concerned about direct local impacts.

In practice, while a steady stream of institutions of higher learning and religious institutions have been lending their support to the movement, we have yet to see a cascade develop on the scale of the campaign against the apartheid regime of South Africa. Major institutions of higher learning that have history of participation in previous divestment movements, such as Harvard, have also been holding out. Even Stanford and Columbia Universities, both of which announced their decisions to divest from select coal companies to help combat climate change, have not shifted their investments away from oil or natural gas.

Neither have well-endowed pension funds in major states, which have been a target for divestment activists. In this sense, small wins notwithstanding, it is too early to conclude that the movement has had a significant impact on major investors, much less on policy. We think that the most promising avenue for the divestment movement is in the world of finance, where terms such as *stranded assets* used to describe fossil fuel investments have begun to make inroads. The remaining challenge is to devise alternative green energy investments that are both stable and attractive options for those looking to divest and reinvest their capital.

As a recent Oxford University study has defined it, *divestment* is a socially motivated activity of private wealth owners, either individuals or groups, such as university endowments, public pension funds, or their appointed asset managers. Owners can decide to withhold their capital – such as selling stock market-listed shares, private equities, or debt – from firms seen to be engaged in a socially reprehensible activity (Ansar et al., 2013). That divestment has historically been an effective platform for making a political statement was not lost on the opponents of fossil fuel industry. Indeed, divestment is akin to an economic sanction that has immediate financial repercussions for the firms it targets, being denied the particular capital that they would otherwise benefit from. However, proponents of divestment recognized that its explicitly social dimension – that of stigmatizing the target or target industry – may hold even more powerful economic repercussions in the long run. This is particularly pertinent in the current fight against the fossil fuel industry. At the heart of the activist message is the notion that if the fossil fuel industry is allowed to burn the proven coal, oil, and gas reserves that they have, climate apocalypse will ensue. Divestment, then, represents an apt instrument for bringing this reality of the ecological paradigm to light, placing the blame for anthropogenic climate change squarely at the door of the fossil fuel industry.

Unlike in the case of Keystone XL, this is achieved not by opposing a particular pipeline or infrastructure, but by influencing the portfolios of prominent institutions of power, such as universities, cities, and religious assemblies. Not all of them boast Harvard's $30 billion endowment, nor do they always have significant holdings in fossil fuels-related stocks. More important than the immediate financial impact of denying the fossil fuel industry the investments are the moral victories achieved in having these institutions reaffirm the values and principles of the ecological paradigm. In short, divestment is a battle for hearts and minds against the fossil fuel industry. As McKibben writes:

> Divestment won't do this by directly affecting share prices, at least in the short run – these companies are the richest enterprises in history. Instead, as

the country's colleges, cities and denominations begin to cut their ties, we'll start to revoke the social license of these firms. Many of the nation's elites sit on college boards, forcing them to grapple with the fact that the fossil fuel industry is now an outlaw against the laws of physics.

(McKibben, 2014, February 11)

As hinted above, this is not to say that divestment will have only negligible economic impact. The eventual goal of divestment is to sway the greatest institutions of power, namely governments themselves. Governments are different from universities, cities, and religious assemblies in that their legislation has the potential to debilitate the fossil fuel industry. The mere possibility of such concerted action by governments against the fossil fuel industry is enough to add uncertainty to future investments in fossil fuel companies. Perhaps the most significant endorsement from a regulator, the Bank of England is conducting an inquiry into the risk of fossil fuel companies causing a major economic crash if future climate change rules render their coal, oil, and gas assets worthless. The concept of a "carbon bubble" has gained traction since 2013, and is being taken more seriously by major financial companies, including Citibank, HSBC, and Moody's (Carrington, 2014, December 1).

However, there are also skeptical voices, particularly on the divestment campaign's actual impact. First, skeptics note that Big Carbon has already lost its social license with no apparent effect on its real operations. Oil already shows up as the most disliked industry in America in Gallup surveys every year, with a 61 percent disapproval rating in 2012.

Unless governments act, however, divestment alone can achieve little. Second, advocates of shareholder activism argue that instead of divesting their stocks, organizations seeking to combat climate change should use their voting power to enact change from within through shareholder resolutions. Those who divest merely cede their stocks to those who may not have moral compunctions about profiting from fossil fuels. Third, others advise caution in drawing analogies between the divestment campaign of the present and those of the past, such as the one against the South African apartheid regime, as the success of past campaigns could be attributed to a combination of factors rather than divestment alone (*The New York Times*, 2013, January 27).

The first point, while a criticism of some methods pursued by divestment activists, seems to be in fundamental agreement that governments must somehow be made to legislate against the fossil fuel industry. Whether the divestment campaign represents a necessary or even useful step is contingent on the presence of a better alternative. The second point of influencing the fossil fuel industry from within presents challenges of its own, such as how much pull shareholders will actually have in how businesses are run and under what circumstances it is realistic to expect shareholders to prioritize the ecological paradigm over profit. Careful weighing of the two alternatives – divestment and shareholder activism – will require a much more in-depth discussion of the latter, which is beyond the scope of this chapter.

The third point, while valid, is one that warrants some familiarity with divestment campaign and its precedents, a subject to which we now turn.

5.2 Overview

Historical precedents of divestment as a method of protest are numerous, including but not limited to alcohol (1970s-), arms, munitions, and landmines (1970s-), gambling (1970s-), pornography (1970s-), tobacco (1980s-), nuclear power (1980s-), the South African apartheid (1978–1990), and Darfur, Sudan (early 2000s–2011) (Ansar et al., 2013: 40). An even more recent example is aimed at Israel's occupation of the Palestinian territories, particularly in the West Bank (Beinin, 2015, January 28). The most heralded examples include the campaign against the South African apartheid, as well as the highly successful campaign against the tobacco industry. The Oxford study nicely boils these campaigns down to three waves. In the first wave, religious groups and industry-related public organizations divest from the target industry. Universities, cities, and select public institutions join in the second wave. In the third wave, the wider market responds.

In the 1980s, divestment activists sought to pressure the South African government to end apartheid. The first wave came in 1980, when Protestant and Roman Catholic churches pledged to disinvest $250 million from banks with ties to South Africa. In the second wave, Harvard and Columbia University endowments sold off shares in companies with operations in South Africa in 1986 and 1987, respectively. The Bank of Boston and Chase Manhattan stopped new loan activities in South Africa, and the US government enacted the comprehensive Anti-Apartheid Act of 1986. Thereafter, 1998 could be the third wave, when US pension funds and universities continued to divest and the campaign went global. Britain's Barclay's Bank divested and stopped lending, as Japanese and other foreign companies began to halt operations in South Africa (Ansar et al., 2013: 10). In hindsight, the success of the South African campaign may seem obvious. This is not the case. The issue then was whether divestment, potentially costly, would have any real impact on companies doing business in South Africa. Debate persists among historians today. What is less subject to dispute, however, is the fact that prominent institutions and individuals were forced to grapple with the morality of the apartheid as a result of the campaign (Gillis, 2012, December 4).

In many ways, the anti-apartheid divestment campaign resembles that against the tobacco industry. In the first wave, public health organizations including the American Public Health Association, American Cancer Society, and World Health Organization in 1980 found tobacco products to be contrary to their missions and divested. In the second wave, Harvard president Derek Bok announced in May 1990 that the university had divested nearly $58 million of investments in tobacco companies. For the third wave, in the mid-1990s, several US public pension funds began to divest tobacco holdings, as the 1994 announcement of increased regulation by the US Food and Drug Administration created uncertainty about future financial performance of tobacco stocks. Mississippi led a lawsuit against the tobacco industry to retrieve Medicaid funds for tobacco-related illness, and Massachusetts enacted legislation requiring complete divestment (Ansar et al., 2013: 10). More than a data point, the tobacco case represents a source of hope for the activists.

So far, the astounding success of its predecessors is yet to be replicated. Harvard, for instance, has not yet lent its support to the fossil fuel divestment campaign, despite public protests from students exemplified by the episode that opened our chapter. Like all previous divestment campaigns, fossil fuel divestment started in the US and in the short term focused on US-based investors. Perhaps it needs time. The Oxford study notes that the fossil fuel campaign has entered its second wave in the relatively short time since its inception in 2010: colleges, universities, cities, counties, religious institutions, and foundations have committed to divesting. While observers may disagree on when the movement truly gathered steam, high on the short list is the unanimous decision by the Unity College Board of Trustees to divest from fossil fuels in the fall of 2012. Stephen Mulkey, the president of Unity College and a climate scientist himself, stood on stage with McKibben to announce that his would be the first institution of higher learning to rid its endowment of all fossil fuel holdings (Toomey, 2014, June 9). Mulkey offered as the main rationale the need to develop a collective approach to addressing global climate change with systematic, comprehensive, and scientifically informed policies. Dozens of media outlets across the United States covered the ensuing divestment movement, which continues today, with student groups petitioning college and university administrations all over the country.[2]

Unity College's decision to divest was the fruit of a nationwide "Do The Math" campaign waged on the open road, as well as in the pages of the *Rolling Stone*. As McKibben writes:

> I had a front row seat to watch this explosion – actually, I was up on stage, on a nationwide tour that sold out concert halls across the country early this winter. With a bevy of progressive heroes (author Naomi Klein, indigenous activist Winona LaDuke, filmmaker Josh Fox, Hip Hop Caucus founder Lennox Yearwood) and with *Rolling Stone* as a media sponsor, we took our biodiesel tour bus from Seattle to Atlanta, Maine to Utah, trying to spark a new front in the climate fight. Unknowingly, we'd timed this Do The Math tour pretty well: Post-Sandy, as the hottest year in American history was drawing to a close, we had no trouble finding allies. In fact, we were serving less as a virus then as a vector, letting activists glimpse their emerging strength. Every night, kids from a dozen local colleges would shout out their resolve, and then gather in "Aftermath" parties to get down to organizing. By the time we finally finished, in December [2012] in Salt Lake City, 192 college campuses had active divestment fights underway, a number that's since grown to 256.
>
> *(McKibben, 2013, February 22)*

The central message behind McKibben's Do The Math campaign is deceptively simple and revolves around three numbers. As mentioned in previous chapters, the first number is 2 degree Celsius. As mentioned in Chapter 2, 114 countries including the United States, China, India, and the United Arab Emirates at the 2009 United Nations Climate Change Conference (later joined by 27 additional countries) agreed to enhance their long-term cooperative action to combat climate change, recognizing the scientific view that the increase in global temperature should be below 2 degrees Celsius.[3]

The second number is 565 gigatons, as scientists estimate that humans can pour roughly 565 more gigatons of carbon dioxide into the atmosphere by midcentury and still have some reasonable hope of staying below two degrees. The third number is 2,795 gigatons, which describes the amount of carbon already contained in the proven coal, oil, and gas reserves of fossil fuel companies. McKibben's key point is that this number – 2,795 – is five times higher than 565. Should the fossil fuel companies be allowed to burn their fossil fuels, that will be enough to cause climate catastrophe five times over (McKibben, 2012, August 2).

Does it follow from this that activists should wage a divestment campaign targeting major institutional endowments? While the message is clear about who is to be held responsible and that something should be done, it does not quite tell us what. That is the reason McKibben visits college campuses all over the country, not only rousing crowds, but also calling them to buy into what is, in essence, a grassroots political campaign. A recurrent theme in McKibben's speeches is the direct hold, a golden lock if you will, the fossil fuel industry and its lobbyists seem to have on the nation's policymakers. The divestment campaign seeks to weaken the fossil fuel industry's grip on power through continuous symbolic and public victories. When it comes to politics, there can be great strength in numbers, and the calculation is that the best way to mobilize the masses is to appeal to their sense of morality. It is not an accident that the key targets of this campaign include colleges, universities, and religious authorities, all of which are institutions that take part, whether implicitly or explicitly, in weaving the moral fabric of society. Each small victory on this front contributes momentum to the movement and renders the pro-fossil fuels position of politicians more precarious.

Tracking the progress made thus far, Figure 5.1 is instructive. The left panel displays the total count of divestment commitments by colleges, universities, and cities over time based on data from the Fossil Free campaign website.[4] This tally of successful outcomes does not include the battles that are currently being waged at campuses and city halls all over the country. In that sense, it understates the degree of mobilization.

Religious authorities have also been instrumental to the movement. Based on data drawn from GreenFaith, we have put together a similar time count graph for religious judicatories (governing bodies for religious organizations) on the right panel of Figure 5.1.[5]

The GreenFaith data consider not only commitments, but also actions on divestment more broadly.[6] The similarity between the two timelines is striking, especially in terms of how the actions on divestment came in fits and starts for both (mostly) secular colleges and cities and religious judicatories. Particularly notable months for

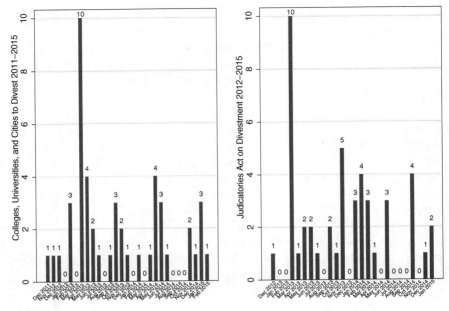

FIGURE 5.1   Colleges, universities, and cities and faith-based judicatories act on divestment.

Source: Fossil Free and GreenFaith

religious judicatories are March and November 2013, followed by February and October 2014. Such evidence of clustering may suggest that organizations committing to divestment mutually reinforce each other, as one organization's decision to join influences the decisions of its peers. This is precisely the kind of cascading dynamic that McKibben and his followers hope to see.

Figure 5.1 perhaps captures religious divestment movement on a high level of aggregation. The reason is that it is the individual congregations that often initiate resolutions on divestment on local or regional levels (to be sent to national governing bodies represented by judicatories), and they are absent from this graph. While individual congregations do not carry the same weight as the judicatories, there are notable exceptions, such as the Union Theological Seminary in New York City. Moreover, by attending various interfaith meetings at the New York City Chapter of Divestment campaign, we befriended individuals from various faith backgrounds who are united by their shared concerns for the environment and disdain for the fossil fuel industry.

Many of these discussions dealt less with interfaith dialogue. While participants shared tips from their experiences with their respective congregations, many of these meetings were organizational in character. Including Episcopalians, Unitarians, Buddhists, Catholics, Evangelicals, Jews, and Muslims, the participants from various religious backgrounds shared the belief that they were stewards of the environment with a moral responsibility to act against the damage the fossil fuel industry is doing. In that sense, their motivations, while rooted in various faiths, largely converge with those of their secular counterparts. One major characteristic that distinguishes the religious activists, however, is their target audience: Their activism begins with their own congregations. It is through the followers of these religions, and secondarily through outside observers, that these organizations serve as sociocultural guideposts for society.

Far from being limited to the lecterns and pulpits of the United States, the divestment movement has gone global. It has thrived in maritime countries, such as the United Kingdom, New Zealand, and Australia. Participating universities abroad include University of Glasgow (United Kingdom), Victoria University (New Zealand), College of Marshall Islands, and Australian National University. Foreign cities to act on divestment include Boxtel (Netherlands), Dunedin (New Zealand), Örebro (Sweden), Oxford (United Kingdom), and Moreland (Australia).

GreenFaith data suggest a similar pattern for judicatories all over the world that have acted on divestment, such as Melbourne Unitarian Peace Memorial Church, Anglican Church in Aotearoa, New Zealand, and Polynesia, Anglican Church of Australia, and Church of England.

Even a former oil dynasty is rising to the challenge. On September 22, 2014, the heirs to the oil fortune, Rockefeller Brothers Fund, which controls about $860 million in assets (around 7 percent of which are in fossil fuels), withdrew their funds from fossil fuel investments. With their divestment, the divestment movement boasted more than 800 global investors strong with a pledge to withdraw a total of $50 billion from fossil fuel investments over the next five years. The decision is a major symbolic victory, the kind that divestment activists can trumpet as they convince other institutions to join the movement.

"John D. Rockefeller, the founder of Standard Oil, moved America out of whale oil and into petroleum," Stephen Heintz, president of the Rockefeller Brothers Fund, said in a statement. "We are quite convinced that if he were alive today, as an astute businessman looking out to the future, he would be moving out of fossil fuels and investing in clean, renewable energy" (Goldenberg, 2014, September 22). Speaking at a forum at Columbia Law School – "Should universities and pension funds divest from fossil fuel stocks?" – Heintz pointed out that the decision was not an easy one. On the moral dimension, the fund believed it needed to set value-driven, programmatic goals. On the economic dimension, the fund believed that further investments in fossil fuel industries are bad investments with fewer returns, and that the market value will shrink. He echoed the environmentalist position that oil, gas, and coal need to stay in the ground to avoid major disruptions to the climate. He also noted that the Rockefellers, while progenitors of ExxonMobil and Chevron, have little sway over the decisions of the oil giants today.

Though largely a sociopolitical movement, the divestment campaign has made an economic impact in non-obvious ways, and is expected to do so for the foreseeable future. Perhaps the biggest impact has been that of introducing uncertainty around fossil fuel investments through stigmatization. As investors look forward and reason backward, they must now consider the possibility that governments, based on the kind of dismal math that McKibben has championed, will eventually legislate against carbon emissions. In such a case, much of the oil, natural gas, and coal proven reserves will be forced to stay "in the ground," nullifying the billions of dollars that fossil fuel companies have spent on exploration and development. Fossil fuel assets, in effect, become stranded assets.

Continually raising this possibility to cast a dark cloud over fossil fuel stocks is the long-term promise of the divestment movement, and its success will be manifested in financial metrics. As the Oxford study points out, stigmatization can lead to a permanent compression in the trading multiples, such as the share price to earnings (P/E) ratio, of a target company. For instance, Rosneft (RNFTF) produces 2.3 million barrels of oil per day, slightly more than ExxonMobil (XOM). Rosneft was, however, valued at $88 billion versus $407 billion for ExxonMobil as of June 2013. Because Rosneft suffers from the stigma of weak corporate governance, investors place a lower probability on its reserves being converted into positive cash flows (Ansar et al., 2013: 14).

To be sure, this will be a hard-fought battle. A recent report by Bloomberg New Energy Finance offers a cool-headed analysis of the challenges that lie ahead for the divestment movement. For starters, the activists are indeed up against a Goliath, as oil, gas, and coal companies form one of the world's largest asset classes, worth nearly $5 trillion at current stock market values (1,469 listed oil and gas firms are worth $4.65 trillion, whereas 275 coal firms are worth $233 billion. ExxonMobil, the largest oil and gas firm, has a market capitalization of $425 billion) (Bullard, 2014).

Moreover, fossil fuel investments, particularly their attractive attributes, such as overall scale, liquidity, value growth, and dividend yield, are difficult to replace. Information technology, for instance, albeit significantly larger than oil and gas as a sector at $7 trillion, pays low dividends as a proportion of post-tax profits. Real estate investment trusts are only $1.4 trillion in total market capitalization, but currently have average dividend yields of more than 4 percent. As for clean energy projects, public equities, YieldCos and green bonds offer stability, growth, and yield, but not in one package (Bullard, 2014).

In fact, significant divestment from coal would be much easier than significant divestment from oil and gas. Listed coal companies are small enough in the aggregate that investors could divest and reinvest without unbalancing portfolios. Oil and gas companies are too large and too widely held for divestment to be easy or fast. A robust architecture for fossil fuel divestment will require alternative investment structures or asset classes. The report concludes that in order to attract trillions of reinvested institutional dollars, clean energy will need a vast expansion of its YieldCo and green bond structures or new instruments (Bullard, 2014).

The talk of the town among divestment activists today seems to be that of reinvestment. Simply removing funds from fossil fuels does not imply investments in clean energy. How to achieve meaningful reinvestment in clean energy has made asset management a pertinent issue in the divestment debate. As exemplified by Calvert Research and Management, represented at the Columbia Law School forum, there are now asset management firms that can assist major funds as they move their investments away from fossil fuels to clean energy with minimal loss to their profits. We expect reinvestment to be the next big debate in what *The Guardian* had once called "a campaign launched by scrappy activists on college campuses."[7]

5.3 Activism in motion

We aim to shed light on the successful tactics of the campaign by examining key developments at the frontlines, such as the Union Theological Seminary, the Episcopalian Church, municipal chapters of 350.org, and collegiate chapters at Harvard and Stanford Universities. How does the idea of divestment take root within an institution? By what procedures does it climb up the institutional hierarchy? Under what conditions do these ideas successfully translate into action?

To preview, our conclusions are three-fold. First, the initial motivations for and reservations against the divestment campaign can be complex, although successful cases are underscored by a sense of moral urgency. Second, the opponents seek to dilute this sense of moral urgency by dissociating the problem – climate change – from the tool to combat it – divestment from fossil fuels. Third, institutional investors with sizeable endowments are unlikely to be convinced until financial instruments begin to emerge that render fossil fuels investments less attractive than the alternatives.

On June 10, 2014, the trustees of Columbia-affiliated Union Theological Seminary (UTS), which has an endowment of $108.4 million, voted unanimously to divest from fossil fuels, becoming the world's first seminary to do so.[8] Considered the intellectual home of socially conscious theologians such as Reinhold Niebuhr and Dietrich Bonhoeffer, UTS has represented progressive mainline Protestantism in America. The sense of moral urgency was palpable, as Michael Johnston, the chair of Union's investment committee and a former executive vice president with Capital Group Companies, expressed in the press release:

> Climate change is affecting this globe, it's killing people, and it's going to destroy what the world looks like as we know it. As a seminary we have a moral obligation to no longer profit from the production of fossil fuels. I hope that people see our actions as a beacon of hope, and recognize that there are things we can do as a country and as a people to cut down on our greenhouse gas emissions.
>
> *(Union Theological Seminary, 2015, February 2)*

In some ways, however, the seminary represents a best-case scenario. In 2012, a graduating student representative from the investment committee met with a group of concerned students. In 2013, the student group wanted to make divestment a top priority – i.e., demand a resolution from the administration to divest. At the time, the UTS had been no stranger to social divestment policy, as there had been previous divestment efforts against alcohol and tobacco, as well as some environmental language against UTS investments in mutual funds. As such, divestment moved forward. In September 2014, the Union Forum initiative organized a conference on faith and the environment. By the spring 2014, there was a petition for the Board of Trustees to review investments and make a resolution before the conference. Serene Jones, the president of UTS, emailed a student campaigner, indicating that the administration and board of trustees were excited about divestment.

According to students who participated in the campaign, the administration was probably aware of the petition, and it may have influenced the board's divestment decision. In June 2014, the board unanimously decided on divestment from fossil fuels. The proponents of divestment, however, were careful to avoid conflictual language in the petition. Their particular emphasis was on framing climate change as a social justice issue. UTS was a best-case scenario, given its legacy of cutting-edge activism on social justice. Moreover, there were no board members with corporate connections.

Even from an insider's perspective, therefore, it seems the UTS as an institution was especially well positioned to lead on divestment. Indeed, the main concern of the UTS community was already on how individual action on campus could match the spirit of divestment. Since divestment was not in the hands of the student community per se, students felt the need to make changes in lifestyle to maintain consistency and avoid hypocrisy.

The language of the announcement makes it clear that the UTS views its decision in moral terms. Jones wrote in a *Times* article: "As a seminary we are familiar with the scriptural warning that 'the wages of sin is death,' and this could not be more literally true than in the case of fossil fuels. As vulnerable communities have been swallowed by rising shorelines, as potable water has become a commodity of increasing rarity, as hundreds of thousands of people have been killed by violent weather, it is ever clear that humanity's addiction to fossil fuels is death-dealing – or as Christians would say, profoundly sinful" (Jones, 2014, June 10). The moral argument continues: "For Christians, sin is the word that describes anything that prevents us from having a faithful relationship with God, with each other, with ourselves, and with creation. We have sinned, and we see this divestment as an act of repentance for Union. All of the world is God's precious creation, and our place within it is to care for and respect the health of the whole." Not only do these statements by Jones highlight the centrality of social justice, such as protection of vulnerable communities, to the mission of UTS, but they also reaffirm its "inescapable moral, spiritual responsibility" to "encourag[e] other seminaries and universities" to act on divestment (Jones, 2014, June 10).

The UTS decision was widely praised by divestment activists, though its actual impact is difficult to assess. "Now that divestment has a firm foothold in Manhattan, the pressure is building on New York City to divest its pension funds from fossil fuels. Union Theological Seminary has helped make the moral case crystal clear: it is wrong to invest in companies that are wrecking the planet and imperiling the future of NYC," Lyna Hinkel from 350NYC stated. "Union's vote to divest is prophetic and strong," said Reverend Fletcher Harper of GreenFaith, an interfaith environmental group that has advocated fossil fuel divestment and clean energy reinvestment by religious institutions. "The seminary's commitment highlights the grave danger posed by climate change and the fossil fuel industry, and is a model for seminaries globally."[9] Our own preliminary assessment is that while the UTS decision represents a major symbolic victory for the divestment campaign and an important source of momentum going forward, it will be a difficult model for other seminaries to emulate given the institution's unique history and extraordinary commitment to social justice.

Indeed, a comparison of draft resolutions to the 78th General Convention of the Episcopal Church (slated for 2015), circulated among members of the Episcopal Diocese of New York and those of the Diocese of Newark, aptly illustrates how fossil fuels divestment among religious organizations, particularly on a national level, may be a more divisive issue than the case of UTS suggests.[10] The draft resolution prepared on behalf of the 238th Convention of the Episcopal Diocese of New York exemplifies "weaker" language in mainly encouraging debate on the issue of fossil fuel divestment further down the road, whereas the "stronger" draft prepared for the 141st Convention of the Episcopal Diocese of Newark directly calls for immediate action on a national level. A comparison of these versions sheds light not only on the diversity of opinions that may exist within religious institutions considering divestment, but reading between the lines also sheds light on the institutional politics of fossil fuels divestment.

The weak New York resolution contains the following elements – rhetorical endorsement of climate action and encouragement (albeit postponement) of informed debate on divestment. The resolution begins by praising the June 2014 release of the Environmental Protection Agency's proposed carbon rule for existing power plants: "Power plants are the single largest source of carbon dioxide pollution in the United States and major contributors to climate change. These emissions not only threaten the environmental stability of our planet, but also the health of young children and their families, disproportionately affecting the poorest among us and all of God's good Creation." Then follows the indictment of the fossil fuel industry: "Coal, gas, oil, and uranium extraction and subsequent transportation threaten the health, sanctity of communities, and the livelihood of future generations. We seek to eliminate the practice of locating such industries disproportionately near neighborhoods inhabited by people of color and low income communities."

The prescription, however, does not seem commensurate with the gravity of the diagnosis: "Resolved, That there continue to be diverse opinions and voices concerning whether the Church should divest its holdings in fossil fuel extraction companies as well as those that use substantial amounts of such fuels. It is important that we as a Church have extensive conversations on this critical issue." By "resolving" to have "diverse opinions and voices," the resolution is essentially agreeing to disagree. Instead of directly calling on national bodies for immediate action, the resolution sets a curiously long time frame: "We ask that the Committee on Corporate Social Responsibility of the Executive Council and the Church Pension Fund, in consultation with experts in the fields of economics and investing, ethics, and renewable energy development, jointly assess whether the benefit of a divestment strategy would be in compliance with our values and issue a report thereon by the Summer of 2016, and we call on upon the Executive Council to facilitate church wide dialogue on this subject following the issuance of this report and communicate the results of the dialogue to the 79th General Convention." Given that General Conventions happen every three years, the 79th General Convention would take place in the year 2018.

On the other hand, the Newark version, "as a matter of moral and theological urgency, in obedience to God's command to 'tend and keep the earth' and consistent with Jesus' injunction that we care for those who are most vulnerable," directly calls on the Church Pension Fund, the Investment Committee of the Executive Council and the Episcopal Church Foundation to adopt a policy "to refrain from this time forward from purchasing any new holdings of public equities and corporate bonds of the world's leading 200 fossil fuel companies" identified by Carbon Underground. The resolution also calls on the same institutions to "develop and implement a plan to divest within five years from direct ownership of public equities and corporate bonds of the world's leading 200 fossil fuel companies" and "to develop and implement a strategy to invest 5% within two years and 10% within four years of their overall holdings in 'impact investments' in the clean energy sector." The resolution seeks divestment and reinvestment on a national level, clean and simple. Lastly, it calls on the 78th General Convention of the Episcopal Church to "encourage all dioceses and the Consortium of Endowed Episcopal Parishes to engage within the coming year the topic of divestment from fossil fuels and clean energy reinvestment."

The difference between the New York and Newark versions suggests the role of conflicting interests — politics — at play. Given that both New York and Newark dioceses are part of the Episcopal Church, it is less likely that the difference in their positions on divestment are theologically grounded. It was only on July 6, 2015, that the leaders of Episcopal Church declared that fossil fuel investments would be purged from its holdings, approximately $380 million in value. This does not include the denomination's $9 billion pension fund or the $4 billion controlled by parishes and dioceses (Goldenberg, 2015, July 3).

Meanwhile, Pope Francis of the Catholic Church waded deep into the climate debate, striking an activist tone similar to that adopted by the anti-fossil fuel movement. In a 150-page encyclical, the pope calls on the rich nations to act: "In different ways, developing countries, where the most important reserves of the biosphere are found, continue to fuel the development of richer countries at the cost of their own present and future. . . . The developed countries ought to help pay this debt by significantly limiting their consumption of non-renewable energy and by assisting poorer countries to support policies and programmes of sustainable development" (Catholic Church & McDonagh, 2016). As Austen Ivereigh, a biographer of the pope, observed: "This is his signature teaching. . . . Francis has made it not just safe to be Catholic and green; he's made it obligatory" (Kirchgaessner, 2015, June 18).

The pope has also instituted a global prayer day for the environment, September 1, reaffirming his legacy as the "climate pope" and providing a veritable forum for Catholics all over the world to mobilize as stewards of the environment (Agence France-Presse, 2015, August 10).

Bringing it all together, GreenFaith data offer a glimpse into the composition of religious organizations acting on divestment. Figure 5.2 counts the number of congregations within faiths that have thus far acted on divestment. To be sure, this is by no means a perfect measure of institutional interest in divestment, as some denominations, such as the Roman Catholic Church, are likely to be more centralized than others. Moreover, with the exception of Unitarian-Universalist, the denominations listed profess to be Christian, and divestment by organizations that belong to other religions – such as Buddhism, Judaism, and Islam – are not represented. Nonetheless, some details stand out. The number of Unitarian-Universalist organizations acting on investment is most notable, and is perhaps consistent with its historically liberal outlook. Not far behind are Society of Friends (Quakers), Presbyterians, and the United Church of Christ. Fewer in number are Episcopal, non-denominational, and Roman Catholic organizations.

Another battleground for winning hearts and minds is among states and cities. Particularly illustrative is New York City, where the authors had numerous chances to participate firsthand in divestment meetings and planning sessions. 350NYC

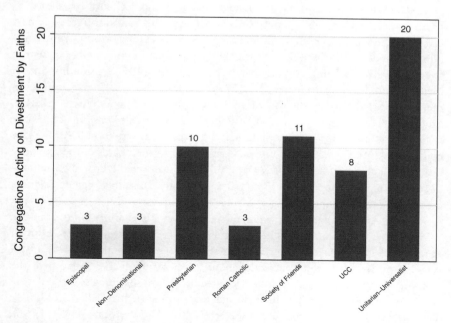

FIGURE 5.2 Divestment actions by faiths.

Source: GreenFaith

brings the same message, but contextualizes it at the local level. Particularly salient for New York City's climate debate is Hurricane Sandy, which claimed the lives of at least 53 New Yorkers:

> Hurricane Sandy decimated the New York City area, causing $65 billion in damage, causing power outages, destroying homes and leaving a path of wreckage from the Rockaways to Riverside Park. It's time for NYC to stop investing our pension funds in oil, gas and coal, and go fossil free! We know that Sandy was fueled in part by Atlantic waters that were 5 degrees warmer than average, a result of human-induced climate change. Mayor Bloomberg has taken steps to make our city an example of low-carbon urban living, from painting bike lanes to mandating energy retrofits – and much much more must be done.
>
> *(Schumer, n.d.)*[11]

To further contextualize climate change, 350NYC notes that average temperatures across the northeastern United States have risen by over 2°F since 1970, winter temperatures are 4°F warmer, and the change in temperature is more noticeable at the extremes. New Yorkers have seen an increase in the number of extremely hot summer days (above 90°F) and a decrease in the number of cold winter days (below 32°F). In the future to come, they are warned against the usual suspects, such as changing precipitation patterns, increasing mosquito populations, and declining agriculture.[12]

To combat this, 350NYC wants New York City to immediately freeze any new investment in fossil fuel companies, and divest from direct ownership and any commingled funds that include fossil fuel public equities and corporate bonds within five years. Particularly high on 350 NYC's agenda is the NYC Pension Fund, with total assets under its management at $127,458,000,000 as of 2012, which includes the city's cash balances, the Board of Education Retirement System (BERS), Employees' Retirement System (NYCERS), Fire Department Pension Fund (Fire), Police Pension Fund (Police), and Teachers' Retirement System (TRS). The city comptroller is the custodian and investment advisor to the boards of the five pension funds, and therefore can exert powerful influence over the boards on responsible investment issues. Thus, 350NYC is currently collecting signatures for a petition to NYC comptroller Scott Stringer. The success of this campaign, at least in comparison to the national movement, seems to have been more limited thus far.

Similar efforts are underway in New England, as 350Vermont also takes aim at the pension fund, which is the state's largest publicly managed fund, with a total value of nearly $4 billion. Currently, about 2.5 percent (or $98 million) of the pension fund is invested in the energy sector through common stock and corporate bonds, all of which is in fossil fuel companies, such as BP ($5,051,504), Total ($6,373,831), Royal Dutch Shell ($5,536,033), Petrobras ($4,214,506), ExxonMobil ($2,912,915), and Chevron ($2,535,247).[13] 350Vermont encourages citizens to let Treasurer Beth Pearce know about their support for fossil fuel divestment and pen letters to the editors for local papers.

There is a difference between what the campaign seeks to achieve and what it has actually been able to achieve, even on a symbolic level. There is no doubt that the activists are aiming for the institutions and funds with large endowments, often unsuccessfully. This is not entirely inconsistent with the moral and symbolic dimensions of the campaign, as larger institutions are likely to make a bigger splash on the national stage. 350Vermont counts among its victories in New England a successful Youth Day of Climate Action at the State House, where high school students were given the opportunity to learn about divestment and connect with legislators and the press, and a Valentine's Day rally, where activists demanded that the legislature break up with fossil fuels and divest.

Colorado is another battleground state, given its abundant fossil fuel reserves and potential for wind and solar energy development. 350Coloardo assumes a multi-pronged strategy, and its three main goals are movement building, opposing "extreme energy" (i.e., fracking and tar sands), and promoting local solutions (i.e., municipally-owned local power utility and local food systems).[14] 350 Colorado also has an ongoing petition campaign calling on the Colorado State Treasury, which has less than .01 percent of its $7 billion invested in oil and gas, to divest.

The State Treasury is no stranger to divestment, as a bill was passed in 2007 requiring divestment from companies supporting atrocities in Sudan.[15] University of Colorado and its $2.7 billion investment pool is the next target. Any victory in the nation's No. 7 energy output state, where its coal, oil, and gas industries produce billions of dollars in revenue and employ thousands, would be significant. Despite its liberal reputation, the regents elected from across the state have a 5–4 Republican majority (Kuta, 2015, April 16).

Harvard and Stanford Universities can further illustrate some of the challenges facing collegiate chapters of divestment. Harvard boasts a $37.6 billion endowment, whereas Stanford endowment is to the tune of $22.2 billion as of October 2015 (Olkowski and Skinner, 2015, September 23; Stuber, 2015, September 25). Given the sizes of endowments, convincing them to divest would not be easy. Indeed, divestment has brought to the fore some of the tensions inherent in these prominent universities' dual role as wealthy financial institutions and leading institutions of higher learning. While students, alumni, and faculty often point to the leadership role they must assume in shaping and guiding debates on pressing issues such as climate change, their boards of trustees are entrusted with maximizing returns on investments for the functioning and advancement of universities. Given the latter has the last word, divestment debate tends to play out in public, as students, alumni, and faculty sign petitions and publicly pressure university administrators and trustees. According to Chloe Maxmin, a student leader in the Divest Harvard campaign, the group intentionally designed an action that could appeal to a broad audience and allow people to participate (Maxmin, 2015: 112).

There is no question that student advocates of divestment at Harvard and Stanford, like many of the activists chronicled in this book, face an uphill battle. The bigger the endowment, the taller the order. Nonetheless, they have capitalized on symbolic victories to build public momentum. On April 11, 2013, Divest Harvard held its first big rally outside Massachusetts Hall. The rally featured speakers Hannah Borowsky (Divest Harvard), Reverend Fred Small (First Parish in Cambridge), Tara Raghuveer (Undergraduate Council president), Professor David Keith (Applied Physics Department), and Ben Franta (Divest Harvard). At the event, around 150 enthusiastic supporters presented 1,300 petition signatures to the administration. Under police supervision, two student representatives managed to enter the building and meet with Secretary of the University and Vice President Marc Goodheart. He offered to collect their petitions inside. At this point, Divestment Harvard notes that "This wasn't acceptable for us: we wanted our administration to acknowledge us publicly." The two students said "no" and walked out, and Goodheart followed them. Once in view of the public, they gladly presented him with the petition signatures on the doorstep of Massachusetts Hall.[16]

President Drew Gilpin Faust was not convinced: "While I share their belief in the importance of addressing climate change, I do not believe, nor do my colleagues on the Corporation, that university divestment from the fossil fuel industry is warranted or wise." Her main argument is that Harvard is an academic institution with an academic mission − "to carry out the best possible programs of education and research" − and that its endowment should not serve other purposes that would "position the University as a political actor rather than an academic institution," risking the "independence of academic enterprise." This represents a break from Harvard's divestment against apartheid. Her statement also expresses concerns about constraints on investment returns, the moral consistency of boycotting a class of companies on whose products and services Harvard relies, as well as the efficacy of divestment as a tool to influence fossil fuel companies. She proposes that Harvard fight climate change through cutting-edge research and teaching on environmental and climate issues.[17]

That is the reason the movement, which began almost three years ago, continues today, and sit-in campaigns outside of President Faust's office have become a fixture. The campaign draws strength from growing support among students, alumni, and faculty. In an Undergraduate Council referendum in 2012, 72 percent of participating Harvard College students supported divestment. Since then, more than 200 faculty members, almost 1,100 alumni, and around 65,000 community members have come on board. Nonetheless, Divest Harvard claims that the university has ignored requests to discuss divestment: "Now, Divest Harvard will accept nothing short of full divestment. After three years of conversations that led nowhere, merely requesting further discussion is both insufficient and disrespectful to the communities who bear the direct consequences of the fossil-fuel industry's actions. Harvard's actions must reflect the urgency of the global need for action" (Divest Harvard, 2015, February 12).

Divest Harvard has also taken the fight to the court of law. On November 19, 2014, seven law students and undergraduates filed a lawsuit against the university, claiming that Harvard has a duty to fight climate change by divesting from fossil fuels: "Such investments contribute to current and future damage to the University's reputation and to that of its students and graduates, to the ability of students to study and thrive free from the threat of catastrophic climate change, and to future damage to the university's physical campus as a result of sea-level rise and increased storm activity" (Goldenberg, 2015, February 19). The goal is for Harvard to withdraw from an estimated $79 million in direct investments in coal, oil, and gas companies, and begin phasing out all other investments containing fossil fuel stocks. The lawsuit is another example highlighting the role of publicity.

In an open letter released on the date of Harvard's first court appearance, more than 30 prominent alumni publicly expressed their support for the campaign. Among this group were Natalie Portman, Cornel West, Robert Kennedy Jr., Maya Lin, Nobel laureate Eric Chivian, Pulitzer winner Susan Faludi, and Bill McKibben. The letter is direct: "As Harvard's own researchers have done so much to show, global warming is the greatest threat the planet faces . . . From the typhoon-battered Philippines to the disappearing islands of the Pacific to the water-starved towns of California's drought-ridden Central Valley, this issue demands we all make changes to business as usual – especially those of us who have prospered from the systems driving climate change" (Goldenberg, 2015, February 20). The alumni called for an old-style teach-in at Harvard followed by several days of sit-ins and rallies (Goldenberg, 2015, February 20). The Massachusetts Supreme Court, however, dismissed the lawsuit after Harvard and the State Attorney General's office filed motions to dismiss (Delwiche and Klein, 2015, March 24). Divest Harvard appealed the dismissal to the Massachusetts Appeals Court, the group's second attempt to use legal action to prompt Harvard to divest (Klein, 2015, October 13).

On the other hand, the board of trustees at Stanford made quite a splash in May 2014, announcing that the university will not make direct investments of endowment funds in publicly traded companies whose principal business is the mining of coal for use in energy generation.[18] According to the press release, divestment from coal is consistent with Stanford's investment policy adopted in 1971, which states that while the trustees' primary obligation in investing endowment assets is to maximize the financial return of those assets to support the university, when "corporate policies or practices create substantial social injury," the trustees may include this factor in their investment decisions. "Stanford has a responsibility as a global citizen to promote sustainability for our planet, and we work intensively to do so through our research, our educational programs and our campus operations," said Stanford President John Hennessy. "The university's review has concluded that coal is one of the most carbon-intensive methods of energy generation and that other sources can be readily substituted for it. Moving away from coal in the investment context is a small, but constructive, step while work continues, at Stanford and elsewhere, to develop broadly viable sustainable energy solutions for the future."

As we have emphasized throughout, the symbolic nature of this campaign makes this small gesture from Stanford, a premier university with one of the largest endowments in America, quite significant. Though Stanford's coal holdings are known to be a small fraction of its endowment (the exact amount is private), when we consider Harvard's unqualified rejection, Stanford showcases a "third way" in which the academic mission of a university can be consistent with divestment from a particular industry as an expression of its concerns about climate change. For a campaign that draws as much momentum from symbolic victories as divestment, this is a welcome development.

Yari Greaney, a Fossil Free Stanford organizer, said the group was "very proud of Stanford taking this leadership position." Maura Cowley, the executive director of Energy Action Coalition, an assemblage of groups active on climate change issues, called the decision "a huge, huge victory." In an interview, she said that "their decision, coming from such a major university and from such a huge endowment, shows that the coal industry and other fossil fuel industries are quickly becoming relics of the past." McKibben, noting that Stanford "knows the havoc that climate change creates around our planet," was also pleased: "Other forward-looking and internationally minded institutions will follow, I'm sure" (Wines, 2014, May 6). Indeed, Columbia University almost three years later would announce its intention to divest from companies deriving more than 35 percent of their revenue from thermal coal production.[19]

Stanford's decision was not costly or a radical departure for the board of trustees and the administration. *The New Republic*'s interview of President John Hennessy is telling. While student activists had initially asked Stanford to divest shares in any of 200 publicly traded fossil fuel companies, the university decided that doing so would hit the school's coffers too hard and be "hypocritical," since Stanford runs mostly on fossil fuels. Thus, Stanford divested only from companies that mine coal. That step was small enough, the university decided, that it would leave Stanford's investment returns unharmed and deflect criticisms of intellectual dishonesty, since California, unlike many other states such as Massachusetts, gets a very small percentage of its electricity from coal. Stanford remains invested in coal consumption, as divestment does not apply to stocks of power companies that burn coal or steel makers for whom coal is a key fuel source. "We don't expect this to solve global warming or put coal out of business," Hennessy said. "We're not on a campaign to end it. We're just on a campaign to prevent ourselves from being complicit in the continued use" (Ball, 2014, May 22).

A few months after announcing it would end direct investments in coal mining companies, Stanford invested in three oil and gas companies, namely Rex Energy Corp., YPF SA, and Petrobras Argentina SA. "This doesn't run counter to Stanford's commitment because they made it clear they would divest from coal, but it certainly isn't in the spirit of the commitment they made," said Jamie Henn, communications director for 350.org (Streib, 2014, November 14). In January 2015, almost 300 professors at Stanford, including Nobel laureates and the 2014 Fields medal winner, called on the university to rid itself of all fossil fuel investments: "The urgency and magnitude of climate change call not for partial solutions, however admirable; they demand the more profound and thorough commitment embodied in divestment from all fossil-fuel companies" (Goldenberg, 2015, January 11). In February, three professors arguing for divestment met with President Hennessy. Representing the 369 faculty signatories, they presented Hennessy with a letter and provided verbal arguments for divestment. Hennessy's response was neutral, according to Paul Ehrlich, Bing Professor of Population Studies. Hennessy cautioned that divestment from fossil fuels would be a "tough sell" to the Board of Trustees. "He was, I would say, taking the position that he was an intermediary between us and the Board of Trustees, and the decision was with the Board of Trustees," Ehrlich said (Xu, 2015, February 17).

The protests would continue. In November 2015, 100 students at Stanford University attempted to enter Hennessy's office to begin a sit-in demanding full divestment. The administration refused them entrance to the building. Some 275 other students joined them for the largest rally in Fossil Free Stanford's history.[20] The sit-in would last for days as students, alumni, faculty members, and other employees, including the executive director and president of the Stanford workers union and representatives of the Student Health Center provided food and support to the protesters.[21]

The Harvard and Stanford cases serve to highlight the weight of practical considerations that preoccupy any university with prominent endowments. Some point out that Stanford's case of coal divestment may be uniquely favorable, given that the school has a history of engagement in environmental issues and one of its trustees and big donor, Thomas F. Steyer, is a hedge fund billionaire who spends hundreds of millions to finance candidates to address global warming. Though Stanford and Columbia are prominent exceptions, the list of schools to divest has been mostly limited to small institutions (Solomon, 2015, February 10). Divestment campaigns continue all over the nation, and even in places where they have met limited success, such as Harvard and Swarthmore College, students are raising the profile of the movement (Gillis, 2012, December 4).

5.4 Motives

The motivations behind the campaign on divestment share many similarities with those behind the Keystone XL campaign. In both cases, activists target the global fossil fuel industry, highlight the discrepancy between continued extraction and climate change mitigation, and achieve a series of small wins in the process. This is not altogether shocking, given that the same organizations and organizers have started both campaigns. And yet, there are also notable differences. The intrinsic motivations that drive activists to get arrested in a rally against Keystone XL are significantly different from those that turn people into divestment activists. Whereas Keystone XL motivates activists by promising concrete action against a single prominent target, divestment offers an opportunity to take action for principled and ethical reasons.

Research on the divestment campaign also raises a series of new challenges. In particular, because the divestment campaign is more recent than Keystone XL, our research relied heavily on continuous observation, both participatory and non-participatory. Besides collecting data from websites, online fora, and activist publications, we attended activist meetings, spoke to divestment activists, and participated in public rallies. We joined mailing lists that were open to the public. We also asked divestment activists questions about their motivations and views of the campaign. The data collection began in spring 2014 and continued until the end of the year.

In the case of divestment, the idea of fossil fuels as a root cause is a powerful one. Similar to Keystone XL, the divestment campaign is ultimately about fossil fuels, and not just climate change. Although the idea that divestment is an effective strategy to reduce the use of coal, oil, and gas has been widely ridiculed by economists, activists are enthusiastic about an opportunity to make a clear and unambiguous statement about fossil fuels. To them, the notion that climate change is ultimately a problem that stems from our excessive reliance on fossil fuels is a powerful motivation to act.

Another clear similarity in motivation is the symbolism of going after a powerful enemy. As we have seen, fossil fuel divestment is the exact opposite of the typical climate policy strategy of controlling the consumption of fossil fuels by a large number of consumers. Indeed, fossil fuel divestment does not even attempt to target all producers of fossil fuels: the campaign is firmly anchored in the notion that the 200 largest fossil fuel companies – the carbon majors – are the real problem. They are, divestment activists argue, responsible for almost all of global greenhouse gas emissions; their economic strategies and political clout are driving us toward climate disruption. While the Keystone XL is a campaign against a pipeline, the divestment campaign is a campaign against the fossil fuel juggernauts.

Where the divestment campaign differs from Keystone XL is the former's much stronger emphasis on removing the social license of the fossil fuel industry. The Keystone XL campaign has been framed around the concrete effects that tar sands oil would bring to American and global markets. It has only touched upon the legitimacy of the fossil fuel industry indirectly, whereas divestment activists seek to undermine the legitimacy of fossil fuels. According to the activists, every divestment decision challenges the very idea that the continued and growing extraction of fossil fuels is a legitimate business activity. This belief is a direct consequence of seeing the world through the lens of the ecological paradigm.

That said, divestment activists are also motivated by the notion of stranded assets. While all divestment activists are motivated by their concern about the ecological destruction caused by the fossil fuel industry, the possibility that fossil fuel reserves become useless due to carbon constraints is a core reason these activists believe they can win. Divestment activists believe that as the pressure for national and international climate policy intensifies, there will be a shadow of doubt cast on the profitability of fossil fuel extraction. This triggers a virtuous cycle: climate advocacy reduces the profits of fossil fuel industry, and this reduced profitability reduces the political clout of the industry, allowing more effective climate advocacy – a dynamic that may ultimately result in a fossil fuel-free world. While stranded assets are neither exciting nor motivating for divestment activists themselves, the notion offers a pathway from campaigning to transformative change.

Here we also see a stark contrast between divestment and conventional climate policy, such as carbon taxes. Advocates of carbon taxes do not by any means challenge the legitimacy of the fossil fuel industry; their claim is that fossil fuel extraction can continue, provided the industry agrees to pay for the damage it is causing. The divestment activists instead rally around the idea that further fossil fuel extraction today is simply wrong. Even if carbon tax is more effective than divestment in terms of emissions reductions, divestment seems to capture the imagination of large groups of people who are not interested in mobilizing for a portfolio of economically optimal carbon pricing policies.

Besides the goal of removing the social license of the fossil fuel industry, divestment activists share a strong sense of historical continuity. The first historical precedent that divestment activists commonly invoke is the campaign against apartheid in South Africa. As we attended various meetings and events on divestment, activists of all stripes brought up the precedent set by the anti-apartheid divestment campaign. At the demonstration on the 2015 Global Divestment Day, student activists held speeches emphasizing how many of the nation's top universities, including Harvard and Yale, had divested to protest South Africa's racist regime. At a Sunday morning seminar in the Riverside Church, where one of us was invited to discuss divestment and climate policy, both the participants and various presenters delved into the congregation's history and brainstormed ways to replicate the spirit of the anti-apartheid campaign.

From a direct historical precedent, divestment activists often build a bridge to the broader notion of peaceful protest that is reflected in Mahatma Gandhi's work, as well as Martin Luther King Jr.'s. Indeed, some members of the divestment campaign specifically said that they joined because they saw clear similarities between King's work and today's divestment campaign. In an *EcoWatch* column, Reverend Lennox Yearwood, who directs the Hip Hop Caucus, explains why his organization had joined forces with the divestment campaign:

> This new strategy calls on institutions to divest their assets from fossil fuels and invest instead in a clean energy economy. Modeled on the innovation of the anti-Apartheid movement, and on similar efforts against tobacco companies, divestment spread rapidly from college campuses into the faith community, where it has historical resonance. Fossil fuel divestment has more in common with the creative energy and moral imperative of the early Civil Rights movement than any major environmental campaign in modern times. Activists remember that Martin Luther King, Jr., did not change history by calling for more white-papers. Like King, the new divestment movement confronts its powerful opponent head on.
>
> (Yearwood Jr., 2015, February 15)

Interestingly, Yearwood connects divestment activism to the civil rights movement by arguing that both the divestment activists and Dr. King were willing to take on a powerful, systematically privileged opponent.

Speaking of King, motivations behind divestment are not fully comprehensible without a consideration of their relationship to justice and religious morality. Both among student and religious activists, the idea of "climate justice" is clearly a guiding principle. According to the student activists we met, a key rationale for divestment is the immorality of investing in companies that cause ecological destruction in marginalized communities. While climate change as a scientific or technical problem does not make too many people's blood boil, the idea that one's own college is funding companies that are responsible for the sea level rise, drought, oil spills, and air pollution is a strong argument for immediate action. In religious communities, divestment activists search for motivation in holy scriptures, such as the Bible, or the teachings of religious leaders, such as Buddha. These teachings provide a clear moral basis for divestment as an integral component of an ethical society. To again cite Yearwood of the Hip Hop Caucus:

> Since Hurricane Katrina destroyed much of New Orleans and the Gulf Coast, America's poor urban populations have known that climate change is more than a cause for the liberal, college-educated elite. Communities of color also suffer far higher rates of cancer, asthma and other diseases because pollution in their neighborhoods is worse. Yet for too long, the mainstream environmental movement has failed to reach demographics outside a narrow, self-defined 'base.' In the process, it has limited its political power and missed opportunities to build the kind of majority needed to secure fundamental change in energy use and our broader economy.
>
> *(Yearwood Jr., 2015, February 15)*

The strong historical continuities and ethical foundations have allowed divestment activists to frame their campaign as standing in solidarity with the broader movement on climate change. On the Columbia University campus, where we had the opportunity to follow the Barnard-Columbia Divest for Climate Justice Campaign, student leaders repeatedly emphasized the importance of the "solidarity tactics" in the divestment movement. In their view, the simultaneous actions of dozens of campus campaigns across the country, along with the broader climate movement, are a critically important force behind the sustained interest in the issue. This recognition is not specific to the Morningside Heights neighborhood in Manhattan. In September 2014, the campaigning organization Fossil Free arranged a web workshop to explore "how divestment can be used as a solidarity tactic, and how climate change is innately intertwined with social justice."[22] This emphasis on solidarity shows that divestment activists do not see their campaign in isolation or as an alternative to other campaigns.

In addition to these moral and ethical arguments, divestment activists have over time also begun to emphasize the positive opportunities that divestment creates. Already in spring 2014, divestment activists learned that a message of reinvestment would allow them to reach out to various progressive groups looking for economic strategies to improve the lot of marginalized and economically regressing communities. Consider, for example, reactions to the divestment campaign among organizers in communities of color in New York. Divestment activists have been able to secure the support of a wide range of such organizers by connecting divestment to investments in green infrastructure and clean technology.

On a final note, we would not do justice to the divestment campaign if we did not underscore the awareness of counterarguments among the activists. If there was one thing that divestment activists obsessed over in the various meetings we attended, it was the necessity of being able to rebut counterarguments. At one strategy retreat of 350NYC, for example, one of us witnessed a grueling two-hour practice "office visit" to a local politician. In the practice session, experienced activists played the role of a New York City council member, asking tough questions about the effectiveness, cost, and feasibility of divestment. According to the activists, the goal of such practice was to ensure that all members of the divestment movement were able to explain to others the logic behind the campaign and present it in a positive light.

Consider, for instance, the divestment movement's response to a critical column by Ivo Welch, a professor of economics at the University of California, Los Angeles, whose research shows that divestment activism did not reduce the value of the stock of targeted companies invested in South Africa (Welch, 2014, May 9). While Welch's article was titled "Why Divestment Fails," *The New York Times* also published three responses under the heading "Why Divestment Can Be Successful" (Weinstein et al., 2014, May 13). In one of them, student activists Ophir Bruck, Chloe Maxmin, and Krishan Dasaratha note:

> The divestment campaign does not aim to affect the share prices of fossil fuel companies. Divestment aims to stigmatize the fossil fuel industry; to spark dialogue about its role in polluting politics, harming communities and driving the climate crisis; and to build a powerful, organized climate movement.
>
> *(Weinstein et al., 2014, May 13)*

By this logic, the activists conclude that "[t]he divestment movement is already amplifying the dialogue around climate solutions, engaging thousands of students worldwide, and bolstering a fast-growing climate change movement. To us, that is why divestment succeeds" (Weinstein et al, 2014, May 13).

5.5 Mobilization potential

Evaluating the divestment campaign is admittedly more difficult than evaluating the Keystone XL campaign. Concerns about the relevance of the Keystone XL pipeline for the climate notwithstanding, activists can easily see whether or not they have managed to delay or stop the pipeline. Such clarity of outcomes does not hold for divestment. Divestment resolutions and actions are individual decisions. They may contribute momentum to the divestment campaign, but none of them is large enough to influence the valuation of fossil fuel companies. Therefore, any effects and successes of the divestment campaign must lie elsewhere. A further challenge is the ongoing nature of the campaign. As we saw above, the first divestment decisions were made in December 2011, but before the year 2013 few major institutions in the United States had made a divestment resolution. Since then, divestment resolutions have come in steadily, and the campaign has also become international, but it is clear that the campaign remains at an early stage. If activists fail to secure divestment resolutions at a growing pace, the campaign may not have a notable impact.

With these caveats in mind, we believe this is an opportune time to evaluate the divestment campaign. It is, after all, an ongoing campaign that is still searching for a long-term direction. In this context, analyzing and evaluating its patterns of mobilization is a natural point of departure.

To understand mobilization for divestment, it is important to remember that the targets of divestment are institutions with funds. Since much of the divestment activism has taken place on campuses and in religious congregations, the importance of the institutional environment is difficult to overstate. From discussions with divestment activists, we can infer that many of them were drawn to this form of campaigning because it allowed them to operate in a familiar environment. In this regard, the divestment campaign appears to have successfully exploited the opportunities that tightly knit student communities on campuses present for activism, an observation familiar to scholars of social movements (Zhao, 1998).

College administrations and congregations may not be among the wealthiest institutions on the planet, but any organizations with tens of millions of dollars or more in endowment will certainly have an asset management plan and at least some say over how those funds are managed. If individual students tried to divest their own paltry savings from fossil fuels, they would not draw the attention of financial institutions, whereas compelling a university administration to divest would be enough to secure the cooperation of investment bankers. After all, these bankers make their living by serving their clients, and a client who wants to divest is still a client with money to invest.

Given this targeting, concrete victory is possible locally. At various divestment events at Barnard, Columbia, NYU, the City University of New York, and the New School, student activists have been inspired and motivated by the prospect of changing university policy through their actions. When New School decided to divest in February 2015, other New York City universities and colleges immediately seized the opportunity to rally the troops and engage in a new, vigorous push at their institutions to promote divestment.

Even where calls for divestment fail, activists can turn an institution's refusal to act into momentum. The student divestment campaign on Harvard campus is perhaps the best example. The Harvard administration revealed its readiness to hit back hard by arresting an undergraduate student for blocking an entrance to Massachusetts Hall (Hashimi, 2014, May 1). Since the incident, the Harvard administration has repeatedly stated that it is not interested in divestment, yet the campaign has become increasingly vocal over time. The gap between the administration's position and what a large segment of the students believe it should be motivates current activists to persist and new ones to join.

But what happens to activists who win their divestment fights? For example, if student activists participate in a successful campaign, what can they do next? In our experience, successful divestment activists often become traveling salesmen or preachers for divestment. Their success draws the attention of other activists and results in salaried opportunities as organizers, invitations to advise others, and prominence in the anti-fossil fuel community. For example, many of the organizers of divestment that we met during the weekend of the People's Climate March in September 2014 were successful divestment activists who had become full-time organizers for various organizations that are participating in the national campaign. This possibility of graduation ensures that divestment activism does not implode under its own logic, as local victories create opportunities for wider and more sustained engagement. This is essential for the movement's ability to generate a series of small wins that sustain, not undermine, the activism.

During the weekend of People's Climate March, we saw this dynamic in action. On the day before the march, divestment activists around the country gathered in the offices of the New York Society for Ethical Culture for networking, brainstorming, and socializing. One notable pattern was that most of the professional, salaried divestment activists who had traveled to New York had a background in student organizing. We met the next generation of activists from Vermont, where the divestment campaign is strong because of Bill McKibben's local presence, as well as California, where divestment campaigns have mushroomed on University of California campuses. For example, one of the student activists who participated in the successful campaign to make Pitzer College divest, Jess Grady-Benson, came to the People's Climate March as a young alumni organizer for the Responsible Endowments Coalition. Her path from student activism to national organizing shows how successful divestment campaigns can jumpstart a longer career in climate activism.

5.6 Impact

Having looked at patterns of mobilization, we begin our evaluation of impact by examining the justifications for the goals of the campaign. Have divestment activists set for themselves immediate, concrete goals that are worth pursuing? We believe the divestment campaign has been successful in setting its immediate goals; if anything, the goals of the divestment campaign are more appropriate than the goals of the Keystone XL campaign. While much of the attraction of the Keystone XL came from the existence of a single concrete target, the divestment campaign sets a series of small goals, institutional decisions to remove investments from the fossil fuel industry. While we have seen that divestment wins do not directly threaten the profitability of fossil fuel companies, every such win still contributes to the overall goal of stigmatizing the fossil fuel industry. Every time an institution divests, the fossil fuel industry will be surrounded by negative publicity of the most credible kind: People are actively betting against the sustainability of the fossil fuel industry.

This positive evaluation may come as a surprise to economists who emphasize the irrelevance of divestment for the operation of the fossil fuel industry. Here, it is important to recall that virtually all divestment activists are aware of these counterarguments. The immediate goal of the divestment campaign has never been to undermine the valuation of any particular companies, or even the valuation of the entire industry. Divestment activists have, instead, focused on the social license of the industry and undertaken efforts to stigmatize the carbon majors. Seen through the lens of the ecological paradigm, this approach is a necessary step toward more ambitious climate policy in the future. According to the Do The Math logic, the fossil fuel industry has already reached an unsustainable position and must begin to scale back its operations. Anyone who believes this premise accepts that the industry's current business model is not legitimate, and the purpose of the divestment campaign is to spread the word. As Rev. Fletcher Harper of GreenFaith, a progressive religious organization dedicated to environmental protection, puts it:

> A final reason religious groups divest is that they view divestment, and the processes and public engagement it involves, as a way to redefine society's moral code. From this perspective, divestment isn't just for religious institutions to maintain their own integrity or to respond to intractable stubbornness. It is to delegitimize and de-normalize divestments target and to demonstrate the repugnance of certain industries or governments. This is a fundamental part of the process of social change. Very few social changes of significance happen without public disgust being attached to the status quo.
> *(Harper, 2013)*

This quote clearly summarizes the importance of stigmatizing the fossil fuel industry as a motor of social change.

Also notable is the campaign's ability to reach its target audience. For divestment activists, the target audience is clearly a progressive community of citizens who make decisions based on ethical and moral considerations. The institutions that express interest in fossil fuel divestment do so, almost without exception, out of moral concern. While both the divestment activists and their allies have become quite fluent in the language of finance and often offer economic arguments, their intrinsic interest in divestment has moral origins. To put it bluntly, people who do not base their financial decisions on some ethical standard of conduct are not interested in fossil fuel divestment. A cursory inspection of divestment campaigns in the United States shows that, although most of them have yet to effect any investment policy change, they have spread widely in colleges, religious communities, and even municipalities. In fact, they seem to have reached a broader audience than the Keystone XL campaign. The combination of ethical considerations and the opportunity to act on one's home turf appears attractive. For example, student activists told us that it would be hard for them to join the Keystone XL campaign without risking their academic success; for these activists, it is more natural to work hard on campus to promote divestment, as the target here is the university administration and the context of debate and action is familiar.

Indeed, the reasons behind the campaign's success in reaching the target audience relate to a clear and inspiring message. Divestment is a clear statement based on firm moral principles. It allows people to act in their own community, in a familiar environment and together with people from the same community. Divestment activists have a local target and can clearly aim for a small win. In this sense, the very same factors that make divestment activists tick are also a major factor behind the dynamism and the success of the campaign. Moreover, the historical reference points provided by campaigns against South Africa's apartheid and other issues clearly reinforce this dynamic and are frequently invoked by both divestment activists and the people listening to them.

To be sure, the target audience of the divestment campaign is itself smaller and more limited than one would infer from the activists' promotional materials. Our review of the publicity surrounding divestment and participation in various divestment events shows that the issue has not become a hot topic for the broader American audience. Divestment draws progressive liberals whose values and ideologies are predisposed to worrying about fossil fuels, climate change, and corporate influence in politics. While divestment activists have done an admirable job in reaching beyond the Keystone XL activist community, they have not made their voices heard among conservatives or people sitting on the fence. Divestment ultimately relies on tactics that mobilize one part of the progressive base for climate action.

But has the divestment campaign achieved its immediate goals? Based on the data we have reviewed, we believe the answer to be a cautious "yes." Over time, the divestment campaign has managed to create a steady stream of divestment decisions, including some major ones, such as the Rockefeller or Stanford divestments. This stream of divestment decisions has allowed the divestment campaign to maintain its momentum, raise difficult ethical and financial questions about the fossil fuel industry, and draw public attention to the need to find alternatives to fossil fuel extraction.

The reason we qualify our positive answer with some caution lies with the lack of a genuine snowball effect. Although the divestment campaign has managed to trigger several divestment decisions, there is not yet evidence of exponential growth. The divestment decisions continue to be made on a regular basis and the numbers are impressive, but the divestment campaign has not broken the bank. At this rate of diffusion, individual divestment decisions will only achieve the critical mass required for policy influence over a very long period of time. In light of the common activist argument that climate change requires urgent action, this slow motion is troubling for divestment activists.

Besides the inherent challenges of convincing financiers to divest from fossil fuels, one reason the divestment campaign has not spread like wildfire is the challenge of moving from small to large players. So far, colleges and smaller religious communities have led the divestment wave. Another key target of the campaign, municipal funds, have reacted much less aggressively. Even those municipalities that have made divestment resolutions have faced difficulties in the actual implementation. This reflects the complexity of designing financial arrangements for municipalities, the endowments of which are generally much larger than those of universities.

Any decision to divest by a municipality is the outcome of a complex political process featuring interest groups, investment bankers, municipal politicians, city officials, and the people living in the city. These kinds of difficulties mean that the effort and energy required to carry out divestment by a municipality are much greater than those required for a college, university, or small congregation. Unless divestment activists find practical solutions to overcoming these barriers, divestment may remain the domain of a select group of highly specialized institutions – as opposed to a moral and ethical campaign that large players can join.

In this regard, it is certainly encouraging that divestment activists have begun to offer concrete advice to municipalities about how to divest. In an October 2014 report, Alex Lenferna, writing on behalf of 350Seattle and Divest University of Washington, recommends a three-stage strategy to the Seattle City Employee's Retirement System: determine the carbon risk of the pensions portfolio, commit to divestment and clearly specify the extent of the commitment, and then create a divestment plan and instruct financial advisors and portfolio managers to implement it within a specific time frame (Lenferna, 2014: 2). We believe this is exactly the kind of concrete advice that can help the divestment movement attract the attention of larger institutional investors.

Having evaluated the achievement of immediate goals, we must next consider their relevance to the ultimate goal of climate mitigation. Because divestment does not directly affect the demand for fossil fuels or the profitability of their operations, we must look for indirect mechanisms of change. As we saw above, divestment events and actions have been frequently covered in the media and drawn a lot of attention. They have successfully depicted the fossil fuel industry as one that relies on hypocrisy for profits: the divestment activists have shown that, barring major advances in technologies such as carbon capture and storage, aggressive climate mitigation measures are inconsistent with the business plans, strategies, and projects of the fossil fuel industry. By depicting the fossil fuel industry as one that relies on hypocrisy, the activists have succeeded in forcing the fossil fuel industry to admit that their profitability depends on delaying, or perhaps altogether forgoing, climate action.

Consider the 2013 strategic report of the oil company Shell (2013). In the report, the company warns that "[r]ising climate change concerns could lead to additional regulatory measures that may result in project delays and higher costs" (Shell, 2013: 8). When the company launched the report, 350.org issued a press release with the following comment by Tim Ratcliffe, the group's European Divestment Coordinator:

> Shell's most recent announcement should serve as a stark warning for investors to pull their funds out of fossil fuels. Especially public institutions like universities, municipalities, religious institutions and pension funds have a

fiduciary duty to exercise responsible stewardship of the public funds they are entrusted with. First of all, it is inherently wrong to support an industry whose business model is based on wrecking our future. Secondly, fossil fuel companies are currently grossly overvalued. Eighty percent of their oil, coal and gas reserves need to stay underground to limit global warming below 2°C, which will turn them into stranded assets. This makes these investments a highly risky gamble.

(Henn, 2014, March 14)

The divestment campaign draws attention to this argument, allowing it to reach a broader audience than do individual press releases.

Furthermore, the divestment campaign has also appeared in statements of prominent politicians. Of these, the most important is undoubtedly President Obama. Already in June 2013, the early days of the divestment campaign, President Obama gave a public speech at Georgetown University and discussed his plan to deal with climate change through executive action. In his speech, he urged the students to become climate activists in the following words:

Convince those in power to reduce our carbon pollution. Push your own communities to adopt smarter practices. Invest. Divest. Remind folks there's no contradiction between a sound environment and strong economic growth. And remind everyone who represents you at every level of government that sheltering future generations against the ravages of climate change is a prerequisite for your vote. Make yourself heard on this issue.

(Randall, 2013, June 25)

While one word on divestment may not be much in terms of concrete action, it shows that President Obama was aware of the divestment campaign and considered it worth mentioning to a student audience – the kind of people who could become climate activists.

Besides stigmatization and change in the public discourse, divestment activists have arguably brought to the limelight the idea of fossil fuels as stranded assets. Before the campaign, progressive financial analysts, such as Carbon Tracker, had already begun to sound the alarm about the dependence of fossil fuel profits on high energy prices. However, it was the divestment campaign that brought this argument into mainstream climate debates. In their efforts to encourage institutions to divest, the activists showed that fossil fuels carry hidden risks that could compromise endowments, pensions, and savings in the future. More worryingly, the hidden risks are related to climate policy: institutions that support climate policy should not invest in fossil fuel companies unless they believe climate change mitigation to be truly hopeless. And now that oil prices have crashed since the end of 2014, sounding the alarm about stranded assets has proven to be prescient.

The challenge for divestment activists is, similar to Keystone XL, to connect the nascent removal of the social license of the fossil fuel industry to actual policy change. Even if divestment activists succeed in framing the fossil fuel industry as unworthy of investment, this does not automatically result in improved climate policy. The moral outrage directed at the industry must become wide and deep enough to actually influence politics. In the context of American democracy, this means that the public must begin to punish politicians for allying with the fossil fuel industry. As far as we can see, this kind of transformative change has yet to occur, and so divestment activists still have a lot of hard thinking to do to use their achievements to bring about real policy change.

And yet, the divestment campaign's emphasis on local victories and knack for broadcasting them to their target audience do not mean that divestment activists are unaware of the need for legislation in the future. They understand that divestment does not itself stop the extraction of fossil fuels, even if more and more investors begin to worry about stranded assets. For divestment activists, their campaign is an important tool in a portfolio of strategies adopted by the larger American climate movement.

One of the most interesting things we learned during our examination of the campaign was that divestment activists have increasingly begun to emphasize the reinvestment aspect of their campaign. In the spring of 2014 and toward the People's Climate March, more local groups working on divestment began to emphasize reinvestment. While the divestment campaign had initially placed little emphasis on what to do with the released funds, divestment activists began to see the necessity of offering a positive vision to their target audience. Although reinvestment itself is a complicated and perhaps even ambiguous concept, activists have turned it into a positive message that allows various institutions to explore proactive measures to channel their funds into positive investments.

For example, a church that divests from fossil fuels could choose to use some of the money to invest in energy efficiency measures that pay themselves back over time; alternatively, they could invest in funds that specifically invest money in companies and projects that use renewables to mitigate energy poverty in the developing world. Besides the benefit of empowering divestment activists themselves with a positive message, the reinvestment approach has also allowed divestment activists to overcome the challenge of offering a constructive alternative to fossil fuel development.

To summarize, the divestment campaign is in many ways a strategically savvy move beyond the simple and practical logic underlying the Keystone XL campaign. By focusing on moral principles and social justice, the divestment campaign has mobilized a new group of activists and reached an expanded target audience. For the future, the increased activities of the progressive financial community and the religious community are particularly important achievements. In this sense, we also believe that there is a natural synergy between Keystone XL and divestment. The campaign on Keystone XL mobilizes enthusiastic activists who yearn for action and are willing to be arrested, whereas divestment inspires people who have dedicated their lives to following moral principles. Without the other, each could be less impressive in its own right.

Notes

1 See full statement available at the Harvard website: www.harvard.edu/president/fossil-fuels (accessed February 13, 2015).
2 See the official account available at www.unity.edu/about-unity/sustainability-science/fossil-fuel-divestment (accessed May 28, 2017).
3 See the official documentation available at http://unfccc.int/resource/docs/2009/cop15/eng/11a01.pdf (accessed December 12, 2014).
4 See the official list of commitments available at http://gofossilfree.org/commitments/ (accessed February 13, 2015).
5 See the official list of divestment efforts available at www.greenfaith.org/programs/divest-and-reinvest/listing-of-known-religious-divestment-efforts (accessed February 13, 2015).
6 The GreenFaith database offers seven categories: (1) Divest own fund(s); (2) Recommend resolution for national judicatory; (3) Passed resolution for local judicatory, congregations, or specific funds; (4) Under consideration; (5) Reinvestment alone; (6) No action/resolution failed to pass; and (7) Pension fund takes divestment or reinvestment action. We exclude (4) and (6), defining divestment action as the remaining categories.
7 For an example, see the guides for investors available at www.ussif.org/climatereinvestment (accessed February 13, 2015).
8 See the official announcement available at: www.utsnyc.edu/divestment (accessed February 24, 2015).
9 See the official statement by 350.org available at: http://350.org/union-theological-seminary-in-nyc-divests/ (accessed February 24, 2015).
10 We thank Steve Knight, for providing these documents at one of the interfaith meetings held in Union Theological Seminary. Knight participates in the divestment campaign through GreenFaith, and is an active member of an Episcopal congregation on the Upper East Side of New York City, where his roles have included board member, Christian education director, and co-founder of a peace & restorative justice community.
11 See the official petition available at: http://campaigns.gofossilfree.org/petitions/divest-new-york-city-from-fossil-fuels (accessed February 24, 2015).
12 See the official position of 350NYC available at: https://350nyc.files.wordpress.com/2013/08/fossilfreenycintroduction.pdf (accessed February 24, 2015).
13 See the official 350Vermont assessment available at http://350vermont.org/current-campaigns/divestment/ (accessed February 24, 2015).
14 See the official 350Colorado website available at http://350colorado.org/about/ (accessed February 24, 2015).
15 See the official petition available at http://campaigns.gofossilfree.org/petitions/divest colorado-state-from-fossil-fuels (accessed February 24, 2015).
16 See the Divest Harvard blog entry available at http://divestharvard.com/15-people gather-for-divest-harvard-petition-delivery/ (accessed February 24, 2015).
17 See the official statement by the university president available at www.harvard.edu/president/fossil-fuels (accessed February 24, 2015).
18 See the official statement available at http://news.stanford.edu/news/2014/may/divest coal-trustees-050714.html (accessed February 24, 2015).
19 See the official press release available at http://news.columbia.edu/coal (accessed April 29, 2017).
20 See the official press release available at www.fossilfreestanford.org/press-release-november-11–2015.html (accessed January 29, 2016).
21 See the official press release available at www.fossilfreestanford.org/press-release-november-19–2015.html (accessed January 29, 2016).
22 See http://gofossilfree.org/september-3rd-web-workshop-divestment-as-a-solidarity-tactic/ (accessed February 15, 2015).

6

THE CAMPAIGN AGAINST COAL IN THE UNITED STATES

The campaign against coal precedes all other fossil fuels campaigns chronicled in this book. While pockets of local protests against surface mining precede the more climate-oriented anti-coal campaign, we should be careful not to overemphasize continuity. Indeed, during the oil crisis of the 1970s, there was widespread acceptance of coal as a viable alternative to foreign oil. Only recently, as national concerns about climate change gained steam, the campaign against coal has become a highly successful anti-fossil fuel campaign.

Given the significance of King Coal in climate politics and the long and varied history of opposition to it, we dedicate this chapter to the campaign against the production and use of coal. The returning cast include James Hansen and Bill McKibben, though the anti-coal campaign precedes the founding of 350.org. The Sierra Club and the Rainforest Action Network are at the forefront of the campaign, mobilizing grassroots activists to impose financial and social costs on the coal industry, as well as opposing, quite successfully, the building and operation of hundreds of coal plants all over the country.

The anti-coal campaign shows what activists can achieve under an ideal set of conditions for mobilization. It combines the defining strengths of campaigns against fossil fuels – targeting the root cause, going after a clear enemy – with exceptional potential for hybrid activism and meaningful small wins. From Appalachia to Montana, local activists have forged effective alliances with national organizers to challenge coal mines and power plants. Impact has been significant under the Obama administration, though President Trump seeks to steer the country back toward coal (Egan, 2017, April 25).

President Obama in 2012 enacted a regulation to reduce mercury emissions from power plants, with significant cost implications for the use of coal in the power sector. In 2014, the president again used executive authority under the Clean Air Act to enact the Clean Power Plan, a comprehensive policy to reduce carbon and other pollution from the power sector. Because coal contributes more carbon emissions per kilowatt hour than does any alternative fuel, this clearly represents pressure on electric utilities to reduce the use of coal.

6.1 Significance

The famed NASA climatologist James Hansen once told the governor of Nevada that phasing out coal emissions "is 80 percent of the solution to the global warming crisis."[1] Hansen's research is unequivocal: "Coal is the largest reservoir of conventional fossil fuels, exceeding combined reserves of oil and gas. The only realistic way to sharply curtail CO2 emissions is to phase out coal use except where CO2 is captured and sequestered" (Hansen et al., 2008).

There are good reasons that Hansen and other activists have targeted coal (Nace, 2010: 9). First, the amount of carbon remaining in the ground in oil and gas reserves is much smaller than the amount of carbon contained in coal reserves. Second, coal is also the most carbon intensive of the fossil fuels. Producing a kilowatt hour of electricity from coal produces about 2.4 pounds of carbon dioxide, while producing the same from natural gas produces about 1 pound of carbon dioxide. While coal produces half of the electricity used in the United States, it is responsible for 80 percent of the carbon dioxide released by electric utilities (Nace, 2010: 9).

Third, coal consumption is far more concentrated than the use of other fossil fuels. Instead of the tens of millions of cars, trucks, planes, homes, businesses, and factories that burn oil and gas, coal activists can concentrate their (f)ire on several hundred stationary plants. Fourth, production of oil and gas is scattered throughout the world, while the United States represents the world leader in the size of its coal reserves.

Thus, coal represents a critical front in the fight against fossil fuels, and all the better for the mostly American activists that it also happens to be the home front (Nace, 2010: 9). Hansen's ultimatum is unequivocal: "Present policies, with continued construction of coal-fired power plants without CO2 capture, suggest that decision-makers do not appreciate the gravity of the situation. We must begin to move now toward the era beyond fossil fuels. Continued growth of greenhouse gas emissions, for just another decade, practically eliminates the possibility of near-term return of atmospheric composition beneath the tipping level for catastrophic effects" (Hansen et al., 2008: 17).

6.2 Overview

In 1965, Ollie Combs, a 61-year-old widow, sat in front of a bulldozer with her two sons to stop their Kentucky land from being mined by Caperton Coal. A photograph of her eating Thanksgiving dinner behind bars went viral, marking the birth of Appalachian Group to Save the Land and People. The organization staged several acts of civil disobedience, such as a much-publicized strip mine occupation by 20 women in Knott County, Kentucky, in 1972 (Nace, 2010: 74). Kentucky also saw violent protests against coal, such as the dynamiting of diesel-powered shovels in April 1967 and, in the months following, the exchange of gunfire between snipers and workers; the use of carbon nitrate to destroy trucks, auger, and bulldozer; and the establishment of shooting ranges to discourage miners (Nace, 2010: 75).

Surface mining of coal, which involves removing the soil and rock overlying the mineral deposit, often leads to significant disruptions in traditional land uses and environmental damage on a large scale. Several years of activism by affected citizens in Appalachia and elsewhere to control the ravages of strip mining led to the passage of the Surface Mining Control and Reclamation Act of 1977 (SMCRA), a legislative initiative to bring the environmental impact of surface mining under federal control.[2] Before SMCRA, the regulation of surface mining and reclamation practices had been the diffuse responsibility of state governments, often undermining enforcement and uniformity in standards. Federal regulation would allow coal mine operators to pass on the costs of environmental protection to consumers of coal without the fear of losing their market share to rivals in states with less strict standards (Edgmon and Menze, 1981: 245).

To be sure, SMCRA did not resolve all problems. It does not control impacts of the surface effects of longwall mining except at the mouth of the mine. Coal mining companies do not reclaim water resources because the Office of Surface Mining Reclamation and Enforcement, the administering agency, has inadequately enforced the law. Most important, the act did not anticipate the expansion of mountaintop removal.[3]

Despite pockets of discontent, coal itself had not yet attained the notoriety it has today. During the oil crisis of the 1970s, coal was often considered a "good" fuel, an alternative energy source not subject to the kind of volatility that characterizes oil. In a survey administered across multiple years asking which, among a list of energy sources, "do you think are realistically possible to use for replacing foreign oil during the next five years?" respondents selected coal most frequently in 1977, and its reign at the top – followed by solar – continued through 1979, 1981, and 1982 (Farhar, 1994: 610, 627). These trends – robust support for coal as a realistic alternative through the 1970s and early 1980s – were consistent with the politics of energy security at the time. Faced with an oil crisis, President Jimmy Carter made the following announcement in 1979:[4]

> To give us energy security, I am asking for the most massive peacetime commitment of funds and resources in our Nation's history to develop America's own alternative sources of fuel – from coal, from oil shale, from plant products for gasohol, from unconventional gas, from the Sun. I propose the creation of an energy security corporation to lead this effort to replace 2 1/2 million barrels of imported oil per day by 1990. The corporation will issue up to $5 billion in energy bonds, and I especially want them to be in small denominations so that average Americans can invest directly in America's energy security. Just as a similar synthetic rubber corporation helped us win

World War II, so will we mobilize American determination and ability to win the energy war.

(Carter, 1979, July 15)

In this sense, coal was viewed as a crucial alternative to sustain America through its period of energy crisis both by the American public and the president himself.

Coal's popularity only began to fall amid growing national concerns about global warming in the 1980s, when the oil crisis was firmly in the rearview mirror. The multi-year survey of "realistic alternatives" to oil, for instance, suggests that it was in March 1983 that solar began to outstrip coal as a realistic alternative, though coal maintained a comfortable second place through 1983, 1984, and 1985. It was only in 1987 that coal saw a significant drop-off, as the percentage of respondents who selected coal dropped from a majority to the 30 percent range. By 1989, coal had fallen behind solar, nuclear, and offshore oil (Farhar, 1994: 610, 627).

Leading today's charge against the coal industry are two environmental organizations, the Sierra Club and the Rainforest Action Network (RAN). Tracing its origins to 1892, the Sierra Club is an environmental organization rooted in the tradition of environmental conservation, and it has grown to encompass more than 60 active chapters across the United States. In 2004, the Sierra Club and allied organizations launched a grassroots campaign called "Beyond Coal" to oppose every proposal for a new coal-fired electric plant. They have since prevented more than 100 coal plants from being built.[5]

Rainforest Action Network, also adopting a grassroots approach, has concentrated its efforts on strategic targets, such as the Environmental Protection Agency (EPA), which has oversight over mountaintop removal, and the major commercial banks, which represent the industry's purse strings.[6] These widely publicized efforts have capitalized on theatrics, such as staging die-ins at the EPA headquarters in DC, occupying treetops at mountaintop removal sites, hanging banners in highly strategic locations, protesting in front of banks, shutting down ATMs, and infiltrating energy conferences.

Other environmental organizations were sometimes out of step with the grassroots base of the campaign. Initially absent on the frontlines were powerhouses such as National Wildlife Federation, Natural Resources Defense Council (NRDC), and Environmental Defense Fund (EDF), as well as Nature Conservancy, Wilderness Society, and the Audubon Society (Nace, 2010: 16). When the NRDC and the EDF signed an agreement with a private equity firm Kohlberg Kravis Roberts & Co. LP (KKR), the future owner of the Texas utility TXU, the grassroots base of the anti-coal movement was skeptical of KKR's promise to drop eight of 11 planned new coal plants in Texas. KKR would not have given up the eight plants, the critics argued, if it had been serious about pursuing them in the first place. Such a compromise would only serve to blunt the momentum for activists, since their campaign had thrived on its crystal clear and uncompromising message (Nace, 2010: 55).

By 2007, the defeat of coal plants in Minnesota and Delaware had breathed new life into the campaign. The US Supreme Court decided in April 2007 to give the EPA both the authority and the responsibility to regulate greenhouse gases (Nace, 2010: 53). The momentum built quickly, as activists swayed one regulator after another to take into account future restrictions on carbon emissions before approving new power plants. Local regulators were put on notice by the opponents of the Big Stone II Power Plant in South Dakota, as well as the opponents of the Glades Power Plant in Florida (Nace, 2010: 54). In May 2007, Progress Energy, with its network of 3.1 million customers, announced a two-year moratorium on new coal plants. Other utilities quietly began to distance themselves from coal (Nace, 2010: 55).

Washington state, like California a year before, signed into law a de facto moratorium on conventional coal plants (Nace, 2010: 54). The September decision of Kansas to block the Sunflower project was another major victory, soon to be followed by derailed projects in Montana, Oklahoma, Kentucky, and Michigan. In North Dakota, Arizona, Washington, and New York, companies were the first to retract their plans to build coal plants in light of mounting concerns about costs, public opposition, and anticipated carbon dioxide regulation. Lending an official voice to a widespread sentiment at the time, Senate Majority Leader Harry Reid publicly spoke out against the building of coal-fired power plants (Nace, 2010: 73).

In 2007, the National Energy Technology Laboratory, a division of the US Department of Energy keeping track of new coal-fired power plants, published a list that included 151 coal-fired power plants either newly built or in various stages of proposal and construction. The list went viral, stoking demands for a coal moratorium.[7] The number had jumped from 92 in 2004 to more than 150, the result of the G. W. Bush administration and its coal subsidies as part of its 2005 Energy Act, estimated to be anywhere from \$4.8 billion to \$9 billion. Under the G. W. Bush administration, Vice President Dick Cheney had convened a secret energy task force, and among its recommendations was that 1,300 to 1,800 new power plants be built in the United States by 2020, with an emphasis on new coal-fired plants (Nace, 2010: 20).

In February 2007, James Hansen told the National Press Club in Washington, DC, that the opportunity to avoid a runaway global warming – whereby human actions trigger enough amplifying feedback loops to ultimately produce "a different planet" – was fast slipping and called for an immediate moratorium on any new coal-fired power plants unless they are capable of carbon capture (Nace, 2008, January). Hansen broke down the rationale for such a moratorium as follows. First, one-quarter of fossil fuel CO_2 emissions remains in the air for more than 500 years. Second, though conventional oil and gas reserves are sufficient to take atmospheric CO_2 at least close to the "dangerous" level, it is not practical to capture their CO_2 emissions, as it is mostly from small, dispersed sources, such as vehicles. Third, coal reserves are far greater in supply than oil and gas reserves, and most coal use is at power plants, where it is feasible to capture and permanently sequester the CO_2 underground. Thus, the only practical way to keep CO_2 below or close to the "dangerous level" is to phase out the "dirty" use of coal during the next few decades.

Hansen acknowledged the global nature of the problem, stating that a surge in global coal use in the last few years has converted a potential slowdown of CO_2 emissions into a more rapid increase. However, he argued that the moratorium must begin in the West, which is responsible for three-quarters of climate change – 75 percent of the present atmospheric CO_2 excess, above the pre-industrial level (Romm, 2007, July 6). The moratorium must extend to developing countries within a decade, which can only happen if developed countries take the lead. If Britain should initiate this moratorium, for instance, Germany, Europe, and the United States could follow, soon to be joined by developing countries. As Hansen wrote: "A spreading moratorium on construction of dirty (no CCS) coal plants is the *sine quo non* for stabilizing climate and preserving creation" (Romm, 2007, July 6).

Responding to Hansen's call, Bill McKibben also launched his Step It Up! campaign in 2007, the predecessor to his highly successful organization 350.org, and one of its key goals was a moratorium on coal (Nace, 2010: 100). The Step It Up! campaign contributed to and eventually celebrated Representative Henry Waxman's (D, California) announcement of a coal moratorium in November 2007.[8]

The timeline of the moratorium campaign is summarized by Figure 6.1, which traces the recent and planned retirements and conversions – often to natural gas – of

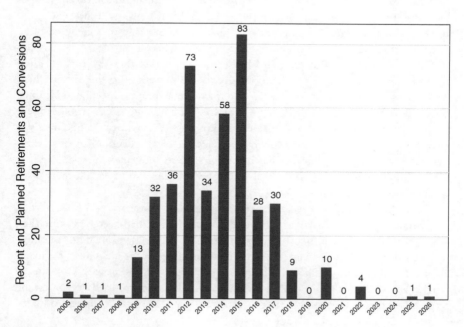

FIGURE 6.1 Recent and planned retirements of coal plants.

Source: SourceWatch

existing coal plants as recorded by SourceWatch. The figure interestingly follows a bell-shaped curve.

While there is some volatility between the years, it is around 2009 that the retirements gather steam with 13 planned, soon to reach 32 in 2010, 73 in 2012, and peaking at 83 in 2015. The number begins to diminish thereafter, dropping to 28 in 2016 and 9 in 2018. The timing, of course, overlaps with that of the shale revolution. America's domestic production of oil and gas began to accelerate around 2009, as methods of extracting "tight" oil and gas from shale rock and other "unconventional" sources revolutionized energy production (Howard, 2014, July 11). It was also in 2012, the same year 73 plants were up for retirement or conversion, that President Obama proudly declared in his State of the Union address: "We have a supply of natural gas that can last America nearly 100 years" (Inman, 2014).

While the timing was certainly fortuitous given the arrival of fracking, the success of the coal campaign was ultimately a bottom-up process. Anti-coal organizations and their allies had staged countless direct action protests across the nation, particularly in the years 2004–2007.[9] As mentioned above, the Sierra Club launched the "Beyond Coal" campaign in 2004, with the initial aim of opposing every proposal for a new coal-fired electric plant. What is not evident in Figure 6.1, therefore, is that as of July 2010, the Sierra Club campaign had already kept 132 proposed plants from being built, with others in limbo, imposing what Lester Brown, a prominent environmentalist, called "a de facto moratorium on new coal-fired power plants" (Hertsgaard, 2012, April 2). It was only later that the campaign took on the goal of closing existing coal-fired plants. By the end of 2013, 158 plants, 20 percent of the total coal-powered generating capacity in the United States, were scheduled to be closed, and no new plants had come online for three years.[10]

The Beyond Coal campaign also had some help along the way. In 2011, former New York mayor Michael Bloomberg gave $50 million to the Sierra Club's Beyond Coal initiative. In April 2015, the former mayor announced an additional $30 million to reduce US reliance on coal. In a ringing endorsement, Bloomberg wrote: "Imagine hearing about a health breakthrough that will save 5,500 lives this year. An innovative new drug? An advanced new medical procedure? A new miracle diet? No. The breakthrough has been a grassroots movement to clean up the air we breathe by closing down coal-fired power plants and replacing them with cleaner energy" (Bloomberg, 2015, April 8).

To be sure, donations have also been a cause for controversy, as *TIME* learned that between 2007 and 2010, the Beyond Coal campaign had accepted more than $25 million from the gas industry, mostly from Aubrey McClendon, CEO of Chesapeake Energy, one of the biggest gas drilling companies in the US and a firm heavily involved in fracking. Though the group ended its relationship with Chesapeake Energy in 2010, turning away an additional $30 million in promised donations, the revelation called into question Sierra Club's independence and its support of natural gas in the past (Walsh, 2012, February 2).

Rainforest Action Network made a splash on April 1, 2008, blockading Citibank's Upper West Side headquarters in New York City. Two members chained themselves to the door, while others drew attention to Citibank's funding of new coal power plant development and mountaintop removal mining.[11] Their activism continued through the National Day of Action Against Coal Finance protests against coal mining, power plants, and financiers through November 14–15, 2008. Activists placed anti-coal banners in strategic locations across the country, protested at Bank of America and Citibank branches, shut down ATMs with crime scene tape, and infiltrated Bank of America's Energy Conference.

On October 30, 2009, RAN activists protested against mountaintop removal at EPA offices in DC and throughout the United States, including Atlanta, Boston, Dallas, Kansas City, and San Francisco. They called for immediate action to stop mountaintop removal coal mining, particularly targeting the Massey Energy blasting site at West Virginia's Coal River Mountain. Similar protests against mountaintop removal at EPA headquarters took place in March 2010. In April, RAN staged a die-in at a downtown Chicago JPMorgan Chase bank to protest its investment in mountaintop removal. It was RAN's first such direct action campaign to pressure the company to abandon its investments.

In July 2010, RAN again staged a sit-in at the EPA headquarters in DC, demanding an end to mountaintop removal coal mining, citing in particular the Pine Creek permit authorized a week prior for a project in West Virginia. That same month, RAN also disrupted Massey CEO Don Blankenship's talk at the National Press Club in DC, holding signs that stated, "Massey Coal: Not Clean, Safe or Forever." The protest focused on Massey's mountaintop removal strip mines and their ongoing safety violations, which led to the death of 29 miners in the Upper Big Branch Mine Disaster in West Virginia. In September, RAN dumped 1,000 pounds of Appalachian dirt on the sidewalk of EPA headquarters in Washington, DC. RAN's message was "EPA: Don't Let King Coal Dump On Appalachia."

The EPA, to be sure, attempted to tighten regulations on coal mining.[12] In March 2009, the EPA under the Obama administration moved to stall the issuance of mountaintop removal permits in West Virginia and Kentucky from the US Army Corps of Engineers. In April, the EPA objected to three additional permits – two in West Virginia and one in Virginia – pending approval from the Army Corps of Engineers, citing concerns about burying eight miles of streams. In May, the Army Corps suspended its approval of A&G Coal Corp.'s Ison Rock Ridge Surface Mine in Wise County, Virginia, following a lawsuit filed by the Sierra Club and Southern Appalachian Mountain Stewards to block the permit. A more comprehensive effort, albeit short of a complete ban, came in June 2009, when the Obama administration vowed to toughen standards on mountaintop removal. Officials from the EPA, the Army Corps of Engineers, the Interior Department, and the White House Council on Environmental Quality promised a more rigorous environmental and legal review of pending and future permit applications for mountaintop removal projects.

In August, US District Judge Henry H. Kennedy Jr. overturned an effort by Obama's Interior Secretary Ken Salazar to repeal a G. W. Bush regulation that made it easier for coal mining companies to dump debris into valley streams (Pear and Barringer, 2008, December 2). Undeterred, the EPA issued a letter to the Army Corps of Engineers identifying problems with a permit issued for a strip mining project in Logan County, West Virginia, the largest permit issued in the state. The EPA specifically cited the Clean Water Act, voicing concerns about degradation of downstream water quality. In September, the EPA identified 79 mountaintop removal permits issued by the Army Corps of Engineers in Kentucky, Ohio, Tennessee, and West Virginia that would likely affect water quality. The agency then put the permits on hold for further study.

In October, in an unprecedented move since the Clean Water Act of 1972, the EPA announced its plans to unilaterally revoke the permit for Mingo Logan Coal's Spruce No. 1 mine owned by Arch Coal, the largest authorized mountaintop-removal operation in Appalachia. In March 2010, the EPA officially announced the veto. In April, the EPA administrator Lisa Jackson laid out new mountaintop removal guidelines, which may halt its practice in Appalachia and wherever valleys are filled with mining debris. Jackson stated that valley fills likely violate Clean Water Act requirements in most cases. Jackson remarked that the new guidelines were not meant to end coal mining, but the gradual tightening of regulations would change mining practices for the betterment of water quality. In June 2010, the Army Corps of Engineers suspended the expedited process for obtaining surface mining permits across much of the nation's eastern coalfields.

The EPA would face significant backlash. In July 2010, the National Mining Association sued the EPA and the Army Corps to slow down efforts to regulate mountaintop removal. The suit concerned the EPA's more detailed review of mining permit applications for valley fills, and a new set of recommended water quality guidelines for surface coal mining in Appalachia. In October, West Virginia set out to sue the EPA over mountaintop removal coal mine permits.

"In 2009, the U.S. Environmental Protection Agency began interfering with the surface coal mine permitting process in West Virginia," said Governor Joe Manchin in a statement. The governor argued that certain federal government entities including the EPA, the US Army Corps of Engineers, and the Department of the Interior delayed the issuance of 23 pending coal mining permits in West Virginia, with only two being approved since 2009.

In October 2011, US District Judge Reggie B. Walton ruled that the EPA had overstepped its authority when it began a more intense review of individual Clean Water Act permits normally handled by the US Army Corps of Engineers. In January 2012, Walton dismissed the EPA's plans to work with other agencies to more closely scrutinize certain mining-related water pollution permits for valley fill waste piles. In March, US District Judge Amy Berman Jackson overturned the EPA's veto of Spruce No. 1 Mine, the largest mountaintop removal permit in West Virginia history. In July 2012, Judge Walton ruled that the EPA had overstepped its authority under federal water protection and strip mining laws when it issued the water quality guidance and that the EPA administrator Lisa Jackson had "infringed on the authority" of state regulators to govern their own pollution permit and water quality standard programs.

Though the EPA's efforts to regulate coal mining were repeatedly frustrated by lawsuits and questions of overstepping boundaries, they demonstrate the extent to which environmental concerns surrounding coal had found support among policymakers and bureaucrats at the highest level of government. A more comprehensive assessment of the anti-coal campaign would require a detailed examination of tactics.

6.3 Activism in motion

Figure 6.2 displays the numerical distribution of defeated coal plants across the United States using data obtained from the Sierra Club. Figure 6.3 maps the geographical distribution based on the same data.

While how much each plant would have contributed to carbon emissions is not evident from either graph, they illustrate the rationale behind our choice of cases to examine activist tactics. First, in Figure 6.3, there is a cluster of darker blue states in the Appalachian region, namely Pennsylvania, West Virginia, Ohio, and Kentucky. The region represents a core constituency for the anti-coal movement with a strong local following. Thus, our first case study will cover the Appalachian region and its local campaigns.

Second, among the states with defeated plants, while Montana and Wyoming do not quite match the level of Texas or Illinois, they are the battlegrounds on which

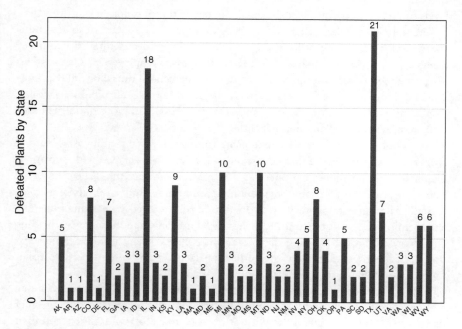

FIGURE 6.2 Defeated coal plants by state.

Source: Sierra Club

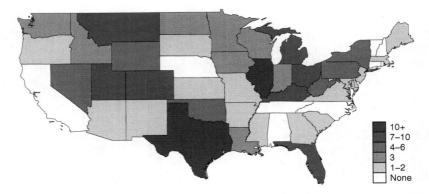

FIGURE 6.3 Map of defeated coal plants.

Source: Sierra Club

a professional environmental organization, Western Organization of Resource Councils (WORC), is actively engaged in a fierce battle against coal. Thus, our second case will trace the campaign from the perspective of WORC. Third, Illinois and Texas stand out for the sheer number of plants they have seen defeated. How did these two very different states, a southern oil patch Republican heartland and the Midwestern political base of the then-Democratic president, achieve similar levels of success in defeating coal plants? We tackle this question in our third case.

Central Appalachia's widely acknowledged importance to American coal mining, as well as its legacy of local protests, renders it an ideal setting to begin our analysis of activist tactics. In 2008, the coal industry employed 37,000 workers across the region, accounting for 1 percent to 40 percent of the labor force in individual counties. The coal severance tax generates hundreds of millions of dollars in state revenues across the region every year, with tens of millions of dollars being distributed to counties and municipalities (McIlmoil and Hansen, 2009: 1).

To be sure, the costs are also significant. Mountaintop removal involves blasting apart mountains to expose thin coal seams, which are then scraped with enormous draglines. The enormous quantities of excess rock are dumped into valleys, covering hundreds of miles of streams. Surrounding communities suffer the consequences, including flooding, respiratory disorders from coal dust, well water contamination, and technological disasters from breaches or failures in impoundments containing coal waste from coal-cleaning or coal-burning plants. Many residents argue that they are forced to suffer because Central Appalachia is an "energy sacrifice zone" for the rest of the nation (Bell and Braun, 2010: 800).

Given that technological and political developments have done little to lessen the environmental and local grievances, Central Appalachia remains the epicenter of anti-coal conflict. There is "a civil war of sorts over coal, with miners and their families pitted against environmental activists" (Howard, 2012, July 8). The coal industry has been framing mountaintop removal as an economic boon for the region, a powerful source of job security in hard times, whereas activists have been emphasizing its impact on the surrounding environment, such as more than 2,000 miles of streams buried and more than 500 mountains destroyed, as well as increased chances of cancer and birth defects among residents of neighboring communities (Howard, 2012, July 8).

Various grassroots organizations have formed. The Central Appalachian coal-field environmental justice movement began in the early 1990s, started in large part by white working-class women fighting to protect their families from the toxins, flooding, air pollution, and other dangers associated with the increasing impacts of mountaintop removal coal mining and coal processing (Bell and Braun, 2010: 800). These pockets of resistance along the Appalachia have not gone unnoticed by major environmental organizations. The story of Scott Parkin, senior climate campaigner at Rainforest Action Network (RAN), illustrates RAN's deliberate strategy of enlisting local resistance groups in its fight against coal (Eshelman, 2010, April 15).

Since joining RAN in 2006, Parkin has traveled across the Appalachia, meeting with local organizations such as Coal River Mountain Watch, Kentuckians for the Commonwealth, and Appalachian Voices fighting to end mountaintop removal. Parkin said of the experience: "The people who live and work there are some of the more inspiring figures you're going to meet in the environmental justice move-ment. . . . Once you experience the situation there and the way they struggle, you don't want to let go; you want to do everything you can to support these people and work on this campaign" (Eshelman, 2010, April 15). He has been actively working to foster relationships between RAN and local and regional groups – many of them women led or whose rank and file include former unionized underground mine workers – and nonviolent direct-action organizations, such as Climate Ground Zero and Rising Tide North America.

Parkin also leads the Global Finance campaign, which targets banks, such as JPMorgan Chase, that fund mountaintop removal or coal-fired power plants con-struction. RAN's all-of-the-above strategy, touching upon every step from the extraction of coal and electricity production to climate change, ranges from public education, corporate pressure, leadership development of locals, to nonviolent civil disobedience against mining companies and the EPA. Parkin calls it "swarming," for its diversity of tactics and targets. Rejecting a single, silver bullet solution, such as a binding UN climate agreement or a comprehensive climate bill in the Senate, the movement sees the coal industry's broad reach and its central role in energy production as a weakness.

Indispensable to this strategy have been the links between the poor and working-class Appalachians and the mainstream environmentalists, which Parkin, among others, has spent years cultivating. These links have instilled purpose in the main-stream environmental justice movement and brought attention to the coal indus-try's economic impacts. Despite the industry's attempt to frame coal as the crucial engine of the economy, poverty and infant mortality rates in Appalachia are among the highest in the nation, and schools and government offices are often shut down.

Mining increased 22 percent between 1985 and 2005, but the number of mining jobs decreased 55 percent, as surface and mountaintop removal mining became increasingly automated (Plumer, 2013, November 4).

By focusing on the effects of coal on Appalachia, the mainstream environmental justice movement has subtly transformed the debate from esoteric discussions about the fate of the world several decades from now to one highlighting the immediate impact of the coal industry on the environment and community, particularly the poor and the working-class. Other groups in Appalachia are targeting state legislatures and Congress, pushing for passage of an array of environmental protections, including the Clean Water Protection Act in the House and the Appalachia Restoration Act in the Senate, which would strengthen existing water pollution regulations by prohibiting valley fills.

Other grassroots initiatives capitalized on the Obama presidency to push for revisions of outdated laws that are inconsistent with its outlook. This tactic of using Obama's campaign rhetoric to elicit social change was illustrated by WORC, Friends of the Earth, and philanthropist Paul G. Allen, who collectively filed a lawsuit on November 25, 2014 to require the US Department of the Interior's Bureau of Land Management (BLM) to prepare a programmatic environmental impact statement for the federal coal leasing program.

Under the federal coal management program, the BLM had managed 309 existing leases in 10 states across the United States as of 2013 and continually processed applications for new leases and modifications to existing leases. The substance of WORC et al.'s complaint was that there had not been a comprehensive environmental review of the federal coal leasing program since 1979. This represents a violation of National Environmental Policy Act, "our basic national charter for protection of the environment," which ensures informed decision-making by federal agencies, requiring them to study and evaluate the environmental impacts of proposed major federal actions.[13]

This is particularly problematic, critics argue, as scientific evidence since 1979 has established that greenhouse gases produced by coal mining and combustion endanger public health and welfare. "More than 80 percent of federal coal comes from the Powder River Basin in Montana and Wyoming. People living in the Powder River Basin have endured many hardships not predicted in the outdated environmental studies, including lack of access to grazing lands, unrestored groundwater aquifers, toxic emissions from explosions, costly and dangerous railroad traffic in major cities to name a few," said Bob LeResche, vice chair of WORC and rancher from Clearmont, Wyoming. "A full environmental study will enable the BLM to fulfill their duty to promote environmentally responsible management of public lands in light of climate change on behalf of the citizens of the United States" (Colwell, 2014, November 25).

The activists took the matter to the court of public opinion, as well as the court of law. In the *Huffington Post*, Paul Allen cites the US Government Accountability Office in claiming that the BLM has failed to ensure that the coal industry pays fair-market value for coal mined on public lands, subsidizing coal industry profits at taxpayer expense. The coal industry, in direct competition with natural gas, has focused on exports, and Allen thinks "exporting subsidized coal compounds the offense, benefitting coal companies, and foreign polluters – everyone except the American people." Allen's most salient argument is that the "leasing of coal from federal lands undermines President Obama's climate policy goals" (Allen, 2014, November 24).

We finally examine two states from Figure 6.2 with the largest number of defeated plants, Illinois (18) and Texas (21). The large number of defeated plants in these states may suggest the active presence of grassroots campaigns by organizations such as the Sierra Club, as well as the traditional importance of these states to the American coal industry. These states are not only very different from each other – an oil patch Republican state and the political home of the then-Democratic president – but their differences also illustrate quite effectively the current trends in American coal.

Texas represents a major coal state. It ranked third in the nation in coal power production in 2005 and ranks as the highest-emitting state or province in the world for carbon emissions, producing 290 million tons per year. Coal plants produce about 36.5 percent of the electricity generated in Texas, where the average retail cost of electricity is the 14th highest in the US at 10.34 cents per kilowatt hour. Texas also has an estimated 13.7 billion tons of coal reserves. The most significant areas for bituminous coal mining are in the southern and north-central parts of the state, although lignite constitutes approximately 97 percent of near-surface coal resources.[14]

It is no accident that Texas also represents a major battleground state for anti-coal activists. Coal combustion produces mercury and other harmful pollutants, and old plants are especially damaging to the climate and health of the community. Big Brown in Freestone County and two other 1970s-era coal plants in East Texas – Martin Lake in Rusk County and Monticello in Titus County – are prime targets, and the Sierra Club is mounting pressure on their owner, Dallas-based Energy Future Holdings (EFH). EFH, which also happens to own the state's largest power generation company, Luminant, insists that its plants are up to environmental standards (Galbraith, 2013, February 10).

The attack on Texas coal plants has also come from an unlikely source, those concerned about water. Diverse interests, including farmers, environmentalists, and others concerned with the availability of the drinking supply, have cobbled together an alliance against proposed coal plants across the state, from Abilene to Corpus Christi. Their shared concern is that plants will use up too much water, which is already under strain. With the state's population expected to double by 2060, there will be more neighborhoods, businesses, lights, and air conditioners. Meanwhile, the water supply is projected to decrease by 18 percent because of aquifer depletion and sediment accumulation in reservoirs.

Thermoelectric power plants using heat to generate power – such as nuclear, coal, and natural gas – are the single largest user of water in the United States. A recent University of Texas at Austin study found that in Texas alone, the plants consume 157 billion gallons annually, enough water for more than 3 million people, each using 140 gallons per day. Burning coal produces heat that turns water into steam, which spins turbines that produce electricity. Even more water is used in the cooling process at some power plants, in which steam is condensed back into water for reuse. There is a less water-intensive alternative, called dry cooling, that uses fans and heat exchangers like a car's radiator, but the first proposed such coal plant, Tenaska Trailblazer Energy Center, had asked nearby Abilene for up to 2 million gallons of treated wastewater each day.

The activists are catching on. "Water is where they are most vulnerable," said a representative of Public Citizen's anti-coal campaign in Texas. In case of a water embargo from water agencies, "we don't know where else they can get it" (Tresaugue, 2010, October 25). The hope is that if their carbon emissions were insufficient to mobilize opposition against coal plants, then water just might do the trick. "We felt we could influence people by talking more about water than pollution," the organizer of Abilenians Against Tenaska said of West Texas (Tresaugue, 2010, October 25). "This is a conservative area, and there are not a lot of people who believe in global warming or worry about air pollution," he said. "But they feel strongly about water."

People who rely on the Colorado River for water are rallying against the potential sale of as much as 7 billion gallons a year of water to the White Stallion Energy Center, a proposed coal-fired plant in Matagorda County, about 90 miles southwest of Houston. The White Stallion plant would require about the same amount of water as Cedar Park, an Austin suburb with a population of 65,000. Rice farmers are now the largest users in the basin. But their supply is interruptible during a period of drought, unlike the amount for cities and industry, and they are fearful that there won't be enough for them in dry times if the power plant is built. Environmentalists are also concerned that there will not be enough water to protect the estuaries that lie at the river's mouth. The region provides a critical habitat for wintering birds and nurseries for fish and shrimp (Tresaugue, 2010, October 25).

Thus, the anti-coal movement received a major boost when it was announced that the White Stallion coal plant had suspended development, in light of mounting litigation costs and potential federal environmental regulations. The White Stallion would have violated the Obama administration's new federal limits on emissions of mercury and toxic pollutants, and the plant needed the court to block or scale back the mercury rules so the plant could be built before April 2013. Building it before then would mean it avoids the EPA's first-ever limits on power plant emissions of carbon dioxide and greenhouse gases. As the role of coal in Texas continued to diminish – coal's share of power generation fell from 49 percent in 2007 to 42 percent in 2011 – the anti-coal activists had been aided by the presence of a willing Obama administration, as well as the growing competitiveness of natural gas (Bastasch, 2013, February 18).

We now turn to Illinois. According to SourceWatch, total Illinois coal output was 47.2 million tons in 2012, up from 37.8 million tons in 2011, making Illinois the fifth largest coal-producing state in the US. In 2004, Illinois had been ninth nationally in coal production, with more than 31 million short tons of coal produced. There are 37,000 square miles of coal deposits in Illinois, about two-thirds of the entire state. Recoverable coal reserves are estimated to total 30 billion tons, accounting for almost one-eighth of the nation's total coal reserves and one-quarter of bituminous coal reserves. In comparison to western coal, Illinois coal is high in sulfur, and even when cleaned the sulfur content averages 2 to 3 percent by weight.

The state consumed more than 54 million short tons of coal for electricity in 2004, making up roughly 48 percent of the electricity generated in Illinois. The state's average retail price of electricity is 7.07 cents per kilowatt hour, the 20th lowest rate in the nation. In 2003, Illinois emitted 230 million metric tons of carbon dioxide, seventh in the nation. A 2011 report by Adrian Wilson (the University of Massachusetts at Amherst), NAACP, Little Village Environmental Justice Organization (LVEJO), and the Indigenous Environmental Network found 90 coal-fired plants to have a disproportionate impact on people of color and low-income, with 4.7 million people living within three miles of the 90 plants, with an average per capita income of $17,600 (25 percent lower than state average), and more than half (52.5 percent) people of color. The highest was Illinois, with 12 highly polluting plants in populous areas with low-income families and people of color.[15]

The coal industry seems to have found a safe haven of sorts in the Midwest. In 2010, Peabody Energy Corporation opened a new coal mine in Sullivan County, Indiana, called Bear Run, which is the largest surface mine in the eastern United States and a symbol of revival for one of America's historical coal fields. Interestingly, this trend is the byproduct of more stringent regulations on pollution. Midwestern fields and the Illinois Basin are attracting coal investors from traditional heartlands, such as Appalachia, partly based on more efficient anti-pollution technology at coal-fired power plants. As a Johnson Rice coal industry analyst told the *Chicago Tribune*, "It's probably the fastest growing region because now utilities have scrubbers, they can burn that nasty coal" (James, 2012, May 11).

Scrubbers using limestone or lime can remove as much as 97 percent of sulfur dioxide (SO2) emissions. Most utilities have now installed scrubbers following the 2005 Clean Air Interstate Rule that required further reduction in SO2 emissions in the eastern United States. Coal industry actors are responding to these changed dynamics. Foresight Energy and producers like Peabody and Alliance Coal are some of the companies counting on an Illinois Basin boom. In the central and northern Appalachian region of West Virginia, Virginia, eastern Kentucky, and Pennsylvania, on the other hand, mines are depleted or increasingly difficult and expensive to work with. Illinois Basin coal is cheaper to mine, as coal seams are closer to the surface and are well-positioned to be shipped overseas via Gulf ports (James, 2012, May 11).

One symbol of the coal industry is the Prairie State Energy Campus, located in the farm fields and woods of southwestern Illinois. Commissioned in 2012, Prairie State represents the largest coal-fired power plant built in the United States in the last 30 years. What stands out about Prairie State is that it sits next to its own coal mine. The company projects enough coal to run the plant for 30 years, providing electricity for 2.5 million households. Peabody Energy, the world's largest private coal company, financed the plant, creating a customer for its own Illinois coal. Peabody later sold 95 percent of the project to eight Midwestern public power agencies (Schoof, 2012, March 1).

The Prairie State plant, however, has not gone unchallenged. It has come under the scrutiny of the US Securities and Exchange Commission (SEC), as cost overruns from construction delays and equipment problems resulted in higher-than-market electricity prices for consumers in several states. The coal industry lobby has gone to work, as the American Legislative Exchange Council (ALEC) sought to block federal pollution regulations by proposing a bill of their own. The "Intrastate Coal and Use Act," created within ALEC's Energy, Environment, and Agriculture task force, would exempt the EPA from overseeing permits for projects such as Prairie State, and leave regulation to state agencies, which may have weaker pollution standards or capacity (Gibson, 2013, February 26).

Others have tried to take up the Prairie State model of bundling coal mines with power plants in-state. In 2013, billionaire Foresight CEO Michael Beyer made an unsuccessful proposal to invest nearly $500 million to complete Dynegy's half-built scrubbers at the Newton and Coffeen plants. If Dynegy did not like the plan, Foresight also offered to take over both plants. In return for financing the scrubber, Foresight would insist on a long-term contract to supply the Newton plant with coal from its own mines nearby. While Illinois coal found its way to Illinois power plants in the past, this has not been the case since the Clean Air Act of 1992. Illinois coal is high in sulfur content, so power generator companies without scrubbers had abandoned it in favor of low-sulfur coal mined in the Powder River Basin of Wyoming.

As Beyer told *Forbes*, "Our coal miners come out of the mine and can see smokestacks, but we're not selling coal to them because they've not been retrofitted with scrubbers to burn high-sulfur coal mined in Illinois … we sell more coal to Europe, India and China than to our neighbors in Illinois" (Helman, 2013, September 18). Because the Wyoming coal burns clean enough, plants like Newton did not adopt scrubber technology. With scrubbers, the plant would be able to burn Illinois coal and have even cleaner emissions. Illinois residents would end up with cheaper electricity as a result. Foresight's Illinois coal production costs of about $22 per ton are believed to be cheaper (on an energy equivalence basis) than any other coal mined in the United States, and transporting it would cost a fraction of getting coal from Wyoming (Helman, 2013, September 18).

To be sure, anti-coal activism is also underway in Illinois. Residents of Saline County in southern Illinois presented the state's environmental agency and attorney general with a 5,000-signature petition to curb coal-mining in their community. The substance of their complaint was that Peabody's Cottage Grove Strip Mine pollutes the air and water and should be investigated. They also called for a probe into the Illinois Department of Natural Resources' issuance of permits. There was also an earlier controversy in the farming community of Rocky Branch, where Peabody Energy sought to extend its Cottage Grove coal mine, "within 300 feet of homes." Residents of Rocky Branch have joined those of Cottage Grove, who have been complaining about blasts resembling "small earthquakes," clouds of toxic coal dust, and polluted waterways, in opposing the proposed 1,019-acre mine (Foster, 2014, March 19).

The grievances are not limited to farmers or locals who are directly affected by mines. High electric bills sent shockwaves across towns in the Midwest, as customers wondered whether they had been duped as power suppliers tried to recoup their investments in a financially troubled Prairie State Energy Campus. By 2012, its development had cost $4.9 billion, more than twice the original estimate, forcing rate hikes and fees in many of the 217 municipalities and 17 electric cooperatives that invested in the project. Rate increases and equipment breakdowns were the opposite of what they had been promised – affordable and reliable supply of energy for the future. Customers in Galion, Ohio, as well as those in Batavia, Illinois, demanded accountability and compensation from their cities for hiding the financial risks associated with the Peabody energy project. In Paducah, Kentucky, customer complaints almost drove a municipal power provider to bankruptcy (Smyth, 2015, February 8).

Alex Epstein, the author of *The Moral Case for Fossil Fuels*, addressed the political tactics of anti-coal campaign at an annual Illinois Mining Institute meeting: "We need to change how we talk about coal. Coal is the most promising fuel of the future right now. . . . Like any technology, you have risks and side effects but the solution is to minimize those, not use them as a pretext for starving people of energy" (Malkovich, 2014, September 11). Arguing that the industry is often "dehumanized," Epstein categorically rejected the notion that owners are "greedy" and that miners are "bumpkins who can't do anything but be stuck in a coal mine and who don't know the catastrophe they are bringing into the world" (Malkovich, 2014, September 11).

6.4 Motives

The campaign against coal in the United States provides a useful contrast to Keystone XL and divestment for evaluating the activists' motivations. Unlike the two previously mentioned campaigns, mobilization against coal has not been primarily driven by 350.org and the organizations around it. On the contrary, the campaign began earlier and was in full swing by 2007. Led by the Sierra Club, it has been much less coordinated than the campaigns on Keystone XL and divestment. While we began our analysis with Keystone XL, a campaign that only really began in August 2011, by that time an entire book had been written about the track record of Sierra Club's Beyond Coal campaign (Nace, 2010). Thus, the analysis of the motivations behind activism against coal offers a genuine opportunity for comparative analysis.

To begin the evaluation, it is easy to see that the notion of fossil fuels as the root of our environmental problems has been an important motivation for activism aimed at coal. Although anti-coal activists have strategically emphasized global issues, the core campaigners share a profound understanding of coal, and fossil fuels more generally, as central to stopping climate change. Similar to Keystone XL and divestment, the recognition of fossil fuels as the core of the climate problem has inspired and driven activists to take concrete action. Coal has been a prime target for environmental activists not only because it has more global warming potential than oil or gas, but also because global coal reserves are so large that they alone could raise global temperatures by several degrees (Plumer, 2015, July 9).

Indeed, the idea of attacking the root cause of climate change and other forms of environmental destruction manifests itself differently from Keystone XL and divestment in the case of coal. For Keystone XL and divestment, even the most ardent activists concede the point that their campaign is ultimately symbolic and political. In the 350.org campaigns, activists were motivated by the idea that a full-frontal assault on the fossil fuel industry could stigmatize dirty energy and turn public opinion against fossil fuels.

Anti-coal activists have another, more direct rationale for their work: each and every coal power plant is a significant contributor to climate change. Given that one-third of America's carbon dioxide emissions come from coal and there were only 633 active coal power plants in 2002, the closure of a single coal power plant would itself be a notable achievement. Due to the massive economies of scale of coal-powered electricity generation, coal power plants are significant targets for climate activism. As we have noted above, the Beyond Coal campaign has a list of more than 200 cancelled or defeated coal power plants in the United States.

While we cannot directly link activism to the cancellation or defeat of these plants, it would be impossible to criticize the anti-coal activists for focusing on an irrelevant sideshow. There is a broad consensus among energy analysts that reducing coal use is an essential step toward halting climate disruption, and this observation is powerful motivation for anti-coal activists. As the Sierra Club executive director Michael Brune put it, stopping coal is "the fastest and easiest way to slash the carbon pollution that is changing our climate" (Brune, 2015, April 8).

Moreover, the entire anti-coal campaign is based on the idea that hundreds of anti-coal campaigns together add up to a swarm that first halts and then stops the production and use of coal in the United States and elsewhere. Tellingly, the information clearinghouse for anti-coal activists is called CoalSwarm – an explicit recognition that the activists are confident about their ability to win the war on coal through grassroots mobilization. This emphasis on coordinating grassroots activism, instead of a centralized nationwide campaign, is a major difference between Beyond Coal and the other campaigns we have reviewed earlier.

The second component of our evaluation matrix focuses on the presence of a clear enemy or opponent. In the case of the campaign against coal, and the Sierra Club's Beyond Coal in particular, the answer is again a definite "yes." Due to significant economies of scale, both coal mining and power generation from coal are concentrated in the hands of large industrial and corporate actors. Financial institutions, such as investment banks, also play a notable role in the coal ecosystem because of the massive size of the investments required. All these corporate interests are ideal targets for anti-fossil fuel activists looking for small but significant wins in the larger battle against the fossil fuel industry.

The "us versus them" logic applies both to the national campaign leadership and to the local organizers. At the national level, anti-coal organizers see coal as their golden opportunity: the world's worst fossil fuel is excavated and used by an economically troubled industry with an already-tarnished public image. At the local level, concerns about public health and the local environment, both in terms of water and air pollution, drive a large number of potential activists to join the campaign and contribute significant amounts of time and energy.

In terms of symbolism, the anti-coal campaign is mostly similar to Keystone XL and divestment. Combusted in massive, centralized power plants for the transmission of power over long distances, coal is a powerful symbol of the fossil fuel economy. More remarkably, the symbolism of the anti-coal campaign is rarely used in a derisive or belittling fashion by policy analysts. In the case of Keystone XL and divestment, we saw repeated attacks on the campaigns and campaigners by both academic economists and mainstream policy analysts. In the case of coal, there has been no such backlash. There appears to be a broad consensus among energy specialists that replacing coal with other fuels is ideal, even though the same analysts may have very different views on oil and gas.

What about the ecological paradigm? Here, we find only partial support for our analytical framework. On the one hand, it is true that the core campaigners and the national movement are strongly committed to the ecological paradigm. Consider again James Hansen, who played an important role in the Keystone XL campaign and offered ecological arguments to justify his position. He has also played an important role in providing the intellectual and analytical foundation for the anti-coal campaign, with a clear reliance on ecological arguments. In *Climate Hope*, a book that documents the early years of the contemporary campaign against coal, Nace (2010: 9–10) cites Hansen saying that coal is "80 percent of the solution to the global warming crisis," noting that Hansen gives four reasons for his emphasis on coal:

1 Of all fossil fuel reserves that remain underground, coal contains the most carbon.
2 Coal has a higher carbon intensity than any other fossil fuel.
3 Coal is burned in large plants, and therefore presents a natural target for action.
4 Coal is a natural target for American activists in particular, given the country's large coal reserves.

Together, these arguments constitute an ecological logic. Instead of emphasizing economic arguments on the demand side for technology-neutral policies such as carbon pricing, Hansen zooms in on a specific fossil fuel, claiming that coal presents a natural target for campaigning.

At the same time, it is not clear that the ecological paradigm is necessary to understand the motivations of local groups mobilizing against power plants and coal mines. Even a cursory examination of Beyond Coal website[16] shows not much discourse on ecology or planetary conditions (Sierra Club, 2013). The website largely focuses on local environmental issues, emphasizing the negative effects of the coal economy on American communities. It has separate sections for "water pollution" and "air pollution," but there is no section for "climate change" or "global warming." Even a subsection on "carbon pollution and climate disruption" makes only a passing reference to "climate disruption," instead focusing on how "even though carbon pollution threatens our health, our economy, and our children's future, we currently have no national protections on how much carbon can be released into our air by dirty power plants" (Sierra Club, n.d.).[17]

6.5 Mobilization potential

Overall, the pattern of mobilization against coal suggests cause for considerable optimism. Though local activism against surface mining and mountaintop removal has a longer history, the recent campaign against coal has blossomed under the leadership of Sierra Club and Rainforest Action Network. Given the actual climate implications of coal, as exemplified by James Hansen's "80 percent of the solution" claim, as well as the concreteness of the target, as exemplified by the coal plants, it should come as no surprise that anti-coal activists have been able to recruit well. Recognizing also that the coal industry has many individual weak points along its value chain and that grassroots activism is best suited to exploit them, activists have effectively used a "swarming" strategy.

Indeed, activist tactics illustrated the strength of combining local concerns with a coordinated national campaign. From Appalachia to Montana, local activists have forged effective alliances with national organizers to challenge coal mines and power plants. Under our analytical framework, these local concerns underscore the potential of anti-coal campaigns for hybrid activism. Those areas of the United States that are ideal targets for anti-coal campaigning because of coal deposits and suitable sites for coal power plants are not populated by urban West or East Coast progressives. Hybrid activism has been, and continues to be, an absolute necessity for the anti-coal campaigns.

Consider the case of WORC. In most respects, this organization and its members are as far removed from the typical climate activist as one can possibly imagine. In Montana and Wyoming, for example, the organization's members are ranchers living in rural communities. Their values, beliefs, and lifestyle differ from the typical urban climate activist in every possible respect, and yet they are attacking coal mines and power plants with considerable enthusiasm. Organizations such as WORC are, despite their rural and conservative membership, popular allies to progressive environmentalists around the country. This popularity stems from a combination of necessity and effectiveness. In states such as Montana or Wyoming, conventional environmental groups cannot mobilize the local population, whereas WORC has a track record of effective campaigning and activism.

The genius of the national anti-coal campaign lies with the aggregation of a diverse set of local campaigns into a coherent and powerful national narrative.

While the local communities fighting against coal are a diverse group, their concerns are shared and largely relate to the detrimental effects of coal production and consumption on human settlements and the natural environment. These shared concerns can, in turn, be linked to the planetary issue of climate disruption because they all stem from the same practice. And since coal is a fossil fuel mined and burned mostly by large industrial interests, the narrative of swarming to stop greedy corporate interests comes together.

The final component of our evaluation matrix is the availability of small wins. Here, we can easily conclude that this potential is great. Over the past years, the anti-coal activists have taken pride in the large and rapidly growing number of defeated coal power plants, as well as several victories in local battles against coal mining and transportation. Despite the difficulty of attributing these outcomes to activism, the campaign has successfully presented them as concrete, meaningful steps toward a coal-free America. In doing so, the campaign has succeeded in motivating the activists to continue the campaign. In what is almost a textbook illustration of Weick's (1984) small wins in action, the continued troubles of the coal industry have allowed the campaign to maintain a positive outlook and create a cycle of positive reinforcement over time. Though "small wins" may have limited direct impact on climate, they do serve the role of mobilizing additional activists and sustaining momentum.

To summarize, while the coal campaign differs from Keystone XL and divestment in several important respects, it also shows what an ideal set of conditions for mobilization can achieve. It combines the defining strengths of the campaign against fossil fuels – targeting the root cause, going after a clear enemy – with exceptional potential for hybrid activism and a stream of meaningful small wins. Against this backdrop, it is easy to understand why the campaign against coal was the original campaign against fossil fuels and still continues to thrive, year after year.

6.6 Impact

In evaluating the effects of the campaign, the first question is again whether the goals of the campaign are justified. The answer is a definite "yes," as coal is the worst of all fossil fuels in terms of greenhouse gas emissions generated and is still the most important fuel used for power generation in the United States. If the anti-coal activists succeed in their goal of progressively closing old plants and stopping the construction of new plants, there is no question that this achievement will induce a reduction in national carbon dioxide emissions. If the activists further manage to stop exports of coal, then the vast deposits of coal found in the United States remain underground, greatly facilitating the world's goal of climate change mitigation during this century.

Given that the anti-coal campaign has solid overall goals, we must next consider the campaign's ability to achieve these goals. Anti-coal campaigns have set laudable goals, but are they in a position to achieve them? Here, again, our evaluation is positive. The anti-coal campaign has already had significant success in delaying and even stopping plans to expand coal mining, transportation, and combustion by electric utilities. The swarming strategies of the anti-coal activists have not made coal projects impossible, but, unlike in the past, today there is opposition to coal in every state of the United States. Even areas that are highly dependent on coal, such as Wyoming, have seen the rise of dynamic opposition movements that undermine coal projects. While we cannot accept the activist claim that all, even most, cancellations of coal power construction in the United States can be attributed to social mobilization, it is indisputable that the vibrant opposition to coal power plants makes investments in coal riskier and less profitable. Combined with other challenges to coal, such as inexpensive shale gas and federal environmental regulations, this opposition has made coal the most vulnerable of all fossil fuels. Indeed, the Sierra Club announced in July 2015 that 200 coal plants nationwide had been shut down, representing the phase out of nearly 40 percent of the 523 US coal plants that were in operation the previous five years.[18]

Besides the clearly positive, direct effect of stopping planned coal power plants on the climate, are there other, less direct benefits to this kind of campaigning? We believe the significance of stopping coal production and burning goes beyond the fuel's direct warming effect. If American anti-coal activists continue to win their battles, they may succeed in removing an important political obstacle to more comprehensive climate policy at the state and federal levels. To see the relevance of this idea, consider patterns of environmental voting in the US Congress. In 2013, House Representatives and Senators from the 3 leading coal-producing states – Wyoming, West Virginia, and Kentucky – voted in favor of what the League of Conservation Voters (2013) considers the "pro-environment" position in 20 percent of the significant environment and energy votes. This contrasts sharply with a mean of 45 percent elsewhere in the country in 2013.

Indeed, federal energy policies under President Obama certainly moved the country in the direction of less reliance on coal. Already in 2012, the president had enacted a regulation to reduce mercury emissions from power plants, with significant cost implications for the use of coal in the power sector. In 2014, the president again used executive authority under the Clean Air Act to enact the Clean Power Plan, a comprehensive policy to reduce carbon and other pollution from the power sector.[19] The goal of the plan was to reduce carbon emissions from the power sector by 30 percent relative to the base year 2005. Because coal generates much more carbon emissions for each kilowatt hour than any alternative fuel, Obama's plan pressures electric utilities to reduce the use of coal.

For anti-coal activists, President Obama's "Clean Power Plan" offered a golden opportunity to consolidate and expand their wins. An important feature of the plan was to allow individual states to submit plans for meeting the federal requirements. While it remains to be seen to what extent anti-coal activists can access and shape state-level regulatory proceedings, the very existence and institutional design of Obama's plan suggest that it closely reflects the preferences of anti-coal activists. His successor, President Trump, has begun what is expected to be a "complex and lengthy" legal process of unwinding these policies (Davenport and Rubin, 2017, March 28). Though only time will tell, the forces put in motion during the Obama presidency, as well as competitiveness of natural gas, are likely to make coal's revival difficult (Egan, 2017, April 25).

It is also important to note that the significance of anti-coal mobilization may also reach beyond the United States. The organizations whose activities we have covered are not only concerned with coal use in the United States. They have also targeted transportation infrastructure, with a particular emphasis on plans to export American coal through Pacific export terminals to Asia. While there is some debate on the net effects of US coal exports on global carbon dioxide emissions, with some experts such as Stanford energy economist Frank Wolak arguing that these exports would not significantly raise global temperatures,[20] it is important to remember that such arguments do not make much sense to the activists whose approach is based on the ecological paradigm. From the ecological perspective, stopping US coal exports is imperative in the context of falling domestic demand for coal. After all, stopping coal exports means that the coal deposits will not be used at all. Therefore, while we acknowledge the possible complexity of the effects of increased US coal exports on global energy markets, we also must remember that the analysis predicting such complexity is not based on the core assumptions of the ecological paradigm.

Moreover, the recent developments in the global coal industry have been largely favorable to those who subscribe to the ecological paradigm, though some qualifications apply. First, there has been a growing political recognition of the role that coal plays in contributing to climate change. In September 2013, Nordic countries announced their intention to join the US, UK, and the World Bank Group in restricting financing for coal-fired power plants. In the lead-up to the Conference of Parties (COP 21) in Paris, 34 OECD nations, including historically recalcitrant Japan and Australia, agreed to limit financing for coal plants (Northrop, 2016, January 11).

In some ways, COP 21 crystallized the widespread recognition among the international community, particularly the 196 countries represented in Paris, that fossil fuels, such as coal, contribute to climate change and that something must be done to limit their use (Coday, 2015, December 23). One hundred and eighty-eight nations submitted national climate action plans and agreed to review and improve them every five years. There was also a call to stabilize the global temperature increase at 1.5 °C, 0.5 below the previous threshold 2°C. However, climate activists, James Hansen among them, continue to express skepticism that the agreements reached at the conference are up to the task of phasing out fossil fuels, particularly because of their heavy reliance on voluntary agreements and the cooperation of emerging economies (Clemente, 2015, December 16).

Second, at the time of writing, the sustained decline in global oil price and stricter environmental regulations, which made natural gas much more competitive, have put the coal industry on the defensive. A major coal producer, Arch Coal, which bought the International Coal Group for $3.4 billion at its peak, is seeking bankruptcy protection to reduce $4.5 billion of debt (Mouawad, 2016, January 11). Latest Energy Information Administration estimates suggest that US coal production in 2015 was about 900 million short tons (MMst), 10 percent lower than in 2014 and the lowest level in three decades (since 1986). US coal exports also declined in 2015, especially to major coal export destinations such as Europe and China (US Energy Information Administration, 2016, January 8).[21] To be sure, the decline in exports can partly be explained by the growing focus among emerging economies on ramping up their domestic coal production (Das, 2016, January 8).

Having discussed the anti-coal campaign's substantive goals and their achievements, we now turn to the question of target audience. Here, we again see a clear contrast to divestment and Keystone XL: the anti-coal campaign is deliberately not targeting climate activists or progressives wedded to the ecological paradigm. To understand the issue of target audience, it is critical to understand that anti-coal mobilization is much less politicized along the traditional left–right, or progressive–conservative, lines. Divestment has driven a sharp wedge between progressives and conservatives. Keystone XL is, with the exception of isolated landowner groups along the planned route for the pipeline, a project adopted by progressives. But the anti-coal campaign has mobilized large numbers of local groups in different states to fight against the coal industry, regardless of their partisan identification, political ideology, or other views. Concerns about coal are shared by Americans of all political stripes, and politically controversial topics such as climate change or economic freedom have had much less polarizing influence than in the other campaigns we have analyzed so far.

This is not to say that Republicans are not using every opportunity to fight back. When President Obama announced his Clean Power Plan, Fox News announced that the White House had declared a "war on coal" (Fox News, 2014, June 2). Similarly, the Senate Republican leader Mitch McConnell, who hails from Kentucky, said that the regulation is a "dagger in the heart of the American middle class." In March 2017, President Trump promised to put "our coal miners back to work" at a rally in Kentucky, a state he won on hopes for a coal revival (Egan, 2017, April 25). But at the same time, we have seen that conservative communities have mobilized against the coal industry across the country. To us, this discrepancy between local actions and national conservative leadership suggests that, while the conservative elite is not sympathetic to the anti-coal campaign, the issue resonates with at least some conservative communities – something that can hardly be said about Keystone XL or divestment.

The other constituency that appears sympathetic to the anti-coal campaign are energy policy experts. The same experts who have ridiculed Keystone XL opposition and divestment efforts have offered analyses that support actions that focus on coal. Michael Levi of the Council on Foreign Relations, whom we saw earlier criticizing the Keystone XL campaign, writes elsewhere that "[w]e need to move forward with gas, using it to edge aside coal, even as we push ahead on a host of zero-carbon opportunities" (Levi, 2013, April 29). Harvard economist Robert Stavins, whose arguments against divestment we covered earlier, writes that "natural gas is the crucial transition fuel to address climate change. A major reason for the recent drop in US CO2 emissions is the increased use of natural gas rather than coal to generate electricity" (Stavins, 2014, March 20). While these energy analysts do not mention the campaign by name, they clearly agree with the premise that targeting coal is important for effective climate policy.

Given the successful targeting of different audiences, the anti-coal campaign suggests that our analytical framework may be grounded in overly pessimistic assumptions about the ability of activists to reach out to the public. Whereas we find evidence for the relevance of the ecological paradigm in the motivations of the core activists, there is no comparable evidence to suggest that the numerous local grassroots campaigns follow the ecological reasoning. The evidence suggests, instead, that the anti-coal campaign has successfully reached beyond the typical audience for ecological arguments, taking hybrid activism to the next level and showing that there is a way to escape the trap of a progressive "echo chamber" among passionate followers of ecological reasoning.

What explains this stark difference from Keystone XL and divestment? There are several possible reasons for this difference. First, of course, is the generally weak economic performance of the coal industry. Unlike the oil and gas industry, coal is struggling in today's economic circumstances – and this is nowhere as true as in the United States, where cheap shale gas is challenging King Coal in the power sector. Besides that, the local damage caused by coal, both in mining and combustion, is immediately obvious to anyone. In the case of Keystone XL, the opposite is true except where the tar sands are located; in the case of divestment, there is no direct damage to observe at all. Coal is, in a sense, both an easier opponent than gas or oil and one that already suffers from a bad public image.

Before we finish this evaluation, we must comment on one notable challenge that the anti-coal campaign has recently been facing. As the campaign against coal has achieved great success, both because of its own actions and because of other forces that undermine the staying power of coal in the American energy economy, fracking of shale gas for electricity generation – the topic of the next chapter – has presented new challenges. While waging war against coal, the Sierra Club came under criticism from anti-fracking activists for fraternizing with the natural gas industry. Controversy erupted when the *TIME* magazine revealed that the Sierra Club Beyond Coal campaign had accepted more than $25 million in donations from the gas industry between 2007 and 2010, mostly from Chesapeake Energy, one of the biggest gas drilling companies in the US and a firm heavily involved in fracking (Walsh, 2012, February 2).

In a public break-up letter addressing the Sierra Club, the environmentalist Sandra Steinberger described her reaction as follows: "The Sierra Club had taken money, gobs of it, from an industry that we in the grassroots have been in the fight of our lives to oppose. The largest, most venerable environmental organization in the United States secretly aligned with the very company that seeks to occupy our land, turn it inside out, blow it apart, fill it with poison. All for the goal of extract-ing a powerful heat-trapping gas, methane, that plays a significant role in climate change. . . . It was as if, on the eve of D-Day, the anti-fascist partisans had discovered that Churchill was actually in cahoots with the Axis forces" (Steingraber, 2012,

March 26). The Sierra Club has since attempted to distance itself from natural gas, emphasizing that it declined further donations from the said company, but in the eyes of some fracking activists, irreparable damage had been done to its credibility (Laskow, 2012, April 3).

More generally, speaking of *the* campaign against fossil fuels itself obscures important cleavages and divisions. The case of coal and fracking clearly illustrates the energy trade-offs that the American public is now facing. Especially for local activists worried about a surface coal mine in the Appalachian Mountains, it is not at all obvious that a few natural gas wells in Pennsylvania are a bad thing. While anti-fracking activists are concerned about water supplies in their own areas, anti-coal activists are concerned about water and air pollution in different states. And yet, there is no easy way to replace the entire conventional power sector with renewable energy. Every time the anti-coal activists win, the demand for shale gas increases; and every time the anti-fracking activists win, the future of coal looks a little brighter, at least when measured in stock market prices. When anti-fossil fuel activists downplay these conflicts, they strategically emphasize the unity and coherence of their movement, but we have seen that such claims obscure important conflicts and disagreements among self-declared anti-fossil fuel campaigners.

Still, our overall evaluation is positive, on balance. Of all the campaigns evaluated so far, the anti-coal campaign has the strongest track record in terms of motivating activists, holding meaningful substantive goals, being able to shape policy at the federal and even international levels, and reaching beyond the typical progressive target audience of committed environmentalists. Next, we will finish our comparative analysis of the campaign against fossil fuels by investigating the case of fracking.

Notes

1 See original letter from James Hansen to Nevada Governor Jim Gibbons available at www. columbia.edu/~jeh1/mailings/2008/20080414_GovernorGibbons.pdf (accessed April 9, 2015).
2 See the Western Organization of Resource Council discussion of the SMCRA available at www.worc.org/media/SMCRA-Report.pdf (accessed May 28, 2017).
3 See the Western Organization of Resource Council discussion of the SMCRA available at www.worc.org/media/SMCRA-Report.pdf (accessed May 28, 2017).
4 See the full transcript available at www.presidency.ucsb.edu/ws/?pid=32596 (accessed May 28, 2017).
5 See the official campaign description available at the Sierra Club website http://content.sierraclub.org/coal/victories (accessed April 27, 2015).
6 SourceWatch has an extensive record of Rainforest Action Network and its activities on its website. See www.sourcewatch.org/index.php/Rainforest_Action_Network (accessed April 27, 2015).
7 See SourceWatch account of the events surrounding the list of 151 plants available at www.sourcewatch.org/index.php/What_happened_to_the_151_proposed_coal_plants%3F (accessed April 27, 2015).
8 See evidence of Step It Up! efforts on coal available at www.stepitup2007.org/article.php-id=709.html (accessed April 27, 2015).
9 See SourceWatch timeline of nonviolent direct actions available at www.sourcewatch.org/index.php/Nonviolent_direct_actions_against_coal:_2004-2007 (accessed April 27, 2015).

10 See the official press release on the year 2013 available at http://content.sierraclub. org/press-releases/2013/12/2013-landmark-year-clean-energy-twilight-coal (accessed April 28, 2015).

11 The timeline presented here relies heavily on CoalSwarm documentation available at www.sourcewatch.org/index.php/Rainforest_Action_Network (accessed April 28, 2015).

12 This section relies heavily on SourceWatch coverage of the political battle against mountaintop removal available at www.sourcewatch.org/index.php/Mountaintop_removal (accessed April 27, 2015).

13 See the official complaint (legal document) available at http://libcloud.s3.amazonaws. com/93/c0/a/4968/BLM-complaint-asfiled-11–24–2014.pdf (accessed May 28, 2017).

14 See SourceWatch description of the coal industry in Texas available at www.source watch.org/index.php/Texas_and_coal (accessed April 30, 2015).

15 See SourceWatch description of the coal industry in Illinois available at www.source watch.org/index.php/Illinois_and_coal (accessed May 1, 2015).

16 See http://content.sierraclub.org/coal/ (accessed April 26, 2015).

17 See http://content.sierraclub.org/coal/burning-carbon-pollution-and-climate-disrup tion (accessed April 26, 2015).

18 See the Sierra Club official press release available at http://content.sierraclub.org/press-releases/2015/07/united-states-phases-out-200th-coal-plant-momentum-renewable-energy-grows (accessed January 14, 2016).

19 See EPA Clean Power Plan Overview available at www.epa.gov/sites/production/ files/2014–05/documents/20140602fs-overview.pdf (accessed May 28, 2017).

20 See "Reduce Greenhouse Gas by Exporting Coal, Says Frank Wolak." Available at https://energy.stanford.edu/news/reduce-greenhouse-gas-exporting-coal-says-frank-wolak (accessed May 3, 2015).

21 See www.eia.gov/todayinenergy/detail.cfm?id=24472 (accessed January 12, 2016).

7

MOBILIZING AGAINST FRACKING

We have seen the decline of coal coincide with the rise of natural gas, as an increasing number of electricity generating plants underwent conversion from the "dirty fuel" to the "bridge fuel" in the late 2000s. A major contributor to this trend has been technological breakthroughs in an unconventional drilling technique called *hydraulic fracturing*, otherwise known as *fracking*. The drilling technique involves injecting water and chemicals at high pressure to break up rocks located thousands of feet below aquifers.

The campaign against fracking in America has a strong community component. As a loose coalition of local communities with shared concerns about the capacity of fracking to harm their immediate environments, whether via contaminated water supply, diseases, or earthquakes, anti-fracking activists (*fractivists*) strive to find their place in the larger climate movement. While the climate implications of fracking may not be as well established, that has not stopped fractivists from contributing momentum and political will to the larger movement. They bring to the movement "a never-surrender, battle-tested spirit" and have notched a number of legislative victories at the local level (Steingraber, 2014, August 26).

Their contributions notwithstanding, the inclusion of fractivists in the climate movement introduces interesting contradictions. Depending on one's beliefs about the complex linkage between fracking and the climate, natural gas could also be considered a more environmentally friendly alternative to coal. Therefore, some environmentalists, even those partaking in the anti-fracking campaign, are willing to support fracking under tighter regulations. From their perspective, unconditional opposition to fracking does more harm than good for the climate. While conflicting views on fracking rarely stop climate activists from marching together in New York or DC, they also make headlines from time to time (Phillips, 2013, May 21).

7.1 Significance

The shale gas revolution that is now underway in America and other parts of the world has forever changed the landscape of global energy markets. North America has been the primary beneficiary, as its surfeit of natural gas is shifting the balance of power away from traditional producers in the Middle East and Russia.

The seed of the revolution was planted in the Barnett Shale, an underground geological structure near Fort Worth, Texas. There, a small firm of wildcat drillers called Mitchell Energy pioneered the application of two oilfield techniques, hydraulic fracturing and horizontal drilling, to release natural gas trapped in shalerock formations. Fracking blasts chemicals and other materials into the rock, creating cracks that allow the gas to seep to the well. Horizontal drilling allows the drill bit to penetrate the earth vertically before moving sideways for hundreds or thousands of meters.

Thus, while the ideas were not new, gas price surges in recent years made such drilling commercially viable. Economies of scale and improvements in techniques halved the production costs of shale gas, making unconventional sources cheaper than conventional ones. The widespread adoption of these techniques has unlocked vast tracts of shale across North America, from Texas to British Columbia. The Barnett Shale alone accounts for 7 percent of American gas supplies. Drawn to these opportunities, ExxonMobil paid $41 billion for XTO, a "pure-play" gas firm with a large shale business. BP, Statoil, Total, and others are signing joint ventures with unconventional producers such as Chesapeake Energy (*The Economist*, 2010, March 11).

The federal government had not regulated fracking in its nascent stage, and as it gained traction, the government even lent a helping hand. Over opposition from within the Environmental Protection Agency (EPA), the George W. Bush Administration, led by Vice President Dick Cheney, passed the Energy Policy Act of 2005, exempting the fracking industry from the Safe Drinking Water Act, the Clean Air Act, and the Clean Water Act. One of its provisions, known as the Halliburton Loophole, allows gas companies to pump millions of gallons of fluid containing chemicals into shale rock formations without disclosing the content (Bateman, 2010, June 21).

Critics of fracking emphasize its potential harms for communities, such as the contamination of the drinking water supply, as well as various ailments and earthquakes. As one fractivist puts it, "Families with nose bleeds and rashes. Sick pets. Horses and livestock with mysterious ailments. Devastated landscapes. . . . Most of all, we came together to protect our drinking water." These concerns, she claims, are buttressed by a growing body of scientific research and an "ever-expanding collection of empirical data" (Steingraber, 2014, August 26).

Fracking's impact on climate change primarily concerns the integrity of fracking wells, the disintegration of which has been linked to methane leakage. A Cornell University scientist, Robert Howarth, argues that we are at a tipping point of "climate catastrophe," singling out methane leakage as a greater contributor to climate change than carbon dioxide emissions (Howarth, 2014). These climate implications are the subject of a heated debate among academics, and are often emphasized by fractivists.

7.2 Overview

The environmental organizations mobilized against fracking are scattered and local. Efforts to institutionalize opposition have often been bottom-up, as exemplified by FracTracker Alliance, a multi-state nonprofit that originated in 2010 as a website focused on southwest Pennsylvania. Other notable organizations include Americans Against Fracking, which plays a pivotal role in organizing opposition to fracking on a national level. Americans Against Fracking also operates as part of a global movement called Global Frackdown. As a global network, members of Global Frackdown often compare notes on tactics and operate in Canada, United States, Europe, and Argentina.

The larger campaign, from the perspective of its organizers, is a counter-response to the powerful pro-fracking narrative of the oil and gas industry, and mirrors some of the industry's tactics, such as lobbying of politicians and shaping of public opinion. The end goal for them, however, is a renewable future without fracking.[1] Broadly construed, the campaign calls on "governmental officials at all levels to pursue a renewable energy future and not allow fracking or any of the associated infrastructure in our communities or any communities." The word *communities* is key, as the organization can be described as a loose coalition of "communities fighting fracking, frac sand mining, pipelines, compressor stations, LNG terminals, exports of natural gas, coal seam gas, coal bed methane and more."[2]

Environmental concerns about hydraulic fracturing originated in the 1990s with its early usage to extract gas from coal, before the technique was applied to extract gas from shales. In this sense, the 2010 documentary that went viral, *Gasland*, cannot be solely credited with starting the anti-fracking movement. Nonetheless, through vivid imagery, such as that of a man setting his tap water alight, *Gasland* neatly packaged and widely disseminated activists' primary concerns about the dangers of hydraulic fracturing. Particularly scathing is the political commentary behind the film, which shows politicians bowing to the pressure of the oil and gas industry. According to Google's analytics, searches for *Gasland* tend to precede rising search activity for "fracking" (Wood, 2012).

As a recent study commissioned by the fracking industry points out, however, this movement is by no means a monolith, and it encompasses a variety of motivations, which tend to vary according to local priorities and group composition. On the one hand, there are concerned voices advocating further study into the environmental and economic consequences of unconventional gas development. Calls for further study often go hand-in-hand with demands for a complete ban or a temporary moratorium on hydraulic fracturing. On the other hand, there are those who are not fundamentally opposed to fracking, but desire a better deal for the communities from the gas industry or tighter regulations of gas development from the government. The former group is readily compatible with the anti-fossil fuel movement, while the latter is not (Wood, 2012).

Those calling for further study point to existing research on water contamination, seismic activity, and other issues surrounding fracking to make their case. For these fractivists and their industry opponents, the so-called impact studies being conducted by government agencies (such as the EPA) represent arenas for political contestation. In Parker County, Texas, the EPA began an investigation after a homeowner reported that his drinking water was bubbling like champagne. The EPA, however, shelved the report connecting methane migration to fracking under pressure, allegedly due to the pressure from Range Resources, the independent natural gas company under investigation.

In another case, the mid-Atlantic EPA began testing the water in Dimock, Pennsylvania, after residents complained of contamination, but the federal EPA closed the investigation in July 2012 even after the investigators warned of methane, manganese, and arsenic contamination. In Pavilion, Wyoming, the EPA released a draft report in 2011 linking fracking to the contamination of an underground aquifer. Under pressure from the industry, the EPA handed the investigation over to the state in June 2013 to be completed with funding from EnCana, the drilling company charged with contamination. Thus, Americans Against Fracking has been consistently petitioning for more transparent investigations.[3]

Calls for further study often go hand-in-hand with demands for a complete ban or a temporary moratorium on hydraulic fracturing. While fractivists' success in implementing fracking bans in New York and Maryland may not be easily replicated elsewhere, moratoriums even at the county or municipal level – whether to accommodate impact studies, mediate political disputes, or develop regulatory frameworks – can be part of a larger strategy of halting unconventional gas development, while buying the time to build political will against the industry (Wood, 2012).

Not surprisingly, it is those fundamentally opposed to fracking who contribute the most fire to the anti-fossil fuel movement. As a fractivist wrote in her open letter to the climate movement: "We bring to all of you, to this larger climate justice movement, a never-surrender, battle-tested spirit. America's fractivists have been fighting for our lives in the gas fields. Now we are ready to fight for life itself" (Steingraber, 2014, August 26). While attending the People's Climate March 2014 in New York City and associated events, the authors witnessed firsthand the palpable enthusiasm of the fractivists.

Those who are not fundamentally opposed to fracking introduce interesting contradictions to the climate movement. Depending on one's beliefs about the linkage between fracking and the climate, natural gas could also be considered a more environmentally friendly alternative to coal. Therefore, some environmentalists, even those partaking in the anti-fracking campaign, are willing to support fracking under tighter regulations. From their perspective, unconditional opposition to fracking does more harm than good for the climate.

In 2013, for instance, the Environmental Defense Fund (EDF) angered fractivists by announcing its participation in the Center for Sustainable Shale Gas Development (CSSD), a collaboration with energy companies and philanthropical organizations to develop performance standards related to protecting air and water quality. The EDF's critics perceive CSSD as an opportunity for the industry to gain good publicity, sending the false message that environmentalists are on board with fracking. While these fractivists view the EDF as co-opted by industry interests, the EDF seems genuinely convinced that tighter regulations is the answer (Phillips, 2013, May 21). These internal disagreements are likely to persist for some time.

The available scientific evidence does not lend decisive support to either of the opposing views. Die-hard fractivists emphasize the release of methane and its impact on the climate, and they do tell a compelling story:

> It turns out that the same unfixable engineering problem that sets the table for contaminating our water also contaminates the atmosphere with climate-killing methane. The problem is that fracked wells are fragile wells. Too often, they leak. The brutal actions of fracking itself, which uses a slurry of highly pressurized water, chemicals, and sand as a club to shatter the shale in order to free the oil or gas can sometimes deform or crack the cement gasket around the wellbore. That's how fracked wells can lose their integrity. That's how they leak. And once they start leaking, you can't turn them off. In short, each wellhead is an inextinguishable methane cigarette in the Earth. And there are no non-smoking sections. That leakage can include natural gas itself – methane – which wafts from the wellhead, or from the compressor station, or from pipelines and flarestacks, into our atmosphere.
>
> *(Steingraber, 2014, August 26)*

Many of these claims rely on the findings of Cornell's professor Robert Howarth, who warns that the production of fossil fuels, particularly natural gas, is the largest methane pollution source in America, and that it will eventually lead to a "tipping point" of climate catastrophe (Howarth, 2014).

Howarth singles out natural gas production as having a greater effect on the climate than carbon dioxide emissions: "Over a 100-year timeframe, methane is about 34 times as potent as a climate change-driving greenhouse gas than carbon dioxide, and over 20 years, it's 86 times more potent. Of all the greenhouse gases released by humans globally, methane contributes more than 40 percent of all radiative forcing, a measure of trapped heat in the atmosphere and a measuring stick of a changing climate" (Howarth, 2014).

Howarth's conclusions remain subject to much dispute. There has been a slew of recent studies suggesting either that methane emissions from oil and gas fields have been underestimated, or that the impact those emissions will have on climate change is extremely complex and difficult to determine. Even many scientists who agree with Howarth's research say there are other ways to curb methane emissions without shutting down natural gas production (Magill, 2014, May 15).

Rigorous research on this question has not kept pace, partly because there is not enough data available. Scientists at the fall 2013 meeting of the American Geophysical Union opined that it is difficult to determine the effects of fracking on water and the climate because little data are available and energy companies keep their energy extraction and production technology under wraps. They called on both state and federal governments and the oil and gas industry to be more transparent about drilling and production practices (Magill, 2013, December 10). The EPA's Greenhouse Gas Reporting Program currently requires energy companies to report only those emissions from fracking operations that involve flaring – the industry's practice of burning off excess natural gas at a well site (Magill, 2015, January 8).

Five years in the making, the EPA has recently released a draft study that finds no evidence of fracking's widespread impact on the nation's water supply. It is careful to note, however, that the technique does have the potential to contaminate the drinking water. While the study notes specific instances of water contamination, it points out that the number of cases was small relative to the number of fracked wells. The issue of data availability is relevant, as environmental groups, such as the Sierra Club, have challenged the findings of the report, arguing that they rely on data supplied by the companies themselves and that data limitations "preclude a determination of the frequency of impacts with any certainty" (Davenport, 2015, June 4).

7.3 Activism in motion

Comparisons across states present a more dynamic picture of the campaign, the forces working to expand its reach and the forces working to contain it. New York and Pennsylvania present interesting comparisons because they are both geographically positioned to benefit from the Marcellus Shale, which holds tremendous promise for the industry. The two states have made very different choices so far: The state of New York chose to ban fracking altogether, while the fracking industry is booming in Pennsylvania. However, neither victory nor defeat seems permanent, as New York's fracking ban is under pressure from the fossil fuel lobby, while Pennsylvania's booming fracking industry is also under attack by fractivists.

In Texas, where it all started, the industry has decisively fired back at the fractivists. After what seemed to be a victory for grassroots fractivists in the city of Denton, which opted to ban fracking after voting on the issue, the legal advocates of the industry in Texas immediately went to work. The result was a statewide ban on anti-fracking bans, nullifying the efforts of Denton fractivists, and solidifying the hold of the industry in the oil-patch state. The fractivists are now exploring other legal avenues to move their agenda forward. We discuss each of these states in turn.

We begin our discussion with New York, where extensive data are available on anti-fracking activism. While New York has a statewide ban on fracking, the distribution of fractivism across counties paints a more nuanced picture of the varying degrees of their involvement. Based on FracTracker data, Figures 7.1, 7.2, and 7.3 present statistics on municipal bans, moratoriums, and current movements organized by county. Figure 7.4 depicts municipal bans and moratoriums over time. Not all 62 New York counties are represented, but all of the counties represented have seen fractivist action in some capacity.[4]

As Figure 7.1 demonstrates, progress has been uneven. Some counties stand out as epicenters of progress. Onondaga and Otsego counties have seen more than 10 municipalities ban fracking, while Oneida and Ulster counties have seen seven each. Sullivan and Tompkins counties boast six apiece. Interestingly, at least 19 of the counties represented have seen no municipal bans whatsoever. While we cannot make too much of these statistics, it is clear that some counties have been more successful than others in implementing bans.

Progress is also uneven for moratoriums, as evident in Figure 7.2. Interestingly, counties that comprised the middle of the pack or the bottom for fracking bans now take the lead.

Particularly notable is Oneida County, with a whopping 19 moratoriums (seven bans), followed by Livingston County, with 12 moratoriums (zero bans) and Ontario County with nine moratoriums (four bans). Not surprisingly, more counties have implemented moratoriums than bans. Only 13 of the counties represented have seen no municipal moratoriums.

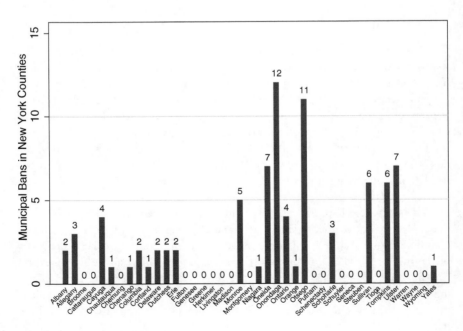

FIGURE 7.1 Municipal bans by county.

Source: FracTracker

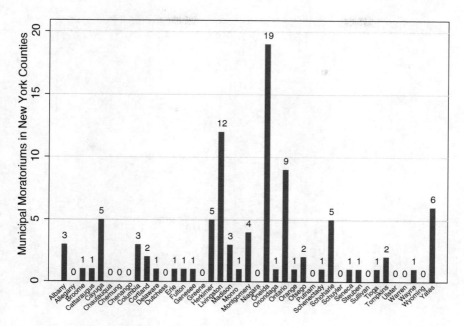

FIGURE 7.2 Municipal moratoriums by county.

Source: FracTracker

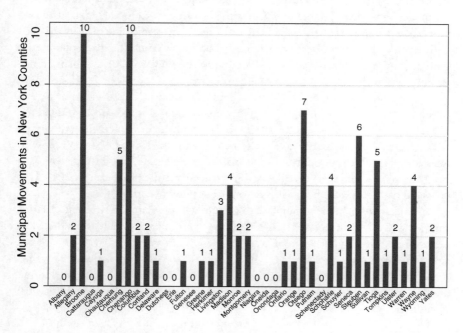

FIGURE 7.3 Municipal anti-fracking movements by county.

Source: FracTracker

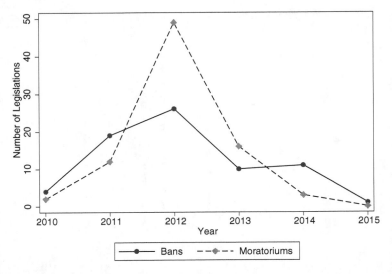

FIGURE 7.4 Municipal bans and moratoriums over time.

Source: FracTracker

The third graph, Figure 7.3, shows counties that are fiercely playing catch up. Broome (zero bans and one moratorium) and Chenango (one ban and zero moratoriums) boast at least 10 ongoing municipal movements. Otsego (11 bans and two moratoriums) and Steuben (zero bans and one moratorium) are also in the race with seven and six movements, respectively. Too much cannot be made of counties with zero municipal movements, however, since the three categories – bans, moratoriums, and movements – are mutually exclusive.

Last but not least, Figure 7.4 depicts bans and moratoriums over time. Not all of the bans and moratoriums tallied in the previous three figures are accounted for, as the time of legislation is not available for some of them. Nonetheless, the graph is suggestive. The year 2012 was a watershed year for fractivists in New York, with legislations for both moratoriums and bans at their peak. Though this may have been the product of their own success in achieving a statewide ban in 2014 – or censored data – the number of legislations trends downward.

When gas companies first applied to the New York State Department of Environmental Conservation (DEC) in 2008 for permits to horizontally mine the Marcellus Shale, the southern tier of western New York was faced with an historic recession. While the permits were under review, six gas companies already had landmen on the ground asking landowners to sign leases, especially in Sullivan and Delaware Counties, for hundreds to thousands of dollars an acre and potential royalties.

The leases prompted community meetings throughout the state, as the locals collectively weighed the costs and benefits of partaking in the shale boom. A meeting organized by the nonprofit Catskill Mountainkeeper in June 2008 brought together environmentalists and concerned citizens. Women from Wyoming and Colorado shared what the shale boom brought their hometowns, such as environmental damage and gentrification. One woman near the front remarked: "And if anybody wants me to make nice to someone who's going to come and rape my land, that's not going to happen. I don't want to live in an industrial zone. I don't want them here" (Applebome, 2008, July 3).

On July 23, 2008, Governor David Paterson signed a bill to streamline the application process for drilling in New York's Marcellus Shale, while simultaneously ordering an update of the 1992 Generic Environmental Impact Statement (GEIS). The new DEC regulations would have made it easier for gas companies to dig wells using sophisticated horizontal drilling. At the same time, the GEIS update would have entailed hearings across the southern and western parts of the state and a subsequent analysis in preparation for new permit statements. Drilling applications would also have been required to undergo an ad hoc review reflecting broader environmental concerns.

While the environmentalists had not achieved a decisive victory, their voice had been heard by the governor. Not yet reassured, eight environmental groups, including the Sierra Club, the Natural Resources Defense Council (NRDC), the Wilderness Society, the Catskill Mountainkeeper, and the Riverkeeper, sent Governor Paterson a letter seeking a moratorium on drilling activity until the environmental impact statement. By this point, gas companies had already paid hundreds of millions of dollars in leasing fees to landowners, some of them in the New York City watershed, with the obvious intention to drill. The state of New York had to quickly formulate a position (Applebome, 2008, July 27).

The issue would soon be put to a vote, as the State Assembly passed a bill in November 2010 intended to place a moratorium on new permits for gas drilling that relies on fracking. In December, Governor Paterson vetoed the bill and instituted a moratorium of his own via an executive order that more narrowly defines the types of drilling to be restricted. The governor proposed that the moratorium be in place until July 1, 2011, going beyond the date specified in the proposed bill, May 15, 2011. The distinction to be made concerned vertical wells and newer horizontal drilling techniques, in which gas drillers plumb the underground shale seams laterally. The governor's order only restricts permits for "high-volume, horizontal hydraulic fracturing." While the industry seemed to appreciate the gesture, it appears to have been largely symbolic, as most modern wells that use fracking are horizontal ones (Zeller Jr., 2010, December 11).

This moratorium extended well beyond the deadlines envisioned by its architects (Sadasivam, 2014, July 22). Governor Andrew Cuomo, who assumed office in 2011, allowed a pending health impact review by national experts to put a further hold on new fracking regulations, postponing the decision until 2013 (Rudegeair, 2012, November 29). The State Assembly passed legislation on March 6, 2013, that extended the moratorium on high-volume hydraulic fracturing in the state until May 2015, pending further studies on the environmental impact of fracking (Krudy, 2013, March 6). It was not until June 2015, when State Environmental

Conservation Commissioner Joe Martens issued a 43-page "findings statement," that the state's fracking prohibition was put into place and given the force of law (Campbell, 2015, June 29).

The Siena College poll released in September 2013 showed 45 percent of New York voters against natural gas fracking and 37 percent in favor. According to Siena College pollster Steve Greenberg, a majority of upstate residents and Democrats opposed the technique, while a plurality of Republicans and downstate suburbanites supported it (Campbell, 2013, September 30). New York City Mayor Bill DeBlasio also expressed his reservations about fracking on January 24, 2014: "I don't see any place for fracking. . . . The science simply isn't reliable enough. The technology isn't reliable enough. And, there's too much danger to our water supply, to our environment in general" (Obley, 2014, January 24).

After a six-year review process by the DEC, including a study from the New York State Department of Health, Governor Cuomo announced a state-wide fracking ban on December 17, 2014: "Let's bring the emotion down and let's ask the qualified experts" (Gerken, 2014, December 17). At a press conference, DEC Commissioner Joseph Martens and Acting Health Commissioner Howard Zucker said the potential harms are too great to allow fracking to proceed at this time, pointing to a dearth of studies regarding its long-term safety. New Yorkers Against Fracking issued a statement praising Cuomo's decision: "On behalf of millions of New Yorkers, we would like to thank the Governor for his leadership and keeping his word in listening to the science and protecting the health and safety of New Yorkers over the special interests of the oil and gas industry" (Gerken, 2014, December 17).

The New York State Petroleum Council, a program of the American Petroleum Institute, issued a statement calling the decision "the wrong direction for New York." The group's executive director, Karen Moreau, called it a "politically motivated and equally misinformed ban on a proven technology" (Gerken, 2014, December 17). While the fracking ban is by no means a small accomplishment for the anti-fracking campaign, the gas industry is currently prioritizing other states with access to the Marcellus Shale that have greater gas reserves than New York, particularly Pennsylvania and West Virginia (Esch, 2015, January 10).

Interestingly, there are even casual talks of secession in the southern tier of New York to join Pennsylvania. As one Broome County resident and chairman of pro-fracking Kirkwood Gas Coalition remarked: "I'm looking out my window right now and I see Pennsylvania. . . . The drills are right there, not three miles away. I see several drilling rigs from my window. It's pretty disappointing" (Nikolewski, 2015, June 9). They ponder the possibilities that could have been – anywhere between 25,000 to 54,000 jobs, with a 2011 study conducted by the state calculating economic value at $2.5 billion annually. Though obtaining approval from the New York Legislature, which also includes the Democrat-dominated State Assembly, Pennsylvania Legislature, and the US Congress is an unlikely prospect, "[I]t's a feel-good thing to talk about it and to let the governor know that we are not happy with what he's done to us" (Nikolewski, 2015, June 9).

Others have pointed out that New York's fracking ban is hypocritical: "Upper estimates have the Marcellus Formation in New York containing 75–100 trillion cubic feet of recoverable gas, but shale energy continues to prove previous assessments greatly understated as the resources get developed. Since 2008, interstate gas receipts from Pennsylvania have increased from 226 Bcf to about 1,200 Bcf. So, it appears that many New Yorkers enjoy using fracked gas . . . as long as it's produced somewhere else" (Clemente, 2015, June 7). Contending that the Southern Tier's vast supply of untapped natural gas reserves are a "gift," Karen Moreau, executive director of the American Petroleum Institute's New York branch, points to the recent EPA study that found "no widespread systemic" water pollution associated with the practice (Karlin, 2015, June 10).

Pennsylvania brings a different perspective. Since 1859, more than 350,000 wells have been drilled for natural gas. The shale revolution arrived in earnest in 2008, and the state has taken full advantage.[5] By its own account, the economic impact of the Marcellus Shale in 2009 has ranged between 23,385 and 23,884 jobs and between $3.1 and $3.2 billion. This impact included about $1.2 billion in labor income and $1.9 billion in value added to the economy. It also foresaw additional economic benefits in future years as mineral right owners spend the leasing and royalty income. The Pennsylvania Department of Labor and Industry (DLI) also presented the much-disputed figure of 245,000 direct and indirect jobs created by shale gas development, 4 percent of total employment in a state with 5.7 million jobs.

Mark Price, a labor economist with the Keystone Research Center, finds 20,000 direct jobs created from Marcellus Shale, while a 2013 report by the Multi-State Shale Research Collaborative concluded that the DLI overstated the industry's effect on employment by including ancillary jobs in its counts. The collaborative offered its own estimate of 29,856 jobs in 2012.[6] The American Petroleum Institute has chimed in, claiming that the natural gas industry in Pennsylvania is contributing $34.7 billion, 5.8 percent of the state's total economic activity. The DLI's *Marcellus Shale Fast Facts*, dated April 7, 2015, reports that in the third quarter of 2014, Pennsylvania shale-related employment totaled 249,436 jobs.

Much less disputed is the fact that the shale revolution is well underway in Pennsylvania. Figure 7.5 presents a county-by-county breakdown of Marcellus Shale gas wells reported to the Pennsylvania Department of Environmental Protection (DEP) for the second half of 2014.[7] Bradford, Susquehanna, and Washington counties represent front-runners in this regard, tallying more than 1,000 wells. They are followed by Greene and Lycoming counties that boast more than 800 wells. Natural gas drilling companies in Pennsylvania set another record in 2014, as shale gas production jumped 30 percent (Seltzer and Povilaitis, 2015, June 8).

Being "all in" may have its benefits, but it also has its costs. Indeed, the state seems to be coming to grips with the environmental consequences after the fact. Under pressure from various competing interest groups, the state has offered ad hoc and partial solutions that contrast sharply with New York's statewide ban. In 2011, facing mounting pressure from environmentalists and scientists, Pennsylvania asked

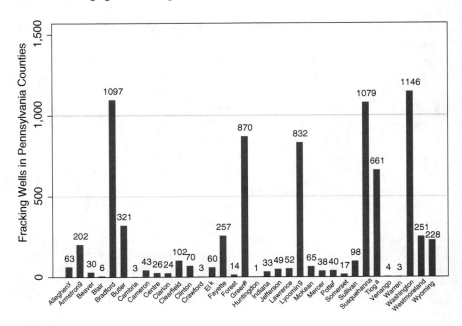

FIGURE 7.5   Fracking wells by county.

Source: StateImpact

the industry to halt disposing millions of gallons of contaminated drilling wastewater through treatment plants that discharge into rivers and streams. The DEP cited recent water tests, suggesting the discharges could harm the drinking water (Levy, 2011, April 19).

On February 14, 2012, Pennsylvania Governor Tom Corbett signed into law Act 13, which allows counties to assess an "impact fee" for each new well drilled that goes mostly to the community where it is located. Over three years, impact fee yielded $13.5 million for Tioga County, which in 2013 had a base budget of $19.6 million (DePillis, 2015, January 15). However, these benefits came with strings attached. Act 13 also revoked local zoning authority, allowing municipalities to adopt rules on drilling, but preventing them from banning it. The law also allows the state's Public Utilities Commission to overturn local zoning and decide whether a community is eligible for a share in impact fee revenues and enables the industry to seize private property for a drilling operation.[8]

Meanwhile, evidence of environmental damage had begun to accumulate. In August 2014, DEP made public 243 cases of contamination of private drinking wells from oil and gas drilling operations. The cases occurred in 22 counties, with Susquehanna, Tioga, Lycoming, and Bradford counties having the most incidences (Valentine, 2014, August 29). Courtesy of recent government efforts to increase transparency, Figure 7.6 presents drilling violations reported to the DEP from January 2009 through March 2015 on any wells that were active during the second half of

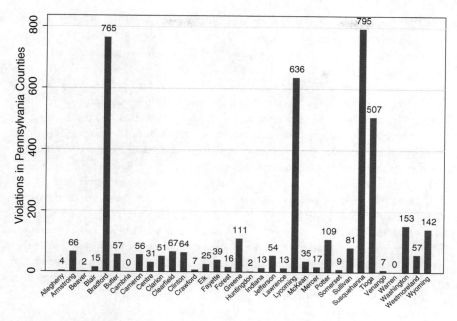

FIGURE 7.6 Drilling violations by county.

Source: StateImpact

2014. Particularly alarming are Bradford and Susquehanna counties, with more than 700 violations each. They are followed by Lycoming with 636 and Tioga with 507.[9]

Among those to raise alarm is Pennsylvania's former health secretary, Eli Avila, who says the state has failed to seriously study the potential health impacts of one of the nation's biggest natural gas drilling booms. Avila says the state's current strategy is a disservice to people and the industry because health officials need to be proactive in protecting the public. Without coordinated statewide research, he argues, it is impossible to know how widespread or dangerous the problems are and whether drilling is indeed responsible. Another public health expert, Bernard Goldstein, who has five decades of public health experience at hospitals and universities, says Pennsylvania is "simply not doing" serious studies on possible health impacts of drilling (Gerken, 2014, July 12).

The last state, Texas, is a feel-good story gone awry, a cautionary tale about the limits of local, community-based activism. The story begins in the city of Denton, which sits on the northern edge of the Barnett Shale. Two weeks after moving to Denton, Cathy McMullen noticed Range Resources hunting for a gas site across the street from a park. She sought recourse from local authorities, but the council permitted the development. The city added 200 feet to its previous 1,000-foot buffer between drilling sites and homes, schools, parks, and hospitals in 2013, but houses continued to be built near existing wells, and the operators found the loopholes to drill where they wished. EagleRidge Energy went so far as to drill wells only 200 feet from homes. When the city sued the company, the judge denied its request for a temporary injunction.

In search of a more powerful remedy, McMullen collected almost 2,000 signatures to put a city-wide fracking ban to a vote. When all was said and done, her grassroots group, Frack Free Denton, had successfully persuaded 59 percent of Denton voters to approve a fracking ban by knocking on doors, staging puppet shows, and performing song and dance numbers. Though McMullen had the backing of Earthworks, a national environmental group, she had triumphed over a Goliath of an opponent, an oil and gas lobby that had raised more than $700,000 – 10 times her own budget – for mailers, advertisements, and a public relations firm (Malewitz, 2014, December 15). This was no small feat in a right-wing, oil-patch state.

The oil and gas lobby put up a fight, allying with Texas lawmakers in an eleventh-hour effort to oppose the ban (Gold, 2015, May 18). Voters were told that the ban would ruin Denton's economy and expose the city to millions in legal claims. There were even accusations that the grassroots activists were working with the Kremlin to protect Russia's natural gas market share. Jones, a general contractor and rancher, led an organization funded by energy companies – Denton Taxpayers for a Strong Economy – to oppose the ban (Malewitz, 2014, December 15). Though the citizens of Denton had voted in favor of a ban, the Texas Oil and Gas Association and the Texas General Land Office filed suits against the city only hours after the votes were tallied, calling the ban unconstitutional (Malewitz, 2015, June 3).

The NPR's Wade Goodwyn offers an apt description of what transpired next: "In frustration, the citizens of Denton voted last year by 59 percent to ban fracking inside the city limits altogether. But that turned out to be the mouse waking the lion. And the lion pounced and ate the mouse all up" (Goodwyn, 2015, May 20. Todd Staples, the president of the Texas Oil and Gas Association, believed that Denton had acted in violation of the property rights of the oil and gas industry, taking their property's value without any compensation. The industry turned to the Republican-dominated state legislature for help. The resulting new law would strip from Texas cities and towns the power not only to ban fracking, but also to regulate many other aspects of the industry, such as wastewater disposal (Goodwyn, 2015, May 20).

Republican Governor Greg Abbott signed House Bill 40 into law, effective immediately, forbidding any Texas town or city from passing local limits or restrictions on any gas or oil drilling operations deemed "commercially reasonable" by private developers and state regulators (Queally, 2015, May 19). Frustrated Denton residents were faced with an unenviable choice: "remove the now-toothless ordinance from its books to stave off further legal trouble [or] keep it to strike a symbolic blow for local control on the off chance that the law will prove useful again some day" (Malewitz, 2015, June 3). Vantage Energy, a natural gas operator, resumed fracking operations inside the city, the final nail in the coffin of an ordinance that Denton officials say they can no longer enforce. On the first two days of fracking's return, the police arrested a small number of protesters who tried to block the company's access to its work site (Malewitz, 2015, June 3).

7.4 Motives

Unlike divestment and more similar to coal or Keystone XL, the anti-fracking campaign has a clear local focus. Ironically, the arguments to justify such a local focus are best conveyed in the film that first brought the issue to a global audience, *Gasland*. The vivid imagery of tap water being set on fire is disturbing for anyone, but the audience it ought to disturb the most are communities located closer to fracking activity.

This includes communities such as Pavillion, Wyoming, where the EPA found evidence of water contamination; Killdear, North Dakota, where fracking fluids were released on the land surface and possibly the aquifer; Bainbridge, Ohio, where natural gas eventually moved into local drinking water aquifers; and Mamm Creek gas field, where methane and benzene migrated along the production well and through natural faults and fractures to drinking water resources. In short, the message of the burning tap water is likely to resonate most where it can be observed firsthand.

However, the campaign cannot be dismissed as a loose coalition of disparate communities responding to threats to their immediate environments. There is a tie that also binds the anti-fracking campaign to the larger climate movement – the ecological paradigm as a worldview that emphasizes the primacy of life and nature over economic growth. Unconventional methods of natural gas extraction require vast quantities of water, potentially contaminate water systems, and release methane into the atmosphere, none of which is compatible with ecological preservation and the sanctity of nature.

Failing to recognize this, the fossil fuel industry's approach has been to argue that the environmental concerns are products of misperceptions propagated by *Gasland*. This has largely missed the mark, as many anti-fracking activists are concerned about more than the contamination of their drinking water. They are disturbed by the idea of fracking itself, deliberately putting in harm's way life and nature they hold dear. Consequences may involve venereal diseases, earthquakes, climate change, or social injustice, all for the fossil fuel industry's relentless drive for profit. The fracking companies have also eroded their public trust by discounting the legitimacy of these grievances, prioritizing proprietary technology over transparency and engaging governments rather than communities (Wood, 2012).

The ecological paradigm also helps explain why, internal disagreements on natural gas notwithstanding, the anti-fracking campaign still feels at home within the larger climate movement. Shared concerns over the climate impact of methane released from fracking wells do not constitute the only tie binding the anti-fracking campaign to the climate movement. Sandra Steingraber's statement is telling in this regard: "We bring to all of you, to this larger climate justice movement, a never-surrender, battle-tested spirit. America's fractivists have been fighting for our lives in the gas fields. Now we are ready to fight for life itself" (Steingraber, 2014, August 26).

The shared belief in the ecological paradigm has concrete organizational implications. The anti-fracking activists will continue to cite studies and employ rhetoric emphasizing methane's contribution to global warming, linking their struggle to the larger debate on climate. That the actual impact of methane emissions on the climate remains subject to scientific dispute will matter less, since many of the anti-fracking activists are already convinced that they share common destiny with other contingents of the climate movement. The ties that bind them are therefore fundamentally normative, and they are reinforced through joint participation in civil disobedience and direct action. These ties could certainly benefit from the backing of rigorous climate science, but they are by no means contingent on it.

This is one reason Steingraber's rousing speech on the "fighting spirit" of the anti-fracking activists, regardless of one's position on the role of fracking and natural gas within the larger climate movement, is likely to find resonance:

> I saw it in upstate New York when I watched a man named Jeremy Alderson respectfully turned down (sic) a judge's offer of community service and accept instead a 15-day jail sentence, saying quietly, "Your Honor, my act of community service was accomplished when I chained myself to the compressor station gate." . . . Friends, it is Friday night, the sun has set, and Jeremy is observing the Sabbath. Tonight, we are the Shabbat candles for Jeremy, who sits alone in a cell in Watkins Glen, New York, for a peaceful act of civil disobedience at a fracking infrastructure site.
>
> *(Steingraber, 2014, August 26)*

What she invokes is principled action, standing up for one's beliefs. Activists may meaningfully disagree on the role of natural gas and how the fight against climate change should proceed. Nonetheless, a shared belief in the ecological paradigm serves as the glue that keeps the movement, despite its internal contradictions, ostensibly coherent.

The anti-fracking campaign, despite its bottom-up character, did not arise from a vacuum. The campaign is the product of deliberate efforts of professional organizations.[10] Converting grassroots opposition into anti-fracking advocacy is the province of environmental and other pressure groups. Americans Against Fracking plays the main role in organizing opposition to fracking across the country. In New York, the advocacy group Frack Action – staffed by veterans of various progressive campaigns – documents how grassroots mobilization through petitions and awareness campaigns was instrumental in passing a local hydraulic fracturing ban in Albany. Pressure groups provide organizational infrastructure, information, technical assistance, and political savvy to the anti-fracking movement (Wood, 2012).

7.5 Mobilization potential

Though we illustrated earlier through a detailed look at New York, Pennsylvania, and Texas how efforts to impose restrictions on fracking have seen mixed results at best, the campaign as a whole undeniably ranks among the more successful anti-fossil fuel movements in terms of drawing participants and building momentum.

In addition to the popular success of *Gasland*, the movement has put together a highly effective advocacy coalition through grassroots mobilization, social media, direct action, and networking (Wood, 2012). Grassroots activists, such as those tied to farm bureau organizations and resident activists, bring legitimacy, credibility, and authenticity to the anti-fracking movement. The use of social media, such as YouTube and Facebook, has allowed for rapid dissemination of information and grassroots mobilization. Indeed, many coordinating groups at the center of the movement started out as forum groups, petitions, or blogs.

Although direct action – denying access to project sites, equipment occupations, and demonstrations – has had limited impact on the gas industry operations, it attracts media attention and raises public awareness of fracking, building a more receptive public audience and aiding activist recruitment. Demonstrations, days of action, and nonviolent civil disobedience help reconfirm principles among activists, mobilizing further grassroots support and generating solidarity. Extensive cross-cutting networks and communication among various environmental organizations at all levels – county, state, and national – make for a smarter campaign overall, as fractivists compare notes on what works and what doesn't.

Fractivists are justly proud of their achievements: "While 2014 has seen some major milestones for our efforts, perhaps the most important of these is the evidence that our movement is growing. . . . In New York, our efforts to birddog Governor Cuomo have proven successful. The Governor himself commented on the tenacious and persistent nature of our efforts to remind him that we don't want fracking in the Empire State. So far, mainly due to the determination of this movement, we've kept fracking out of New York" (Hauter, 2014, October 1). Credit should be given where it is due, and leading organizations have successfully utilized local communities and the increasingly receptive segments of the public to increase their numbers.

As we will elaborate below, a key test will be whether the fractivists can sustain their momentum as the contradictions within the climate movement, particularly between those who view natural gas as part of the climate solution and those who do not, become more apparent. Also important is the fact that commercialization of fracking is a relatively recent development. As more data are generated and we learn more about the impact of fracking on our immediate environments and the climate, it would be interesting to see how the anti-fracking movement processes and responds to new information.

7.6 Impact

Taking stock of policy impact, the most notable victories of the anti-fracking campaign have been on the state level, such as fracking bans in New York and Maryland. Smaller victories have also been achieved on the county level and may pave the way for victories similar to New York and Maryland in other states. The fracking industry has been put on notice, as Jonathan Wood, the author of a study they commissioned, advises gas companies to acknowledge local grievances, engage communities, work to reduce the damage fracking does to the environment, and "create more winners" to avoid stoking further blockades and moratoriums. If momentum continues to build, a cascade of public opinion may lead to a nation-wide fracking ban (Wood, 2012).

The key for the anti-fracking campaign, therefore, is to keep up the pressure on the fossil fuel industry and governments, while holding fast to their central message. As Wood points out, though fracking may not pose environmental problems when executed properly, continued political pressure from activists means that even occasional mistakes in drilling practices will not go unscrutinized. With every well blowout and water contamination story in the newspaper, the anti-fracking campaign grows stronger. Though Wood also notes that the anti-fracking campaign may grow complacent, grappling with the consequences of its own success, the report represents a forthright acknowledgment of the policy inroads made by the campaign, as well as the potential for policy change to come (Rabeler, 2013, March 26).

The target audiences important for the anti-fracking campaign to succeed politically are two-fold – the local communities and the general public. The former is more important than the latter in the short term, as local communities have greater capacity to act to secure county and state level bans and moratoriums. The latter, however, will be necessary to sustain the movement in the long run as a source of recruits and political capital to bring about policy change. While environmental organizations spearheading the movement certainly target and draw strength from existing grievances at the community level, they also make deliberate efforts at mass appeal.

In this regard, a recent study suggesting that the public views both the natural gas industry and the film *Gasland* among the least trustworthy sources of information is instructive (Theodoria et al., 2014). Based on telephone and mail surveys conducted in Pennsylvania's Marcellus Shale region over the summer of 2012, the paper ranked the order of trustworthiness as follows: university professors, environmental groups, newspapers, landowner groups, regulatory agencies, cooperative extensions, the natural gas industry, and then *Gasland*. The findings suggest that the public parses through the flurry of arguments from various stakeholders in the media with a dose of skepticism. While *Gasland* may have been useful for rallying the troops, sustained engagement of the public with thoughtful arguments and compelling stories will be key for the environmentalists.

The policy changes made so far bode well for the movement, and they also have the potential to shape the fracking industry's outlook. In addition to the much trumpeted victories in New York and Maryland, Global Frackdown has also highlighted passing of more than 400 measures against fracking, wastewater injection, and frac sand mining in communities across the United States, keeping fracking out of the Delaware River Basin, passing ballot measures banning or placing a moratorium on fracking in Colorado, Ohio, and Vermont, as well as launching Americans Against Fracking and strong statewide coalitions in New York, California, Colorado, Oregon, Ohio, and Maryland.[11] Each political victory brings greater legitimacy to the campaign.

Nonetheless, the campaign is not without critics, and the backlash tends to come from two sources – the gas industry and those in the climate movement who accept unconventional natural gas development as inevitable. The gas industry has often targeted *Gasland*, blaming it for wildly exaggerating the environmental repercussions of fracking. The industry has also argued that fracking produces employment and promotes economic growth (Efstathiou Jr., 2012, October 23). The more interesting disagreement, however, comes from within the environmental establishment itself. There are quarters of the movement that do not fundamentally oppose fracking and are willing to accept it under tighter regulations.

Given that natural gas represents a compelling alternative to coal, and the impact of methane emissions on climate is still under dispute, these tensions are not likely to go away any time soon (Lynch, 2013, January 29). In the eyes of activists who believe that natural gas may be part of the climate solution, the fracking campaign is actually doing more harm than good. While the ecological paradigm will help keep many of these contradictions under the rug, our final evaluation is that difficult conversations will need to take place among anti-fracking activists, as well as within the larger anti-fossil fuel community itself, to clarify the long-term policy goals for this campaign and the necessary means to sustain the momentum.

Notes

1 See the official Americans Against Fracking website available at www.americansagainst fracking.org/take-action/global-frackdown/ (accessed June 18, 2015).
2 See the official Global Frackdown website available at www.globalfrackdown.org/org-endorsement-form/ (accessed June 18, 2015).
3 See the official statements available at www.americansagainstfracking.org/take-action/ (accessed June 18, 2015) and http://frackfreeworld.org/about-us/statements (accessed June 18, 2015).
4 The data from FracTracker are available at http://maps.fractracker.org/latest/?appid=68 f3de3fc2a1462aaf700fff5ec0ab47 (accessed June 21, 2015).
5 See the Pennsylvania Fracking website available at www.pennsylvaniafracking.com (accessed June 18, 2015).
6 See the SourceWatch description available at www.sourcewatch.org/index.php/Penn sylvania_and_fracking#Jobs (accessed June 18, 2015).
7 The data from StateImpact are available at http://stateimpact.npr.org/pennsylvania/ drilling/counties/ (accessed June 21, 2015).
8 See the Source Watch entry on Pennsylvania and fracking available at www.source watch.org/index.php/Pennsylvania_and_fracking#Jobs (accessed June 18, 2015).
9 The data from StateImpact are available at http://stateimpact.npr.org/pennsylvania/ drilling/counties/ (accessed June 21, 2015).
10 For a list of these organizations, consult www.fractracker.org/resources/the-alliance-map/
11 See the official Global Frackdown website available at www.globalfrackdown.org/ about/ (accessed June 19, 2015).

8

CAMPAIGNS AGAINST FOSSIL FUELS

A global view

We have so far focused on the United States, but even the original campaign against Keystone XL was ultimately an international issue, a pipeline intended to transport oil extracted from Canadian tar sands to and through the United States. More generally, campaigns against fossil fuels are common across the world. Consider, for example, the bittersweet irony of increased oil and gas exploration in the Arctic as a result of climate change, which is melting away the ice. The international environmental NGO Greenpeace draws on this irony in their slogan for the campaign to "Save the Arctic," which says that "no matter how bad your #worstjoke may be, drilling for oil in the Arctic is worse" (Craighill, 2015, March 3).

To shed light on the global aspects of campaigns against fossil fuels and evaluate the applicability of our argument, we now offer a brief overview of developments in other regions of the world. Specifically, the goal of this chapter is to show that our theory can be applied outside the American context. After all, the primary problem with fossil fuels is their contribution to the global environmental problem of climate change. If the campaign against fossil fuels is to succeed in the long run, it must score a series of victories not only in America, but also in other major economies. Even if North American anti-fossil fuel campaigners succeeded in achieving all of their goals, high and rapidly growing carbon dioxide emissions from emerging economies would assure rapid global warming over this century.

What does the global landscape for anti-fossil fuel campaigns look like? To summarize, it turns out that the United States is in many ways a special case. Campaigns against pipelines are common across the world, but they are based on an altogether different logic than Keystone XL. There are very few fracking campaigns, probably because fracking is not yet at all common outside the United States. The global divestment campaign very much reflects the American campaign, but this is only so because the global divestment campaign is a direct extension of the North American original. Of all the global campaigns we review here, only the global anti-coal campaign has independently developed strategies, frames, and outcomes similar to those of its American counterpart. In light of these findings, it appears that the North American anti-fossil fuel campaign is a national effort that is not easy to replicate elsewhere.

We begin with a brief overview of what the literature on activism says about opposition to fossil fuels in different countries. There is by now a large, if fragmented, body of case studies on such opposition written under the banner of "political ecology" (Martinez-Alier, 2002). While these case studies do not focus on fossil fuels in particular, campaigning against fossil fuel extraction has been common both in industrialized and developing countries. Drawing on this literature and our own analytical framework, we analyze the international dimensions of today's campaign against fossil fuels. As hinted above, we find that the prospects for a globalization of the American anti-fossil fuel movement are not bright, mainly because the logic and outcomes of the anti-fossil fuel movement reflect the American national context. With the exception of the rapid evolution of a coordinated and effective global anti-coal campaign, a truly global strategy would require organizations such as 350.org to develop a new set of targets, tactics, and strategies.

The chapter ends with a case study of the environmental campaign against the funding of coal by development agencies. Many American and European environmental organizations have aggressively targeted these development agencies and fought to reduce, or even ban, the funding of coal mining and coal power plants. These campaigns have been relatively successful and offer a powerful illustration of the broader campaign against fossil fuels. On the other hand, the campaigns also highlight the need to graduate from opposing individual projects to focus on comprehensive policy. In this specific case, construction of coal power plants in many emerging economies continues unabated because these countries are not dependent on development agencies for finance. Therefore, the victories of the campaign against development agencies are partial only and raise many questions about the future of the campaign against fossil fuels.

8.1 Historical precedents

The literature on campaigns against fossil fuels on different continents is limited. Most of the earlier studies actually focus on two different energy problems: nuclear power and large dams. In the industrialized countries, the first major movements that specifically targeted energy projects were in opposition to nuclear power plants. Concerned about nuclear safety – accidents, radiation, and waste – activists have for decades vigorously opposed both government and corporate efforts to build new nuclear power plants. With the exception of France, where the anti-nuclear movement was unable to stop the rapid construction of 58 nuclear reactors by the public electric utility Electricité de France,[1] the anti-nuclear movement has achieved a high level of success across the industrialized countries (World Nuclear Association, 2017, October). In the United States, no construction permits were given between the years 1979–2012, and many already permitted construction plans were abandoned (US Energy Information Administration, 2012, September 27).[2] According to Kitschelt (1986) and Baumgartner (1989), anti-nuclear activists were able to permeate the relatively open regulatory system and challenge the initially pro-nuclear consensus among American experts.

There is no question that the anti-nuclear movement has been successful, but one must keep in mind that the movement's activism was greatly facilitated by nuclear accidents in the United States and Europe. In the United States, the Three Mile Island accident was a tipping point that turned the American public and polit-ical establishment against nuclear power after decades of consistent support (Rees, 2009). In Europe, the Chernobyl accident left an abiding impression on Germany and other countries (Jahn, 1992; Joppke, 1990; Rudig, 1990). The desperation and fears that Chernobyl provoked were further strengthened by the 2011 Fukushima incident in Japan, a country long admired for its engineering and technological prowess. It was in the aftermath of Japan's tragedy that the German Chancellor Angela Merkel finally decided to phase out nuclear power by 2022 – a historic energy policy decision that put a lot of pressure on the country to deliver on renewable energy (Dempsey, 2011, August 13).

More recently, the anti-nuclear movement has grown increasingly transnational. Today's anti-nuclear advocates operate on a global scale, trying to stop nuclear power projects not only in Europe or America, but also in Asia. In China, for example, anti-nuclear protests have become increasingly frequent in the aftermath of the 2011 Fukushima incident in Japan (Yue, 2014, September 23). In India, efforts to build the country's largest nuclear power reactor in Tamil Nadu sparked large protests in 2012, with activists drawing inspiration from the global backlash against nuclear due to Fukushima (Lakshmi and Denyer, 2012, September 15). In both countries, international organizations such as Greenpeace also do active anti-nuclear work, enabling international coordination of local and national protests.

The anti-nuclear case offers a few important insights into a global analysis of anti-fossil fuel campaigns. First, the nuclear case shows the role of accidents that are widely publicized, as well as the power of local concerns. Without the Three Mile Island and Chernobyl accidents, the fate of nuclear power in North America and Western Europe could have been very different. However, the analysis also highlights the importance of accounting for the local political context. The success of nuclear power first in France and then in China shows that the national constel-lation of political institutions cannot be ignored as a factor in understanding why even vigorous campaigns sometimes fail to stem the tide. Countries faced with the same reality of dependence on fossil fuels and its contribution to climate change may respond with different measures, depending on political context.

The other major historical precedent for campaigns against energy projects is popular resistance to large dams in the developing world (Leslie, 2007; McCully, 2001). In his review of the international anti-dam movement, McCully (2001: 281) writes, "The decade since the mid-1980s has seen the emergence of an interna-tional movement against current dam-building practices . . . [comprising] thou-sands of environmental, human rights and social activist groups on all the world's inhabited continents." The movement began decades ago in the United States and focused on protesting the environmental consequences of dam construction especially in the Southwest, with charismatic leaders such as the late environmental writer Edward Abbey. Today, however, opposition to large dams is concentrated in developing countries that still have untapped hydroelectric potential. Since 1985, the global campaign has been coordinated by the organization International Rivers, whose staff:

> work with an international network of dam-affected people, grassroots organizations, environmentalists, human rights advocates and others who are committed to stopping destructive river projects and promoting better options. . . . We seek a world where healthy rivers and the rights of local communities are valued and protected. We envision a world where water and energy needs are met without degrading nature or increasing poverty, and where people have the right to participate in decisions that affect their lives."[3]

The anti-dam movement has been active across a wide range of countries. Many of the iconic anti-dam campaigns have been mounted in India, where the country's dreams of economic modernization through access to hydroelectric power have frequently clashed with a vibrant civil society operating in a democratic environment conducive to grassroots mobilization. Activists in the *Narmada Bachao Andalon*, or Save Narmada Movement, forced the World Bank to withdraw from funding the planned massive Sardar Sarovar Dam, citing concerns about forced displacement of marginalized groups, such as tribal communities (Khagram, 2004; Pallas and Urpelainen, 2012). These local groups also engaged in deep collaboration with international organizations such as the Environmental Defense Fund, increasing their access to powerful policymakers in the West (McCully, 2001: 302).

Similar to the pipeline campaigns, local concerns prove critical to understanding anti-dam mobilization. In her ethnographic account of tribal life and politics in the threatened areas, Baviskar (1995) recounts the hostile relations between tribal communities and government officials. Besides the immediate issue of displacement, Baviskar emphasizes the local government's lack of interest in the welfare and concerns of the tribal communities, writing that "[a]lthough the government plans to drastically alter the lives of so many people with the Sardar Sarovar Project, it has not bothered to consult or even inform them about their fate. . . . [T]he planning and implementation process of the Project does not include the participation of the affected population and is a callous violation of their right to information, cultural autonomy and choice" (Baviskar, 1995: 202). Although the dam has now been approved by Indian authorities, popular opposition has delayed the project by three decades and resulted in changes in the design of the hydroelectric infrastructure.

Another country that has seen much activism against dams is Brazil (Carvalho, 2006). As early as in 1975, the public electric utility Eletronorte had proposed a massive hydroelectric dam with a planned generation capacity of 14,700 MW, called Belo Monte, in the Xingu River. However, concerns about the displacement

of indigenous tribes living along the river soon resulted in "extensive mobilization at the grassroots level (especially among the indigenous organizations in the
Xingu), and national and international NGOs" (Carvalho, 2006: 257). In 1989, an
alliance between environmentalists and indigenous peoples was able to force the
World Bank to cancel a loan to Eletronorte. Again, though dam construction is set
to begin soon, this mobilization resulted in considerable delays and a considerable
reduction in the size of the dam's reservation. As McCully (2001: 296) summarizes,
"The Brazilian anti-dams movement has combined with the country's economic
woes to slow down drastically the country's ambitious dam-building plans."

With the singular exception of China, where the construction of both large and
small hydroelectric dams has advanced rapidly and without constraints imposed
by the civil society, the campaign against dams has been at least as successful as the
anti-nuclear campaign. Despite considerable remaining potential, the construction
of large hydroelectric dams has come to a grinding halt over the past three decades.
One of the reasons behind the campaign's success appears to be the dependence of
most developing countries, which hold most of the untapped hydroelectric potential, on international funders and developers. These transnational linkages have
allowed anti-dam activists to score political victories in national contexts that do
not initially appear favorable to environmental activism.

8.2 Against fossil fuels: international dimensions

As we have already noted, our research strategy is to focus on the very same campaigns that we have analyzed in the American context: pipelines, divestment, fracking, and anti-coal activism. Though our treatment of the global campaigns is less
extensive than that of the American case, we keep the structure of the discussion
similar. After all, our goal here is to use our analytical framework to shed light on
developments outside the United States, and focusing on the same set of issues
allows meaningful comparisons across borders. Given the diversity of campaigns at
the global level, we also refrain from making categorical statements about impact.

As we shall see, there are considerable differences in the motivations and effects
of these campaigns. Pipelines are a major concern for environmental activists across
the globe, but their planetary significance is rarely highlighted in the campaigns.
The global divestment campaign is but an extension of the original campaign and,
unsurprisingly, follows the same logic. Fracking campaigns outside the United State
are mostly fragmented and weak, if only because there is not yet much fracking outside the United States. Among the North American campaigns we have analyzed,
the anti-coal campaign has the strongest counterpart on the global scene, with
environmental activists skillfully combining global and local concerns to mobilize
against coal mines and power plants.

While opposition to oil extraction by local communities is widespread, we focus
our review here on efforts that specifically target pipelines, in an effort to paral-
lel our chapter on the Keystone XL. Efforts against pipelines are also common in
other parts of the world, but their motivations and operations turn out to be quite

different from those of the Keystone XL campaign. To illustrate this, we consider two recent case studies, one from Africa and the other from Latin America: the Chad-Cameroon pipeline and the Urucu natural gas pipeline.

The Chad-Cameroon pipeline is one of the more famous examples of activism against oil infrastructure. At the time of its development, this joint project of ExxonMobil, Petronas, and Chevron was to be the largest infrastructure project in Africa, with a $4.2 billion price tag (African Forum and Network on Debt and Development, 2007: 15). Between 1993 and 1999, the World Bank and other development agencies supported the governments of Chad and Cameroon in the design of the project. The project was approved in the year 2000 and, in 2003, Chad became an oil exporter. As Pegg (2009: 314) notes, however, in January 2006 the Bank responded to Chad's worsening governance problems and "suspended all new loans and grants to Chad and all disbursements ($124 million) yet to be released from its eight active loans in Chad. Suspending the loan disbursements automatically triggered a freeze on the oil revenues in Chad's escrow account in London." After a series of failed negotiations and in the face of political instability in Chad, in August 2008, the World Bank complained to Chad. In September 2006, Chad pre-paid "all outstanding World Bank loans relating to the pipeline project, . . . effectively ending the Bank's involvement in this project" (Pegg, 2009: 319).

Throughout the development of this project, environmentalists launched attacks on the bank for supporting the pipeline. Per usual, the campaign against the pipeline was a joint effort between international groups, such as the EDF in the United States, and local organizations, such as the Center for Environment and Development (Cameroon) and the Chadian Association for the Promotion and Defense of Human Rights. In April 2007, these groups published a "project non-completion report" that summarizes what they believe to be the major problems with the project. In the section on "environment and livelihoods," the authors Horta et al. (2007: 17–21) raise the following issues: large ecological footprint, health risks, and damage to crops and trees because of lack of dust control, water problems, toxic waste, erosion, commercial logging near a rainforest, poaching and threat of invasive species, oil flaring, delays and insufficient funding for biodiversity off-set areas, and lack of alternative livelihood strategies.

What is most interesting about the report is that, in 2007, at the peak of global attention to climate change, the words "climate," "global," "warming," and "carbon" are not mentioned at all. In a stark contrast to the Keystone XL case, the organizations campaigning against the pipeline have nothing to say about the problem of climate change. The entire campaign is based on concerns about local impacts, despite the participation of major environmental NGOs such as the EDF. As we shall see, this pattern is common across campaigns against pipelines, with the singular exception of Keystone XL.

In Brazil, the Urucu-Manaus natural gas pipeline did not face the same governance problems that undermined Chad's plans to grow wealthy with oil exports, but this project also met with organized environmental opposition. The Urucu gas reserves in central Amazonia were discovered already in 1986, and in 1988 the

Brazilian national oil and gas company Petrobras, in collaboration with the state government of Amazonas and the Ministry of Mines and Energy, saw it as "a solution to the chronic problem of supplying energy to Manaus and areas in the western Amazon" (Carvalho, 2006). The project has faced considerable delays, however, and it was only in November 2009 that the pipeline was finally inaugurated.

The mobilization against the pipeline began in earnest in 1999, when an international coalition of NGOs "orchestrated a media campaign" (Carvalho, 2006: 254). The opposition was sparked by the 1997 construction of a small segment of the pipeline from Urucu to Coari, which created "known environmental and social impacts" (Carvalho, 2006: 253). The coalition against the pipeline comprised organizations such as Friends of the Earth International, Pastoral Land Commission (an organization of the Brazilian Catholic Church), and various indigenous rights groups such as Coordination of the Indigenous Organization of the Brazilian Amazon (Carvalho, 2006: 253–254). While the coalition did not manage to stop the construction of the pipeline, it delayed it by several years through lawsuits related to the pipeline's environmental license and forging of alliances with local politicians.

For our purposes, the most notable feature of this activism is again the lack of emphasis on climate change. The activists did not use climate change or the global problems associated with fossil fuels as an argument in their campaign. Instead, they focused exclusively on the local impacts. Neither the local nor the international partners of the anti-pipeline coalition tried to link the pipeline to the issue of climate change. This lack of attention to climate change can be seen in a Friends of the Earth International report (2002) entitled *Clashes with Corporate Giants*. The report expresses concerns about water pollution, the disappearance of fish, and even child prostitution in the city of Coari because of the Urucu-Coari construction. In the future, the report claims:

> The Urucu gas pipeline would open the door to loggers, miners, farmers and agriculturalists from Rondonia to intact areas of the Amazon. This could deforest one of the region's most preserved sites, inhabited by extremely isolated and vulnerable indigenous groups such as the Apurinã, Paumari, Deni and the remaining Juma.
>
> *(Friends of the Earth International, 2002: 35)*

Climate change or carbon dioxide emissions are never mentioned, however.

To summarize, these two campaigns against oil and gas pipelines, respectively, highlight stark differences between the motivations and goals of Keystone XL and those of international campaigns. Keystone XL has been, first and foremost, about climate change and leaving fossil fuels underground. International campaigns against oil and gas pipelines do criticize the fossil fuel industry, but the emphasis is almost exclusively on the local social and ecological effects of the infrastructure project. This means that the deliberate use of a pipeline as a larger symbol, which made the Keystone XL campaign so potent in the US context, is conspicuously absent in these international campaigns.

Although there are historical precedents to divestment, in the case of fossil fuels, it turns out that the global campaign is an outgrowth of the North American version. As of May 6, 2015, the website Fossil Free, the online hub for the divestment campaign, lists the United States, Canada, Europe, South Africa, Australia, and New Zealand as locations of active divestment campaigns.[4] The website also does not differentiate between the campaigns of different countries, but instead refers to "an international network of campaigns and campaigners working toward fossil fuel divestment in our communities."[5] Furthermore, Fossil Free acknowledges that it is "a project of 350.org." By and large, these campaigns rely on the list of top 200 publicly traded fossil fuel companies – the carbon majors. The arguments given on the website are common across the campaigns and cite the troubling ethics of fossil fuels, the importance of undermining the legitimacy of the fossil fuel industry, and keeps track of divestment commitments and actions both in the United States and elsewhere in the world. To summarize, there is no functional differentiation between the American and other campaigns. There was no international fossil fuel divestment campaign before the American campaign, and the international campaigns largely follow the American example.

The reason behind the integrated logic of these campaigns is that divestment is, for environmental activists, a new tactic. While divestment became prominent first in the anti-apartheid campaign and then in the boycotts against Israel, it is not a tactic that has played a major role in environmental or energy campaigns in the past. Because of this institutional vacuum, 350.org has been able to rapidly fill the global space and draw followers outside its home base in the United States. The end result is an integrated global campaign.

In the case of fracking, the current situation is the opposite from the integrated international divestment campaign. At the time of writing, fracking is only conducted on a commercial scale in North America. Although countries such as China may have larger shale gas reserves than the United States, their energy industries do not currently have the technological ability to tap into these resources, despite high energy prices. In Europe, countries such as Bulgaria, France, Germany, and the Netherlands have put formal or *de facto* moratoria on fracking. As a result of these national bans and the lack of commercial fracking even in countries that allow it, there is no international campaign against fracking that could be compared to the groundswell of local activism in North America.

To be sure, it is important not to conflate the lack of local activism in many countries with a lack of success. In countries that have either enacted a moratorium on fracking or have no significant commercial activity, it is unsurprising that fracking protests are rare. When a ban is already in place, there is not much that the anti-fracking movement can do, except for monitoring government policy and preparing for mobilization in case political leaders propose to remove the moratorium. When there is no commercial activity, local communities may feel little need to become active to stop fracking. This is a very different situation from, say, New York State, where local fracking activism has been fueled by concerns about the rapid development and expansion of fracking in neighboring Pennsylvania.

The most important exception to the pattern of relative inaction must be Argentina, a country that is currently in the middle of rapid shale gas development. According to the US EIA, Argentina has the world's third-largest "technically recoverable shale gas resources," ahead of both the United States (#4) and Canada (#5).[6] The *Buenos Aires Herald* reported:

> Argentina will try to reverse a long decline in natural gas and oil production with the deal YPF energy company signed on Tuesday with Chevron to invest US$1.24 billion in developing the country's shale deposits. Nevertheless, environmental groups and organizations complain about the risks of using the hydraulic fracturing technique, also known as fracking, to recover hydrocarbons.
>
> *(Buenos Aires Herald, 2013, July 21)*

In a pattern quite different from the United States, the anti-fracking coalition comprises not only environmentalists, but also a large number of indigenous peoples' activists, with anti-corporate arguments aimed at multinational energy majors. The anti-capitalist website PopularResistance.org, for example, reports that the indigenous Mapuche communities, who live in the shale play areas, began protesting against the drilling by the national oil and gas company YPF in 2010 (Frayssinet, 2014, November 19). The environmental journal *Earth Island Journal* reports that the Mapuche were never consulted about the Chevron-YPF deal to begin fracking in southern Argentina (O'Neill, 2013, October 7). According to the same source, indigenous activists are concerned about the local ecology and water. As Lautaro Nahuel, of the Mapuche Confederation of Neuquén puts it: "It's not just the land they are taking . . . All the natural life in this region is interconnected. Here, they'll affect the Neuquén River, which is the river we drink out of." While these concerns clearly stem from an ecological paradigm, they also have an indigenous basis that has not played a major role in United States.

To be sure, some American environmental organizations have made efforts to internationalize their campaign. Consider the Global Frackdown event on October 11, 2014.[7] On this date, anti-fracking campaigns around the world organized events against the fracking industry. A large majority of the events were held in North America and most of the remaining events were organized in Western Europe. The website of this action day, which was also held in 2012 and 2013, notes that "The Global Frackdown is an international day of action initiated by Food & Water Watch to ban fracking" (Global Frackdown, n.d.). While one action day a year is still modest, it is nonetheless notable that one of the leading national anti-fracking organizations in the United States is now also spearheading efforts to create a global campaign.

Despite the partial Argentine exception and recent efforts to create an international campaign, it is safe to say that anti-fracking activism at the global level is both diverse and highly localized. It is not organized to the same extent as the campaign in the United States, and the level and nature of activism vary widely across countries. While many of the concerns about fracking are similar to those raised by American activists, there is, with the partial exception of efforts such as the Global Frackdown, no overarching international campaign against fracking. The conditions and policies in different countries are too diverse for a more organized campaign.

The international campaign against coal, on the other hand, is organized and coordinated. Among the American environmental groups, Sierra Club has an "international climate and energy" campaign that targets coal projects across the world using tactics borrowed from their American-focused Beyond Coal campaign.[8] In the campaign's 2014 annual report, written in collaboration with Greenpeace and other activists, the organization highlights, besides the United States, campaigns from Australia, India, Kosovo, Philippines, Thailand, and Turkey (Sierra Club, 2014). The 2013 report highlighted campaigns in Alaska, Germany, India, Bangladesh, China, Indonesia, and Australia (Sierra Club, 2013). Notably, most of the case studies are actually contributed by Greenpeace's national activists, highlighting the international connections of these campaigns.

In a similar vein, the Rainforest Action Network's coal campaign is not limited to the United States, but often targets international projects, especially through attacks on finance. In May 2015, RAN triumphantly announced that Bank of America, which the NGO had called "Bank of Coal" in the past, had decided to reduce its investments in coal mining (Rainforest Action Network, 2015, May 6).[9] Already in March 2011, RAN had created a list of six major banks that invested large amounts of money in coal mining, with Bank of America topping the list. After four years of campaigning, RAN appears to have won the contest.

But the international campaign against coal is not limited to extensions of American campaigns. Indeed, the most important similarity between the American and international anti-coal campaigns is their strong emphasis on grassroots mobilization. Across the world, the success or failure of campaigns against coal ultimately hinges on local communities. While international activists concerned about climate change play an important supporting role, the vast majority of the actual campaign work is done by citizens living in communities threatened by coal.

An enlightening example of such campaigning is found on the Germany–Poland border. According to what Greenpeace activists based in Warsaw told us, the backbone of the campaign against a proposed open-cast lignite coal mine in the border region of Lusatia is a grassroots campaign from 20 villages in the area, where 6,000 Polish and German people are under the threat of displacement. These people are much less motivated by climate change than by the imminent threat that coal mining poses to their communities and livelihoods. As Marzena Dera, from the village of Grabice, told Greenpeace Energydesk:

> For 18 years we have wanted to buy this farmland from the state, but each year there is a different excuse. The government are only protecting the coal underneath us. We are unlikely to be able to even renew the lease next year.
> *(Abelvik-Lawson, 2014, August 26)*

At the same time, the Polish government is strongly in favor of increased coal mining and burning as a way to promote economic development (Kania, 2014, April 28).

Another widely publicized example of anti-coal campaigning is found in Mahan, Madhya Pradesh, India, where two Indian companies, Hindalco Industries and Essar Energy, have planned "to mine local coal to feed their $3.8 billion Mahan aluminum smelter and power plants." A controversy erupted when the previous cabinet's Tribal Affairs Minister, V. Kishore Chandra Deo, said that the companies had tried to force villagers to agree to coal mining in the forest area. According to a February 2015 article in the *Hindustan Times*, villagers in the area disagree on the merits of the project (Santoshi, 2015, February 4). Some support the Mahan Sangarash Samiti, a local organization that opposes coal mining. For example, Virenda Singh, who lives in the village of Amelia, says: "It takes a lifetime for a tree to grow and centuries for a forest to come alive, but they will cut all these trees and destroy the home of wild animals and birds" (Santoshi, 2015, February 4). But others, such as Byasji Jaiswal from the village of Budher, support coal mining and say:

> We are poor and nobody gives a damn about us. I don't think we can save these forests. And I don't care now. We want money and jobs. The reality is that the mining project will come here. And it is good if it brings more benefits to us.
>
> *(Santoshi, 2015, February 4)*

These are but some examples of a recurring pattern. Coal mining and burning are polluting activities, with clear negative consequences for local communities. At the same time, coal can fuel economic development, bringing industry and employment to deprived areas. The anti-coal campaign relies heavily on the ability of local opposition movements to win their struggles with a little help from their international friends.

The global anti-coal campaign shares many features with the American campaign, even though the two are not tightly integrated. Both American and international activists are concerned about climate disruption, yet much of the rhetoric on the battlefield – in local communities and national campaigns – focuses on local concerns. This strategy has been successfully used in the United States. While the international coordinators and professional activists are largely motivated by planetary concerns, their ability to score victories against coal mines and power plants depends on mobilizing local communities.

It is the combination of careful international coordination and vigorous local activism that allows the anti-coal activists to win their fights, both in America and elsewhere. These wins, in turn, keep the campaign alive and ensure sustained interest among environmental movements of all stripes. After all, it is hard for an environmentalist to argue against a successful campaign that simultaneously deals with climate change and addresses local problems ranging from air pollution and water use to public health and land use. Despite the stark contrast between the American socio-economic context and those of developing countries, the characteristics of coal drive a large number of environmental activists toward similar tactics, and for similar reasons.

Overall, some anti-fossil fuel campaigns we examined in the American context have found greater resonance on the global stage than did others. Divestment boasts a somewhat integrated campaign, with a presence in the United States, Canada, Europe, South Africa, Australia, and New Zealand. Similarly, there is evidence of international coordination among anti-coal activists, who seek to strike a balance between combating global climate change and addressing more local concerns. On the other hand, unlike the Keystone XL campaign, protests against oil and gas pipelines abroad do not seem to place the same emphasis on climate change or the role of the fossil fuel industry. The anti-fracking campaign has also found limited resonance abroad, perhaps due to more practical considerations, such as pre-existing national bans on hydraulic fracking and the lack of commercial fracking even in countries that allow it.

8.3 Case study: coal and development

Of all the international campaigns against fossil fuels, perhaps the most widely publicized is the call for a moratorium on development finance for coal projects. During the past decade, international environmental groups have targeted the financing schemes of development agencies in particular, in an ambitious effort to stop development assistance for what these groups call "dirty coal" projects once and for all. The idea behind this campaign, activists say, is that development agencies should stop paying lip service to sustainability and instead incorporate mainstream environmental and climate mitigation considerations into all of their activities. Because coal is the most carbon-intensive fossil fuel, activists seek to replace it with more sustainable alternatives, and renewable energy in particular.

From a strategic perspective, this campaign makes sense for environmental groups. Coal is a relatively easy target, development agencies have faced a lot of pressure to improve their sustainability record, and the most important development agencies – especially the World Bank – depend on funding by liberal democracies with influential environmental groups. At the same time, the focus on development agencies raises some difficult ethical questions and has not been received well among the possible recipients of aid. If the mandate of development agencies is to eradicate extreme poverty, is it reasonable that environmental groups target such projects in particular? From an environmentalist's perspective, the answer is probably "yes," as environmentalists do not believe coal to be compatible with sustainable human development. But what about the governments and people of the countries whose plans to build power plants are buried because of environmental activism?

These dilemmas are readily seen in the case of the World Bank, which in 2013 promised to stop funding coal-fired power plants, except in "rare circumstances," such as in the case of least-developed countries without other viable options (Yukhananov and Volcovici, 2013, July 16). The bank had been under heavy pressure to stop funding coal projects at least since it approved a $3.75 billion loan to

South Africa, a middle-income country with high levels of industrialization, that allowed the country's monopoly electric utility, Eskom, "to move forward with a 4,800 megawatt power plant. . . . Environmental groups condemned the loan, calling the Medupi power plant a disaster for climate change that will enrich industry while keeping poor South Africans condemned to energy poverty" (Friedman, 2010, April 9). In an official news feature on July 7, 2013, the president of the World Bank Group, Jim Yong Kim, stated: "We need affordable energy to help end poverty and to build shared prosperity. . . . We will also scale up efforts to improve energy efficiency and increase renewable energy – according to countries' needs and opportunities" (World Bank, 2013, July 16).[10]

In this case, the bank's leadership responded to pressure by environmentalists from industrialized Western countries, along with their local allies, mobilizing against coal. However, the response from recipients was very different. In 2010, when the World Bank voted on the Eskom loan, the developing countries formed a unified front against the industrialized countries in favor of the loan. Given that climate change hurts many of the least developed countries in Sub-Saharan Africa and South Africa is not among the world's poorest countries, it is striking how unanimous the developing countries were in their support for using development assistance to support the Medupi power project. Indeed, explaining any variation among developing countries in their views on coal may be an interesting avenue for future research. As economists Scott Morris and Billy Pizer write in an online essay for the Center for Global Development, rejecting coal:

> would be bad for development and would also undermine the very goals that the bank's coal critics espouse by further pitting developing and developed countries against each other in the climate debate occurring within the bank. . . . [T]he World Bank's rejection of an outright ban on coal financing and embrace of a thoughtful, well-defined, limited role could support, rather than contradict, greater progress on the broader climate change agenda at the bank.
>
> *(Morris and Pizer, 2013)*

The case shows the difficulties that environmental frames and arguments face in the context of development. For poorer countries, economic development is a top priority. Even if they recognize the disadvantages of burning coal, they are genuinely concerned about the possibility that their ability to finance power generation and rural electrification is jeopardized. No wonder, then, that the coal industry itself has tried to use economic development as an argument in favor of coal. Peabody Energy, one of the world's largest coal companies, introduces on its website a plan to promote the use of coal to eradicate energy poverty:

> Access to electricity fuels progress and drives health and longevity. Yet today, more than half of the people across the globe lack proper electricity, and another 2 billion people will require power as the population grows. This

means that as many as 5 billion to 6 billion people will lack proper energy in as little as two decades. We have the power to solve this crisis.

(Ritter, 2015)

While such an argument would be hard to make in an industrialized country context, the connection between energy and economic development offers the coal industry an opportunity to fight against those who are attacking coal as a dirty fuel of the past.

In the United States, anti-fossil fuel activists, led by Greenpeace and Friends of the Earth, have also attacked the Overseas Private Investment Corporation (OPIC), a public credit agency that offers credit and guarantees to private investors to enable American investments in developing countries.[11] In 2009, a lawsuit filed by these two organizations and the city of Boulder, Colorado, "was settled . . . after more than six years" and forced the United States Export-Import Bank to consider carbon dioxide emissions and OPIC to set a 10-year emissions reductions goal.[12] Of the two targets, OPIC has taken its goal of low-carbon development seriously and started to prioritize renewable energy. Some development experts, however, have expressed concerns about this approach. In a report written for the Center for Global Development, development economists Moss and Leo (2014) note that "[t]here has been a general bias toward using OPIC to invest principally in solar, wind, and other low-emissions energy projects. . . . [W]e estimate that more than 60 million additional people in poor nations could gain access to electricity if OPIC is allowed to invest in natural gas projects, not just renewables." Whether one accepts this computation as valid or not, the principal argument about the possible costs of restricting public finance to energy project stands as a possibility.

In this case, the rule against investment in fossil fuels has drawn significant criticism, especially in the context of President Obama's "Power Africa" plan, which aims to provide the least-developed countries of Sub-Saharan Africa with electric power for development and industrialization (USAID, n.d.).[13] While the criticisms are not focused on coal in particular, they highlight the downside of preventing development agencies from investing in fossil fuels. It is one thing to require that the world's wealthy societies increase the pace of their sustainable energy transitions; it is another to enact policies that prevent the world's destitute from gaining access to the electricity that their societies need to grow.

Again, we face the same trade-off: if economic development results in environmental deterioration, how much damage is acceptable? For the anti-fossil fuel activists, whose actions are strongly influenced by the ecological paradigm, the answer is often that economic development must be environmentally sustainable, and therefore organizations such as OPIC must focus their efforts on supporting renewable energy and other sustainable technologies. But for the development community and the governments of the least-developed countries, this answer is not good enough.

Many of the environmentalist arguments for excluding fossil fuels from development finance hinge on the promise of renewable energy. To cite the Sierra Club again, Craine et al. (2014) present a report on what they call the "Clean Energy for All (CE4ALL)" model. They write:

> The investment needs for achieving energy access have been vastly over-estimated. This is largely due to embedded assumptions of poor energy efficiency leading to high energy demand and poor cost-modelling of off-grid solutions which, in turn, reduce the projected utilization of off-grid solutions. Moreover, simplistic models for the patterns of market development imply much more front-loaded investment than is actually required.
>
> *(Craine et al., 2014: 12)*

The claim is that it is time for the world to move away from conventional power sector planning, which emphasizes large power plants and grid extension as the key to removing energy poverty. According to Sierra Club's analysis, technological progress allows the world to guarantee energy access through renewable energy to everyone without expensive capital investments into ecologically destructive fossil fuels.

These claims have not gone uncontested. The Breakthrough Institute, which believes in the necessity of increasing energy consumption for economic development, has argued that Sierra Club's approach would leave the world's poor without the energy they need. Alex Trembath, an energy analyst at the institute, writes in a blog post that CE4ALL "is a vision of, at best, charity for the world's poor, not the kind of economic development that results in longer lives, higher standards of living, and stronger and more inclusive socioeconomic institutions. . . . [L]evels of energy consumption in poor countries will rise 50 to 100 times higher through urbanization, agricultural intensification, industrialization, and the broader process of modernization" (Trembath, 2014, June 30). In a similar vein, one of the world's most influential private development philanthropists, Bill Gates, writes that "we should not try to solve the problem [of climate change] on the backs of the poor; . . . they desperately need cheap sources of energy now to fuel the economic growth that lifts families out of poverty. They can't afford today's expensive clean energy solutions."[14]

It is striking how sharply views on the viability of distributed renewable energy are split between advocates and opponents of banning fossil fuels from development finance. Environmental activists do not attack fossil fuels because they are desperate to create markets for solar and wind power; rather, their interest is in stopping environmental destruction caused by the fossil fuel industry. Similarly, governments of developing countries are not captured by the fossil fuel industry; they are genuinely concerned about their ability to provide their people with abundant energy for growth. Because of these concerns, the debate on development finance for fossil fuels has become aggressive and hostile. Whereas anti-fossil fuel activists can attack the mighty and powerful energy industry in the United States, similar attacks raise more difficult questions about who should bear the burden for weaning the world off fossil fuels. For environmentalists, renewable energy and conservation present an opportunity for leapfrogging, but many governments and development experts object to the idea that the least-developed countries should limit their choices in a world in which others accumulated their wealth by burning fossil fuels.

8.4 Summary: from America to the world

As we have seen, our analytical framework can be applied outside North America. However, the findings show that anti-fossil fuel campaigns outside the United States follow a rather different set of logics. In particular, among the different campaigns, only the anti-coal movement can be considered a global equivalent of the North American movement. There is a global campaign against coal that is more than a direct extension of the North American campaign, and yet the global campaign has adopted very similar strategies, frames, and actions to those that have been popular in North America. While the global divestment campaign is a direct extension of the American campaign, there is no global fracking campaign to speak of, and global struggles against pipelines have been far removed from concerns about climate change.

The similarities and differences between American and global campaigns are summarized in Table 8.1. What are the drivers behind these differences? Overall, the evidence suggests the centrality of two factors: differing local contexts and coordination challenges. With the exception of divestment, which is essentially one American-led global campaign, in all other three cases there are differences. However, the differences are not the same across categories. Fracking is the extreme comparison, as the lack of fracking activity outside North America has made organized

TABLE 8.1 Summary of similarities and differences between American and international campaigns against fossil fuels.

	American Campaign	Origin of International Campaign	Nature of International Campaign
Pipelines	Combines fossil fuel, climate disruption concerns with local land, water issues	Independent from American campaign	Exclusively motivated by local issues
Divestment	Removing the social license of the fossil fuel industry	Outgrowth of American campaign	Similar to American campaign
Fracking	Partly about fossil fuel, climate disruption concerns; strong local component	No organized campaign	High variation across local contexts; strong local component
Coal	Partly about fossil fuel, climate disruption concerns; strong local component	Independent from American campaign	Partly about fossil fuel, climate disruption concerns; strong local component

campaigning both possibly unnecessary and very hard. The difference between the large number of international pipeline campaigns and the Keystone XL is also clear, as only the Keystone XL relies on arguments about climate disruption, global warming, and the fossil fuel industry. In contrast, the international record of pipeline campaigns largely focuses on local concerns, ecological justice, indigenous rights, and alternative visions of development. Among the different campaigns, only coal shows significant similarities between the American and international campaign. In this regard, we conclude that many features of the American campaign are shaped by the national energy, economic, social, and political context.

The similarities between the various coal campaigns provide another perspective on this comparison. In this case, differences between national contexts are overwhelmed by the similarity in the concerns about public health, air pollution, and water resources. Unlike fracking operations, coal power plants and mines are common across the world, and the weak economics of coal provide activists with an opportunity to effect meaningful change in a large number of different countries. At the same time, coal is the one fossil fuel that is by now widely regarded as a problem even outside the environmentalist circles, meaning that a global campaign against coal is much easier to justify than, say, a global campaign against pipelines or natural gas. In this sense, the global campaign against coal shares many similarities with the campaign against hydroelectric dams.

The campaign against funding for coal by multilateral and bilateral development agencies sheds further light on these similarities and differences. The assault led by American environmental organizations has achieved some success in reducing funding for fossil fuels, especially coal, but these victories have come at a high price. The American environmental establishment is often perceived as imperialistic and hypocritical in developing countries, and even many American commentators in the development community are questioning the goals and foci of this campaign. At the same time, countries such as China and India are offering financing for fossil fuel development when organizations such as the World Bank are unwilling to do so because of the political pressure they face. This campaign highlights the challenges of relying on the ecological paradigm in campaigns against fossil fuels in the world's poorer countries, where the eradication of poverty and continuation of economic growth are pressing priorities for policymakers and most of the population.

Overall, it is clear that the prospects for a globalization of the American anti-fossil fuel movement are not bright. Our investigation has shown that the logic and outcomes of the anti-fossil fuel movement reflect the American national context. With the exception of the rapid evolution of a coordinated and effective global anti-coal campaign, a truly global strategy would require organizations such as 350. org to develop a new set of targets, tactics, and strategies. The American campaign against fossil fuels is important as a case mostly because of America's global centrality and paralysis of climate policy, not because it is a model that could be easily replicated elsewhere in the world.

Notes

1 See www.world-nuclear.org/info/Country-Profiles/Countries-A-F/France/ for an over-view of nuclear power in France (accessed April 19, 2015).
2 See www.eia.gov/totalenergy/data/annual/showtext.cfm?t=ptb0901 for information about nuclear reactor permits in the United States (accessed April 19, 20105).
3 See the organization website at www.internationalrivers.org/resources/about-international-rivers-3679 (accessed May 5, 2015).
4 See http://gofossilfree.org/ (accessed May 6, 2015).
5 See http://gofossilfree.org/about-fossil-free/ (accessed May 6, 2015).
6 See Table 6 in www.eia.gov/analysis/studies/worldshalegas/ (accessed May 8, 2015).
7 See www.globalfrackdown.org/ (accessed May 8, 2015).
8 See www.sierraclub.org/international (accessed May 10, 2015).
9 See press release at www.ran.org/breaking_bank_of_america_dumps_coal_mining_in_sweeping_new_policy (accessed May 6, 2015).
10 See https://goo.gl/w27fWW (accessed May 28, 2017).
11 See www.opic.gov/ (accessed May 10, 2015).
12 The Greenpeace press release on the settlement is available at www.greenpeace.org/usa/news/landmark-global-warming-lawsui/ (accessed May 28, 2017).
13 See www.usaid.gov/powerafrica (accessed May 10, 2015).
14 His blog post is available at www.gatesnotes.com/Energy/Two-Videos-Illuminate-Energy-Poverty-Bjorn-Lomborg (accessed May 10, 2015). The blog post also includes links to videos about fossil fuels and energy poverty by Bjorn Lomborg, a Danish social scientist and a self-declared environmentalist famous for challenging the view that the world is in a crisis of sustainability (Lomborg, 2001).

9

CONCLUSION

Climate change is perhaps the world's greatest collective action problem, but governments have little reason to act on it unless they face domestic political pressure to do so. Unfortunately, mobilizing people to demand climate action from their governments has also proven to be difficult. The threat is distant, complex, and overwhelmingly global. Recognizing this problem, a large segment of American environmental activists has now set its sights on a more concrete target: the fossil fuel industry. Anti-fossil fuel activists now have an enemy, a concrete target to attack under the ecological paradigm. The Keystone Principle, the activists say, precludes any new fossil fuel extraction.

This change of strategy comes at a time when the cumulative emissions among the 20 largest energy companies between 1854 and 2010 have reached 428,439 metric tons of carbon dioxide equivalent (MtCO2e), or 29.5 percent of global industrial emissions from 1751 to 2010. Ninety companies are responsible for contributing 63.04 percent of global industrial CO2 and methane between 1751 and 2010 (Heede, 2014). At current pace, the global mean temperature may increase by more than four degrees Celsius by some estimates, disrupting ecosystems and bringing about crop decline, freshwater depletion, diseases, flooding, and rising sea levels (IPCC, 2013: 20–21; World Bank, 2014).

The fossil fuel industry is not only important because it extracts the fossil fuels that generate carbon dioxide emissions, but also because of its tremendous political influence. With millions of dollars in annual spending and an official outpost on K Street, ExxonMobil deploys career lobbyists to secure meetings, executive orders, and favorable laws in Washington (Coll, 2012). According to OpenSecrets.org, the vast majority of campaign contributions from the oil, gas, electricity, and mining industries have found their way to Republican candidates, at least since the 1990 election cycle (OpenSecrets.org, 2016). By explicitly targeting the fossil fuel industry, activists are doing political work to level the playing field against this goliath of an opponent.

Recognizing the significance of the activists' strategic shift toward attacking the fossil fuel industry, this book has shown that the change of focus can be a source of motivation and inspiration. The proposed construction of the Keystone XL pipeline, which President Obama rejected in the fall of 2015, served as the initial lightning rod for activists mobilized against unconventional energy. The divestment campaign now morally challenges the very idea that the continued and growing extraction of fossil fuels is a legitimate business activity, seeing its arguments validated every time a prominent endowment, institution of higher learning, or faith group joins the movement.

Coal activists move beyond symbolism and moral arguments by concentrating their fire on coal power plants. Coal, a contributor to one-third of America's carbon emissions, as well as local water and air pollution, has had no shortage of enemies. Similarly, concerns about the local water supply has created a vibrant movement against hydraulic fracturing (fracking), though the scientific uncertainty surrounding methane emissions makes it an awkward fit within the climate movement.

The other advantage of campaigning against fossil fuels is that the strategy promises effectiveness over time. Stopping Keystone XL would allow activists to declare a major victory at the national level and send a clear message to national decision-makers and prospective investors. So far, virtually all Keystone XL events both in the national and local contexts have been smash hits in mobilizing ordinary Americans. Though the demand for fossil fuels or their profitability may not have been directly affected, high-profile divestments by Rockefeller Foundation and Stanford University have helped raise difficult ethical and financial questions about the industry's practices.

The anti-coal campaign has enjoyed considerable success in delaying and even stopping plans to expand coal mining, transportation, and combustion by electric utilities. Combined with other challenges to coal, such as inexpensive shale gas, and federal environmental regulations, this opposition has made coal the most vulnerable of all fossil fuels. Though not to coal's extent, the anti-fracking movement has thus far been widely successful in drawing participants and building momentum. They have passed more than 400 measures against fracking, wastewater injection, and frac sand mining in communities across the nation. New York's recent statewide ban on fracking was the icing on the anti-fracking cake.

On the other hand, our analysis has also revealed a series of limitations of the anti-fossil fuel campaign. The substantive impact of the divestment and Keystone XL campaigns on climate change mitigation remains unclear. The political impact of the anti-fossil fuel campaign appears to be limited to mobilizing the progressive base, and there are few signs that the movement could shape public opinion on the political right or even in the center.

This concluding chapter summarizes our argument, reflects on it, and fleshes out its implications for climate change. We believe that the examination of the fossil fuel movement has been a fruitful one for researchers interested in social change and that the movement itself has a bright future. The early success of the movement against fossil fuels suggests that a combative strategy emphasizing both ethical issues confronting oil, gas, and coal producers and the very real danger of stranded assets under increasingly stringent constraints on greenhouse gas emissions has a good chance of success in the future.

After summarizing our argument, we continue with the lessons of the anti-fossil fuel campaign for the study of social movements in the context of anthropogenic climate change. Departing from standard grievance models, we show how the substance of the campaign serves as an important source of motivation for activists. In this case of climate change, there is clearly an underlying grievance, but the lack of an actionable target or opponent has until recently prevented the grievance from turning into social mobilization. The reframing of the problem as one of stopping the extraction and use of fossil fuels has inspired activists to take action. Hybrid activism has been crucial, as the global nature of climate change has paralyzed past environmental movements. In response, the anti-fossil fuel activists have formed a motley coalition highlighting the local environmental and social effects of fossil fuel extraction and use. For these activists, small wins are significant because they validate the Keystone Principle – if activists are to stop the use and extraction of fossil fuels, they must categorically refuse to accept new fossil fuel projects.

We finish this concluding chapter with what we consider the most important question: what can the campaign against fossil fuels do to mitigate climate change? Going forward, the anti-fossil fuel movement must sustain its momentum and dynamism. Small wins and stigmatization represent its bread and butter, and they should stay the course as the stakes continue to increase. A combative strategy focusing on shaming and stigmatizing the fossil fuel industry has met with considerable success, and in the future an increased emphasis on stranded assets can further strengthen this strategy. As the need to mitigate climate change grows clearer over time, anti-fossil fuel activists can force the industry to change by broadcasting an economic message: the economic case for oil, gas, and coal is getting weaker and weaker over time.

The activists must also look inward to ensure dynamism of their movement going forward. Strengthening the broader green coalition by forging tight linkages with advocates of feasible, pragmatic alternatives to fossil fuels, such as renewable energy, energy efficiency, and technological development. This may involve coordinated campaigns with other contingents of the green coalition, as well as establishing career paths for activists who may be interested in transitioning from anti-fossil fuel activism to green advocacy. The modest success of the Paris Agreement provides an excellent opportunity to highlight these green alternatives, as the reality of climate change takes hold of governments and the fossil fuel industry faces increasing social and economic pressure.

As for the fossil fuel industry, our prescription is that it must begin by acknowledging the reality of climate change because denial is a self-defeating strategy, and the industry badly needs a better image to avoid the fate of tobacco industry. By continuing to deny climate change, energy companies strengthen the argument of activists, as it serves as an additional piece of evidence that the companies are "merchants of doubt" driven by profits rather than science or any concern for human welfare. As energy prices decline and the wisdom of investing in unconventional energy is increasingly called into question, we argue that now is the time to stop extreme energy projects. The fossil fuel industry can make sound, level-headed business decisions at a time of uncertainty and also take credit for being socially responsible while at it.

This is not to say that all of the burden falls on either the activists or the industry to help us escape the climate conundrum. It is up to the activists to better understand the major energy companies and their cost-benefit calculus and identify high-impact targets for shaming as well as constructive dialogue. If activists are able to moderate their demands and present more specific solutions for gradually reducing our reliance on fossil fuels, then the major energy companies for their part can also benefit from taking these activists seriously. Changing the energy mix will take time, but many (though not all) companies are aware that it must be done. The two sides can thus benefit each other. The activists can influence company decisions by pointing them in positive, constructive directions, and the companies can take concrete measures to ensure their own long-term profitability while taking credit for doing so.

Considering all this, the campaign against fossil fuels is an important addition to the broader effort to stop, or at least slow down, climate disruption. Whether the effort succeeds will depend on the strategies and actions of climate activists, businesses, government officials, and ordinary citizens of all stripes. The anti-fossil fuel campaign has reinvigorated climate activism in North America, brought in a new generation of grassroots climate activists, and raised the profile of climate change among progressive groups and leaders. This in itself will not be enough to achieve the movement's substantive goals, but, then again, it is hard to imagine a global solution to the problem of global warming without American leadership. The campaign against fossil fuels is off to a good start and now faces a series of important strategic choices that will in large part determine the movement's long-run impact in the evolving global politics of climate change. If the movement can adapt to changing circumstances and continue mobilizing millions around the world, then it can contribute to progress in the global effort to halt climate change and avoid irreversible damage to the planet, its ecosystems, and human societies.

9.1 Understanding and evaluating the campaign against fossil fuels

Our evaluation of the four campaigns is summarized in Table 9.1. This matrix compares activist motives, mobilization potential, impacts, and weaknesses of each campaign across the four campaigns. As the table shows, the two key motives for activists across the four campaigns are the symbolic significance of the target (Keystone XL, divestment) and local concerns (Keystone XL, coal, fracking). Given

TABLE 9.1 Evaluation matrix for the four campaigns.

	Activist Motives	*Mobilization Potential*	*Impact*	*Weaknesses*
Keystone XL	Symbolic target; widespread local concerns	Pivotal campaign for ecological activists; hybrid coalitions at local level	Policy impact high during Obama's tenure, partly thanks to political opportunity	Single target; dependent on political opportunity structure
Divestment	Symbolic target; clear, moral enemy	Attractive target for religious, student activists	Successful challenge to legitimacy of fossil fuel industry	Tangible impact on fossil fuel extraction unclear
Coal	Widespread local concerns	Attractive target both at national and local levels	Clear decline in US coal use; activism contributed to plant retirements	N/A
Fracking	Widespread local concerns	Substantial potential for local anti-fracking coalition formation	High level of local success (municipal, state policy)	Broader impact unclear; effect of fracking on climate change unclear

these motivations, all four campaigns have lots of mobilization potential, as the campaigns prove attractive to different activists under the unifying framework of the ecological paradigm. The impacts of these campaigns vary substantially, however, as the coal and fracking campaigns have arguably had the most tangible and robust effects on the fossil fuel industry. While President Obama ultimately rejected Keystone XL, this decision did not survive under the Trump administration and, in any case, the importance of Keystone XL for climate policy is disputed. Divestment, on the other hand, has challenged the legitimacy of the fossil fuel industry and drawn attention to the problem of stranded assets, but there is little evidence to suggest that it has directly reduced the profitability or influence of the fossil fuel industry. The campaigns have weaknesses, too. From Keystone XL's focus on a single pipeline and dependence on favorable political opportunity structures to divestment's lack of tangible impact and the anti-fracking movement's exclusive focus on local outcomes, all campaigns except coal have at least one clear weakness.

Overall, though, it is clear the movement against fossil fuels has had a successful start. The Keystone XL campaign demonstrates how the strategic framing of a single pipeline, among many others, could engender a large activist coalition organized around core ecological principles. Stretching from Alberta, Canada, to the Gulf of Mexico, the pipeline has been framed by activists as the ultimate enabler of tar sands development in North America, essentially "game over" for the climate if constructed. This rhetorical move has allowed local anti-pipeline activists to join forces with those who worry about the global problem of climate change, allowing the 350.org leadership and their allies to reap huge benefits in the form of grassroots mobilization and movement building. Even in the worst case, the activists can celebrate President Obama's decision to reject the Keystone XL application.

While the divestment campaign has also benefited from the presence of a clear opponent, it draws more strongly on moral and ethical principles. Emphasizing the discrepancy between the continued extraction of the fossil fuels and the urgency of meeting elusive international climate targets, the divestment campaign has found many adherents on college campuses, among religious communities, and, more recently, even in cities. Combining ethical arguments with financial ones, such as the possibility that huge fossil fuel deposits become "stranded assets" under international climate policy, divestment activists have begun to shake the confidence of the fossil fuel industry.

The most successful campaign has been against the coal industry, as anti-coal activists have laid siege to hundreds of existing and planned coal power plants across America, often with considerable success. Buoyed by secular trends, such as the rise of natural gas as a viable alternative, anti-coal activists have successfully built and sustained considerable momentum against the "dirty fuel." While shutting down coal power plants, some of the biggest contributors of greenhouse gases, has concrete climate implications often lacking in the more symbolic Keystone XL or divestment campaigns, the anti-coal activists have been more strongly oriented toward local goals.

Fracking, through the widely disseminated documentary *Gasland*, has jumpstarted a movement with considerable staying power. Opposition against fracking appears to be even more locally rooted than the anti-coal campaign, and it is likely to persist in many communities, regardless of the scientific verdict on fracking's actual climate impact. These potent local grievances, particularly those surrounding contamination of the drinking water, are themselves consistent with the ecological paradigm, which reaffirms the sanctity of nature and life over economic growth. Thus, the argument that natural gas is a "bridge fuel," a cleaner alternative to coal and a pathway to a sustainable future, is unlikely to blunt its momentum.

This positive evaluation, however, requires at least a partial acceptance of the ecological paradigm, a worldview that emphasizes the primacy of life and nature over economic growth. For its adherents, activism against fossil fuels is rooted in their identity and fundamental beliefs about the world. Anti-fossil fuel campaign taps directly into the frustrations, needs, and wishes of those who felt the urgency of climate change, but were alienated by the professionalism, pragmatism, and rigid structure of what Naomi Klein calls "Big Green" in America (Klein, 2014). As soon as leaders such as Bill McKibben created an organization and a strategy to combat the fossil fuel industry, they found a way to transform their energy and urge to do something into concrete action.

The fossil fuel industry, for these activists, represents a clearly identifiable opponent responsible for the vast majority of global greenhouse gas emissions. By setting their sights on the world's largest fossil fuel producers, frequently called carbon majors (Heede, 2014), they turn climate change from a complex global problem into a simple battle between good and evil. Given that the activists are outmatched in terms of resources and political connections, the goal is to stigmatize the industry and remove the "social license to pollute," make *coal*, *oil*, and *gas* dirty words that provoke unpleasant images in the eyes of the public. This change in public perceptions, activists believe, will force policymakers to enact policies that put an end to fossil fuel extraction.

Across all four campaigns that we have evaluated, we see the kind of motivation and inspiration that cannot be drawn from, say, a campaign for a carbon tax. The technicalities of economic policies, such as carbon tax and emissions trading schemes are not likely to receive the most "Facebook likes," save from the most enthusiastic of policy wonks. The campaign against fossil fuels offers a more exciting prospect: tackling the root cause of climate change. While advocates of carbon taxes do not challenge the legitimacy of the fossil fuel industry, so long as it pays for the damage, anti-fossil fuel activists maintain that further extraction is simply wrong. Moreover, activists believe that the primary obstacle to effective climate policy is the ability of oil, gas, and coal companies to capture politicians. Unless activists can mobilize people's power to counter these industries, debates about optimal economic approaches to climate change are purely academic.

In terms of effectiveness, contrasting the anti-fossil fuel campaign and more conventional climate advocacy is difficult. Though the campaign against fossil fuels has not run its course, it has done more to raise the visibility and provoke concern about climate change and the practices of the fossil fuel industry than any other campaign, reinvigorating environmental activism in the United States with a series of important victories. The Sierra Club has played an important role in defeating planned coal power plants across the nation, preventing the construction of costly infrastructure that would lock in high levels of emissions. The Keystone XL campaign has established a vibrant base and prompted President Obama to reject the pipeline, while the divestment campaign has convinced high-profile institutions, such as Stanford University and the Episcopal Church, to join. We have brief remarks about the motivation and effectiveness of each campaign.

We begin with motivations. The Keystone XL pipeline has many attractive features for mobilizing activists who rely on the ecological paradigm for understanding the world. A large pipeline to transport oil extracted from the tar sands to and from the United States, Keystone XL symbolizes the environmental destruction associated with nonconventional fossil fuels activists call "extreme energy." Activists invoke destroyed landscapes, massive amounts of greenhouse gases, excessive water use, and risks of oil leakages across the entire North America, best summed up by

James Hansen's claim that its construction would be "game over" for the climate. Keystone XL symbolizes the threat nonconventional fossil fuels pose to climate stability, and this is what motivates Keystone XL activists.

Whereas Keystone XL motivates activists by promising concrete action against a single large target, divestment offers an opportunity to take actions for principled and ethical reasons. In the case of divestment, the idea of fossil fuels as an unambiguous cause is a powerful one. Although the idea that divestment from fossil fuels is an effective strategy to reduce the use of coal, oil, and gas has been widely ridiculed by economists, activists are enthusiastic about an opportunity to make a clear and unambiguous statement about fossil fuels. This enthusiasm is on display in the large number of faith-based communities that have joined. The notion that climate change is ultimately a problem that stems from our excessive reliance on fossil fuels is a powerful motivation to act.

Following the ecological paradigm, the divestment campaign places a stronger emphasis on removing the social license of the fossil fuel industry. Every divestment decision, the argument runs, challenges the very idea that the continued and growing extraction of fossil fuels is a legitimate business activity. The possibility that fossil fuel reserves become useless due to carbon constraints gives them additional hope. As the pressure for climate policy intensifies, activists believe that doubt will be cast over the profitability of fossil fuel extraction. This triggers a virtuous cycle: climate advocacy reduces the profits of fossil fuel industry, and reduced profitability reduces the political clout of the industry, allowing more effective climate advocacy.

Similar to Keystone XL and divestment, the recognition of coal as the core of the climate problem has inspired and driven activists to take concrete action. Unlike Keystone XL and divestment, however, coal activists are not merely seeking to stigmatize dirty energy or turn public opinion against fossil fuels. Given that one-third of America's carbon dioxide emissions come from coal and there were only 633 active coal power plants in 2002, the closure of a single coal power plant would itself be a notable achievement. While we cannot directly link activism to the cancellation or defeat of these plants, it would be impossible to criticize the anti-coal activists for focusing on the margins. There is a broad consensus among energy analysts that reducing coal use is an essential step toward halting climate disruption, and this observation is powerful motivation for anti-coal activists.

Moreover, the entire anti-coal campaign is based on the idea that hundreds of anti-coal campaigns together add up to a swarm that first halts and then stops the production and use of coal in the United States and elsewhere – hence the name of their information clearinghouse, CoalSwarm. Due to significant economies of scale, coal mining and power generation from coal are concentrated in the hands of large corporations, ready targets for swarming. Even for members of the swarm that are not worried about ecology or planetary conditions, local environmental issues, such as water pollution and air pollution provide motivation for activism against coal.

Unlike divestment and more similar to Keystone XL, the anti-fracking campaign has a clear local focus. Concerns about fracking's contamination of the local water supply are best conveyed in the film *Gasland*, particularly in the vivid imagery of tap water being set on fire. However, the campaign cannot be dismissed as a loose coalition of disparate communities responding to threats to their immediate environments. While the actual impact of methane emissions on the climate remains under scientific dispute, many anti-fracking activists subscribe to the ecological paradigm, bringing to the climate movement and the anti-fossil fuel campaign "a never-surrender, battle-tested spirit" developed from years of "fighting for their lives in the gas fields."

We also offer an assessment of the effectiveness of the four campaigns with qualifications. For Keystone XL activists, what is at stake is an avalanche of dirty energy development in North America. As energy experts see it, stopping one pipeline is tinkering at the margins. While this remains an open question, our assessment is positive – If stopping Keystone XL allows the anti-fossil fuels activists to declare a major victory at the national level and send a clear message to national decision-makers, it can change the nature of the climate policy game in the United States. Virtually all Keystone XL events, both in the national and local contexts, have been smash hits in mobilizing ordinary Americans. Moreover, stopping a major pipeline sends the signal that the fossil fuel industry cannot take future infrastructure for granted, reducing the profitability of fossil fuel extraction in the eyes of their investors.

Though critics often point out that divestment does not directly affect the demand for fossil fuels or the profitability of their exploration and extraction, our assessment of the campaign is cautiously optimistic. A cascade is yet to happen, but the campaign has seen a steady stream of divestment decisions, keeping the momentum alive and raising difficult ethical and financial questions about the fossil fuel industry in the public sphere. They have successfully depicted the fossil fuel industry as hypocritical profit-seekers: Barring major advances in technologies such as carbon capture and storage, aggressive climate mitigation measures are inconsistent with the business plans, strategies, and trajectories of the fossil fuel industry. The activists have also brought the idea of fossil fuels as stranded assets to the limelight.

The assessment of the anti-coal campaign is mostly positive. It has already had significant success in delaying and even stopping plans to expand coal mining, transportation, and combustion by electric utilities. The swarming strategies of the anti-coal activists have not made coal projects impossible, but opposition has spread to every state, including coal-dependent Wyoming. While cancellations of coal projects cannot be solely credited to activists, vehement opposition to coal power plants makes investments in coal riskier and less profitable. In 2014, President Obama used executive authority under the Clean Air Act to enact the Clean Power Plan, a comprehensive policy to reduce carbon and other pollution from the power sector. Combined with other challenges to coal, such as inexpensive shale gas, and federal environmental regulations, this opposition has made coal the most vulnerable of all fossil fuels.

As a study commissioned by the gas industry is the first to admit, the anti-fracking movement has thus far been widely successful in drawing participants and building momentum. In addition to the popular success of *Gasland*, which popularized concerns about the impact of fracking on the water supply across communities, the movement has put together a highly effective advocacy coalition using a combination of grassroots mobilization, online and social media, direct action, and networking. Together they have passed more than 400 measures against fracking, wastewater injection and frac sand mining in communities across the nation. Their crowning achievement came in 2014, when Governor Andrew Cuomo of New York announced a state-wide ban on fracking. Though it is less obvious whether the movement has fundamentally shaped public opinion on the issue, it has effectively mobilized the base.

Despite these indications of progress, the anti-fossil fuel movement remains vague on specific policy proposals. This is understandable for a relatively new campaign that has chosen a strategy of raising awareness and mobilizing the progressive base in America, but organizational inertia may ultimately result in missed opportunities. Energy and environmental policy is made in a complex political environment characterized by structural and institutional obstacles to change, not least of which is the industry lobby itself. If the anti-fossil fuel movement cannot transform its potential into concrete policy demands, there may not be a legislative response. Even if rejecting Keystone XL or similar projects has symbolic value and can rally the troops, it is not quite as effective as a carbon tax or other comprehensive federal policies in terms of actual climate mitigation.

To be sure, our assessment of the campaign is different from those of detractors who emphasize the opportunity cost of focusing precious time and energy on an individual pipeline, a college campus, a fracking well, or to a lesser extent, a coal plant. What if activists would have instead pushed for climate policies at the national or state level? As Harvard environmental economist Robert N. Stavins put it in an interview, "The political fight about Keystone is vastly greater than the economic, environmental or energy impact of the pipeline itself. . . . It doesn't make a big difference in energy prices, employment, or climate change either way" (Davenport, 2015, January 8). According to this logic, even if the campaigns we covered are not necessarily counterproductive, the environmental groups are at best wasting their time.

We think this criticism ignores the political reality of the situation. Environmental organizations in America have tried countless other approaches, but none of these has inspired so many to mobilize as the anti-fossil fuel campaigns chronicled in our book. Without Keystone XL, for instance, there might be no movement against fossil fuels, and so the question of opportunity cost would never arise. Without Keystone XL, we might have nothing but deafening silence. Thanks to this movement, American environmentalism has again become a dynamic, vibrant, and lively socio-political force. In a context characterized by the primacy of climate change as an environmental issue, the indirect strategy of attacking fossil fuels instead of carbon emissions has brought environmentalism back to the center of the political game.

In the United States, we foresee two potential future trajectories for the anti-fossil fuel movement. Both scenarios require the consistent pursuit of a coherent strategy by the activists and are contingent on their strategies' influencing the calculations and decisions of major government actors. The first strategy is an overwhelming victory for the activists against the fossil fuel industry. In this world, there is a widespread consensus that the fossil fuel industry has been a key contributor to climate change and that a transition to renewables is necessary. This consensus is seen not only in the public ire against the fossil fuel industry and revocation of its "social license" to pollute, but also crystallized in policy intended to drastically curb carbon emissions.

This scenario is highly unlikely given the significant political influence of the fossil fuel industry, particularly in the political right. As we have shown throughout the book, the fossil fuel industry's access to centers of power and abundance of political and economic resources have allowed for numerous victories. The Republican push against President Obama in favor of Keystone XL is testament to the deeply entrenched influence of the fossil fuel industry in American politics. While the fossil fuel industry has certainly made inroads in problematizing the social license of the fossil fuel industry, the fossil fuel industry's political influence will continue so long as economies, as well as the protestors themselves, remain deeply dependent on these resources.

The other potential trajectory is to force the political right to change their strategy. This strategy is actually more subtle and nuanced than it sounds. There is no buying of politicians or efforts to persuade or compromise. Instead, the intuition is best captured by the term, "radical flank effect," in the study of social movements (Haines, 2013). If liberal activists are loud and visible, they may actually enhance the political clout of moderate conservative climate activists. For example, Martin Luther King Jr. was considered a radical by many until Malcolm X and the Black Panthers showed up (Haines, 1984). The existence of a radical alternative may make a moderate climate activist more acceptable to the public.

Given current trends, this is the more likely scenario. It is no secret that the kind of activists who get noticed at climate marches are very passionate about their views. Mostly left of center, these activists are not particularly eager to tone down their political views to court conservatives or strike compromises with the fossil fuel industry. The ecological paradigm, which fuels and unites these activists, makes matters fairly black and white. The fossil fuel industry is causing environmental destruction, and it must go. Radical fossil fuel activists, by maintaining such a position, do service to moderates and conservatives concerned about climate change, who suddenly seem more reasonable and centrist. Indeed, student activists also now argue that "the climate movement needs to get more political, especially when it comes to electoral politics. . . . The movement needs to mobilize thousands of people to vote for pro-climate candidates and call out candidates who are promoting dangerous climate policies" (Maxmin, 2015: 118).

While a complete takedown of the fossil fuel industry remains far-fetched, and conservative climate activists remain the exception than the rule, incremental movements along the two trajectories are observable today. For instance, a growing number of fossil fuel companies, such as BG Group, BP, Eni, Royal Dutch Shell, Statoil, and Total, are warming up to the idea of a carbon tax. This is a pragmatic move. They realize that something must be done about the climate, though on their own terms – an efficient and predictable policy to limit greenhouse gas emissions that would also ensure their own long-term viability. The fossil fuel industry is clearly on the defensive, and this was hardly a foregone conclusion (*The New York Times*, 2015, June 6). Consistent with the radical flank effect, libertarians and conservatives are also revisiting their position on carbon tax (Tercek, 2015, May 5).

Global problems, however, require global solutions. Even if the movement in the United States remains vibrant, continues to stigmatize fossil fuels, and exerts influence on policy, the global hotspots for energy development are in emerging economies. With rapid economic growth, China and India's energy consumption will grow for decades to come, and their choices will determine the future of the global climate.

9.2 Implications for research on activism and social movements

This book is not the last word on climate activism, but we hope that our findings can inspire and inform future scholarship on the topic. Our findings shed new light on the motivations of activists, the role of hybrid activism in sustaining social movements, the importance of small wins, and the thorny problem that target audiences pose for social movements.

To begin with, our work shows how the substance of the campaign serves as an important source of motivation for activists. In the literature, motivation is often conceptualized as a grievance against a social, political, or economic phenomenon (Bolton, 1972; Klandermans and Oegema, 1987; McAdam and Boudet, 2012). In the movement against fossil fuels, this concept offers only a partial understanding. Many of the anti-fossil fuel activists have for a long time, in the language of the academic literature, held a grievance against climate change, but this grievance has only recently prompted action. In this case, there is clearly an underlying grievance, but the lack of an actionable target or opponent has until recently prevented the grievance from turning into social mobilization.

The reframing of the problem as one of stopping the extraction and use of fossil fuels has inspired activists to take action. Had we only looked at the underlying problem as the grievance, we would have missed this important element of the problem. As long as the grievance was framed as a distant and complex threat requiring techno-economic solutions, the grievance was not enough to generate action. It was a combination of high fossil fuel prices and a competent reframing of the problem of climate change that mobilized the activists. In contrast, our analysis does not lend support to explanations that primarily focus on economic conditions, public opinion, or political opportunity structures. The surge in anti-fossil fuel activism coincides with high fossil fuel prices, but it does not seem very sensitive to the growth of the American economy, public opinion about climate change, or partisan balance in the federal government.

In the field of climate activism, Hadden (2015) reports closely related findings on the evolution of the international movement. As the salience of climate change in society grew in the lead up to the by-now notorious 2009 Copenhagen United Nations Climate Change Conference, the previously unified climate movement began to see cleavages between "climate advocates" and "climate justice activists." While climate advocates continued to focus on conventional advocacy and lobbying for new policy instruments, climate justice activists began emphasizing the moral overtones of the problem. This new framing, shows Hadden (2015), resulted in a split of the movement into two networks that pursued different agendas and, in some instances, began arguing with each other, instead of the opponents of climate action. Here, again, the underlying grievance was the same: why are our political leaders not doing more to stop dangerous climate disruption? The climate justice framing, however, attracted a very different group of climate activists to participate in international climate summits and challenge the previously consensual relations between activists and political leaders.

The fossil fuels framing goes hand-in-hand with a broader turn toward local action and domestic politics in climate policy (Avery, 2013; Betsill and Bulkeley, 2006; Hale, 2011; Hoffmann, 2011; Nace, 2010; Urpelainen, 2013). Although climate change is a global problem, concrete progress to combat it must be made at the national, or even sub-national, level. Our analysis of the four components of the anti-fossil fuel campaign has shown that such local frames can be a powerful source of motivation and create an opening for progress in what initially appears to be a complex and distant problem that only a world government could solve.

For studies of climate activism and social movements more broadly, we see the relationship between framing and motivation as a key research frontier. Framing is, after all, something that entrepreneurial activists can use to shape their campaigns and increase their attractiveness to potential activists. In the environmental field, for example, "environmental justice" advocates have brought environmental issues to the attention of American minority communities by showing how environmental deterioration hurts minorities more severely than it does the white majority (Bullard, 1990). In a similar vein, climate justice activists are now trying to present climate disruption as a fundamental violation of the rights of vulnerable and marginalized populations in the least developed countries and low-lying areas of the world. This emphasis on framing seems to have been a successful strategy, again emphasizing the importance of subjective perceptions in activism, an observation made by McAdam (1999: 48) about how grievances and political opportunities were transformed into civil rights activism by savvy African-American leaders and frustrated citizens in the South.

The study of the anti-fossil fuel campaign also has important implications for the large and growing body of work on hybrid activism. In recent years, a growing body of evidence has shown that hybrid activism is key to understanding the rapid growth of some campaigns. Recent theories of "issue bricolage" in mobilization suggest, for example, that hybrid activism is possible even when different groups have few substantive goals in common, provided they share a common culture of tactics and activities (Jung et al., 2014). Compelling recent evidence can be found in the anti-war movement (Heaney and Rojas, 2014, 2015) and climate activism (Hadden, 2015). Our findings emphasize a specific kind of hybrid activism: the interplay of global and local environmental issues.

The global nature of the climate change problem appears to have contributed to the paralysis of the American environmental movement in the past. The anti-fossil fuel activists have brought climate activism back to life by highlighting the local environmental and social effects of fossil fuel extraction and use. This tactic has proven particularly effective in the case of anti-coal and anti-fracking mobilization. In the case of fracking, this hybrid framing has been so effective that there is now even a debate on whether local concerns about fracking actually raise a barrier to replacing coal with natural gas, as some commentators say that the anti-fracking activists are hurting the cause of decarbonization in North America. On the other hand, the anti-fossil fuel campaign has also brought in progressive, and even anti-corporate, activists by highlighting the fossil fuel industry, as opposed to the users of fossil fuels, as the primary culprit behind climate change. By pointing the finger at the carbon majors, anti-fossil fuel activists have picked a fight that attracts people who have previously shown little interest in climate activism.

The role of hybrid activism in the anti-fossil fuels movement partly confirms the conventional wisdom, yet it also raises new questions. Why was hybrid activism so effective and necessary in the case of coal, despite this fuel's overwhelmingly negative climate effects? How do social movements deal with cases such as fracking, where some activists worry about hybrid activism spoiling the original campaign? What is the role of hybrid activism in cases such as divestment that have very precise and narrow targets? We believe such questions could be raised about other campaigns as well. For example, when and how do anti-war campaigns change because of hybrid themes, such as anti-corporate attacks on the weapons industry? How do moderate critics of trade and investment agreements from the development community deal with anarchist and socialist groups? The analysis of the anti-fossil fuel movement sheds light on the challenges and opportunities of hybrid activism, as activists adhering to the ecological paradigm must work together with local ranchers, farmers, hunters, and landowners to stop fossil fuel extraction.

The next important lesson from our work is the centrality of small wins validating the importance of Weick's (1984) original idea. The dynamic growth of the anti-fossil fuel movement has drawn on a long list of relatively small, yet critical, victories against the fossil fuel industry. Although the anti-fossil fuel industry cannot claim yet that their victories have brought the fossil fuel industry to its knees, or even significantly reduced the rate of growth for fossil fuel extraction and use in North America, the small wins have been frequent and notable enough to keep current activists motivated and draw others to participate. Under the ecological paradigm, small wins are significant because they validate the Keystone Principle: if activists are to stop the use and extraction of fossil fuels, they must categorically refuse to accept new fossil fuel projects. This view of campaigns against fossil fuels effectively turns otherwise minor events into important confirmations and validations of the very principles and values that anti-fossil fuel activists live by.

Among the different strands of the campaign against fossil fuels, divestment offers a particularly vivid illustration of the importance of small wins. As we have seen above, the most common criticism of the divestment campaign is that individual victories, and perhaps even a broadly successful movement capable of prompting many divestment decisions by organizations with endowments, would not undermine the profitability of the fossil fuel industry. Despite these criticisms, leading divestment activists have successfully packaged individual divestment decisions as major moral victories that contribute to the dynamism of the campaign. Every time an organization, be it a college, a municipality, or a church, divests, the activists receive confirmation that their messaging is effective and that their moral call for responsible, sustainable investments works. In a similar vein, the Keystone XL campaign has succeeded in turning delays into small wins. Achieving these goals has been easier for the anti-coal and anti-fracking campaigns, given their strong local emphasis, and yet one cannot help being impressed in seeing how activists have woven local victories into a coherent story of an American, perhaps even global, movement.

On the other hand, the cases of Keystone XL and divestment raise questions about substantive impact. The literature about small wins focuses heavily on sustaining activism and mobilization, but what about substantive effects? In the case of Keystone XL, activists achieved their proximate goal. A conventional approach to social movements might code this as unambiguous success, but what if the pipeline actually would have had limited effects on greenhouse gas emissions? In the case of divestment, the goalposts are perhaps even more difficult to see. Success in divestment does not mean that fossil fuel extraction ends, as the divested assets are purchased by others. And finally, in the case of fracking, progress against natural gas extraction may even have the negative side effect of halting the decline of the coal industry. These issues suggest a need for new approaches to measuring the impact of social movements in a broader sense and call for caution in evaluating the substantive impact, as opposed to mobilization potential, of small wins.

For future studies of the role of small wins in sustaining activism and social movements, the ability of organizations and movement leaders to shape their campaigns in a manner that enables small wins presents an important research question. In the case of the anti-fossil fuel campaign, Bill McKibben and his followers distanced themselves from the conventional frame of climate advocacy and, instead, began to emphasize a direct confrontation with the fossil fuel industry, drawing on the moral urgency created by the cold, hard mathematics of fossil fuel reserves and blame assignment on the world's most powerful corporate interests. When and how is such strategic use of frames possible in social and political activism? To what extent is the case of climate change an exceptional case in this regard? We consider answering these questions to be important next steps for the study of social movements, mobilization, and activism.

Finally, we must comment on the issue of target audience. The literature on social movements has for a long time understood that activists pursue change by targeting specific audiences (Bob, 2005; Gamson, 1975; Gillion, 2013; Haines, 1984; Heaney and Rojas, 2015). In the case of the activism against fossil fuels, we have found that the activism is, both purposefully and as a result of events, mostly focused on drawing the attention of liberals and progressives to climate change. By adopting an explicitly confrontational stance, anti-fossil fuel activists have excluded the possibility of targeting political conservatives, or even the center of the political spectrum. Based on our research, this strategy is seen by the activists as both necessary, because the current polarized political environment does not encourage compromise and dialogue, and useful, because highlighting climate change as a challenge for the progressive and liberal movement could prompt broader political changes. The most important exception to this rule are the local constituencies of the anti-coal and anti-fracking campaigns, and yet the ultimate goals of these campaigns are at the national and, eventually, international levels. Therefore, even their target audience is found somewhere else.

The issue of target audience creates opportunities for future research on social movements. In the case of the anti-fossil fuels campaign, the organizers faced a difficult challenge. By adopting a confrontational stance, they in a sense marginalized themselves. But had they not adopted this stance, they might not have a movement to begin with. Furthermore, it is not clear that a more moderate position would have allowed them to make inroads into other target audiences in a polarized environment. There is also the hope that a "radical flank effect" would force conventional climate advocates to adopt positions and strategies that contribute to the achievement of the policy goals of the anti-fossil fuel advocates. To what extent do organizers of other campaigns face similar challenges, and how do they deal with them? Which factors drive some campaigns toward easy target audiences, such as progressives, and why do other campaigns adopt the strategy of reaching out to a broader audience? In contexts with both kinds of campaigns, such as climate change, what is the joint effect of campaigns with different target audiences?

More broadly, the issue of target audience is critical to understanding the causal pathways from social movements to lasting societal change. In an important recent contribution to the study of social movements, Heaney and Rojas (2015) document how the American anti-war movement lost access to the Democratic Party at the time when political tides turned more favorable to them. When Democrats gained office after the 2008 Obama campaign, they chose to pay less attention to the demands of the anti-war movement. The anti-fossil fuel movement is very, very far from having the kind of access and support that the anti-war campaign enjoyed during the George W. Bush administration years, but the hypothetical scenario is nonetheless intriguing. If the anti-fossil fuel movement manages to force the elite of the Democratic Party to put more emphasis on climate change and reach beyond President Obama's executive authority initiatives, then what is the future of the movement? Can it still play a useful role when its ideas and messages are no longer radical to one half of the political spectrum? Will an American progressive movement that is truly committed to climate change as a core issue make a difference in national politics? If so, will it leave a lasting impression at the international level? These are the kinds of questions that our concluding discussion of this book addresses, and we very much believe that similar questions should be asked in the context of other social movements and issues surrounding activism.

9.3 The campaign against fossil fuels and the politics of climate change

Going forward, we consider the chief objectives of the anti-fossil fuel movement in the US theater to be two-fold. First, revoking the social license of the fossil fuel industry should remain a priority, so long as the fossil fuel industry continues to exercise its political muscle. Small wins and stigmatization represent the bread-and-butter of the movement, and they should stay the course as the stakes continue to increase. So far, this strategy has been successful, and there is every reason to believe that such a campaign can play an even more important role in the future. To sustain its momentum, particularly in the context of today's low and volatile energy prices, we recommend a targeted shaming strategy, as social pressure, properly harnessed and judiciously applied, can force the fossil fuel industry to consider alternatives to continuous expansion. Key to this strategy for the activists is to understand the inner workings and the cost-benefit calculus of the major fossil fuel companies, such that points of vulnerability may be identified. The lesson we draw from the recent trend of coal plants being transitioned to natural gas is that a sophisticated understanding of the industry's changing economic calculus can help activists identify high-impact targets to expedite the phase-out of the more pernicious fossil fuels. In this sense, the recent drop in oil price and the doubts it casts on the continued development and expansion of unconventional energy present a valuable opportunity for activists. As companies begin to second guess the economic merits of unconventional energy in light of cheap and abundant oil, activists can bring additional social pressure to bear on these investments, seeking to directly impact the major fossil fuel firms' cost-benefit calculus.

The second key lesson for the future is the power of the stranded assets argument. The anti-fossil fuel campaign was born at a time of record-high fossil fuel prices, but this commodity price boom turned out to be temporary. From 2014 to 2015, the price (in constant November 2016 dollars) of imported crude oil in the United States, decreased from $91.7 to $47.4.[1] This rapid and unexpected collapse doomed many nonconventional energy projects, such as tar sands and fracking wells, into unprofitable irrelevance. In a surprising turn, the low fossil fuel prices, which generally should discourage campaigning against fossil fuel production, became a powerful message, as the future profitability of the fossil fuel industry now appeared bleak. And when the Bank of England (2015: 35) emphasized the financial risks of climate change and mentioned the possibility of stranded assets in a public discussion paper, nobody could ignore the argument any longer: "For example, could rapid improvements in renewable energy technology, such as energy storage, or the introduction of new financial instruments to manage environmental risk, affect financial markets? Is there a risk that carbon-intensive assets may become 'stranded' as part of a low carbon transition?"

The December 2015 climate summit in Paris prompted, for the first time in history, a global agreement aimed at limiting global warming below two degrees Celsius.[2] Because the agreement relies heavily on decentralized action – countries are allowed to choose their own national action plans, which will then be reviewed periodically – the anti-fossil fuel movement has an opportunity to push governments and other decision-makers to adopt policies and measures that contribute to global climate mitigation. Every time countries come together to review their national actions, following the timeline laid out in the Paris agreement, the anti-fossil fuel movement has an opportunity to demand climate action in a favorable media environment.

Several other trends in the world economy are also shaping the political environment in which the anti-fossil fuel movement broadcasts the message of stranded assets. Perhaps the clearest such trend is the uncertainty surrounding the coal industry. In December 2015, the IEA updated its projections for the global coal market, noting that "[f]ollowing more than a decade of aggressive growth, global coal demand has stalled. . . . [O]versupply and shrinking imports in China and elsewhere suggest prices will remain under pressure through 2020" (US International Energy Agency, 2015, December 18).[3] The economic difficulties faced by the coal industry create an opening for activists to close struggling coal mines and stop the construction of coal-fired power plants. On the other hand, global fluctuation in fossil fuel prices is relevant for capital-intensive energy projects. While oil prices hovered around a $100 per barrel between January–July 2014, by December 2015 they had fallen below $40 per barrel (Federal Reserve Bank of St. Louis, n.d.).[4] These low oil prices have made many fossil fuel extraction projects unprofitable, strengthening the message of stranded assets.

The broader green coalition for climate change mitigation can support – and benefit from – the efforts of anti-fossil fuel activists. In many ways, closer ties between the anti-fossil fuel movement and the green coalition – where champions of feasible and pragmatic alternatives to fossil fuels are to be found – makes logical sense. It is one thing to argue and propagate the notion that the continued burning of fossil fuels is morally wrong, and it is another to suggest plausible alternatives. We argue that anti-fossil fuel activists must be intentional and strategic in forming synergistic linkages with advocates of energy efficiency, green companies, and renewables producers. In the following paragraphs, we lay out the logic behind our argument and propose concrete steps by which activists may pursue this strategy. Broadly, we identify two targets of opportunities, one for the anti-fossil fuel activists and another for the fossil fuel industry. First, for the anti-fossil fuel activists, the recently concluded Paris Agreement, as well as the continued resonance of their fundamentally normative message, provide an unprecedented opportunity to breathe new life into a broader green advocacy coalition that must be at the forefront of the fight to replace fossil fuels with renewables. Second, counterintuitively for the fossil fuel industry, the best way to blunt the momentum of the anti-fossil fuel movement is to acknowledge the reality of anthropogenic climate change and publicize the efforts already underway to include renewables in their long-term energy mix. If both parties pursue these interests, it is our contention that there will be more room for constructive dialogue and potential realization of shared interests. Perhaps the challenge for anti-fossil fuel activists is to convince the fossil fuel industry, particularly by revitalizing and leveraging the broader green coalition, that transitioning to renewables makes good business sense.

If fossil fuel prices remain low in the future, then the demand for oil, gas, and coal may continue to increase and undermine the ongoing global shift to cleaner sources of energy. Thus, vigorous and coordinated activism on behalf of these cleaner sources becomes absolutely critical. The anti-fossil fuel movement has a clear and well-articulated message of the nature of the problem – the contribution of the fossil fuel industry to anthropogenic climate change – but it lacks a coherent and well-articulated message about plausible policy alternatives. As the demand for cheap energy, particularly in emerging economies of Asia, continues to increase, stigmatizing the operations of the fossil fuel industry without proposing a politically and economically viable set of alternatives will not be sufficient. The argument for alternatives must be made not only in the intellectual realm, but also in the political arena. As the anti-fossil fuel message begins to take hold, a powerful advocacy coalition encompassing a wide range of feasible, pragmatic alternatives will need to carry the mantle.

These pragmatic alternatives may include advocates of solar and wind deployment in the context of a renewable energy boom, concerted public and private initiatives to increase energy efficiency, as well as experimental projects geared toward the eventual rollout of electrical vehicles. Particularly promising in this regard is the prospect of forging an alliance between anti-fossil fuel activists and innovative, promising green companies that stand to profit from further deployment of renewables, energy efficiency, and next-generation technologies.

The effectiveness of such a joint strategy – stigmatizing fossil fuels and promoting cleaner alternatives – is likely enhanced by the 2015 Paris Agreement, which relies on member states' national action plans. These action plans, or pledges, are collectively reviewed by the membership every five years. Such a bottom-up pledge-and-review system creates an opening for climate activists. On the one hand, attacks on fossil fuels draw attention to harmful policies, such as subsidies for the production and consumption of fossil fuels.[5] When Oil Change International and 14 other nongovernmental organizations – including, of course, 350. org – launched a report on the need to keep fossil fuels in the ground only a few months before the 22nd Conference of the Parties to the UNFCCC, they deliberately linked the urgency of this strategy to the Paris Agreement's shared goal of preventing global warming in excess of 2 degrees Celsius relative to pre-industrial times (Oil Change International, 2016). To the extent that governments heed this call, it becomes a self-reinforcing message and a virtuous cycle, as expectations about future constraints on carbon emissions discourage fossil fuel exploration and extraction. The Paris Agreement, in a sense, is a global embodiment of the stranded assets argument.

As governments need modern energy to power their economies and people's daily lives, however, attacks on fossil fuels are themselves not enough. No government is going to commit to an action plan that deprives its people of modern energy; the plans, without exception, call for decarbonization and enhanced efficiency (United Nations Framework Convention on Climate Change, n.d.).[6] Therefore, the anti-fossil fuels campaigning at the global level benefits from positive, action-oriented messages that emphasize the benefits and feasibility of cleaner alternatives. The report says as much:

> Renewable power technologies are not only possible; they are already in use at scale in many countries, growing rapidly, and often cost less than gas or coal generation. . . . Electric vehicles are at an earlier stage of development than renewable power, but may be able to penetrate the market more rapidly: whereas a power plant has a typical lifetime of 40 years, cars generally last for around ten years.
>
> *(Oil Change International, 2016: 40)*

Under the Paris Agreement's national climate pledges and collective review, we consider this combined message constructive and powerful.

Another lesson dovetails with the need for cross-cutting linkages and coordination across the broader green coalition. The anti-fossil fuel movement, particularly its simple message and strategy of small wins, has significant recruitment potential. As fans of popular sports are well aware, recruitment potential must be used wisely to have concrete impact on outcomes. Consistent with our observation that the anti-fossil fuel movement must couple its contrarian message with a set of feasible, pragmatic alternatives, we believe that one of the strategies by which activists may achieve this is to turn anti-fossil fuel activism into a recruitment gateway for the broader green coalition. Porousness across the different contingents of the anti-fossil fuel movement was already on display during our participation in the People's Climate Change in New York City. While people may sign on to the movement because they are passionate about a specific cause, such as the construction of a local pipeline and its potential impact on their homelands, or fracking and its potential impact on their drinking water, the shared commitment of these motley activists to the ecological paradigm also ensures mobility across various contingents of the movement. At many events, we met activists who were loyal to more than one cause of the anti-fossil fuel movement, choosing to participate in a divestment organizational meeting one day and attending an anti-fracking rally the next. What its more, there were others whose impressive activist careers spanned multiple decades, covering a wide array of issue areas, such as pacifism and anti-nuclear weapons.

These are encouraging signs, and we further advocate the encouragement of career paths linking the anti-fossil fuel movement and the broader green coalition, whereby ordinary people drawn by the powerful, yet normative message of the anti-fossil fuel movement find ample opportunity to expand their horizon and participate in bringing about the very changes necessary to replace fossil fuels. This will have twin benefits. First, it substantively strengthens the argument of the activists, as they are no longer seen as idealists whose normative criticisms against the industry are not backed by a concrete solution. Rather than being perceived as pointing their proverbial fingers at the fossil fuel industry, they can now claim to be "practicing what they preach" and "walking the walk." Second, it will breathe new life into the broader green coalition, which has been less successful than the new breed of activists we have examined in this book in mobilizing recruits to champion their cause. This disparity is what motivated our analysis of the anti-fossil fuel movement in the first place. What does implementation of this lesson look like? As the topic at hand pertains to the building of careers, perhaps the most obvious place to start is the university. Given the popularity of divestment campaigns across college campuses, one concrete way to link the anti-fossil fuel movement and the broader green coalition is to begin at the chapter level. Workshops and programs designed to introduce student members of divestment to potential career options in green advocacy, such as renewable energy policy, as well as even lucrative positions in green companies may be a useful start.

We now turn our attention to the fossil fuel industry. Given this barrage of public relations attacks from the anti-fossil fuel movement, how should the industry respond? Though prescriptions may differ for each major oil company, we believe that all of them face an historic opportunity. Given the recent election results, which gave the Republicans the presidency and the majority in both houses, perhaps this seems an opportune time for the fossil fuel industry to double down on climate denial. That would be a mistake. Political tides can turn, as reflected in changing administrations, but the episodes we have chronicled throughout this book suggest that the fossil fuel industry has been implicated in climate change to an unprecedented extent. While climate action may be slow, the inevitable increase in global awareness of the problem will continue. Fossil fuel companies, rather than remaining the villain for the better part of this new millennium, can chart a different path for themselves as pioneers in climate change mitigation. As BP (2013) and Shell (2014) have demonstrated by example, acknowledging the reality of climate change is not costly, particularly if it is accompanied by a sound business strategy that balances sustainability with profitability. By continuing to deny climate change, ExxonMobil, for instance, only provides fodder for activists, who have every incentive to capitalize on the narrative that the industry's continued denial of climate change – in the face of incontrovertible scientific evidence – is rooted in its material self-interests (Supran and Oreskes, 2017, August 27). The anti-fossil fuel activists' ultimate goal is to send the industry the way of the tobacco industry, and from the perspective of the industry, acknowledging the problem of climate change is almost a costless way to prevent this worst-case scenario.

What we are advocating here is not that fossil fuel companies transform themselves into renewables companies overnight. Even under the IEA's most ambitious climate policy scenario, in which governments commit to 450 ppm CO_2

equivalent of greenhouse gases, oil and gas still make up 47 percent of the energy mix in 2035. Oil remains the dominant source for transport fuels, accounting for as much as 87 percent of demand in 2035. It suffices to note that clinging to a narrative that has proven time and again to be scientifically suspect only provides additional ammunition for the anti-fossil fuel movement. By conceding this already lost battle, the fossil fuel industry can regroup and seek out other opportunities, as well as potential common ground with activists. Acknowledging the realty of climate change for many firms, to be sure, has not meant a complete change of direction. BP (2013), while acknowledging that action is needed to limit carbon dioxide (CO2) and other greenhouse gases, proposes a "diverse mix" of oil sands, shale gas, deepwater oil and gas, and biofuels. Shell (2014), while calling on government, industry, and society to address the increasing stress placed on our food, water, energy supply, and the climate, regards natural gas as "the sweet spot in the stress/opportunity nexus." Chevron (2013), which invests hundreds of millions of dollars on energy efficiency efforts in their operations, such as upgrading steam traps, installing more efficient heat exchangers, and constructing more efficient power plants, as well as renewable and alternative energy, such as cellulosic biofuels, continues to pour tens of billions into traditional exploration and production projects. We argue that companies may help themselves by going even further.

In the United States, political events complicate such calculations. Many observers were surprised when Donald Trump, who was the underdog in polls over the entire election season, won the presidency on November 8, 2016. After the results were in and the stock markets opened, the prices of fossil fuel industry shares increased rapidly and those of the renewable energy industry tumbled (Olson et al., 2016, November 9). And yet, the fact remains that nonconventional fossil fuels contain great risks. As oil is a global commodity, events in the United States are far from the primary determinant of international market prices. The decline of coal consumption in the United States and elsewhere in the world reflects to a significant extent economics and concerns about local environmental and public health concerns. The price of renewable energy continues to decrease, and electric vehicles promise to displace oil in the future. For the fossil fuel industry, doubling down on expensive and polluting nonconventional energy projects would be a significant future risk despite the Trump presidency.

If the industry does respond in a constructive fashion and makes a serious effort to move away from fossil fuels, then the anti-fossil fuel movement has an opportunity to identify and support promising plans for change. This, ultimately, is how we envision the best-case scenario for both the anti-fossil fuel activists and the fossil fuel industry itself. If the activists are better able to understand the cost-benefit calculus of fossil fuel companies and the fact that replacing fossil fuels in their energy mix requires both time and plausible business alternatives, they should be able to take the long view and encourage burgeoning business ventures that promote sustainability, while condemning those that undermine it. This is how they can cooperate with fossil fuel companies without being complicit in climate change. If the fossil fuel industry is willing and able to adapt their business model to the more modest demands of the activists, it can become a catalyst for change. As costly as this strategy may seem in the short run for the fossil fuel companies, being on the right side of history will help to ensure a more prosperous future, particularly one that avoids the pitfall of stranded assets. While companies such as BP and Chevron have been touting their modest investments in biofuels, it is up to the activists to remind them that they can do much more. The terrifying new math of global warming highlights the problem humanity faces, and shutting down fossil fuel companies is a great rallying cry, but not a plausible solution. Understanding the business models of these companies, particularly the opportunities and constraints they face, will help activists to identify where constructive dialogue must take place and important progress can be made. Through mutual adaptation despite significant differences, the anti-fossil fuel movement and the major energy companies of this century can rise to the challenge of climate change.

Notes

1 See www.eia.gov/forecasts/steo/realprices/ (accessed November 15, 2016).
2 The text of the agreement can be found at https://unfccc.int/resource/docs/2015/cop21/eng/l09r01.pdf (accessed May 28, 2017).
3 See http://goo.gl/h4hgYH (accessed January 29, 2016).
4 See https://research.stlouisfed.org/fred2/series/DCOILWTICO/downloaddata (accessed January 29, 2016).
5 See Benes et al. (2015) and Cheon et al. (2015) for the politics of fossil fuel subsidies.
6 See http://unfccc.int/focus/indc_portal/items/8766.php (accessed November 16, 2016) for Intended Nationally Determined Contributions.

BIBLIOGRAPHY

350.org (2012, February 13). Top climate scientists warn Congress over Keystone XL. *350. org*. URL: https://350.org/top-climate-scientists-warn-congress-over-keystone-xl/

350.org (2013, February 17). Amazing! 35,000+ March at Forward on Climate Rally in DC. *350.org*. URL: https://350.org/amazing-35000-march-forward-climate-rally-dc/

Abelvik-Lawson, H. (2014, August 26). Communities in conflict: Lignite mining on the Poland-Germany border. *Greenpeace Energydesk*. URL: http://energydesk.greenpeace. org/2014/08/26/communities-conflict-lignite-mining-poland-germany-border/

African Forum and Network on Debt and Development (2007). *The contribution of oil to debt and under-development in Africa: The case of the Chad-Cameroon oil pipeline project*. African Forum and Network on Debt and Development, Harare, Zimbabwe.

Agence France-Presse (2015, August 10). Pope creates global prayer day for the environment. *The Guardian*. URL: www.theguardian.com/environment/2015/aug/10/pope-creates-global-prayer-day-for-the-environment

Albert, S. and Whetten, D. A. (1985). Organizational identity, *Research in Organizational Behavior* **7**: 263–295.

Allen, P. (2014, November 24). This land is our land. *The Huffington Post*. URL: www.huff ingtonpost.com/paul-allen/this-land-is-our-land_1_b_6214864.html

Alter, C. (2014, September 22). "Hundreds of Thousands Converge on New York to Demand Climate-Change Action." *Time*. URL: http://ti.me/1wXla3H

Amenta, E. and Caren, N. (2007). The legislative, organizational, and beneficiary consequences of state-oriented challengers, *in* D. A. Snow, S. A. Soule and H. Kriesi (eds), *The Blackwell Companion to Social Movements*, Blackwell Publishing, Malden, chapter 20, pp. 461–488.

Amenta, E., Caren, N., Chiarello, E. and Su, Y. (2010). The political consequences of social movements, *Annual Review of Sociology* **36**: 287–307.

Andrews, K. T. (1997). The impacts of social movements on the political process: The civil rights movement and black electoral politics in Mississippi, *American Sociological Review* **62**(5): 800–819.

Andrews, K. T. (2004). *Freedom Is a Constant Struggle: The Mississippi Civil Rights Movement and Its Legacy*, University of Chicago Press, Chicago.

Ansar, A., Caldecott, B. and Tilbury, J. (2013). *Stranded assets and the fossil fuel divestment campaign: What does divestment mean for the valuation of fossil fuel assets?* Stranded Assets Programme. Smith School of Enterprise and the Environment, University of Oxford, Oxford, UK.

Applebome, P. (2008, July 3). A land rush is likely, so a lawyer gets ready. *The New York Times.* URL: https://nyti.ms/2rcpUpn

Applebome, P. (2008, July 27). The light is green, and yellow, on drilling. *The New York Times.* URL: https://nyti.ms/2saFBeh

Asif, M. and Muneer, T. (2007). Energy supply, its demand and security issues for developed and emerging economies, *Renewable and Sustainable Energy Reviews* **11**(7): 1388–1413.

Auyero, J. and Swistun, D. A. (2009). *Flammable: Environmental Suffering in an Argentine Shantytown,* Oxford University Press, New York.

Avery, S. (2013). *The Pipeline and the Paradigm: Keystone XL, Tar Sands, and the Battle to Defuse the Carbon Bomb,* Ruka Press, Washington DC.

Ball, J. (2014, May 22). The truth about Stanford's coal divestment. *New Republic.* URL: www.newrepublic.com/article/117871/stanfords-coal-divestment-shows-environmental-hurdles-ahead

Bank of England (2015). *One bank research agenda.* Bank of England, Discussion Paper. URL: www.bankofengland.co.uk/research/Documents/onebank/discussion.pdf

Barnes, D. (1984). *Farmers in Rebellion: The Rise and Fall of the Southern Farmers' Alliance,* University of Texas Press, Austin.

Barrett, S. (2003). *Environment and Statecraft: The Strategy of Environmental Treaty-Making,* Oxford University Press, Oxford.

Bastasch, M. (2013, February 18). Regulations, litigation force cancellation of Texas coal-fired power plant construction. *The Daily Caller.* URL: http://dailycaller.com/2013/02/18/regulations-and-litigation-force-cancellation-of-texas-coal-fired-power-plant-construction/

Bateman, C. (2010, June 21). A colossal fracking mess. *Vanity Fair.* URL: www.vanityfair.com/news/2010/06/fracking-in-pennsylvania-201006

Baumgartner, F. R. (1989). Independent and politicized policy communities: Education and nuclear energy in France and in the United States, *Governance* **2**(1): 42–66.

Baviskar, A. (1995). *In the Belly of the River: Tribal Conflicts Over Development in the Narmada Valley,* Oxford University Press, New York.

Beinin, J. (2015, January 28). The divestment campaign is aimed at ending Israel's occupation of Palestinian lands. *The Stanford Daily.* URL: www.stanforddaily.com/2015/01/28/the-divestment-campaign-is-aimed-at-ending-israels-occupation-of-palestinian-lands/

Bell, S. E. and Braun, Y. A. (2010). Coal, identity, and the gendering of environmental justice activism in central Appalachia, *Gender and Society* **24**(6): 794–813.

Benes, K., Cheon, A., Urpelainen, J. and Yang, J. (2015). *Low oil prices: An opportunity for fuel subsidy reform.* A Briefing Paper for Center on Global Energy Policy, Columbia University.

Benford, R. D. and Snow, D. A. (2000). Framing processes and social movements: An overview and assessment, *Annual Review of Sociology* **26**(1): 611–639.

Bergin, N. (2014, September 15). Putting the Bold in Nebraska: Pipeline gave progressive group a cause. *Lincoln Journal Star.* URL: http://journalstar.com/news/state-and-regional/nebraska/putting-the-bold-in-nebraska-pipeline-gave-progressive-group-a/articleee485dce-af50-516e-87de-546350286de2.html

Bergin, N. (2015, September 29). TransCanada suspends efforts to condemn land for pipeline. *Lincoln Journal Star.* URL: http://journalstar.com/news/state-and-regional/federal-politics/transcanada-suspends-efforts-to-condemn-land-for-pipeline/articlea659f5cf-f8a7-5fd3-a9b9-7c6d3830e612.html

Betsill, M. M. and Bulkeley, H. (2006). Cities and the multilevel governance of global climate change, *Global Governance* **12**(2): 141–159.

Beynon, H., Cox, A. W. and Hudson, R. (2000). *Digging Up Trouble: The Environment, Protest and Opencast Coal Mining*, Rivers Oram Press, New York.

Bloomberg (2014, December 2). Oil investors at brink of losing trillions of dollars in assets. Gore: It's that Road Runner moment. *Bloomberg*. URL: http://bloom.bg/1yzJtn6

Bloomberg, M. R. (2015, April 8). Michael Bloomberg: I'm giving $30M to fight Big Coal. *CNN Money*. URL: http://money.cnn.com/2015/04/08/news/economy/bloomberg-coal-sierra-club/

Bob, C. (2005). *The Marketing of Rebellion*, Cambridge University Press, New York.

Bold Nebraska (2010, July 27). Attend pipeline hearings. *BoldNebraska.org*. URL: http://boldnebraska.org/attend-pipeline-hearings/

Bold Nebraska (2011, May 27). TransCanada Pipeline Background and Resources." *BoldNebraska.org*. URL: http://boldnebraska.org/transcanada-pipeline-background-and-resources/

Bold Nebraska (2012, February 6). TransCanada Pipeline. *BoldNebraska.org*. URL: http://boldnebraska.org/transcanada-pipeline/

Bolton, C. D. (1972). Alienation and action: A study of peace-group members, *American Journal of Sociology* **78**(3): 537–561.

Bourdieu, P. (1986). The forms of capital, *in* J. Richardson (ed.), *Handbook of Theory and Research for the Sociology of Education*, Greenwood, New York, pp. 241–258.

BP (2013). *BP Annual Report and Form 20-F 2013*, BP, London, UK.

BP (2015). *BP statistical review of world energy*, 64th edn. URL: www.bp.com/en/global/cor porate/energy-economics/statistical-review-of-world-energy.html

Broder, J. M., Krauss, C. and Austen, I. (2013, February 17). Obama faces risks in pipeline decision. *The New York Times*. URL: www.nytimes.com/2013/02/18/business/energy-environment/obamas-keystone-pipeline-decision-risks-new-problems-either-way.html

Brown, E., Hartman, K., Borick, C., Rabe, B. G. and Ivacko, T. (2013). *Public opinion on fracking: Perspectives from Michigan and Pennsylvania*, Center for Local, State, and Urban Policy, University of Michigan.

Brune, M. (2015, April 8). Winning numbers. *Sierra Club*. URL: www.sierraclub.org/michael-brune/2015/04/beyond-coal-climate-clean-energy

Bullard, N. (2014, 25 August). Fossil fuel divestment: A $5 trillion challenge, *Bloomberg Energy Finance White Paper*, Bloomberg.

Bullard, R. D. (1990). *Dumping in Dixie: Race, Class, and Environmental Quality*, Westview Press, Boulder.

Campbell, D. (2013). Social networks and political participation, *Annual Review of Political Science* **16**: 33–48.

Campbell, J. (2013, September 30). Poll: Fracking opposition at an all-time high in N.Y. *Democrat & Chronicle*. URL: http://on.rocne.ws/19QJLrY

Campbell, J. (2015, June 29). N.Y. makes fracking ban official. *Democrat & Chronicle*. URL: www.democratandchronicle.com/story/tech/science/environment/2015/06/29/fracking-ban-new-york/29492515/

Carrington, D. (2014, December 1). Bank of England investigating risk of 'carbon bubble'. *The Guardian*. URL: http://gu.com/p/43n59/stw

Carroll, W. and Ratner, R. (1996). Master framing and cross-movement networking in contemporary social movements, *Sociological Quarterly* **37**(4): 601–625.

Carson, R. (2002). *Silent Spring: 40th Anniversary Edition*, Mariner Books, New York. Originally published in 1962.

Carter, J. (1979, July 15). Address to the Nation on Energy and National Goals: "The Malaise Speech." *The American Presidency Project*. URL: www.presidency.ucsb.edu/ws/?pid=32596

Carvalho, G. O. (2006). Environmental resistance and the politics of energy development in the Brazilian Amazon, *Journal of Environment and Development* **15**(3): 245–268.

Casper, B. M. and Wellstone, P. D. (1981). *Powerline: The First Battle of America's Energy War*, University of Massachusetts Press, Amherst.

Catholic Church and McDonagh, S. (2016). *On care for our common home: The encyclical of Pope Francis on the environment, Laudato Si*.

Chan, C. K. and Yao, X. (2008). Air pollution in mega cities in China, *Atmospheric environment* **42**(1): 1–42.

Cheon, A., Lackner, M. and Urpelainen, J. (2015). Instruments of political control: National oil companies, oil prices, and petroleum subsidies, *Comparative Political Studies* **48**(3): 370–402.

Chevron (2013). *Chevron 2013 Annual Report*, Chevron Corporation, San Ramon, CA.

Clark, S. (2014, June 30). Why we are blocking the office of Harvard's president. *The Huffington Post*. URL: www.huffingtonpost.com/stacy-clark/why-we-are-blocking-the-o_b_5237319.html

Clemente, J. (2015, June 7). Why New York's fracking ban for natural gas is unsustainable. *Forbes*. URL: www.forbes.com/sites/judeclemente/2015/06/07/why-new-yorks-fracking-ban-for-natural-gas-is-unsustainable/

Clemente, J. (2015, December 16). COP21 doesn't change our more coal, oil, and natural gas reality. *Forbes*. URL: www.forbes.com/sites/judeclemente/2015/12/16/cop21-doesnt-change-our-more-coal-oil-and-natural-gas-reality/#39e4c055ae8e

Coday, M. (2015, December 23). COP21, coal exports at odds. *The Olympian*. URL: www.theolympian.com/opinion/letters-to-the-editor/article51272905.html

Coll, S. (2012). *Private Empire: ExxonMobil and American Power*, Penguin Press, New York.

Colwell, K. (2014, November 25). Groups file lawsuit against BLM on coal leasing program. *Friends of the Earth*. URL: www.foe.org/projects/climate-and-energy/blog/2014-11-groups-file-lawsuit-against-blm-on-coal-leasing-program

Cooley, A. and Ron, J. (2002). The NGO scramble: Organizational insecurity and the political economy of transnational action, *International Security* **27**(1): 5–39.

Corell, E. and Betsill, M. M. (2001). A comparative look at NGO influence in international environmental negotiations: Desertification and climate change, *Global Environmental Politics* **1**(4): 86–107.

Craighill, C. (2015, March 3). Despite the good, the bad and the unfunny, Arctic drilling still the #WorstJoke we know. *Greenpeace*. URL: www.greenpeace.org/usa/despite-good-bad-unfunny-arctic-drilling-still-worstjoke-know/

Craine, S., Mills, E. and Guay, J. (2014). *Clean energy services for all: Financing universal electrification*. Sierra Club, San Francisco and Washington, DC.

Cress, D. M. and Snow, D. A. (1996). Mobilization at the margins: Resources, benefactors, and the viability of homeless social movement organizations, *American Sociological Review* **61**(6): 1089–1109.

CTI (2014). *Carbon Supply Cost Curves: Evaluating Financial Risks to Oil Capital Expenditures*, Carbon Tracker Initiative, London, UK.

Das, K. N. (2016, January 8). EXCLUSIVE: After 40 years, India set to re-open commercial coal mining to private firms. *Reuters*. URL: http://in.reuters.com/article/india-coal-idINKBN0UM1K520160108

Davenport, C. (2015, January 8). Experts say that battle on Keystone pipeline is over politics, not facts. *The New York Times*. URL: https://nyti.ms/2rPRsOq

Davenport, C. (2015, January 29). Senate approves Keystone XL pipeline bill, testing Obama. *The New York Times*. URL: www.nytimes.com/2015/01/30/us/politics/keystone-xl-pipeline-bill-senate-vote.html

Davenport, C. (2015, February 11). House passes Keystone bill despite Obama's opposition. *The New York Times*. URL: www.nytimes.com/2015/02/12/us/politics/house-passes-keystone-bill.html

Davenport, C. (2015, June 4). Fracking has not had big effect on water supply, E.P.A. says while noting risks. *The New York Times*. URL: https://nyti.ms/2s7DCHv

Davenport, C. and Rubin, A. J. (2017, March 28). Trump signs executive order unwinding Obama climate policies. *The New York Times*. URL: https://nyti.ms/2ovruhs

Davenport, C. and Smith, M. (2015, January 9). Obama facing rising pressure on Keystone oil pipeline. *The New York Times*. URL: https://nyti.ms/2qnFwWK

Davies, J. C. (1962). Toward a theory of revolution, *American Sociological Review* **27**(1): 5–19.

Davis, C. (2012). The politics of 'fracking': Regulating natural gas drilling practices in Colorado and Texas, *Review of Policy Research* **29**(2): 177–191.

Davis, J. H. (2015, November 2). TransCanada suspends request for permit to build Keystone pipeline. *The New York Times*. URL: www.nytimes.com/2015/11/03/us/politics/transcanada-suspends-request-for-permit-to-build-keystone-pipeline.html

Davis, J. H. (2015, November 3). Obama won't yield to company's bid to delay Keystone pipeline decision. *The New York Times*. URL: www.nytimes.com/2015/11/04/us/politics/obama-wont-yield-to-companys-bid-to-delay-keystone-pipeline-decision.html

Delwiche, T. R. and Klein, M. A. (2015, March 24). Judge dismisses divestment lawsuit. *The Harvard Crimson*. URL: www.thecrimson.com/article/2015/3/24/judge-dismisses-divestment-lawsuit/

DemocracyNow.org (2014, March 10). 2 million submit objections as Keystone comment period closes. *DemocracyNow.org*. URL: www.democracynow.org/2014/3/10/headlines/2_million_submit_objections_as_keystone_comment_period_closes

DemocracyNow.org (2014, March 11). Senate Dems stage landmark filibuster for climate action; scant mention of Keystone decision. *DemocracyNow.org*. URL: www.democracynow.org/2014/3/11/headlines/senate_dems_stage_landmark_filibuster_for_climate_action_scant_mention_for_keystone_decision

DemocracyNow.org (2014, April 28a). Cowboy Indian Alliance protests Keystone XL pipeline in D.C. after latest Obama admin delay. *DemocracyNow.org*. URL: www.democracynow.org/2014/4/28/cowboy_indian_alliance_protests_keystone_xl

DemocracyNow.org (2014, April 28b). 'We need to end the fossil fuel age': Music legend Neil Young protests Keystone XL oil pipeline. *DemocracyNow.org*. URL: www.democracynow.org/2014/4/28/we_need_to_end_the_fossil

DemocracyNow.org (2014, May 13). Senate GOP blocks bipartisan energy efficiency bill. *DemocracyNow.org*. URL: www.democracynow.org/2014/5/13/headlines/senate_gop_blocks_bipartisan_energy_efficiency_bill

DemocracyNow.org (2014, November 6). White House to await State Dept. review of Keystone XL. *DemocracyNow.org*. URL: www.democracynow.org/2014/11/6/headlines/white_house_to_await_state_dept_review_of_keystone_xl

DemocracyNow.org (2014, November 17). House OKs Keystone XL pipeline; Senate to vote this week. *DemocracyNow.org*. URL: www.democracynow.org/2014/11/17/headlines/house_oks_keystone_xl_pipeline_senate_to_vote_this_week

DemocracyNow.org (2014, November 20). Keystone, climate change and the cold. *DemocracyNow.org*. URL: www.democracynow.org/2014/11/20/keystone_climate_change_and_the_cold

DemocracyNow.org (2014, December 8). Sen. Landrieu loses runoff vote in Louisiana. *DemocracyNow.org*. URL: www.democracynow.org/2014/12/8/headlines/sen_landrieu_loses_runoff_vote_in_louisiana

Dempsey, J. (2011, August 13). How Merkel decided to end nuclear power. *The New York Times*. URL: www.nytimes.com/2011/08/13/world/europe/13iht-germany.html

DePillis, L. (2015, January 15). How local government played catch-up as a fracking boom rolled through. *The Washington Post*. *DemocracyNow.org*. URL: www.washingtonpost.com/

news/storyline/wp/2015/01/15/how-local-government-played-catch-up-as-a-frack
ing-boom-rolled-through/

Diani, M. (2007). Networks and participation, *in* D. A. Snow, S. A. Soule and H. Kriesi (eds), *The Blackwell Companion to Social Movements*, Blackwell Publishing, Malden, chapter 15, pp. 339–359.

Divest Harvard (2015, February 12). Why Harvard students are sitting-in outside Drew Faust's office. *The Nation. DemocracyNow.org.* URL: www.thenation.com/article/why-harvard-students-are-sitting-outside-drew-fausts-office/

Dokshin, F. A. (2016). Whose backyard and what's at issue? Spatial and ideological dynamics of local opposition to fracking in New York State, 2010 to 2013, *American Sociological Review* **81**(5): 921–948.

Dowie, M. (1995). *Losing Ground: American Environmentalism at the Close of the Twentieth Century*, MIT Press, Cambridge.

Dryzek, J. and Goodin, R. E. (1986). Risk-sharing and social justice: The motivational foundations of the post-war welfare state, *British Journal of Political Science* **16**(1): 1–34.

Duara, N. (2015, February 12). Keystone XL pipeline on hold after Nebraska judge grants injunction. URL: http://fw.to/aZm1qGZ

The Economist (2010, March 11). An unconventional glut. *The Economist.* URL: www.econo mist.com/node/15661889

Edgmon, T. D. and Menze, D. C. (1981). The regulation of coal surface mining in a federal system, *Natural Resources Journal* **21**(2).

Edwards, B. and McCarthy, J. D. (2007). Resources and social movement mobilization, *in* D. A. Snow, S. A. Soule and H. Kriesi (eds), *The Blackwell Companion to Social Movements*, Blackwell Publishing, Malden, chapter 6, pp. 116–152.

Efstathiou Jr., J. (2012, October 23). Fracking will support 1.7 million jobs, study shows. *Bloomberg Businessweek.* URL: www.bloomberg.com/news/articles/2012-10-23/fracking-will-support-1-7-million-jobs-study-shows

Egan, M. (2017, April 25). Why Trump's coal promises are doomed. *CNN Money.* URL: http://money.cnn.com/2017/04/25/investing/coal-trump-jobs-promise/

Eilperin, J. (2012, February 13). Senate GOP tries to restore Keystone pipeline. *The Washington Post.* URL: www.washingtonpost.com/national/health-science/senate-gop-tries-to-restore-keystone-pipeline/2012/02/13/gIQAlje2BR_story.html

Energy Intelligence (n.d.). PIW ranks the world's top 50 oil companies. URL: http://www2. energyintel.com/PIW_Top_50_ranking_about

Esch, M. (2015, January 10). NY fracking ban seen as having little impact on supply. *Fuel Fix.* URL: http://fuelfix.com/blog/2015/01/10/ny-fracking-ban-seen-as-having-little-impact-on-supply/

Eshelman, R. S. (2010, April 15). Cracking Big Coal. *The Nation.* URL: www.thenation. com/article/cracking-big-coal

European Climate Foundation. (n.d.). Addressing the need for low-carbon development in Poland. URL: https://europeanclimate.org/initiatives/regional/poland/

ExxonMobil (2013). *ExxonMobil Summary Annual Report 2013*, Exxon Mobil Corporation, Irving, TX.

Fang, H., Wu, J. and Zeng, C. (2009). Comparative study on efficiency performance of listed coalmining companies in China and the US, *Energy Policy* **37**(12): 5140–5148.

Farhar, B. C. (1994). Trends: Public opinion about energy, *Public Opinion Quarterly* **58**(4): 603–632.

Federal Reserve Bank of St. Louis. (n.d.). Crude oil prices: West Texas Intermediate. *FRED Economic Data.* URL: https://research.stlouisfed.org/fred2/series/DCOILWTICO/down loaddata

Fisher, D. R. (2014). Studying large-scale protest: Understanding mobilization and participation at the People's Climate March. URL: https://climateaccess.org/system/files/Fisher_PCM.pdf

Foster, J. M. (2014, March 19). Illinois residents fight back against the state's coal industry. *ThinkProgress*. URL: https://thinkprogress.org/illinois-residents-fight-back-against-the-states-coal-industry-7408641cd2b7

Fox News (2014, June 2). Obama administration targets coal with controversial emissions regulation. *Fox News*. URL: www.foxnews.com/politics/2014/06/02/obama-to-announce-rule-to-limit-emissions-from-fossil-burning-plants-part-his/

Frayssinet, F. (2014, November 19). Shale oil fuels indigenous conflict in Argentina. *Popular Resistance.Org*. URL: https://popularresistance.org/shale-oil-fuels-indigenous-conflict-in-argentina/

Friedman, L. (2010, April 9). South Africa wins $3.75 billion coal loan. *The New York Times*. URL: www.nytimes.com/cwire/2010/04/09/09climatewire-south-africa-wins-375-billion-coal-loan-17887.html

Friends of the Earth International (2002). *Clashes with corporate giants: 22 campaigns for biodiversity and community*, Friends of the Earth International, Amsterdam.

Galbraith, K. (2013, February 10). Sierra Club takes aim at coal plants in East Texas. *The Texas Tribune*. URL: www.texastribune.org/2013/02/10/sierra-club-escalates-push-against-luminant-coal-p/

Gamson, W. A. (1975). *The Strategy of Social Protest*, Dorsey Press, Homewood.

Gerken, J. (2013, February 17). 'Forward On Climate' rally brings climate change activists to National Mall in Washington, D.C. *The Huffington Post*. URL: www.huffingtonpost.com/2013/02/17/forward-on-climate-rally_n_2702575.html

Gerken, J. (2014, July 12). Former Pa. health secretary claims state didn't address fracking health impacts. *Penn Live*. URL: http://s.pennlive.com/Sdkpi7H

Gerken, J. (2014, December 17). Gov. Andrew Cuomo to ban fracking in New York State. *The Huffington Post*. URL: www.huffingtonpost.com/2014/12/17/cuomo-fracking-new-york-state_n_6341292.html

Gerring, J. (2004). What is a case study and what is it good for? *American Political Science Review* **98**(2): 341–354.

Gibson, C. (2013, February 26). Will ALEC block EPA coal pollution safeguards at Illinois' controversial Prairie State Energy Campus? *Polluterwatch*. URL: www.polluterwatch.com/blog/will-alec-block-epa-coal-pollution-safeguards-illinois-controversial-prairie-state-energy-campu

Giddens, A. (2009). *The Politics of Climate Change*, Polity Press, Malden.

Gillion, D. Q. (2013). *The Political Power of Protest: Minority Activism and Shifts in Public Policy*, Cambridge University Press, New York.

Gillis, J. (2012, December 4). To stop climate change, students aim at college portfolios. *The New York Times*. URL: http://nyti.ms/SEOw2b

Global Frackdown (n.d.). About the global frackdown. *GlobalFrackdown.org*. URL: https://globalfrackdown.org/about/

Gold, R. (2015, May 18). Texas prohibits local fracking bans. *The Wall Street Journal*. URL: www.wsj.com/articles/texas-moves-to-prohibit-local-fracking-bans-1431967882

Golden, K. C. (2013, February 16). The Keystone Principle: Stop making it worse. *Grist*. URL: http://grist.org/climate-energy/the-keystone-principle/

Goldenberg, S. (2014, September 22). Heirs to Rockefeller oil fortune divest from fossil fuels over climate change. *The Guardian*. URL: www.theguardian.com/environment/2014/sep/22/rockefeller-heirs-divest-fossil-fuels-climate-change

Goldenberg, S. (2015, January 11). Stanford professors urge withdrawal from fossil fuel investments. *The Guardian*. URL: www.theguardian.com/environment/2015/jan/11/stanford-professors-fossil-fuel-investments

Goldenberg, S. (2015, February 19). Harvard prepares to fight fossil fuel divestment case in court. *The Guardian*. URL: www.theguardian.com/environment/2015/feb/19/harvard-prepares-to-fight-fossil-fuel-divestment-case-in-court

Goldenberg, S. (2015, February 20). Harvard's high-profile alumni join fossil fuel divestment campaign in open letter. *The Guardian*. URL: www.theguardian.com/environment/2015/feb/20/harvard-celebrity-alumni-fossil-fuel-divestment-campaign-open-letter

Goldenberg, S. (2015, July 3). Episcopal church votes to divest from fossil fuels: 'This is a moral issue'. *The Guardian*. URL: www.theguardian.com/world/2015/jul/03/episcopal-church-fossil-fuel-divestment?CMP=share_btn_tw

Goldthau, A. (2008). Rhetoric versus reality: Russian threats to European energy supply, *Energy Policy* **36**(2): 686–692.

Gongaware, T. B. (2010). Collective memory anchors: Collective identity and continuity in social movements, *Sociological Focus* **43**(3): 214–239.

Goodwyn, W. (2015, May 20). New Texas law makes local fracking bans illegal. *NPR*. URL: www.npr.org/2015/05/20/408156948/new-texas-law-makes-local-fracking-bans-illegal

Green, J. F. (2014). *Rethinking Private Authority: Agents and Entrepreneurs in Global Environmental Governance*, Princeton University Press, Princeton, NJ.

Greenberg, N. (2011, August 24). Nation's largest environmental organizations stand together to oppose oil pipeline. *Common Dreams*. URL: www.commondreams.org/newswire/2011/08/24/nations-largest-environmental-organizations-stand-together-oppose-oil-pipeline-0

Gullion, J. S. (2015). *Fracking the Neighborhood: Reluctant Activists and Natural Gas Drilling*, MIT Press, Cambridge.

Hadden, J. (2015). *Networks in Contention: The Divisive Politics of Climate Change*, Cambridge University Press, New York.

Haines, H. H. (1984). Black radicalization and the funding of civil rights: 1957–1970, *Social Problems* **32**(1): 31–43.

Haines, H. H. (2013). Radical flank effects, *in* D. A. Snow, D. Della Porta, B. Klandermans and D. McAdam (eds), *Wiley-Blackwell Encyclopedia of Social and Political Movements*, Blackwell Publishing, Malden, pp. 1048–1050.

Hale, T. N. (2011). A climate coalition of the willing, *Washington Quarterly* **34**(1): 89–102.

Haley, A. and X, M. (1992). *The Autobiography of Malcolm X as Told to Alex Haley*, Ballantine Books, New York.

Hamburger, T. (2014, December 7). Fossil-fuel lobbyists, bolstered by GOP wins, work to curb environmental rules. *The Washington Post*. URL: http://wapo.st/12Bj1hl

Hansen, J. (2011). Silence is deadly. URL: www.columbia.edu/~jeh1/mailings/2011/2011 0603_SilenceIsDeadly.pdf

Hansen, J., Sato, M., Kharecha, P., Beerling, D., Berner, R., Masson-Delmotte, V., Pagani, M., Raymo, M., Royer, D. L. and Zachos, J. C. (2008). Target atmospheric co2: Where should humanity aim? *Open Atmospheric Science Journal* **2**: 217–231.

Harper, F. (2013). Divest and reinvest now! the religious imperative for fossil fuel divestment and reinvestment in a clean energy future. *Overview Essay for GreenFaith*. URL: www.greenfaith.org/programs/divest-and-reinvest/divest-reinvest-now-with-discussion-questions

Harris, A. (2015, January 16). TransCanada sued by Nebraska landowners over Keystone path. *Bloomberg*. URL: www.bloomberg.com/news/articles/2015-01-17/transcanada-sued-by-nebraska-landowners-over-keystone-path-1-

Hartmann, B. and Sam, S. (2016, March 28). What low oil prices really mean. *Harvard Business Review*. URL: https://hbr.org/2016/03/what-low-oil-prices-really-mean

Hashimi, A. H. (2014, May 1st). Undergraduate protester arrested for blocking entrance to Mass. Hall. *Harvard Crimson*. URL: www.thecrimson.com/article/2014/5/1/divest-protester-arrested-mass-hall/

Hauter, W. (2014, October 1). Ahead of Global Frackdown, movement to ban deadly gas drilling gains momentum. *Common Dreams*. URL: www.commondreams.org/views/2014/10/01/ahead-global-frackdown-movement-ban-deadly-gas-drilling-gains-momentum

Hawken, P. (2007). *Blessed Unrest: How the Largest Movement in the World Came into Being, and Why No One Saw It Coming*, Penguin Group, New York.

Hayden, T. (2012, November 13). Climate activists hit hard with 'Do the Math' national tour. *The Nation*. URL: www.thenation.com/article/climate-activists-hit-hard-do-math-national-tour/

Heaney, M. T. and Rojas, F. (2014). Hybrid activism: Social movement mobilization in a multimovement environment, *American Journal of Sociology* **119**(4): 1047–1103.

Heaney, M. T. and Rojas, F. (2015). *Party in the Street: The Antiwar Movement and the Democratic Party After 9/11*, Cambridge University Press, New York.

Heede, R. (2014). Tracing anthropogenic carbon dioxide and methane emissions to fossil fuel and cement producers, 1854–2010, *Climatic Change* **122**(1–2): 229–241.

Helman, C. (2013, September 18). Billionaire rejected in novel plan to clean up Illinois coal plants. *Forbes*. URL: www.forbes.com/sites/christopherhelman/2013/09/18/billionaire-rejected-in-novel-plan-to-clean-up-illinois-coal-plants/

Henn, J. (2014, March 14). 350.org reacts to Royal Dutch Shell warning its profits will be hit by climate change regulation. *Common Dreams*. URL: www.commondreams.org/newswire/2014/03/14/350org-reacts-royal-dutch-shell-warning-its-profits-will-be-hit-climate-change

Henn, J. and Kessler, D. (2011, August 24). Nation's largest environmental organizations stand together to oppose oil pipeline. URL: www.commondreams.org/newswire/2011/08/24/nations-largest-environmental-organizations-stand-together-oppose-oil-pipeline

Hertsgaard, M. (2012, April 2). How a grassroots rebellion won the nation's biggest climate victory. *Mother Jones*. URL: www.motherjones.com/environment/2012/04/beyond-coal-plant-activism

Hoffmann, M. J. (2011). *Climate Governance at the Crossroads: Experimenting with a Global Response After Kyoto*, Oxford University Press, Oxford.

Horta, K., Nguiffo, S. and Dijiraibe, D. (2007). *The Chad-Cameroon oil & pipeline project: A project non-completion report*. Association for the Promotion and Defense of Human Rights, Chad; Center for Environment and Development, Cameroon; Environmental Defense, USA.

Howard, J. (2012, July 8). Appalachia turns on itself. *The New York Times*. URL: www.nytimes.com/2012/07/09/opinion/appalachia-turns-on-itself.html

Howard, R. (2014, July 11). Is the U.S. fracking boom a bubble? *Newsweek*. URL: www.newsweek.com/2014/07/18/how-long-will-americas-shale-gas-boom-last-260823.html

Howarth, R. W. (2014). A bridge to nowhere: Methane emissions and the greenhouse gas footprint of natural gas, *Energy Science and Engineering* **2**(2): 47–60.

Howarth, R. W., Santoro, R. and Ingraffea, A. (2011). Methane and the greenhouse-gas footprint of natural gas from shale formations, *Climatic Change* **106**(4): 679–690.

Hulme, M. (2010). *Why We Disagree About Climate Change*, Cambridge University Press, New York.

IEA (2014). *World Energy Outlook*, International Energy Agency, Paris.

Ikelegbe, A. (2005). The economy of conflict in the oil rich Niger Delta region of Nigeria, *Nordic Journal of African Studies* **14**(2): 208–234.

Inman, M. (2014). Natural gas: The fracking fallacy, *Nature* **516**(7529): 28–30.

International Rivers (n.d.). About International Rivers. URL: https://www.international rivers.org/resources/about-international-rivers-3679

IPCC (2013). Summary for policymakers, *in* T. F. Stocker, D. Qin, G.-K. Plattner, M. Tignor, S. Allen, J. Boschung, A. Nauels, Y. Xia, V. Bex and P. Midgley (eds), *Climate Change 2013: The Physical Science Basis. Contribution of Working Group I to the Fifth Assessment Report of the Intergovernmental Panel on Climate Change*, Cambridge University Press, Cambridge, UK.

Jahn, D. (1992). Nuclear power, energy policy and new politics in Sweden and Germany, *Environmental Politics* **1**(3): 383–417.

James, S. (2012, May 11). Coal makes a comeback in Illinois Basin. *Reuters*. URL: www.reuters.com/article/coal-illinois-idUSL1E8G2IWD20120511

Jasper, J. M. (2011). Emotions and social movements: Twenty years of theory and research, *Annual Review of Sociology* **37**: 285–303.

Johnston, A. (2015, February 26). Breaking down the Keystone pipeline fight. *DecodeDC*. URL: www.decodedc.com/breaking-down-the-keystone-pipeline-fight/

Jones, S. (2014, June 10). Union becomes the world's first seminary to divest from fossil fuels. *Time*. URL: http://time.com/2853203/union-fossil-fuels/

Joppke, C. (1990). Nuclear power struggles after Chernobyl: The case of West Germany. *West European Politics* **13**(2): 178–191.

Jung, W., King, B. G. and Soule, S. A. (2014). Issue bricolage: Explaining the configuration of the social movement sector, 1960–1995, *American Journal of Sociology* **120**(1): 187–225.

Kalicki, J. H. and Goldwyn, D. L. (eds) (2013). *Energy and Security: Strategies for a World in Transition*, Woodrow Wilson Center Press, Johns Hopkins University Press, Washington, DC.

Kania, J. (2014, April 28). The future of Polish coal as energy source. *Polish Public Relations Office*.

Karlin, R. (2015, June 10). New York fracking supporters pin hopes on EPA study. *Times Union*. URL: www.timesunion.com/news/article/New-York-fracking-supporters-pin-hopes-on-EPA-6319978.php

Kearney, Diane. (2011). Top four U.S. coal companies supplied more than half of U.S. coal production in 2011. URL: www.eia.gov/todayinenergy/detail.php?id=13211

Khagram, S. (2004). *Dams and Development: Transnational Struggles for Water and Power*, Cornell University Press, Ithaca.

Kilkenny, A. (2013, February 18). Thousands of climate change activists gather in Washington for 'Forward on Climate' rally. *The Nation*. URL: www.thenation.com/article/thousands-climate-change-activists-gather-washington-forward-climate-rally/

King, C. (2015, December 17). TransCanada increases budget for Energy East pipeline. *The Wall Street Journal*. URL: www.wsj.com/articles/transcanada-increases-budget-for-energy-east-pipeline-1450365048

Kirchgaessner, S. (2015, June 18). Pope's climate change encyclical tells rich nations: pay your debt to the poor. *The Guardian*. URL: www.theguardian.com/world/2015/jun/18/popes-climate-change-encyclical-calls-on-rich-nations-to-pay-social-debt

Kitschelt, H. P. (1986). Political opportunity structures and political protest: Anti-nuclear movements in four democracies, *British Journal of Political Science* **16**(1): 57–85.

Klandermans, B. and Oegema, D. (1987). Potentials, networks, motivations, and barriers: Steps towards participation in social movements, *American Sociological Review* **52**(4): 519–531.

Kleeb, Jane. (2014, December 11). Background: Nebraska unconstitutional pipeline process. *BoldNebraska.org*. URL: http://boldnebraska.org/lawsuit/

Klein, M. A. (2015, October 13). Student protesters appeal dismissal of divestment lawsuit. *The Harvard Crimson*. URL: www.thecrimson.com/article/2015/10/13/divestment-appeal-lawsuit-dismiss/

Klein, N. (2014). *This Changes Everything: Capitalism Vs. the Climate*, Simon and Schuster, New York.

Kolbert, E. (2012). Bill McKibben on Keystone, Congress, and Big-Oil Money. *Yale Environment 360*. URL: http://e360.yale.edu/features/bill_mckibben_on_keystone_congress_and_big-oil_money

Koop, F. (2013, July 21). Fracking controversy arrives in Argentina. *Buenos Aires Herald*.

Koopmans, R. (2007). Protest in time and space: The evolution of waves of contention, *in* D. A. Snow, S. A. Soule and H. Kriesi (eds), *The Blackwell Companion to Social Movements*, Blackwell Publishing, Malden, chapter 2, pp. 19–46.

Korpi, W. (1974). Conflict, power and relative deprivation, *American Political Science Review* **68**(4): 1569–1578.

Krauss, C. (2017, March 10). Oil prices: What to make of the volatility. *The New York Times*. URL: www.nytimes.com/interactive/2017/01/09/business/energy-environment/oil-prices.html

Krauss, C. (2017, March 24). U.S., in reversal, issues permit for Keystone oil pipeline. *The New York Times*. URL: https://nyti.ms/2nLpuVC

Kriesi, H. (2007). Political context and opportunity, *in* D. A. Snow, S. A. Soule and H. Kriesi (eds), *The Blackwell Companion to Social Movements*, Blackwell Publishing, Malden, chapter 4, pp. 67–90.

Krudy, E. (2013, March 6). New York State Assembly votes to block fracking until 2015. *Reuters*. URL: www.reuters.com/article/us-energy-fracking-newyork-idUSBRE9251IH20130306

Krupp, F. (2014). Don't just drill, baby – drill carefully, *Foreign Affairs* **93**(3): 15–20.

Kuta, S. (2015, April 16). CU regents say no to fossil-fuel divestment. *Daily Camera*. URL: www.dailycamera.com/cu-news/ci_27924351/cus-board-regents-says-no-fossil-fuel-divestment

Labott, E. and Berman, D. (2015, November 6). Obama rejects Keystone XL pipeline. *CNN Politics*. URL: www.cnn.com/2015/11/06/politics/keystone-xl-pipeline-decision-rejection-kerry/

Lakshmi, R. and Denyer, S. (2012, September 15). Protests disrupt India's nuclear energy plan. *The Washington Post*. URL: www.washingtonpost.com/world/asia_pacific/protests-disrupt-indias-nuclear-energy-plan/2012/09/15/ec75ca58-fdad-11e1–98c6-ec0a0a93f8eb_story.html

Laskow, S. (2012, April 3). Anti-coal campaign is 'the most significant achievement of American environmentalists' since the 1970s. *Grist*. URL: http://grist.org/coal/anti-coal-campaign-is-the-most-significant-achievement-of-american-environmentalists-since-the-1970s/

League of Conservation Voters (2013). *2013 National environmental scorecard: First session of the 113th congress*. League of Conservation Voters, Washington DC.

Lee, M. F. (1995). *Earth First! Environmental Apocalypse*, Syracuse University Press, Syracuse.

Lenferna, A. (2014). *Fossil fuel divestment report for the Seattle city employees' retirement system*. Report written on behalf of 350 Seattle and Divest University of Washington.

Leslie, J. (2007). *Deep Water: The Epic Struggle Over Dams, Displaced People, and the Environment*, Farrar, Straus and Giroux, New York.

Leung, M. D. and Sharkey, A. J. (2013). Out of sight, out of mind? Evidence of perceptual factors in the multiple-category discount, *Organization Science* **25**(1): 171–184.

Levant, E. (2014). *Groundswell: The Case for Fracking*, Random House, New York.

Levi, M. (2012, January 18). Five myths about the Keystone XL pipeline. *The Washington Post.* URL: www.washingtonpost.com/opinions/five-myths-about-the-keystone-xl-pipeline/2011/12/19/gIQApUAX8P_story.html

Levi, M. (2013, April 29). We don't need exotic fuels to cook the earth, coal will do. *The Atlantic.* URL: www.theatlantic.com/technology/archive/2013/04/we-dont-need-exotic-fuels-to-cook-the-earth-coal-will-do/275271/

Levy, M. (2011, April 19). Pa. wants to end gas-drilling wastewater discharge. *The San Diego Union-Tribune.* URL: www.sandiegouniontribune.com/sdut-pa-wants-to-end-gas-drilling-wastewater-discharge-2011apr19-story.html

Lewis, S. (2007). Chinese NOCs and world energy markets: CNPC, SINOPEC, and CNOOC. Research paper written for the Baker Institute's study, *The Changing Role of National Oil Companies in International Energy Markets.*

Lomborg, B. (2001). *The Skeptical Environmentalist: Measuring the Real State of the World*, Cambridge University Press, New York.

Lovins, A. B. (1976). Energy strategy: The road not taken? *Foreign Affairs* **55**: 65–96.

Lukacs, M. (2014, November 18). Keystone XL pipeline opposition forges 'Cowboys and Indians' alliance. *The Guardian.* URL: http://gu.com/p/43cmn/stw

Lynch, M. C. (2013, January 29). Yoko Ono is wrong on fracking. *U.S. News & World Report.* URL: www.usnews.com/opinion/blogs/on-energy/2013/01/29/yoko-ono-is-wrong-on-fracking

MacDonald, J. (2016, February 25). Electric vehicles to be 35% of global new car sales by 2040. *Bloomberg New Energy Finance.* URL: https://about.bnef.com/blog/electric-vehicles-to-be-35-of-global-new-car-sales-by-2040/

Madison, L. (2011, November 30). Senate republicans push bill expediting Keystone XL pipeline decision. *CBS News.*

Magill, B. (2013, December 10). Scientists: Lack of data means fracking impacts unknown. *Climate Central.* URL: www.climatecentral.org/news/scientists-call-for-more-fracking-data-transparency-16816

Magill, B. (2014, May 15th). 'Catastrophe' claim adds fuel to methane debate. *Climate Central.* URL: www.climatecentral.org/news/fracking-methane-emissions-catastrophe-17439

Magill, B. (2015, January 8). EPA moves to count methane emissions from fracking. *Climate Central.* URL: www.climatec entral.org/news/epa-methane-emissions-fracking-18511

Malewitz, J. (2014, December 15). Dissecting Denton: How a Texas city banned fracking. *The Texas Tribune.* URL: www.texastribune.org/2014/12/15/dissecting-denton-how-texas-city-baned-fracking/

Malewitz, J. (2015, June 3). With fracking ban overruled, Denton ponders next steps. *The Texas Tribune.* URL: www.texastribune.org/2015/06/03/more-questions-answers-denton-ponders-next-steps/

Malkovich, B. (2014, September 11). Illinois Mine Institute speakers address political tactics of anti-coal movement. *The Southern Illinoisan.* URL: http://thesouthern.com/news/local/illinois-mine-institute-speakers-address-political-tactics-of-anti-coal/article_c3e51e94-a443-459dd-ae64-69e3a88542bb2.html

Marshall, G. (2014). *Don't Even Think About It: Why Our Brains Are Wired to Ignore Climate Change*, Bloomsbury Press, New York.

Martin, P. L. (2011). Global governance from the Amazon: Leaving oil underground in Yasuní National Park, Ecuador, *Global Environmental Politics* **11**(4): 22–42.

Martinez-Alier, J. (2002). *The Environmentalism of the Poor: A Study of Ecological Conflicts and Valuation*, Edward Elgar, Northampton.

Maxmin, C. S. (2015). *The rising: Political mobilization for climate action.* Senior Thesis, Harvard University.

Mayer, H. (1999). Air pollution in cities, *Atmospheric Environment* **33**(24–25): 4029–4037.

McAdam, D. (1986). Recruitment to high-risk activism: The case of Freedom Summer, *American Journal of Sociology* **92**(1): 64–90.

McAdam, D. (1999). *Political Process and the Development of Black Insurgency, 1930–1970,* University of Chicago Press, Chicago.

McAdam, D. and Boudet, H. (2012). *Putting Social Movements in Their Place: Explaining Opposition to Energy Projects in the United States, 2000–2005,* Cambridge University Press, New York.

McCarthy, J. D. and Zald, M. N. (1977). Resource mobilization and social movements: A partial theory, *American Journal of Sociology* **82**(6): 1212–1241.

McCully, P. (2001). *Silenced Rivers: The Ecology and Politics of Large Dams,* enlarged and updated edn, Zed Books, New York.

McGowan, E. (2011, August 29). NASA's Hansen explains decision to join Keystone pipeline protests. *InsideClimate News.* URL: https://insideclimatenews.org/news/20110826/james-hansen-nasa-climate-change-scientist-keystone-xl-oil-sands-pipeline-protests-mckibben-white-house

McIlmoil, R. and Hansen, E. (2009). *The decline of central Appalachian coal and the need for economic diversification.* Downstream Strategies Thinking Downstream White Paper No. 1.

McKibben, B. (2007). A letter from Bill McKibben. *StepItUp.* URL: www.stepitup2007.org/article.php-id=417.html

McKibben, B. (2011, June 23). Join us in civil disobedience to stop the Keystone XL tarsands pipeline. *Grist.* URL: http://grist.org/climate-change/2011-06-23-join-us-in-civil-disobedience-to-stop-the-keystone-xl-tar-sands/

McKibben, B. (2012, August 2). Global warming's terrifying new math. *Rolling Stone.*

McKibben, B. (2013). *Oil and Honey: The Education of an Unlikely Activist,* Henry Holt, New York.

McKibben, B. (2013, February 22). The case for fossil-fuel divestment. *Rolling Stone.*

McKibben, B. (2014, February 11). Room for debate: Turning colleges' partners into pariahs. *The New York Times.* URL: https://nyti.ms/2qWiYfZ

McKibben, B. (2015, December 13). Falling short on climate in Paris. *The New York Times.* URL: https://nyti.ms/2rvzgg6

McMichael, A. J., Campbell-Lendrum, D., Kovats, S., Edwards, S., Wilkinson, P., Wilson, T., Nicholls, R., Hales, S., Tanser, F., Sueur, D. L., Schlesinger, M. and Andronova, N. (2004). Chapter 20: Global climate change, *in* M. Ezzati, A. D. Lopez, A. Rodgers and C. J. Murray (eds), *Comparative Quantification of Health Risks: Global and Regional Burden of Disease Due to Selected Major Risk Factors,* Vol. 2, World Health Organization, Geneva, pp. 1543–1649.

McNeil, B. T. (2011). *Combating Mountaintop Removal: New Directions in the Fight Against Big Coal,* University of Illinois Press.

Messer, C. M., Shriver, T. E. and Adams, A. E. (2015). Collective identity and memory: A comparative analysis of community response to environmental hazards, *Rural Sociology* **80**(3): 314–339.

Meyer, D. S. (2004). Protest and political opportunities, *Annual Review of Sociology* **30**: 125–145.

Meyer, D. S. (2005). Social movements and public policy: Eggs, chicken, and theory, *in* D. S. Meyer, V. Jenness and H. Ingram (eds), *Routing the Opposition: Social Movements, Public Policy, and Democracy,* University of Minnesota Press, Minneapolis.

Miller, S. (2012, March 8). Senate narrowly rejects the Keystone oil pipeline amendment. *ABC News*. URL: http://abcnews.go.com/blogs/politics/2012/03/senate-narrowly-rejects-the-keystone-oil-pipeline-amendment/

Montrie, C. (2003). *To Save the Land and the People: A History of Opposition to Surface Coal Mining in Appalachia*, University of North Carolina Press, Chapel Hill.

Mooney, C. (2015, February 25). This is the real significance of Obama's Keystone XL veto. *The Washington Post*. URL: www.washingtonpost.com/news/energy-environment/wp/2015/02/25/this-is-the-real-significance-of-obamas-keystone-xl-veto/

Morris, S. and Pizer, B. (2013). Thinking through when the World Bank should fund coal projects. *Center for Global Development*. URL: www.cgdev.org/publication/ft/thinking-through-when-world-bank-should-fund-coal-projects

Moss, T. and Leo, B. (2014). *Maximizing access to energy: Estimates of access and generation for the Overseas Private Investment Corporation's portfolio*. Center for Global Development, Washington, DC.

Mouawad, J. (2016, January 11). Oil prices slide again, and the bottom is not yet in sight. *The New York Times*. URL: https://nyti.ms/2r3aDrd

Muller, N. Z., Mendelsohn, R. and Nordhaus, W. (2011). Environmental accounting for pollution in the United States economy, *American Economic Review* **101**(5): 1649–1675.

Nace, T. (2008, January). Stopping coal in its tracks. *Orion Magazine*. URL: https://orion magazine.org/article/stopping-coal-in-its-tracks/

Nace, T. (2010). *Climate Hope: On the Front Lines of the Fight against Coal*, CoalSwarm, San Francisco.

The New York Times (2013, January 27). Room for debate: Is divestment an effective means of protest? *The New York Times*. URL: https://nyti.ms/2rUhMal

The New York Times (2015, June 6). The case for a carbon tax. *The New York Times*. URL: www.nytimes.com/2015/06/07/opinion/the-case-for-a-carbon-tax.html

Nikolewski, R. (2015, June 9). Escape from New York? Secession talk lingers as fracking ban is finalized. *Watchdog.org*. URL: http://watchdog.org/223020/fracking-ban-secession/

Northrop, M. (2016, January 11). Is the post-fossil fuel era now inevitable? *The Huffington Post*. URL: www.huffingtonpost.com/michael-northrop/is-the-post-fossil-fuel-e_b_8954310.html

Nuttall, W. J. and Manz, D. L. (2008). A new energy security paradigm for the twenty-first century, *Technological Forecasting and Social Change* **75**(8): 1247–1259.

Obley, M. (2014, January 24). De Blasio: Fracking poses 'too much danger to water supply' in New York. *The Huffington Post*. URL: www.huffingtonpost.com/2014/01/24/de-blasio-fracking_n_4660612.html

Oil Change International (2016). *The sky's limit: Why the Paris climate goals require a managed decline of fossil fuel production*. Oil Change International, Washington, DC.

Olkowski, T. S. B. and Skinner, W. C. (2015, September 23). Endowment returns 5.8 percent, growing to $37.6 billion. *The Harvard Crimson*. URL: www.thecrimson.com/article/2015/9/23/hmc-endowment-returns-2015/

Olson, B., Miller, J. W. and Cook, L. (2016, November 9). Oil, coal seen as winners with Donald Trump victory. *Wall Street Journal*. URL: www.wsj.com/articles/oil-coal-seen-as-winners-with-trump-victory-1478693338

Olson, M. (1965). *The Logic of Collective Action: Public Goods and the Theory of Groups*, Harvard University Press, Cambridge.

O'Neill, E. (2013, October 7). The fracking debate moves to Argentina. *Earth Island Journal*. URL: www.earthisland.org/journal/index.php/elist/eListRead/the_fracking_debate_moves_to_argentina/

OpenSecrets.org (2014). Annual lobbying on energy and natural resources. *OpenSecrets.org*. Accessed on December 7th, 2014. URL: www.opensecrets.org/lobby/indus.php?id=E

OpenSecrets.org (2016). Energy/natural resources. *OpenSecrets.org*. Accessed on May 8th, 2017. URL: www.opensecrets.org/industries/indus.php?cycle=2014&ind=E

Opukri, C. and Ibaba, I. S. (2008). Oil induced environmental degradation and internal population displacement in the Nigeria's Niger Delta, *Journal of Sustainable Development in Africa* **10**(1): 173–193.

Oreskes, N. and Conway, E. M. (2010). *Merchants of Doubt: How a Handful of Scientists Obscured the Truth on Issues From Tobacco Smoke to Global Warming*, Bloomsbury Press, New York.

Owolabi, T. (2014, December 3). Shell pipeline leak spills thousands of barrels into Niger Delta. *Reuters*. URL: www.reuters.com/article/2014/12/03/us-shell-oilspill-idUSKCN0JH26Z20141203

Pallas, C. L. and Urpelainen, J. (2012). NGO monitoring and the legitimacy of international cooperation: A strategic analysis, *Review of International Organizations* **7**(1): 1–32.

Pallas, C. L. and Urpelainen, J. (2013). Mission and interests: The strategic formation and function of north-south NGO campaigns, *Global Governance: A Review of Multilateralism and International Organizations* **19**(3): 401–423.

Papousek, T. (2013, September 24). Q&A: Samuel Avery, author of 'the pipeline and the paradigm'. *Daily Nebraskan*.

Pear, R. and Barringer, F. (2008, December 2). Coal mining debris rule is approved. *The New York Times*. URL: www.nytimes.com/2008/12/03/washington/03mining.html

Pegg, S. (2009). Chronicle of a death foretold: The collapse of the Chad-Cameroon pipeline project, *African Affairs* **108**(431): 311–320.

Phillips, S. (2013, May 21). Fractures in the anti-fracking movement. *StateImpact*. URL: https://stateimpact.npr.org/pennsylvania/2013/05/21/fractures-in-the-anti-fracking-movement/

Pipher, M. (2013). *The Green Boat: Reviving Ourselves in Our Capsized Culture*, Riverhead Books, Penguin Group.

Piven, F. F. and Cloward, R. A. (1977). *Poor People's Movements: Why They Succeed, How They Fail*, Random House, New York.

Plumer, B. (2013, November 4). Here's why Central Appalachia's coal industry is dying. *The Washington Post*. URL: www.washingtonpost.com/news/wonk/wp/2013/11/04/heres-why-central-appalachias-coal-industry-is-dying/

Plumer, B. (2015, July 9). There are 2,100 new coal plants being planned worldwide – Enough to cook the planet. *Vox*. URL: www.vox.com/2015/7/7/8908179/coal-global-climate-change

Pooley, E. (2010). *The Climate War: True Believers, Power Brokers, and the Fight to Save the Earth*, Hyperion, New York.

Przeworski, A. and Teune, H. (1970). *The Logic of Comparative Social Inquiry*, Robert E. Krieger, Malabar.

Queally, J. (2015, May 19). By banning fracking bans, Texas picks gas drillers over local democracy. *Common Dreams*. URL: www.commondreams.org/news/2015/05/19/banning-fracking-bans-texas-picks-gas-drillers-over-local-democracy

Rabe, B. (2004). *Statehouse and Greenhouse: The Evolving Politics of American Climate Change Policy*, Brookings Institution Press, Washington, DC.

Rabe, B. G. (2014). Shale play politics: The intergovernmental odyssey of American shale governance, *Environmental Science and Technology* **48**(15): 8369–8375.

Rabe, B. G. and Borick, C. (2013). Conventional politics for unconventional drilling? Lessons from Pennsylvania's early move into fracking policy development, *Review of Policy Research* **30**(3): 321–340.

Rabeler, K. (2013, March 26). Gas industry report calls anti-fracking movement a 'highly effective campaign'. *YES! Magazine.* URL: www.yesmagazine.org/planet/gas-industry-report-calls-anti-fracking-movement-highly-effective

Rainforest Action Network. (2015, May 6). Breaking: Bank of America dumps coal mining in sweeping new policy. *ran.org.* URL: www.ran.org/breaking_bank_of_america_dumps_coal_mining_in_sweeping_new_policy

Randall, T. (2013, June 25). 'We Need to Act': Transcript of Obama's climate change speech. *Bloomberg.* URL: www.bloomberg.com/news/articles/2013-06-25/-we-need-to-act-transcript-of-obama-s-climate-change-speech

Rees, J. V. (2009). *Hostages of Each Other: The Transformation of Nuclear Safety Since Three Mile Island,* University of Chicago Press, Chicago.

Ritter, D. (2015). The forest or the pit? *in* C. Nelson, D. Pike and G. Ledvinka (eds), *On Happiness: New Ideas for the Twenty-First Century,* UWA Publishing, Crawley, Western Australia, pp. 96–115.

Rockström, J., Steffen, W., Noone, K., Persson, Åsa, III, F. S. C., Lambin, E. F., Lenton, T. M., Scheffer, M., Folke, C., Schellnhuber, H. J., Nykvist, B., de Wit, C. A., Hughes, T., van der Leeuw, S., Rodhe, H., Sörlin, S., Snyder, P. K., Costanza, R., Svedin, U., Falkenmark, M., Karlberg, L., Corell, R. W., Fabry, V. J., Hansen, J., Walker, B., Liverman, D., Richardson, K., Crutzen, P. and Foley, J. A. (2009). A safe operating space for humanity, *Nature* **461**(7263): 472–475.

Romm, J. (2007, July 6). James Hansen on stopping new coal plants. *ThinkProgress.* URL: https://thinkprogress.org/james-hansen-on-stopping-new-coal-plants-9e4312a4678d

Rucht, D. (1990). Campaigns, skirmishes and battles: Anti-nuclear movements in the USA, France and West Germany, *Organization and Environment* **4**(3): 193–222.

Rudegeair, P. (2012, November 29). New York fracking decision delayed after state agency requests more time to complete health study. *The Huffington Post.* URL: www.huffingtonpost.com/2012/11/30/new-york-fracking-decision_n_2215138.html

Rudig, W. (1990). *Anti-Nuclear Movements: A World Survey of Opposition to Nuclear Energy,* Longman, Harlow.

Sadasivam, N. (2014, July 22). New York state of fracking: A ProPublica Explainer. *ProPublica.* URL: www.propublica.org/article/new-york-state-of-fracking-a-propublica-explainer

Samuel, S. (2012, November 12). Protestors call on Obama to reject Keystone XL pipeline. *CNN Politics.* URL: www.cnn.com/2012/11/18/politics/keystone-pipeline-protest/index.html

Santoshi, N. (2015, February 4). Madhya Pradesh: Battle for coal divides Mahan villages. *Hindustan Times.* URL: www.hindustantimes.com/india/madhya-pradesh-battle-for-coal-divides-mahan-villages/story-yyKkfeKOULc869B9wUVe3I.html

Schlosberg, D. and Dryzek, J. S. (2002). Political strategies of American environmentalism: Inclusion and beyond, *Society and Natural Resources* **15**(9): 787–804.

Schoof, R. (2012, March 1). Giant new plant shows coal power isn't going away. *McClatchy.* URL: www.mcclatchydc.com/2012/03/01/140544/giant-new-plant-shows-coal-power.html

Schulte, G. (2015, January 20). Keystone XL pipeline developer takes steps to seize land in Nebraska. *The Guardian.* URL: www.theguardian.com/environment/2015/jan/20/keystone-xl-pipeline-developer-seize-land-nebraska

Schumer, N. (n.d.). Divest New York City from Fossil Fuels! Fossil Free. URL: https://campaigns.gofossilfree.org/petitions/divest-new-york-city-from-fossil-fuels

Schweigman, K. (n.d.). South Dakota is the Mississippi of the North. URL: http://hemi.es.its.nyu.edu/journal/2_1/warmwater.html

Seltzer, A. M. and Povilaitis, J. F. (2015, June 8). The 'Pennsylvania Solution' to the fracking boom. *Law360.* URL: www.law360.com/articles/665246/the-pennsylvania-solution-to-the-fracking-boom

Shabecoff, P. (2003). *A Fierce Green Fire: The American Environmental Movement,* Island Press, Washington, DC.

Shell (2013). *Strategic Report of Royal Dutch Shell,* Royal Dutch Shell, London.

Shell (2014). Shell's energy strategy. URL: www.shell.com/global/aboutshell/investor/strategy.html

Sheppard, K. (2011, September 7). Nobel winners call on Obama to reject Keystone XL. *Mother Jones.* URL: www.motherjones.com/blue-marble/2011/09/nobel-winners-call-obama-reject-keystone-xl

Sierra Club (n.d.). Carbon pollution: An urgent threat from coal. *SierraClub.org.* URL: http://content.sierraclub.org/coal/burning-carbon-pollution-and-climate-disruption

Sierra Club (n.d.). International climate and energy. *SierraClub.org.* URL: www.sierraclub.org/international

Sierra Club (2013). *Move beyond coal: The global movement in 2013,* Sierra Club, Washington, DC.

Sierra Club (2014). *Move beyond coal: The global movement in 2014,* Sierra Club, Washington, DC.

Skocpol, T. (1979). *States and Social Revolutions: A Comparative Analysis of France, Russia, and China,* Cambridge University Press, Cambridge, UK.

Skocpol, T. (2013). *Naming the problem: What it will take to counter extremism and engage Americans in the fight against global warming.* Symposium on the Politics of America's Fight Against Global Warming, Harvard University.

Smith, H. J., Pettigrew, T. F., Pippin, G. M. and Bialosiewicz, S. (2012). Relative deprivation: A theoretical and meta-analytic review, *Personality and Social Psychology Review* **16**(3): 203–232.

Smyth, J. C. (2015, February 8). Illinois coal power plant at center of Midwest rate fights. *Northwest Herald.* URL: www.nwherald.com/2015/02/08/illinois-power-plant-at-center-of-midwest-rate-fights/af75kgi/?page=1

Solomon, S. D. (2015, February 10). Colleges use anti-apartheid strategies to battle fossil fuels. *The New York Times.* URL: https://nyti.ms/2r0YlPS

Spear, S. (2013, February 12). Join Forward on Climate solidarity rallies across the U.S. URL: www.ecowatch.com/join-forward-on-climate-solidarity-rallies-across-the-u-s-1881696341.html

Stavins, R. N. (2014, March 20). Divestment is no substitute for real action on climate change. *Yale Environment 360.* URL: http://e360.yale.edu/features/counterpoint_robert_stavins_divestment_no_substitute_for_real_action_on_climate

Steingraber, S. (2012, March 26). Breaking up with the Sierra Club. *Orion Magazine.* URL: https://orionmagazine.org/2012/03/breaking-up-with-the-sierra-club/

Steingraber, S. (2014, August 26). What the anti-fracking movement brings to the climate movement. *Moyers & Company.* URL: http://billmoyers.com/2014/08/26/what-the-anti-fracking-movement-brings-to-the-climate-movement/

Stephenson, E. (2014, March 2). Hundreds of Keystone protesters arrested at White House. *Reuters.* URL: www.reuters.com/article/2014/03/03/us-usa-keystone-protest-idUSBREA210RI20140303

Stouffer, S. A., Suchman, E. A., Devinney, L. C., Star, S. A. and Williams, Jr., R. M. (1949). *The American Soldier: Adjustment During Army Life,* Vol. I, Princeton University Press, Princeton.

Streib, L. (2014, November 14). Stanford adds fracking investments in 3rd quarter. *Bloomberg.* URL: www.bloomberg.com/news/articles/2014-11-14/stanford-endowment-adds-fracking-investments-in-third-quarter

Stuber, S. (2015, September 25). Stanford's endowment shows upward growth. *The Stanford Daily*. URL: www.stanforddaily.com/2015/09/25/stanfords-endowment-shows-upward-growth/

Supran, G. and Oreskes, N. (2017, August 27). What Exxon Mobil Didn't Say About Climate Change. The New York Times. URL: https://nyti.ms/2vn5EQv

Swart, N. C. and Weaver, A. J. (2012). The Alberta oil sands and climate, *Nature Climate Change* **2**(3): 134–136.

Tarrow, S. (1998). *Power in Movement: Social Movements and Contentious Politics*, 2nd edn, Cambridge University Press, New York.

Tarrow, S. (2011). *Power in Movement: Social Movements and Contentious Politics*, 3rd edn, Cambridge University Press, New York.

TarSands Blockade (n.d.). Nonviolent direct action. *TarSandsBlockade.org*. URL: www.tarsandsblockade.org/about-2/non-violent-direct-action/

TarSands Blockade (n.d.). Why oppose KXL? *TarSandsBlockade.org*. URL: www.tarsandsblockade.org/about-2/why-oppose-kxl/

Taylor, I. (2006). China's oil diplomacy in Africa, *International Affairs* **82**(5): 937–959.

Tercek, M. (2015, May 5). The conservative case for a carbon tax: Q&A with Jerry Taylor. *The Huffington Post*. URL: www.huffingtonpost.com/mark-tercek/the-conservative-case-for-a-carbon-tax_b_7214984.html

Theodoria, G. L., Luloff, A., Willits, F. K. and Burnett, D. B. (2014). Hydraulic fracturing and the management, disposal, and reuse of frac flowback waters: Views from the public in the marcellus shale, *Energy Research & Social Science* **2**(1): 66–74.

Tilly, C. (1978). *From Mobilization to Revolution*, McGraw-Hill, New York.

Toomey, D. (2014, June 9). How a small college launched divestment from fossil fuels. *Yale Environment 360*. URL: http://e360.yale.edu/feature/interview_stephen_mulkey_how_a_small_college_launched_divestment_from_fossil_fuels/2773/

TransCanada (2013). Keystone XL Pipeline. *TransCanada*. URL: www.keystone-xl.com/wp-content/uploads/2013/09/Keystone-XL-Pipeline-Factsheet.pdf

Trembath, A. (2014, June 30). The low-energy club. *The Breakthrough Institute*. URL: https://thebreakthrough.org/index.php/programs/energy-and-climate/the-low-energy-club

Tresaugue, M. (2010, October 25). Water emerges as new weapon in Texas coal plant fight. *Houston Chronicle*. URL: www.chron.com/news/houston-texas/article/Water-emerges-as-new-weapon-in-Texas-coal-plant-1603441.php

Union Theological Seminary (2015, February 2). Union Theological Seminary in the City of New York votes unanimously to divest from fossil fuels. *Union News*. URL: https://utsnyc.edu/divestment/

United Nations Framework Convention on Climate Change (n.d.). Intended Nationally Determined Contributions (INDC). *UNFCCC*. URL: http://unfccc.int/focus/indc_portal/items/8766.php

United Nations Framework Convention on Climate Change (2009, December 7–19). Report of the Conference of the Parties on its fifteenth session, held in Copenhagen from 7 to 19 December 2009. Addendum Part Two: Action taken by the Conference of the Parties at its fifteenth session. URL: http://unfccc.int/resource/docs/2009/cop15/eng/11a01.pdf

United Nations Framework Convention on Climate Change (2015, December 12). Adoption of the Paris Agreement. *UNFCCC*. URL: https://unfccc.int/resource/docs/2015/cop21/eng/l09r01.pdf

Urpelainen, J. (2009). Explaining the Schwarzenegger phenomenon: Local frontrunners in climate policy, *Global Environmental Politics* **9**(3): 82–105.

Urpelainen, J. (2013). A model of dynamic climate governance: Dream big, win small, *International Environmental Agreements* **13**(2): 107–125.

US Department of State (2017, March 24). Issuance of Presidential Permit to TransCanada for Keystone XL Pipeline. *Office of the Spokesperson.* URL: https://www.state.gov/r/pa/prs/ps/2017/03/269074.htm

US Energy Information Administration (2012, September 27). Annual energy review. *Today in Energy.* URL: www.eia.gov/totalenergy/data/annual/showtext.cfm?t=ptb0901

US Energy Information Administration (2015, December 18). Global coal demand stalls after more than a decade of relentless growth. *iea.org.* URL: http://goo.gl/h4hgYH

US Energy Information Administration (2016, January 8). Coal production and prices decline in 2015. *Today in Energy.* URL: www.eia.gov/todayinenergy/detail.cfm?id=24472

USAID (n.d.). Power Africa. *USAID.org.* URL: /www.usaid.gov/powerafrica

Valentine, K. (2014, August 29). Pennsylvania finally reveals fracking has contaminated drinking water hundreds of times. *ThinkProgress.* URL: https://thinkprogress.org/pennsylvania-finally-reveals-fracking-has-contaminated-drinking-water-hundreds-of-times-739cf4fc103b

Valentine, K. (2015, January 9). BREAKING: Nebraska Supreme Court ruling upholds Keystone XL pipeline route. *ThinkProgress.* URL: https://thinkprogress.org/breaking-nebraska-supreme-court-ruling-upholds-keystone-xl-pipeline-route-ecaa8c7fa592

Victor, D. G. (2011). *Global Warming Gridlock: Creating More Effective Strategies for Protecting the Planet,* Cambridge University Press, New York.

Victor, D. G. and Kennel, C. F. (2014). Climate policy: Ditch the 2°C warming goal, *Nature* **514**: 30–31.

Volcovici, V. (2013, February 17). Thousands at climate rally in Washington call on Obama to reject Keystone pipeline. *Reuters.* URL: http://reut.rs/VYUqiu

Walsh, B. (2012, February 2). Exclusive: How the Sierra Club took millions from the natural gas industry – and why they stopped. *Time.* URL: http://science.time.com/2012/02/02/exclusive-how-the-sierra-club-took-millions-from-the-natural-gas-industry-and-why-they-stopped/

Walsh, E. J. (1981). Resource mobilization and citizen protest in communities around Three Mile Island, *Social Problems* **29**(1): 1–21.

Weick, K. E. (1984). Small wins: Redefining the scale of social problems, *American Psychologist* **39**(1): 40

Weinstein, S., Bruck, O., Maxmin, C., Dasaratha, K. and Gould, D. P. (2014, May 13). Why divestment can be successful. *The New York Times.* URL: https://nyti.ms/2r1jrxo

Welch, I. (2014, May 9). Why divestment fails. *The New York Times.* URL: www.nytimes.com/2014/05/10/opinion/why-divestment-fails.html

WHO (2014). *Quantitative risk assessment of the effects of climate change on selected causes of death, 2030s and 2050s,* World Health Organization, Geneva, pp. 1–128.

Wines, M. (2014, May 6). Stanford to purge $18 billion endowment of coal stock. *The New York Times.* URL: https://nyti.ms/2r15ekn

Wolfson, M. (2001). *The Fight Against Big Tobacco: The Movement, the State, and the Public's Health,* Transaction Publishers, Piscataway, NJ.

Wood, J. (2012). The global anti-fracking movement: What it wants, how it operates, and what's next. Whitepaper by Control Risks. URL: www.marcellusprotest.org/sites/marcellusprotest.org/files/shale_gas_whitepaper.pdf

World Bank (2013, July 16). World Bank Group Sets Direction for Energy Sector Investments. *WorldBank.org.* URL: www.worldbank.org/en/news/feature/2013/07/16/world-bank-group-direction-for-energy-sector?cid=EXT_WBSocialShare_EXT

World Bank (2014). Turn down the heat: Confronting the new climate normal, *Turn Down The Heat Series*, International Bank for Reconstruction and Development/The World Bank, Washington, DC.

World Nuclear Association. (2017, October). Nuclear power in France. *world-nuclear.org*. URL: http://www.world-nuclear.org/information-library/country-profiles/countries-a-f/france.aspx

Xu, V. (2015, February 17). Faculty meet with Hennessy to discuss divestment from fossil fuels. *The Stanford Daily*. URL: www.stanforddaily.com/2015/02/17/faculty-meet-with-hennessy-to-discuss-divestment-from-fossil-fuels/

Yearwood Jr., L. (2013, February 17). Forward on Climate Rally. Rev. Yearwood's remarks. *C-SPAN.org*. URL: www.c-span.org/video/?c4363223/forward-climate-rally-21713

Yearwood Jr., L. (2015, February 15). Divest or else: How hip-hop can help save the planet. *Ecowatch*. URL: http://ecowatch.com/2014/11/15/divest-hip-hop-save-planet/

Yergin, D. (1991). *The Prize: The Epic Quest for Oil, Money, and Power*, Simon and Schuster, New York.

Yue, Z. (2014, September 23). China's nuclear expansion threatened by public unease. *China Dialogue*. URL: www.chinadialogue.net/article/show/single/en/7336-Chinese-protesters-threaten-nuclear-expansion

Yukhananov, A. and Volcovici, V. (2013, July 16). World Bank to limit financing of coal-fired plants. *Reuters*. URL: www.reuters.com/article/us-worldbank-climate-coal-idUSBRE96F19U20130716

Zeller Jr., T. (2010, December 11). New York Governor vetoes fracking bill. *The New York Times*. URL: https://nyti.ms/2saCtii

Zhao, D. (1998). Ecologies of social movements: Student mobilization during the 1989 pro-democracy movement in Beijing, *American Journal of Sociology* **103**(6): 1493–1529.

Zornick, G. (2013, February). 'Forward on Climate' rally sends a message to Obama: No Keystone. *The Nation*. URL: www.thenation.com/blog/172964/forward-climate-rally-sends-message-obama-no-keystone

Zuckerman, E. W. (1999). The categorical imperative: Securities analysts and the illegitimacy discount, *American Journal of Sociology* **104**(5): 1398–1438.

INDEX

350.org 9, 13, 14, 16, 23, 26, 33, 68, 76, 77, 82–84, 85, 103, 126, 181
350Colorado 109, 125n14
350NYC 104, 107–108, 117, 125n12
350Seattle 122
350Vermont 108–109, 125n13

A&G Coal Corp. Ison Rock Ridge Surface Mine 133
Abacha, Sani (General) 29
Abbey, Edward 177
Abbott, Greg 168
Abilenians Against Tenaska 140
activism: definition 40; divestment 103–113; environmental, before campaigns against fossil fuels 46–51; high-cost 44; hybrid 44; impact of movement 63–64; low-cost 44; religious climate 59; social movements and 203–208; study of 40–46
African National Congress 41
Allen, Paul G. 138–139
Alliance Coal 141
Alpha Natural Resources LLC 30
American Cancer Society 97
American Clean Energy and Security Act 49
American environmentalism 16, 20, 201; campaigns before fossil fuels 46–51
American Geophysical Union 159
American Legislative Exchange Council (ALEC) 32, 142
American Petroleum Institute 164, 165
American Psychologist (journal) 56

Americans Against Fracking 156, 157, 170, 172, 173n1
Americans for Prosperity 32
Amnesty International 44
Anglican Church, Aotearoa, New Zealand 101
Anglican Church of Australia 101
Anti-Apartheid Act (1986) 97
anti-nuclear movement 45, 175–176, 191n1
Aotearoa, New Zealand 101
Appalachian Group to Save the Land and People 127
Appalachian Voices 137
Appalachia Restoration Act 138
Arch Coal Inc. 30, 149
Army Corps of Engineers 133–134
Audubon Nebraska 79
Audubon Society 129
Avery, Samuel 3, 51, 57
Avila, Eli 167

Bach, John 93
bandwagon 74, 77
Bank of America 133, 183
Bank of Boston 97
"Bank of Coal" 183
Bank of England 37, 96, 208
Barclay's Bank 97
Barnard-Columbia Divest for Climate Justice Campaign 116
Barnett Shale 46, 155–156, 167
Bear Run 141
Belo Monte 177

Beyer, Michael 142
"Beyond Coal" campaign 129, 132, 143–144, 146, 151
BG Group 203
Biden, Joseph 71
Big Carbon 96
Big Green 10, 49, 197
Big Stone II Power Plant 130
Big Tobacco 10, 12
Black Panthers 62, 202
Blankenship, Don 133
Blockadia 88
Bloomberg, Michael 132
Bloomberg New Energy Finance 38, 102
Board of Education Retirement System (BERS) 108
Bok, Derek 97
Bold Nebraska 75, 79–82, 89
Bonhoeffer, Dietrich 103
Borowsky, Hannah 110
Boxer, Barbara 72
Boxtel, Netherlands 101
BP 15, 30, 31, 34, 35, 37, 58, 108, 155, 203, 212, 213, 214
Bradford County 165, *166*, *167*
Breakthrough Institute 188
bridge fuel 52, 154, 197
Broome County *160*, *161*, 162, 164
Bruck, Ophir 117
Brune, Michael 83, 86
Buenos Aires Herald (newspaper) 182
Bureau of Land Management (BLM) 138
Bush, George W. 9, 61, 130, 133, 155, 207

Calvert Research and Management 102
campaigns: explaining the momentum 56–63; external logic of 40; goals of 51–56; impact of movement 63–64; internal logic of 40
Canadian Natural Resources Limited 36
cap-and-trade system 46, 49–50, 53, 85
Caperton Coal 127
carbon bubble 37, 96
carbon budget 36, 55
carbon capture 7, 122, 130, 200
carbon dioxide (CO2) 2, 25–27, 30, 34, 130–131, 213
carbon majors 10, 18, 23, 31, 54, 114, 120, 181, 198, 205
carbon tax 3, 11, 13, 39, 53–54, 56, 62, 85, 115, 198, 201, 203
Carbon Tracker Initiative (CTI) 4, 36, 123
Carbon Underground 106
Carrizo-Wilcox Aquifer 70
Carson, Rachel 47
Carter, Jimmy 128–129

Cassidy, Bill 73
Catskill Mountainkeeper 162, 163
Center for Environment and Development (Cameroon) 179
Center for Global Development 186, 187
Center for Sustainable Shale Gas Development (CSSD) 158
Central Appalachian coalfield environmental justice movement 137
Chad-Cameroon pipeline 179
Chadian Association for the Promotion and Defense of Human Rights 179
Chase Manhattan 97
Chenango County *160*, *161*, 162
Cheney, Dick 2, 31, 130, 155
Chernobyl nuclear plant 46, 176
Chesapeake Energy 132, 155
Chevron 30, 35, 101, 108, 179, 214
Chicago Tribune (newspaper) 141
China Coal Energy 30
Chivian, Eric 111
Church of England 101
Citibank 37, 96, 132–133
Clashes with Corporate Giants (Friends of the Earth International) 180
Clean Air Act 47, 48, 126, 142, 148, 155, 200
Clean Energy for All (CE4ALL) model 188
Clean Power Plan 126, 148, 150, 153n19, 200
Clean Water Act 47, 134, 155
Clean Water Protection Act 138
climate change 192; fossil fuels and 26–29; global nature of 13–14, 205; international agreements 16–17; politics of 208–214
Climate Ground Zero 137
Climate Hope (Nace) 145
Climate Solutions 4
Climate War (Pooley) 50
Cloud Peak Energy 30
coal, campaign against 64, 66, 126–127; activism in motion 135–143; coal and development case study 185–189; defeated coal plants by state *135*; evaluation matrix **196**; impact of 147–152; map of defeated coal plants *136*; mobilization potential 146–147; motives of 143–146; overview of 127–135; recent and planned retirements of coal plants *131*; significance of 127; summary of American and international campaigns **189**
Coal India 30
Coal River Mountain Watch 137
CoalSwarm 144, 153n11, 199

Combs, Ollie 127
communities 156
communities at risk 45
Conference of Parties (COP) 149
Consol Energy (US) 30
Coordination of the Indigenous Organization
    of the Brazilian Amazon 180
Copenhagen UN Climate Change
    Conference (2009) 50, 204
Corbett, Tom 166
Cottage Grove Strip Mine 142–143
Council on Foreign Relations 69, 150
Cowboys and Indian Alliance 72, 76
Cowley, Maura 112
Cree 77
Cuomo, Andrew 163, 201
Cuyahoga River fire (Cleveland) 47

Dalai Lama 67, 71, 77
Dasaratha, Krishan 117
DeBlasio, Bill 164
deepwater oil projects 37
de Klerk, Frederik Willem 41
Delaware County 160, 161, 162
Democracy Now (television program) 74
Democratic Party 62, 207
Dene 77, 84
Denton Taxpayers for a Strong Economy 168
Deo, V. Kishore Chandra 184
Department of Environmental
    Conservation (DEC) 162, 163, 164
Department of Environmental Protection
    (DEP) 165
Department of Labor and Industry (DLI) 165
Dera, Marzena 183
dirty fuel 154, 187, 197
Divest Harvard 2, 93, 109–111, 125n16
divestment 93–94; actions by faiths 107;
    activism in motion 103–113; campaign
    64–66; colleges, universities and cities
    100; evaluation matrix **196**; faith-based
    judicatories on 100; impact of campaign
    on 119–124; mobilization potential
    for campaign 117–119; motives of
    campaigns on 113–117; overview of
    97–103; significance of 94–97; summary
    of American and international campaigns
    against **189**
Do The Math campaign 98, 120
Dunedin 101
Dynegy 142

EagleRidge Energy 167
Earth Day (1970) 16, 47
Earth First 49
Earth Island Journal (journal) 182

Earthworks 168
ecological debt, concept of 59
ecological paradigm 4, 9, 10, 51, 58, 85, 145
ecological sustainability 41–42
EcoWatch (news site) 115
Ecuador 7, 28
Ehrlich, Paul 113
Electricité de France 175, 191n1
electric vehicles 38
Enbridge 76
EnCana 157
Energy Act (2005) 130
Energy Action Coalition 112
Energy Future Holdings (EFH) 139
Energy Information Administration (EIA)
    149, 182
Energy Policy Act (2005) 155
Eni 203
environmental activism, campaigns before
    fossil fuels 46–51
Environmental Defense Fund (EDF) 1, 47,
    48, 49, 75, 129, 158, 177
environmentalism 2, 10–11, 15–16, 20;
    American 16, 20, 46–51, 201
environmentalist organizations, definition
    of 41–42
environmental justice movement 48, 204
Environmental Protection Agency (EPA)
    32, 73, 105, 129, 130, 133–135, 155,
    157, 159
Episcopalians 103, 105, 106, 198
Epstein, Alex 143
Eskom 186
Essar Energy 184
European Union 16
extreme energy 15, 85, 109, 195, 198
ExxonMobil 2, 7, 15, 29, 31, 33, 34, 37, 54,
    58, 101, 102, 108, 155, 179, 192, 212

Faludi, Susan 111
Faust, Drew Gilpin 2, 93, 110
Fire Department Pension Plan (Fire) 108
Fisher, Dana 60–61
Food & Water Watch 182
Forward on Climate rally 74–75, 82–83
Fossil Free campaign 99, 100, 112, 113,
    116, 181
fossil fuels 2, 23–24; future of human
    civilization 6–8; future prospects 33–38;
    goals of campaigns against 51–56;
    historical trends in consumption 25;
    industrialization, globalization and
    24–25; industry 29–33; mobilization
    potential and impact against 11–15;
    problem with 25–29; summary of
    American and international campaigns

against **189**; understanding the
movement against 8–11
fossil fuels, campaigns against 174–175;
coal and development case study
185–189; historical precedents 175–178;
international dimensions 178–185;
politics of climate change and 208–214;
summary of 189–190; understanding and
evaluating 195–203
Fox News 150
Frack Action 170
Frack Free Denton 168
fracking 7, 132, 154; activism in motion
159–168; campaign against 64, 66, 154;
current international situation 181; drilling
violations by county *167*; evaluation
matrix **196**; impact of campaign against
171–173; mobilization potential 170–171;
motives 169–170; municipal anti-fracking
movements by county *161*; municipal
bans and moratoriums over time *162*;
municipal bans by county *160*; municipal
moratoriums by county *161*; overview
of 156–159; significance of 155–156;
summary of American and international
campaigns against **189**; wells by county *166*
fractivists (anti-fracking activists) 154
FracTracker Alliance 156, 160, *160*,
161, *162*
Francis (Pope) 106
Franta, Ben 110
Freestone County 139
Friends of the Earth 1, 75, 138, 187
Friends of the Earth International 180
Fukushima incident (2011) 176

Gallup 8, 96
Gandhi, Mahatma 41, 57, 115
Gasland (documentary) 156, 169, 171–173,
197, 200
Gates, Bill 188
Gazprom 31, 33
Generic Environmental Impact Statement
(GEIS) 163
Gibbons, Jim 152n1
Glades Power Plant 130
Global Divestment Day (2015) 115
Global Finance campaign 137
Global Frackdown 156, 172, 182–183
globalization, fossil fuels and 24–25
global warming: coal and 127, 129, 130,
137, 140, 143–146; congressional action
on 72; divestment campaigns 111–113;
fossil fuel industry and 56, 78, 174, 190;
gridlock 14; limiting 37, 123; methane
and 170; public concern *9*; threat of 111

Golden, K. C. 4
Goldtooth, Tom 70
Goodheart, Marc 110
Goodwyn, Wade 168
Gore, Al 37
Grady-Benson, Jess 119
Greaney, Yari 112
Greenberg, Steve 164
GreenFaith 12, 59, 99, *100*, 101, 104, 107,
120, 125n10, 125n6
greenhouse gas (GHG) 36, 85
Greenhouse Gas Reporting Program 159
Greenland 27
Greenpeace 1, 44, 75, 174, 183, 187,
191n12
Greenspan Alan, 36
Groundswell (Levant) 52

Halliburton Loophole 155
Hansen, James 1, 26, 69, 70, 78, 85, 126,
127, 130, 131, 145, 146, 152n1, 199
Harper, Fletcher 104, 120
Harvard Corporation 2, 93
Harvard University 93
Harvard University Police 2
Heineman, Dave 78, 80, 81
Heintz, Stephen 101
Henn, Jamie 112, 123
Hennessy, John 111, 112–113
Hindalco Industries 184
Hinkel, Lyna 104
Hip Hop Caucus 1, 82, 84, 115, 116
Howarth, Robert 155–156, 158
HSBC 37, 96
Huffington Post (online newspaper) 93, 138
human civilization, fossil fuels and future
of 6–8
Hurricane Katrina 116
Hurricane Sandy 108
hybrid activism 16, 44, 194, 205
hydraulic fracturing 154; *see also* fracking

illegitimacy discount 44
Illinois Basin 141
Independent Mail, The (newspaper) 90
Indian National Congress 41
Indigenous Environmental Network 141
industrialization, fossil fuels and 24–25
industrial revolution 41
Intergovernmental Panel on Climate
Change (IPCC) 26
International Coal Group 149
International Energy Agency (IEA) 6, 24,
34, 52, 209, 212
International Rivers 177
Intrastate Coal and Use Act 142

Ison Rock Ridge Surface Mine 133
issue bricolage 204
Ivereigh, Austen 106

Jackson, Amy Berman 134
Jaiswal, Byasji 184
Johnson Rice coal industry 141
Johnston, Abby 90
Johnston, Michael 103
Jones, Serene 104
Jones, Van 72
JPMorgan Chase 133, 137
Judaism 83

Kaine, Tim 72
Keith, David 110
Kennedy, Henry H., Jr. 133
Kennedy, Robert, Jr. 111
Kennel, Charles F. 7
Kentuckians for the Commonwealth 137
Kerry, John 50, 72
Keystone Principle 4, 192, 194, 205
Keystone XL pipeline 1, 3, 5, 7, 11–13,
    20, 21, 28, 67–68, 193; activism in
    motion 74–84; campaign 39, 57, 58,
    61, 63–66; evaluation matrix **196**;
    headlines containing 75; impact of
    campaign 89–91; mobilization potential
    86–89; motives of campaign against
    85–86, 113–114; overview of 70–74;
    significance of 68–70
Kim, Jim Yong 186
King, Martin Luther, Jr. 41, 84, 115, 116, 202
King Coal 126, 151
Kleeb, Jane 80
Klein, Naomi 10, 70, 197
Koch, David and Charles 32
Koch Industries 32
Kohlberg Kravis Roberts & Co. LP
    (KKR) 129
Kolbert, Elizabeth 52
Kozisek, Mark 74, 82
Krupp, Fred 48
K Street 2, 7, 31, 192

Lakota 67
Landrieu, Mary 73
left-wing bias, 61
Lenferna, Alex 122
LeResche, Bob 138
Levant, Ezra 52
Levi, Michael 69, 150
Lin, Maya 111
Little Village Environmental Justice
    Organization (LVEJO) 141
Livingston County 160, 160, 161

Logan County 134
Lomborg, Bjorn 191n14
Lone Eagle, Beth 67
Lycoming County 165–167

Macauley, Boma 29
McClendon, Aubrey 132
McConnell, Mitch 150
McKibben, Bill 1, 4, 9, 10, 16, 20, 33,
    50–51, 52, 70, 75, 76, 83, 86–88, 94,
    95–96, 98–100, 102, 111–112, 119, 126,
    131, 198, 206
McMullen, Cathy 167–168
Mahan Sangarash Samiti 184
Malcolm X 62, 202
Manchin, Joe 134
Mandela, Nelson 41
Marcellus Shale 159, 162–165, 172
Markey, Edward 72
Marshall, George 55
Martens, Joe 164
Marxism 43
Massey Energy 133
Massie, Bob 93
Matagorda County 140
Maxmin, Chloe 50, 109, 117
Melbourne Unitarian Peace Memorial
    Church 101
Merkel, Angela 176
methane (CH4) 26
metric tons of carbon dioxide equivalent
    (MtCO2e) 2, 25, 30–31, 192
Mingo Logan Coal 134
Mitchell Energy 155
mobilization 45
mobilization potential 11; campaign against
    coal 146–147; divestment 117–119;
    Keystone XL 86–89
Moller, Joe 79–80
Moody's 37, 96
Moral Case for Fossil Fuels, The
    (Epstein) 143
moratoriums 9, 130–132, 156–157, 160,
    161, 162, 163, 172, 181, 185
Moreau, Karen 164, 165
Morris, Scott 186
Mulkey, Stephen 98
Multi-State Shale Research
    Collaborative 165

Nahuel, Lautaro 182
Narmada Bachao Andalon 177
National Day of Action Against Coal
    Finance 133
National Energy Technology
    Laboratory 130

National Environmental Policy Act 138
National Iranian Oil Company 30, 31
National Mining Association 134
National Press Club 130
National Resources Defense Council (NRDC) 1, 129
National Wildlife Federation 1, 75, 129
Natural Resources Defense Council (NRDC) 47, 75, 163
Nature Climate Change (journal) 68
Nature Conservancy 129
Nebraska 20
Nebraska Farmers Union 79
Nebraskans for Peace 79
neutral experts 45
New Republic, The (magazine) 112
New Yorkers Against Fracking 164
New York Society for Ethical Culture 119
Niebuhr, Reinhold 103
Niger Delta 29
nitrous oxide (N2O) 26
Nobel laureates 78, 79, 111, 112
Nobel Peace laureates 67, 71, 77, 78
Nobel Peace Prize 41, 55, 67, 78
nonconventional 10, 14, 18, 85, 198–199, 208, 21, 3
non-denominational 107, *107*
nongovernmental 19, 29, 43–44, 210
nonnegotiable 53
non-OECD (Organisation for Economic Co-operation and Development) 6, 24, 34
nonpartisan 60
nonprofit 12, 59, 156, 162
nonviolence 41
NYCERs (Employees' Retirement System) 108
"Not In Anyone's Back Yard" 45
"Not In My Back Yard" 45

Obama, Barack 1, 8, 13, 18, 31, 61, 67, 71–72, 74, 86, 88–90, 123, 132, 138, 139, 148, 150, 187, 193, 196, 197
Obama administration 32, 64, 71–74, 82, 89, 126, 133, 140
OECD (Organisation for Economic Co-operation and Development) 24, 35, 149
Office of Surface Mining Reclamation and Enforcement 128
Ogallala Aquifer 70, 78
Oil and Honey (McKibben) 88–89
Oil Change International 210
oil price 10, 13–14, 37–38, 58, 74, 123, 149, 208–209

Oneida County 160, *160*, *161*
Onondaga County 160, *160*, *161*
Ontario County 160, *160*, *161*
OpenSecrets.org 2–3, 8, 31, *32*, 192
opportunity 10–11, 14–15, 18, 35, 58
Otsego County 160, *160*, *161*, 162
Overseas Private Investment Corporation (OPIC) 187

Paris Agreement 15, 16, 194, 209–211
Parker County 157
Parkin, Scott 137
Pastoral Land Commission 180
Paterson, David 163
Peabody Energy Corporation 30, 32, 54, 141, 142, 143, 186
Peak Oil 37
Pearce, Beth 108
People's Climate March (PCM) 60–61, 65, 84, 119, 124, 157, 211
Petrobras 37, 108, 112
Petronas 179
Pipeline and the Paradigm, The (Avery) 57
pipelines, summary of American and international campaigns against **189**
Pipher, Mary 80, 81
Pizer, Billy 186
Police Pension Fund (Police) 108
political ecology 175
political opportunity 68, 76
political opportunity structure 8, 17–18, 43, 61, **196**
Portman, Natalie 111
"Power Africa" plan 187
Prairie State Energy Campus 141–143
Presbyterians 107
prestige 77
Price, Mark 165
Progress Energy 130
Public Citizen's anti-coal campaign 140

radical flank effect 62, 202–203, 207
Raghuveer, Tara 110
Rainforest Action Network (RAN) 1, 75, 126, 129, 132–133, 137, 146, 152n6, 183
Range Resources 157, 167
Ratcliffe, Tim 122
Raymond, Lee 2, 31, 36
Reagan, Ronald 46–48
Reid, Harry 130
"Reject and Protect" slogan 73
relative deprivation 42
renewables 7, 35, 38
resource mobilization theory 42–43

Responsible Endowments Coalition 119
Rex Energy Corp. 112
Rising Tide North America 137
Riverkeeper 163
Roche, Brett A. 2, 93–94
Rockefeller, John D. 101
Rockefeller Brothers Fund 101
Rockefeller Foundation 193
Rolling Stone (magazine) 4, 50, 94, 98
Roman Catholics 97, 107, *107*
Rosneft (RNFTF) 102
Royal Dutch Shell 30, 31, 108, 203
Rusk County 139

Safe Drinking Water Act 155
Saik'uz First Nation 84
Salazar, Ken 133
Saline County 142
Sandhills Beef 79
Santa Barbara oil spill 47
Sardar Sarovar Dam 177
Sardar Sarovar Project 177
Saro-Wiwa, Ken 29
satyagraha movement, Gandhi 41, 57
Saudi Aramco 30–31
Save Narmada Movement 177
scale shifts 45
Schelling, Thomas 55
Seamans, Paul 67
Securities and Exchange Commission
    (SEC) 142
Shaanxi Coal (China) 30
shareholder activism 96
Shell 15, 29, 30–31, 35, 36, 212
Shenhua 30
Sierra Club 1, 12, 75, 82–84, 86, 126, 129,
    132, 135, 139, 143–144, 146, 151–152,
    153n18, 163, 183, 187–188, 198
Silent Spring (Carson) 47
Singh, Virenda 184
Skocpol, Theda 49–50
Small, Fred 110
small wins 56, 194, 208; concept of 11,
    18–19
social justice 41–42
social media 171
social mobilization 42
social movements, activism and 203–208
Society of Friends (Quakers) 107
soft path 62
SourceWatch 132, 140, 152n6–7, 152n9,
    153n14–15
South Africa 10, 12
Statoil 37, 155, 203

Stavins, Robert N. 86, 150, 201
Steingraber, Sandra 169–170
Step It Up! campaign 131, 152n8
Steuben County *160*, *161*, 162
Steyer, Thomas F. 113
stranded assets 95
substantive impact 11
Sullivan County 141, *160*, *161*, 162,
    166, *167*
Suncor 36
surface mining 7, 28, 126, 128, 134, 146
Susquehanna County 165–167, *166*, *167*
Surface Mining Control and Reclamation
    Act (1977) (SMCRA) 128

Tamil Nadu, nuclear power protests 176
Tar Sands Action 70
Tar Sands Blockade 1, 70, 82–84
tar sands oil 36, 58, 65, 67–72, 80, 82–85,
    89, 114
Teachers' Retirement System (TRS) 108
Tenaska Trailblazer Energy Center 140
Texas General Land Office 168
Texas Oil and Gas Association 168
Thomas, Jacqueline 84
Thompson, Randy 81, 82
Thoreau, Henry 83
threat 8, 10, 18, 42, 58, 72, 85, 88, 169, 179,
    183, 192, 199–200
Three Mile Island 42, 46, 176
TIME (magazine) 132, 151
Tioga County *160*, *161*, 166, *167*
Titus County 139
Tompkins County 160, *160*, *161*
Total 30, 37, 108, 155, 203
TransCanada 13, 67, 71, 73–74, 76, 80–82,
    87–88, 90
Trembath, Alex 188
Trump, Donald J. 5, 9, 13, 76, 91, 126, 148,
    150, 196, 213
Tutu, Desmond 67, 71, 77

Ulster County 160, *160*, *161*
Union Theological Seminary (UTS) 100,
    103–105, 125n10
Unitarian-Universalist 107
United Church of Christ 107
United Nations Climate Change
    Conference (2009) 26, 99
United States Export-Import Bank 187
Upper Big Branch Mine Disaster 133
Urucu-Coari construction 180
Urucu-Manaus natural gas pipeline 179
Urucu natural gas pipeline 179–180

US Food and Drug Administration 97
US Government Accountability Office 138
US Park Police 72

Vantage Energy 168
Victor, David G. 7
visible projects 76

Walmart 48, 49
Walton, Reggie B. 134
Waxman, Henry 131
Waxman-Markey bill 49, 50
Welch, Ivo 117
West, Cornel 111
Western Organization of Resource
    Councils (WORC) 136, 138, 146,
    152n2–3
White Stallion Energy Center 140
Wilderness Society 129, 163
Wilson, Adrian 141
Wise County 133

Wolak, Frank 149
Wood, Jonathan 171–172
World Bank 6, 7, 14, 28, 177, 178, 179,
    185–186, 190
World Bank Group 149, 186
World Health Organization (WHO)
    27, 97

Xingu River 177–178

Yasuni National Park 7, 28
Yearwood, Lennox 84, 115, 116
YieldCos 102
Yinka Dene Alliance of British
    Columbia 84
Young, Neil 73
Youth Day of Climate Action 109
YPF SA 112

Zapatistas of Mexico 44
Zucker, Howard 164